Mandate for Change

Policies and Leadership for 2009 and Beyond

EDITED BY CHESTER W. HARTMAN

LEXINGTON BOOKS

A division of
ROWMAN & LITTLEFIELD PUBLISHERS, INC.
Lanham • Boulder • New York • Toronto • Plymouth, UK

LEXINGTON BOOKS

A division of Rowman & Littlefield Publishers, Inc.
A wholly owned subsidiary of The Rowman & Littlefield Publishing Group, Inc.
4501 Forbes Boulevard, Suite 200
Lanham, MD 20706

Estover Road
Plymouth PL6 7PY
United Kingdom

British Library Cataloguing in Publication Information Available

Library of Congress Cataloging-in-Publication Data

Mandate for change : policies and leadership for 2009 and beyond / edited by
Chester Hartman.
        p. cm.
    Includes bibliographical references and index.
    ISBN-13: 978-0-7391-3167-1 (cloth : alk. paper)
    ISBN-10: 0-7391-3167-2 (cloth : alk. paper)
    ISBN-13: 978-0-7391-3168-8 (pbk. : alk. paper)
    ISBN-10: 0-7391-3168-0 (pbk. : alk. paper)
    ISBN-13: 978-0-7391-3169-5 (electronic)
    ISBN-10: 0-7391-3169-9 (electronic)
  1. United States--Social policy--1993- 2. United States--Economic policy--2001-
3. United States--Foreign relations--21st century. I. Hartman, Chester W.
    HN59.2.M355 2009
    303.48'40973--dc22   2008044526

Printed in the United States of America

♾™ The paper used in this publication meets the minimum requirements of American
National Standard for Information Sciences—Permanence of Paper for Printed Library
Materials, ANSI/NISO Z39.48–1992.

Mandate for Change

Contents

International Issues

Editor's Introduction

Chester Hartman

The American people have made it abundantly clear they want a fundamental change in our nation's policies, both at home and abroad. The level of dissatisfaction, even repugnance, about what the last eight years have wrought is ever more pronounced.

Three decades ago, conservative ideologues at The Heritage Foundation produced a primer for the "Reagan Revolution" entitled *Mandate for Leadership*. It offered a blueprint for the newly elected Reagan Administration, as well as an overarching philosophy of governance. That philosophy was in reality a philosophy against the role of government and in favor of markets (by which they meant large corporations). Philosopher-philanthropist George Soros has called this approach "market fundamentalism"; others have labeled it neoliberalism. The Heritage Foundation's mandate called for the systematic shrinking of government and argued that unfettered markets can better solve most problems.

Today, that overarching framework is bankrupt. The failure of government and markets in New Orleans, for health care, for the housing and financial markets—to name just a few of the outstanding current crises—could not be clearer. In James K. Galbraith's neat phrase titling his new book, we now have a "Predator State." The chapters that follow set forth a fundamental, badly needed "mandate for change" to reinvigorate government and rethink/rework the role of markets and civil society.

Just as neoliberalism has guided our government on the domestic front since the Reagan years, neoconservatism has been the dominant conservative framework for foreign policy. Under the most recent Bush Administration, this overarching doctrine has shunned multilateralism and international law in favor of reckless, destructive, unpopular unilateralism. It has assumed that the United States should be the global cop, and that it knows best how to advance democracy and prosperity abroad. Iraq, Afghanistan and many other foreign policy disasters have exposed the bankruptcy of this approach. The international policy chapters that follow replace neoconservatism with a new role for the United States in the world, one that emphasizes mutual respect, mutual interests, multilateralism, diplomacy and international law.

This volume is modeled after one that I co-edited with Marcus Raskin in 1988, when I was a full-time Fellow at the Institute for Policy Studies—*Winning America: Ideas and Leadership for the 1990s* (South End Press), aimed at strengthening a possible incoming progressive national Administration. The need for progressive policies—and appointing progressive persons to lead such efforts—is even more urgent now than it was two decades ago.

And so we called upon our IPS colleagues and policy experts from around the country to put forward such policies in each of their areas of expertise. The forty-seven chapters that follow (virtually all written specially for this volume) cover the waterfront—and indeed, the waterfront needs to be covered. There are so very many important areas of national policy that need fixing, having been damaged for so long and so severely by past Administrations' ultra-conservative, neoliberal actions.

Each chapter is formatted identically: a set of policy proposals, supported by an essay that provides appropriate background and rationale for those pro-posals, followed by a resource list of relevant readings, organizations, websites.

While the chapters are divided into domestic and international topics, we recognize that this often is a permeable wall—issues like climate change, immi-gration, agriculture, drug policy, terrorism, nuclear weapons, our wars—to name some of the more obvious areas—have clear spillover from one category to the other. In the case of immigration, we opted for chapters in both categories: one dealing with national policy as to who gets to immigrate, how many, from where, under what rules; the other dealing with how these newcomers—regardless of who they are, how they came here, what their status is—get inte-grated into U.S. society.

Another cross-boundary issue relates to the substantive topics as well. Most of the issues covered in individual chapters have spillover to other substantive topics. Housing is closely related to health, education and employment, for ex-ample; drug policy and the criminal justice system is another example. Inevita-bly, then, material in some chapters will overlap with and on occasion repeat what is in another chapter. That's why we've prepared a detailed index, which we encourage readers to use liberally.

As right-on as this set of policy proposals is, we recognize that good ideas by themselves rarely are sufficient to sway the political system and its principal actors. It takes organizing, movement-building to bring about response and change. And so, following our broad set of policy proposals, we asked several of the important figures from the community organizing world to say their piece—in the form of responses to specific questions we posed to them.

As to acknowledgments: First off, to the Institute for Policy Studies, for forty-five years the leading think/do tank of the Left—a place where I spent nine years and still consider my political home. Their wonderful director, John Cavanagh, was a true partner in this effort—as ever, easy and instructive to work with. IPS interns Daniel Scheer, Abby Rapoport and Alyssa Ramsey pro-vided excellent support work in a number of important areas.

And then to our dozens of colleagues and friends who produced their chapters quickly and well, demonstrating once again the strong sense of community among progressive activists. Being connected to so many wonderful public interest workers, academics and others whom we could reliably call on to write the different chapters made this book possible.* Technical back-up and preparation of the index were in the most capable hands of Teri Grimwood, who has worked with me on numerous projects for a quarter-century. Only she knows how central she was to getting this book out on time. And we thank the Wallace Global Fund for their generous support of this project.

Finally, thanks to my wife, Amy Fine, for her constant good judgment, patience, assistance and all the other ways she supports me and my work, and to my sons Ben and Jeremy for their last-minute technological first-aid to their electronically challenged father.

Chester Hartman
August 2008

* An orthographic note: With regard to terminology on race and racial categories, we opt to let each author use whatever is her or his word, punctuation, capitalization preference; such usages embody issues that, for many, have levels of meaning well beyond mere style, and we choose not to impose any arbitrary single format or rule.

Chapter 1

Progressives and the Incoming Administration

Robert L. Borosage and Katrina vanden Heuvel

Electric. The election of Barack Obama to the presidency of the United States unleashes hope and optimism across the country and the world.* It "turns the page" on the Reagan era, the conservative dominance of our politics over the last thirty years. In this country, people desperate for a change of course look with both anticipation and some trepidation about what comes next. Across the world, America's reputation and influence is rising overnight, as peoples and leaders celebrate the repudiation of the mad cowboy policies of the Bush years.

Obama's election both reflects and could strengthen a new and potentially enduring progressive reform majority, while unleashing the energy of the new generation that has fueled his candidacy. Unlike any other American President, he has his own energized base of activists, numbering in the millions, in direct communication and eager to be mobilized in districts across the country. His election is accompanied by increased Democratic majorities in both Houses of Congress—a caucus that will be broader, and thus less liberal than the current caucuses.

The new President inherits a desert: an economy in trouble, a nation in debt, on going occupation and wars in two nations, a broken health care system, a shaken financial system, one in four homes "underwater," families struggling with soaring prices for basics, while incomes stagnate and insecurity rises, an investment deficit in everything from water systems to transport to education that increasingly discolors our lives and burdens our economic prospects, and a public sensibly cynical about whether government can organize a two-car funeral for anyone except the entrenched private interests that plunder it recklessly.

*This essay written in the Summer of 2008 assumes the election of Barack Obama has occurred, as any other result is unthinkable.

1

Obama's election provides a mandate for the central promises of the campaign. Despite widespread progressive concerns about Obama's caution or his "turn to the center," the core of his agenda has been largely driven by progressives in motion: an end to the war, a concerted drive on energy independence and global warming, affordable health care for all, rebuilding America, a new strategy in the global economy, a commitment to empowering workers and to ending the Bush retreat on civil rights and his assault on basic liberties, and much more.

Those central promises, and the collapse of the conservative right, are triggering a new mobilization by the same entrenched corporate interests that have long dominated Washington. Corporate leaders bought into Democrats in the election. Lobbies scramble to hire former Democratic legislators and key staffers. The permanent establishment has been pumping out agenda suggestions, seeking to consolidate consensus on a cautious agenda that might curb Obama's visions. Wall Street warns of excessive regulation; bipartisan corporate retainers bewail any retreat from corporate trade policies; conservatives are reborn as budget hawks, decrying deficits and inflation.

The Better Part of Caution: Bold Action

Accompanying this mobilization of the permanent establishment is the widespread conventional wisdom that the new administration must choose one or two major things to get done, focus on those, and not try to do too much. Too many new administrations, the keepers of opinion intone, think they can change the world, confuse their priorities, and don't understand the limits of the congressional agenda or of public attention. Far better to focus, put forth a sensible, not too ambitious agenda and budget, and demonstrate competence early. This advice is particularly impressed upon the new President, given his youth and relative inexperience.

As with so much conventional wisdom, this serves up more convention than wisdom. In reality, as history Rick Perlstein has argued, periods of significant reform in American politics are rare, but feature when they come spasms of furious activity, generating major, convulsive reforms. Roosevelt's 100 days was marked by day after day of major legislation. In 1964–65, after Kennedy's assassination and the rout of Goldwater, Johnson pushed the Congress to pass the Voting Rights Act, Medicare reform, Comprehensive Immigration reform, aid to education, the War on Poverty and much more in a matter of months.

Our entire political system—the balance of powers, the bicameral legislature, the grotesqueries of Senatorial rules and courtesies, the entrenched permanent corporate lobbies—is designed to stop things, to generate stasis, not reform. The only exception is the area of national security, where modern Presidents have claimed a set of imperial prerogatives.

So when significant reform occurs, it occurs because conditions are ripe, the public demands and expects change, and a President lashes the Congress to act, rolls over the entrenched interests, and gets things done. Inevitably this period doesn't last long; the reaction sets in. So it is vital to move rapidly and boldly and across many areas to have any chance to succeed.

The stunning rise of Barack Obama—with a backdrop of the catastrophic failures of conservatism—sets the stage for exactly that opportunity. Given the conditions he inherits, he can only succeed by being bold, radical in his initiatives, and ambitious in his agenda. Surely, the first advice to the new President is to capture this moment now, and drive a bold new direction for the country.

The First Weeks

If Obama simply were to accomplish his core promises—from ending the war to passing comprehensive health care reform—he would go far to transforming the country. In his first 100 days, he will have to choose his priorities, but some core initiatives seem inescapable—the question not being whether he will address them but how bold he will be.

The first choice the President must make is on the quagmire in Iraq. He should task the Joint Chiefs with developing a sensible plan for withdrawing our forces from Iraq and bringing that misbegotten occupation to an end. If he fails to do this, his administration will be embattled from day one within his own party and base. If he does it, he will have to act boldly to define a broad new security agenda for America.

As Obama confirms his pledge to bring the occupation to an end, he will redefine U.S. security strategy in broad terms. At the core of that, as Al Gore has stated, is a concerted drive for energy independence, so that we stop borrowing billions from the Chinese to send to regimes in the Middle East to purchase oil that is fueling catastrophic climate change. The drive for new energy is also a major source of jobs and growth, as well as the centerpiece of a new global strategy designed to ensure that the United States sustains a vibrant middle class in a global economy. Obama should set a high goal, announce a major investment agenda in weatherizing homes (stimulating a construction industry in collapse), in renewable energy, in driving Detroit to build the hybrid and electric cars and mass transit of the future, in research and development to capture the green industries that will be the growth generators of the next decades.

At the same time, he will address directly the central threat posed by suicidal terrorists—the fear of them gaining possession of a nuclear bomb. Obama will surely launch a major initiative on the proliferation of weapons of mass destruction, joining with the Russians to secure loose nukes, challenging the world to join in a new drive for nuclear disarmament, reviving U.S. leadership in limiting testing of nuclear and biological warfare, and more. This comprehensive initiative can be a centerpiece of a global initiative to re-engage our allies both in a reformulated campaign against al Qaeda's terrorist networks and a multilateral initiative to engage Iraq's neighbors in cooperating on sustaining that nation's unity. He should dispatch a dramatic negotiator—here Bill Clinton could be of service—to the Middle East, making it clear that his administration will pursue peace in the Middle East from day one.

His energy initiative can become the centerpiece for a bold new strategy for getting the economy going. Here he can dramatize his stark departure from the conservative policies that have driven us into the hole we are in. He can announce a growth agenda built on new energy and on investing in America, rebuilding our starved infrastructure from water systems to schools. He can call for new rules to ensure that our markets work for working people, empowering workers to organize, holding executive accountable, regulating the shadow banking system that the Federal Reserve has been forced to bail out, calling for a reassessment of U.S. strategy in the global marketplace.

Obama has pledged to present a comprehensive health care proposal to the Congress in the first 100 days. That will spark a debate likely to last many months, if not years, as the insurance and drug industry lobbies—two of the most powerful in the country—join with conservatives to challenge any plan. He may sensibly also seek to move into law immediately health care for children, a program that already passed the Congress only to be vetoed by Bush, and power to negotiate lower prices on drugs under Medicare, a measure that passed the House only to fall to a filibuster in the Senate.

This focus on core security, economic and social challenges should be followed immediately by a major initiative on Just Democracy, calling on Congress to renovate our electoral system, while moving to curb the influence of money on politics. This should be linked to dramatic call to public service. Obama should decry those who would denigrate those who go into public service, lay out a bold expansion of national service in everything from Democracy to Green Corps, and invite Americans to join in the process of reinventing our government, using new technologies to make it more responsive, more efficient and more interactive.

This clear restatement of our common stake in effective democratic governance should be combined with executive orders rolling back the secrecy, the trampling of liberties in the name of security that have been the hallmark of the last administration. An early order to close Guantanamo and the CIA's secret detention centers, while initiating an executive review of the scope of presidential national security powers would be a first step in lifting the dark cloud on U.S. reputation abroad. His first weeks will also feature a review aimed at reversing many of the reactionary Bush executive orders—from the gag rule on doctors abroad to the gutting of worker protections in OSHA and NLRB.

After this surge of activity, Obama will turn to his budget, where his basic priorities on taxes and spending will be unveiled.

Progressives in the First 100 Days

In the transition and first months of an Obama administration, the role of progressives will be clear. We should organize to help define and claim the mandate of the election. And we should sustain the independent organizing efforts to help Obama fulfill his core promises—and not incidentally, to encourage him to stick to and fight for those promises against great opposition.

Progressives will enjoy their greatest strength mobilizing independently to support Obama's reform priorities. We can organize constituent pressure on politicians that are blocking the way, something a President would be loath to do. We can expose the lobbies and interests and backstage maneuvers designed to limit reforms. With newspapers increasingly without the resources for investigation, progressives will have to assume a greater role in monitoring and tracking the opposition, even as we mobilize activists in targeted districts across the country. In doing this, we can help define the Obama agenda, even as we supply muscle and energy to help pass it. Assuming he fulfills his promise on Iraq, progressives will find it easy to mobilize in support of his first 100 day agenda.

Perhaps the best example is the Health Care for Americans Now Coalition. It has built a broad coalition with the resources to drive the debate on health care. Having done this during the electoral campaign, it is in position to support Obama's reforms—even as it helps insure that he stays with his pledge. That model—claiming the mandate, mobilizing to pressure those who stand in the way, and demonstrating the force of public support for the President, and importantly encouraging the White House to stand up for its own promises—will be vital in the early months of the administration.

This will require concerted independent organizing, linking national monitoring that exposes the opposition (in the Congress, the lobbies, and in the administration itself), with issue campaigns focused on local mobilization. It will also require challenging legislators who stand in the way. SEIU has already taken the lead in announcing a $10 million "accountability project," designed to hold legislators accountable to the core mandate of the voters, with a new organization—They Work for US—as the core vehicle. Progressives should join and complement this effort.

We've already seen its benefits. Ned Lamont's victory over Joe Lieberman in the Democratic primaries in 2006 emboldened Democrats on Iraq, and helped create the victory that year. Donna Edwards' successful challenge to an entrenched Democratic incumbent who represented his donors more than his voters sent a message throughout the caucus. In the context of supporting Obama's progressive reforms, every Democrat should be on notice from their own constituents that they will be held accountable for their votes.

The Pressure for Unity

If Obama backs away from his pledges or compromises for partial reforms rather than forcing a larger battle, progressives will face a harder task. In the first months of his administration, Obama will have the popularity of his historic victory, the stark contrast with Bush's follies, and the force of his own organized base behind him. Much of the progressive activist base and blogosphere will be happy to have dispatched Bush. While retreat on ending the war would generate a firestorm, on many other issues retreats would be difficult to oppose. Moreover, the White House and the Congressional leadership will push hard for unity, pointing to the lesson of Clinton's first two years when Democratic division contributed to the public frustration that led to the election of the Gingrich congress. While Republicans are likely to be in some disarray, the new right will be mobilized in full scale assault on Obama from day one.

Here again, our task is clear—mobilizing popular demand for reforms that force the White House and the Congress to do what they have promised. Bill Moyers, at the time Lyndon Johnson's press secretary, tells a classic story in his January 18, 2008 "Bill Moyers Journal" program about Johnson and Martin Luther King. Upon taking the presidency, Moyers reports, Johnson

> wanted Martin Luther King to call off the marching, demonstrations, and protests. The civil rights movement had met massive resistance in the south, and the south, because of the seniority system, controlled Congress, making it virtually impossible for Congress to enact laws giving full citizenship to black Americans, no matter how desperate their lives. LBJ worried that the mounting demonstrations were hardening white resistance.
>
> As the pressure intensified on each side, Johnson wanted King to wait a little longer and give him a chance to bring Congress around by hook or crook. But Martin Luther King said his people had already waited too long. He talked about the murders and lynchings, the churches set on fire, children brutalized, the law defied, men and women humiliated, their lives exhausted, their hearts broken. LBJ listened, as intently as I ever saw him listen. He listened, and then he put his hand on Martin Luther King's shoulder, and said, in effect: "OK. You go out there, Dr. King, and keep doing what you're doing, and make it possible for me to do the right thing." Lyndon Johnson was no racist, but he had not been a civil rights hero, either. Now, as President, he came down on the side of civil disobedience, believing it might quicken America's conscience until the cry for justice became irresistible, enabling him to turn Congress. So King marched and Johnson maneuvered and Congress folded.

As an organizer, Obama understands that change comes from the bottom up. He has called upon Americans to "keep on marching, and organizing, and knocking on doors, and making phone calls." He has called his own campaign part of building a movement for change that can overcome business as usual in Washington. As President, he will face different pressures, and undoubtedly seek to limit his agenda, pick his fights. The movement that he has called into being will have little choice but to embrace his charge, and mobilize across the country to "make it possible for [him] to do the right thing."

Challenging the Corrosive Consensus

The hardest challenge for progressives will be how to expand the agenda beyond the corrosive consensus that has simply excluded core alternatives from the debate.

Defeating McCain—while challenging his agenda—was vital to ending the conservative hold over American politics. At the same time, progressives should recognize that election of Obama only opens the debate about what comes next. And the current debate is still constipated, constricted by an elite consensus enforced by powerful interests. Consider the core elements of the bipartisan consensus in the election campaign that constricts real change:

Candidates of both parties pledged to increase the size of the military, adding billions to a bloated military budget that already represents nearly one-half the world's military spending. Neither dissented from America's role as globocop; neither challenged the empire of bases, or the covert plumbing that virtually condemns us to foreign conflict, covert or overt.

While Obama made affordable health care for all a centerpiece of his agenda, neither candidate addressed the full unraveling of the private social contract once delivered through corporations and unions. Neither championed a public economic bill of rights, from health care to pensions above Social Security to guaranteed paid vacation, in addition to paid sick days and family leave.

While Obama expressed his support for labor rights and environmental protections in trade accords, and called for a concerted drive for energy independence, neither candidate laid out a bold strategy to insure that the United States can sustain a broad middle class in the global economy.

While both candidates promised more resources for education, both were constrained by their fiscal policies—McCain by supporting tax cuts that will require impossible cuts in domestic programs; Obama by a Rubinomics focus on balanced budgets and understandable timidity about tax increases that will put harsh constraints on any new investment agenda.

While Obama clearly championed social liberalism, neither candidate said much about poverty, nor about our brutal criminal system of injustice that so devastates the lives of young minority men.

While Obama laid out a promising agenda at his Cooper Union speech in the primaries, neither candidate challenged the Wall Street bailout now proceeding nor mobilized support for re-regulating the shadow banking system that has proved so reckless in its greed.

This corrosive agenda reflects the entrenched power of the established order. It is enforced by aggressive lobbies—the military industrial complex, Wall

Street, corporate interests—and rationalized by well-rewarded house scholars. The establishment's strength is its ability to simply exclude alternatives from serious consideration.

After the first flurry of activity, the Obama administration will have to address fundamental questions. What is a global economic strategy than can sustain a broad middle class? How do we really deal with catastrophic climate change? What must be done to curb Wall Street's casino economy? How do we rebuild America, sustain a basic social contract with accumulated public and private debts greater as a percentage of GDP than those at the end of World War II?

Conditions are likely to continue to be a terrible ally. Contrary to McCain and Bush, the fundamentals of the American economy are weak, not strong. An Obama presidency faces stark challenges that will require a far bolder agenda than what is now on the table. To be successful, he will have to be more radical than now imagined.

Progressives should assume that this administration has no alternative but to be one of constant experimentation. Progressives scholars should be developing alternative policies that are now deemed inconceivable—from dismantling our empire of bases, to curbing the imperial presidency, to progressive tax reforms, to strengthening the public commons—from public enterprise to public parks—over private wealth. State and local initiatives need national exposure. Again, independent issue campaigning—particularly on those concerns not high on the immediate agenda—will help lift issues onto the national screen.

Here progressives must continue to strengthen and expand the growing infrastructure on the left. Progressives in the Senate and House, many grouped around the Progressive Caucus, can provide both leadership and a public forum for new ideas. Research institutes can help think outside the establishment box. The blogosphere can both track the limits of the current debate, while giving new ideas greater visibility. The network of progressive state and local officials can provide links that carry good ideas from state to state.

When John Kennedy was elected, he too summoned a new generation into politics. A cautious leader and committed Cold Warrior, Kennedy's agenda was very limited. But the energy he unleashed helped build the civilizing movements of the next decades—the anti-war movement, the civil rights, women's, environmental and gay rights movements—that have transformed this country—and far transcended the limits of the Kennedy politics.

Conditions now are very different from the America of the 1960s. That generation was nurtured in the security of the post-war prosperity. The movements assumed a prosperous America that ought to be more just. This generation grows up with much greater economic insecurity, laden with debt, struggling to find jobs that will afford the security needed for building a family. It faces an economy that cannot be sustained—and must be transformed.

But once more a young and exciting candidate, elected after a long and failed conservative era, can spark the hope and sense of possibility that generate movements that carry far beyond the limits of the current political debate. The opportunity is now ours to seize.

Domestic Issues

Chapter 2

The United States Can Cut Poverty in Half

Angela Glover Blackwell, Peter Edelman and Mark Greenberg

POLICY PROPOSALS

- Declare a federal goal of cutting poverty in half in ten years.
- Develop a revamped modern definition of poverty to track the nation's progress.
- Adopt minimum wage and tax policies to ensure that work is a route out of and a protection from poverty.
- Help more low-income families with children by improving the Child Tax Credit.
- Ensure child care help to millions of low-earning families.
- Make unemployment insurance available to low-wage workers.
- Help homeowners avoid foreclosure and help families move to neighborhoods of opportunity.
- Promote equitable development strategies.
- Connect disadvantaged and disconnected youth with school and work.

* * * * * * * * * * * * * * *

The United States is the richest nation in the history of the world. At the same time, 36.5 million Americans live in poverty, and millions more struggle to make ends meet. The results are tragic for the children, adults and elderly Americans in households who cannot afford adequate food and shelter, and, increasingly, cannot afford to pay for heating, cooling or gas. But the costs of sustained, persistent poverty hurt all of us, in visible and less visible ways. They

13

weaken our nation's capacity to be economically vibrant, to grow and prosper, and to provide opportunity to all.

The incoming President and Congress should join in a commitment to the goal of cutting poverty in half in the United States over the next ten years, and set the nation on course to end poverty in America in a generation. During the recent campaign, Senator Obama expressly committed to the goal of cutting poverty in half in ten years, and Senator McCain declared that eradicating poverty would be a top priority of his Administration. Now that the elections have passed, it is time to translate words to action. That requires both building the commitment into the ongoing priorities of the Administration, and a legislative agenda for Congress to enact.

Cutting poverty in half is not just about enacting federal legislation, though that is part of what must be done. This must be a national cause, with the active engagement of states and cities, communities, businesses, faith-based groups, public and private organizations, and individuals. For it to happen, the incoming President must lead and inspire, helping all Americans to see that it is in their interest, that it is doable and that it should be done.

Moreover, at a time of fear and uncertainty about our economy, when millions of Americans are struggling to hold on to their homes and jobs and to make their paychecks last through the month, the goal of reducing poverty must be seen as integral to, not separate from, the Administration's economic strategy. Much of the agenda to reduce poverty is an agenda to build and strengthen the middle class—to ensure that working families can thrive and prosper, that all children can get a decent education, that lifelong education helps all workers meet the needs of twenty-first-century jobs, that all Americans have good health care coverage and a secure retirement. But if we want to end the scourge of deep, persistent poverty, we must do this and more, and bring opportunity to people and communities that have been left behind even when the economy was far stronger than it is today. Strengthening the middle class and tackling deep poverty must go hand in hand.

The challenge for the incoming Administration is not that we don't know how to reduce poverty. Our nation has learned an enormous amount since the War on Poverty about what does—and doesn't—work. There's strong evidence that Americans wish something could be done to reduce poverty, although many of them doubt whether government can act effectively. The incoming President and congressional leadership should come together to declare a national commitment to halving poverty in ten years and to advancing an agenda grounded in the experience of what works and in American values of work, family, individual and social responsibility, and opportunity.

Drawing on Census Bureau data in this and the following paragraphs, the official measure of poverty in the United States seriously understates the numbers of Americans struggling to get by. The current measure—$21,027 for a family of four in 2007—was set based on studies of family budgets in the early 1960s, and has only been adjusted for inflation since then. Studies and surveys routinely find that the amounts Americans think is needed to make ends meet or lead a reasonably decent life is twice the poverty level or greater. The official measure at best counts the numbers of Americans furthest from having an adequate income to meet their basic needs.

Even with this stringent measure, one in eight Americans—12.3 percent—were living in poverty in 2006. Every racial and ethnic group faces poverty, but the risks are not even. The largest single group of poor people in the United States is comprised of white Americans, but poverty rates for African Americans (24.3 percent), Native Americans (29.3 percent) and Hispanics (21.5 percent) are twice as high or higher than those for whites (8.2 percent) and Asians (10.3 percent).

Americans of every age risk poverty, but the rate is highest for children (17.4 percent, 12.8 million children). Among children, the highest risk is for the youngest. We know that the early ages are critical for child development, and yet one-fifth of children under age three (21 percent) are living in poverty, including 41 percent of African-American and 30 percent of Hispanic children.

When children grow up in poverty, we all pay a price. We all pay a price when young people who could someday make important contributions to our economy fail to do so because they didn't get the education they need. We all pay a price when people turn to crime because they have no other hope. Harry Holzer and his colleagues have estimated that the drag on the U.S. economy from children growing up in persistent poverty is about $500 billion a year, 4 percent of the Gross Domestic Product, from lower adult productivity, higher health care costs and increased crime-related costs.

And we all pay a price when the American Dream no longer seems American. Research tells us that upward mobility in America is much less common than in a number of other developed nations with which we compete. A major reason is that children growing up in the bottom 20 percent are less likely to move up here than elsewhere. That's not just a problem for them—it tells us that in a global economy, we are wasting the potential of millions of Americans who could be contributing to our nation's competitiveness.

It is sometimes suggested that there's not much that can be done that can make a difference. To the contrary, history shows two elements are critical to making progress: a strong economy with low unemployment and a focused national policy commitment. Between 1964 and 1973, amidst the booming economy of the 1960s, the War on Poverty and the Civil Rights Movement, poverty fell by 42 percent. Between 1993 and 2000, when a near-full employment economy was combined with an expanded Earned Income Tax Credit, welfare reform, an increased minimum wage, child care and health care expansions, and other policies, poverty fell for seven consecutive years, dropping by 25 percent.

In sharp contrast, since 2000, our nation has gone backwards, with 4.9 million more people in poverty today than at the beginning of the decade. It is time to go forward again.

An Agenda for Action

What should the incoming President and Congress do to set us on course to end poverty in America? The Center for American Progress Task Force on Poverty proposed a strategy in its report, *From Poverty to Prosperity: A National Strategy to Cut Poverty in Half.* The CAP Task Force looked at the experience of what does and doesn't work, drew from the best available research, and grounded its recommendations in fundamental American values. It began with the premise that we should have a working society in which those who are able to work should be expected to do so, and in return work should be rewarded, and work should be both protection from and a route out of poverty. We need strong unions to improve working conditions for all workers; policies to promote asset-building; strategies to help people live in neighborhoods of opportunity; and efforts to encourage and support responsible parenting. We need universal health care for all of our people. We need to ensure high-quality education through the life cycle, starting with early education, continuing through K-12 and higher education, and providing for the needs of workers in a changing economy. And we need to recognize that there is not a single magic bullet, but that sensible policies that can achieve broad public support can also make a dramatic difference in reducing poverty.

A federal goal to cut poverty in half in ten years

The incoming President should begin by issuing an Executive Order declaring that it is the goal of his Administration to cut poverty in half in ten years and to set the nation on course to end poverty in the next generation. The Executive Order should direct every federal agency to consider and report back as to how its legislative and administrative efforts can contribute to advancing the national goal. Within the White House, the Domestic Policy Council and National Economic Council should have joint responsibility for the goal. In their annual budget justifications, each agency should describe its action plan for advancing the national goal.

The White House office responsible for faith-based and community-based initiatives should be actively involved in efforts to advance the goal. The White House should issue an annual report, describing federal actions, state and local progress, the contributions of private actors, civil initiatives and voluntary efforts. The report should provide an annual scorecard of short-term and long-term measures of progress.

A revamped modern definition of poverty to track the nation's progress

There are many things wrong with the current measure. The thresholds for determining when a family is in poverty are unrealistically low. The measure excludes necessities like taxes, health care, child care and transportation, and fails to count the effects of key programs that help families, such as tax credits, food stamps and subsidized housing. The National Academy of Sciences has recommended improvements in the definition, and the incoming Administration should adopt them to ensure that the measure is realistic and reflects the effects of policies. At the same time, the federal government should also track and seek to address other measures of family well-being: the number of Americans with incomes above the poverty line but unable to afford a reasonably decent life; the number without adequate assets; and better measures of the numbers of people and families outside the social mainstream.

Minimum wage and tax policies to ensure that work is a route out of and a protection from poverty

A starting point for national employment policy should be that work should pay decently. The incoming Administration should develop a comprehensive strategy for increasing the number of good jobs in America. As one piece of that strategy, the minimum wage should be substantially increased. For ten years before 2007, Congress failed to raise the federal minimum wage. As a result of legislative action in 2007, the federal minimum will reach $7.25 in 2009, but will then remain flat until Congress acts again. The federal minimum wage should be raised to half the average wage and then indexed so that it never again falls so far below the wages of other working Americans.

Along with a higher minimum wage, there must be adequate enforcement. The incoming Administration should establish a new Department of Labor task force to target the industries with the worst abuses of minimum wage and over-time laws, and take action against the misclassification of employees as independent contractors and strengthen workplace safety rules.

Even with a significantly increased minimum wage, too many workers and families will be struggling to get by. Tax-based assistance can play a critical role in encouraging and supporting work. The incoming Congress should triple the Earned Income Tax Credit for workers without children. The federal Earned Income Tax Credit has played a critical role in increasing labor force participation by low-income families with children, but provides only a small benefit to workers without children and to non-custodial parents. An expanded credit for these groups would both encourage employment and reduce poverty.

Improving the Child Tax Credit

The federal Child Tax Credit helped 37 million families with children in 2007, but it provides no help to families with the lowest earnings or no earnings. This is because it is only partially "refundable," so families with earnings below $8,500 in 2008 receive no benefit from the credit and other low-earning families receive only partial benefits. As a result, the poorest 8 million children are completely left out, and millions more receive only a partial credit. Just 1 percent of current benefits from the credit go to the poorest 20 percent of families.

The Center for American Progress Task Force on Poverty called for making the Child Tax Credit fully refundable so that all low-income families with children receive the same benefit that is received by middle- and higher-income families. Modeling by the Urban Institute estimated that adopting such a proposal would reduce child poverty by 20 percent, using a definition of poverty drawn from recommendations of the National Academy of Sciences.

Child care help for low-earning families

High-quality child care helps parents work and helps ensure that their children are in safe arrangements that support their healthy development. Wealthy families can afford to purchase this care; millions of other American families cannot. The federal-state child care subsidy program provides important help to those who get it, but only has enough funding to reach one in seven eligible families. It should be expanded to be available to all families with incomes below about $40,000 a year, and federal funding for child care quality initiatives should be doubled. At the same time, the federal tax credit for child care provides too little assistance for middle-class families, and none at all for working families who earn so little that they don't owe taxes. It should be expanded and made refundable.

Unemployment Insurance for low-wage workers

Losing a job shouldn't mean falling into poverty. Rather, it should be fundamental that workers losing their jobs should qualify for unemployment insurance in order to get by while they're looking for or preparing for a new job. But only 37 percent of unemployed workers receive unemployment insurance benefits, and only about 14 percent of unemployed low-wage workers get these benefits—low-wage workers are twice as likely to be unemployed, but less than half as likely as other workers to receive this assistance. A set of sensible policy changes—looking at most recent earnings when a worker applies for benefits, extending assistance to part-time workers and those who leave jobs for compelling family reasons—would all help, and legislation pending in the last Congress would encourage states to adopt these changes. The incoming Administration should encourage adoption of the Unemployment Insurance Modernization Act, and then go further to identify and address other barriers to Unemployment Insurance participation for low-earning workers.

Avoiding foreclosure and helping families move to neighborhoods of opportunity

An estimated 2.2 million homeowners may lose their homes to foreclosure over the next several years, with low-income and minority communities the hardest hit. As families lose their home, communities deteriorate, states and cities lose property tax revenue, and more families slip into poverty.

Meeting the housing crisis head-on is a critical step to salvaging millions of families' financial security and preventing severe damage to the economy. Families struggling with exploding mortgage costs and deceptive or unfair terms need opportunities to renegotiate or refinance into safe, affordable and sustainable mortgages. Cities, towns and non-profits can purchase and rehabilitate foreclosed properties, preventing a downward spiral of falling property values, vandalism, crime and overwhelmed local governments, while creating new affordable housing. Restoring foreclosed properties to productive use as affordable housing will be necessary to counteract demand forces that will drive up rents as former owners return to renting with little new supply of rental housing. And as a last resort, families should be able to modify the terms of their mortgages in bankruptcy, just like they can modify loans on their investment properties, vacation homes and boats, a step that would let 600,000 families keep their homes.

A very high proportion of low-income families are renters, and the incoming Administration and Congress should also do more to help families live in neighborhoods where they have the opportunities enjoyed by most Americans. Over the next ten years, the federal government should fund two million new "opportunity vouchers" to provide a broader range of housing choices to low-income families. These vouchers should be linked to the provision of employment and social services, and additional vouchers should be created for specific units in areas with good schools, high-quality public services and good employment opportunities.

Equitable development strategies

In addition to creating more housing choices in communities rich with opportunity, the incoming Administration must build on the understanding of how metropolitan development patterns have made it more difficult for those living in isolated poverty communities to improve their life chances, and advance principles of equitable development:

- integrating strategies that focus on people with strategies focused on improving places;
- reducing local and regional disparities;
- promoting investments that are equitable, catalytic and coordinated; and
- ensuring meaningful community participation, leadership and ownership within these change efforts.

Applying these principles requires greater availability of public transportation to connect isolated poor neighborhoods to job centers; incentives to attract grocery stores and other essentials to underserved communities; strong efforts to improve neighborhood safety; and high-quality public schools for urban neighborhoods. Additionally, political processes must provide opportunities for disadvantaged communities to have their voices heard regarding decisions in their neighborhoods, communities and regions.

There are many ways in which the incoming Administration can support and advance principles of equitable development in its legislative agenda. For example, it can ensure that there is a strong new commitment to promoting public transportation in transportation reauthorization legislation. It can include provisions in economic stimulus legislation to increase the presence of full-service grocery stores in underserved communities. It can take action to bring more qualified teachers into poor urban communities. And, in any infrastructure initiatives, it can place emphasis on jobs for those marginalized from the workforce.

Connecting disadvantaged and disconnected youth with school and work

Low-income youth continue to be out of school, out of work and ill-prepared to enter adult society in numbers of a magnitude that is deeply distressing—in 2005, 1.7 million poor and near-poor youth were out of school and out of work. The problem is particularly severe in certain distressed rural and urban communities. Disconnected youth are disproportionately minority—African-American, Hispanic and Native American. The disparities in education and early labor market experience exacerbate racial and ethnic inequalities in America. Among young minority men, "disconnection" is heavily associated with high rates of incarceration. Not only is this unfair to the young people themselves, it also imposes a huge social and economic cost on the United States.

The incoming Administration should place a major priority on connecting and reconnecting low-income young people with schools, work and their communities. The Administration should propose comprehensive legislation establishing a national commitment to reduce disconnection. The legislation should significantly expand funding for state and local efforts, engaging schools, community colleges and non-profits, partnerships with employers and others. It should combine resources to help build effective local systems with competitive grant funds to promote new innovative approaches. And it should be grounded in a principle of reciprocity: that youth should complete school and connect to further education and the labor force, and should be encouraged and rewarded for doing so.

Poverty in America means that we are a less prosperous nation, with millions of Americans falling behind. But we know that this is a problem we can tackle. Setting a national goal to cut poverty in half would demonstrate the incoming President's ambition and determination to make this difference, and inspire leaders across the country to make this a national cause.

Resources

ACORN: www.acorn.org
Catholic Charities USA: www.catholiccharitiesusa.org
Center for American Progress: www.americanprogress.org
Center for Community Change: www.ccc.org
Center for Economic and Policy Research: www.cepr.net
Center for Law and Social Policy: www.clasp.org
Center on Budget and Policy Priorities: www.cbpp.org
Childrens Defense Fund: www.childrensdefense.org.
Coalition on Human Needs: www.chn.org
Economic Policy Institute: www.epi.org

Food Research and Action Center: www.frac.org
Half in Ten: www.halfinten.org
Leadership Conference on Civil Rights: www.civilrights.org
National Center for Children in Poverty: www.nccp.org
PolicyLink: www.policylink.org
Sojourners/Call to Renewal: http://www.sojo.net/
Spotlight on Poverty and Opportunity: www.spotlightonpoverty.org

References

The American Prospect. "Ending Poverty in America: Special Report." April 22, 2007. Available at http://www.prospect.org/cs/archive/view_report?reportId =22.

Berlin, Gordon. *Rewarding the Work of Individuals: A Counterintuitive Approach to Reducing Poverty and Strengthening Families.* Vol. 17, No. 2. Brookings Institution and Princeton University, 2007. Available at http://www.futureofchildren.org/usr_doc/7_02_Berlin.pdf.

Blank, Rebecca. "How to Improve Poverty Measurement in the United States.*" Journal of Policy Analysis and Management*, Vol. 27, No. 2, 233–254 (2008). Available at http://www.npc.umich.edu/news/events/pdf/Blank-Poverty Measure%20(2).pdf.

Catholic Charities. *Poverty in America: A Threat to the Common Good.* Catholic Charities USA, 2006. Available at http://www.catholiccharitiesusa.org/Net Commnity/http/community.catholiccharitiesusa.org/NetCommunity/Docum ent.Doc?id=389.

Center for American Progress. *From Poverty to Prosperity: A National Strategy to Cut Poverty in Half.* Center for American Progress Task Force on Poverty, 2007. Available at http://www.americanprogress.org/issues/2007/04/ pdf/poverty_report.pdf.

Danziger, Sheldon. *Fighting Poverty Revisited: What Did Researchers Know 40 Years Ago? What Do We Know Today?* Focus Vol. 25, No. 1. Institute for Research on Poverty, Madison, Wisconsin, 2007. Available at: http://www. irp.wisc.edu/publications/focus/pdfs/foc251a.pdf

Edwards, John, Marion Crain, Arne Kalleberg, eds., *Ending Poverty in America: How to Restore the American Dream.* The New Press, in conjunction with the Center on Poverty, Work and Opportunity, University of North Carolina at Chapel Hill, 2007.

Greenberg, Mark. "Next Steps for Federal Child Care Policy." *The Future of Children Journal*, Vol. 17, No. 2. Brookings Institution and Princeton University, 2007. Available at http://www.futureofchildren.org/usr_doc/04_ 5565-4_greenberg_revised.pdf.

Holzer, Harry J., Dianne Whitmore Schanzenbach, Greg J. Duncan, and Jens Ludwig. *The Economic Costs of Poverty in the United States: Subsequent*

Effects of Children Growing Up Poor. Center for American Progress, January 2007. Available at http://www.americanprogress.org/issues/2007/01/pdf/poverty_report.pdf.

Chapter 3

High-Quality, Affordable Health Care for All

Ron Pollack

POLICY PROPOSALS

- Create new health coverage opportunities for working families through a system, similar to the Federal Employee Health Benefits Program (FEHBP) and the Massachusetts Connector, which would enable families to obtain portable health coverage through a variety of private health plans, including a public plan. Make this option available for small businesses as well, so they can offer affordable coverage to their workers.
- Provide substantial, refundable and advanceable tax credits on a sliding scale to people and families unable to afford health coverage but who are ineligible for Medicaid and the State Children's Health Insurance Program (SCHIP).
- Extend eligibility to Medicaid for low-income people based exclusively on their low-income status, rather than current restrictive eligibility rules that disqualify many low-income adults, especially those without children, from such coverage. Ensure that adequate outreach and streamlined enrollment systems are in place so that eligible low-income people and families actually participate in Medicaid and SCHIP. Reauthorize SCHIP with adequate, additional funds before the program's reauthorization expires in March 2009.
- Eliminate current restrictions that prevent legal immigrants from securing public health coverage.
- In order to curb skyrocketing health care costs while improving quality of care, finance coverage growth by limiting the tax exclusion for employer-sponsored health insurance provided to highest-income employees; eliminating current windfall payments to private health plans in

Medicare; and increasing federal taxation on the purchase of tobacco products. Additionally, Congress should rescind the prohibition that prevents Medicare from bargaining with the pharmaceutical companies for cheaper drug prices.

■ Establish a regulatory nation-wide floor of protections, which states can supplement, to prevent insurance companies from "cherry-picking" and denying coverage to people with pre-existing health care problems. Ensure that such regulatory protections outlaw the use of discriminatory high premiums for people with family histories of health problems or for people with existing health problems.

■ To moderate unsustainable health care cost growth, transform the health care system so it provides more cost-effective and higher-quality care. Such a transformation should be based on research about the best science and analyses about cost-effectiveness as well as new payment systems that encourage providers to treat patients based on the best science and proven cost-effectiveness. It should also be based on care coordination, especially for people with chronic health problems and disabilities.

■ Promote the development and use by medical providers of electronic personal health records, as well as e-prescribing, but do so in a manner that protects privacy.

■ Encourage the greater availability and use of preventive care, as well as more healthy lifestyles, such as the promotion of exercise, good diets and smoking cessation.

* * * * * * * * * * * * * * *

The Opportunities to Secure Historic Health Care Reform

In 2009, there may be an historic opportunity to achieve meaningful health care reform—reform designed to ensure that everyone in the United States has realistic access to high-quality, affordable health care.

As many public surveys showed throughout calendar year 2007, health care was the most significant domestic concern—second, overall, only after the Iraq war—for America's voters.[1] In the past several months (as the economy worsened), public surveys began to show that the state of the economy became a higher priority. However, as many pollsters and survey analysts have indicated, the growing concern about the economy significantly reflects the concerns voters have about the unaffordability of health care; it also reflects the insecurity people have about their access to health care if their employers drop or reduce health coverage or if they experience a job layoff.

There are other clear indications that the need for health care reform has become a salient concern throughout the country and that the time is ripe for meaningful national action. Some of the more visible indicators include:

- A significant number of states (most notably Massachusetts, Illinois, Maryland, Maine, Pennsylvania and Vermont) have either enacted important reforms or are in the process of debating them.
- Numerous business leaders across the country are speaking out about the need for health care reform, motivated mostly by the increasing costs they bear for covering their workers and retirees.[2]
- A noteworthy variety of "strange bedfellow" organizations that span the ideological spectrum have reached incremental agreements that could expand health coverage for people (especially children) who are uninsured, and are prepared to consider more fundamental reforms.[3]
- The leading Democratic Presidential candidates throughout the primary election season indicated that health care reform would receive high-priority attention if they were elected.

Several factors have led the public to conclude that a genuine health care crisis exists that threatens their personal security. First and foremost, health care costs have skyrocketed, especially in comparison to working families' wages. In 2008, Families USA released fifty state-by-state surveys comparing the growth in average insurance premium costs with median earnings for the period 2000–2007. In California, for example, annual family insurance premiums rose from $6,227 to $12,194—an increase of 95.8 percent. In comparison, wages rose by 21.7 percent in that same period. As a result, health insurance premiums rose five times faster than earnings.[4] In Michigan (where the economy is worse than most other regions of the country), insurance premiums rose 17.1 times faster than earnings.[5]

Despite such significant increases in insurance premiums, the coverage that these premiums purchase is considerably less than people received years ago. Deductibles and out-of-pocket co-payments are increasing rapidly; the health care services covered in insurance plans are shrinking; and some employers are dropping coverage for dependents and retirees. As a result, changes over recent years have resulted in working families paying more and more while receiving less and less.

These changes in the economics of health care have fueled a substantial increase in the number of people who are uninsured. The latest Census Bureau Current Population Survey shows that there were 45.7 million Americans who were uninsured *throughout calendar 2007*[6]—more than the aggregate population of twenty-four states plus the District of Columbia.[7] By contrast, in 2000, the number of uninsured people was 38.4 million;[8] thus, the average annual increase in the number of uninsured was over 1 million.

As troublesome as these numbers are, they mask how widespread the uninsured problem has become for families across the country. Families USA recently released a report based on other Census Bureau data showing how many people were uninsured at some point over the previous two years. The numbers are astounding: In that 2006–2007 period, 89.6 million Americans were uninsured for some period of time. This represents more than one out of every three (34.7 percent) Americans under sixty-five years of age.[9] Most of these people were uninsured for significant periods of time: over half (50.2 percent) were uninsured for at least nine months, and nearly two-thirds (63.9 percent) were uninsured for at least six months.[10]

In five states, more than two out of every five people under sixty-five years of age were uninsured at some point during the previous two years. The portion of the non-aged population uninsured in those states is enormous: In Texas, 45.7 percent of the non-elderly population was uninsured at some point in the previous two years; in New Mexico, the percentage was 44.3 percent; in Arizona, it was 41.8 percent; in California, it was 40.5 percent; and in Florida, it was 40.1 percent.[11]

Even among those who are insured, the portions of their incomes devoted to family health expenses have grown enormously. According to a Families USA report issued recently, approximately 62 million Americans are in families that will spend more than 10 percent of their *pre-tax* income on health care in 2008, an increase of 17 million people from the beginning of the decade.[12] Approximately 17 million people will spend more than 25 percent of their *pre-tax* income on health care in 2008.[13] These data vividly illustrate why health care costs have become the single largest cause of bankruptcies in the United States—with the overwhelming majority of these bankrupted individuals experiencing this hardship despite the fact that they had health insurance.[14]

As these problems grow and public concern mounts, the possibility of achieving meaningful health care reform early in the next administration seems increasingly realistic. However, as several Presidents have learned dating back as far as the 1930s—including Franklin Roosevelt, Harry Truman, John Kennedy, Lyndon Johnson, Richard Nixon, Jimmy Carter and Bill Clinton—it is not easy to enact meaningful health care reform. Indeed, all tried with little success to enact major health reforms. Hence, it is important to assess the obstacles that must be overcome if health reform is to succeed this time.

The Key Obstacles to Achieving
Meaningful Health Care Reform

As history shows, it is always much easier to stop health care reforms than it is to pass them. Indeed, the only significant federal reforms in health care occurred in 1965 with the enactment of Medicare and Medicaid. That singular, major success, however, was achieved under rather unusual political circumstances: Lyndon Johnson had just won a landslide victory over Barry Goldwater—a tidal wave that resulted in Democrats controlling two-thirds of the membership in the Senate and House of Representatives. At no time since that period has any political party had such hegemony over national policymaking.

Meaningful health care reform will necessarily be controversial, and its enactment will depend on a super, bipartisan Congressional majority. That is because major health care reform is likely to be subjected to a Senate filibuster, and at least sixty votes will be needed to invoke cloture and end the filibuster. As a result, it will be essential for any health care reform effort to galvanize support among bipartisan and moderate political groups and members of Congress if meaningful health care reform is to be adopted.

To secure meaningful health care reform, it is important to consider four key lessons gleaned from previous failures. *First*, there is a significant likelihood that conservative and special interest groups will spend substantial sums to defeat health care reform. In 1993–1994, for example, the opponents of the Clinton health care plan spent more than $300 million to fight and propagandize against reform.[15] Based on the more recent experience with the limited reauthorization of SCHIP in 2007, we can assume that opposition to much more comprehensive reform is likely to be vigorous. Hence, supporters of reform must coalesce with significant resources and work in a cooperative and disciplined manner.

Second, in earlier reform efforts, the opposition was united and consistent with its messaging. Supporters of reform, on the other hand, were fragmented, and their messaging had little coherence and consistency. Indeed, they exhibited a so-called "yes, but" syndrome—expressing weak overall support for the notion of reform while highlighting the many, inevitable imperfections in the pending reform. As a result, the media portrayed the pending reform as enjoying precious little support. Such fragmentation by the potential supporters of reform must be avoided this time.

Third, all of the major health care stakeholders—including liberal and conservative organizations, groups aligned with the Democratic and Republican parties, as well as public (non-profit) interest and special (commercial) interest groups—exhibited the same destructive behavior during past iterations of (failed) health care reform debates. In all of these debates, the stakeholder organizations came into the process touting their top-priority proposal. However, when it appeared that their top-priority proposal would not be enacted, they opposed or refused to support any other proposal. In effect, therefore, their second-favorite choice was the status quo. Not surprisingly, therefore, we ended up with the status quo, and the opportunities for meaningful health care reform were squandered. A different and more cooperative inter-organizational dynamic needs to occur if the opportunities for historic health care reform in 2009 are to succeed.

Fourth, meaningful health care reform is only likely if the incoming President and Congress make it a very high *and early* priority. Even though President Clinton was deeply committed to meaningful health care reform, the effort to secure such reform occurred late in his first year—after the divisive debate about the North American Free Trade Agreement, the effort to balance the federal budget, and the creation of the "don't ask, don't tell" policy about gays in the military. By the time President Clinton gave his speech about health care reform in September 1993 and subsequently introduced his proposal, much of the President's political capital had been expended. Timeliness in initiating and completing the next iteration of health care reform will be critical to its success.

Expanding Health Coverage

Employer-sponsored health insurance coverage is slowly but steadily declining. In 2000, the portion of the American population with employer-sponsored health insurance was 64.2 percent.[16] As of 2006, the percentage had declined to 59.7 percent.[17] Perhaps more significantly, employer-sponsored health insurance now requires considerably greater financial payments by working families—as employers, saddled with growing costs, shift a greater portion of premiums, deductibles, co-payments and uncovered services onto the shoulders of employees.[18]

This does not mean that employer-sponsored health insurance is near an end—or should come to an end. Approximately 180 million Americans today receive their coverage through their employer or the employer of their family's breadwinner.[19] Most people with employer-sponsored health insurance are satisfied with it.[20] and would feel threatened if a proposal were promoted that resulted in loss of their job-based coverage. Such a proposal would violate a clear lesson learned from previous, failed health reform efforts: Do not threaten the health coverage of those who have it today.

However, the steady erosion of employer-sponsored health coverage suggests that group coverage alternatives should be established. The creation of such alternatives would enable working families to have portable health coverage so that they can keep that coverage if they move from one job to another or if they are laid off. Additionally, such alternatives would protect people from being forced into the individual health insurance market—a market that is largely unregulated,[21] that denies health coverage to those who need it the most, and that constitutes the "wild, wild west" of health insurance.

To foster such alternatives, it makes abundant sense to create a system like the Federal Employee Health Benefit Program (FEHBP), the program that serves Members of Congress and other federal employees. A comparable system, called the Health Care Connector, was established by the historic Massachusetts health reform law. Such a system arrays a number of private plans for selection by individuals as well as small businesses—plans that meet coverage, cost and regulatory standards (such as prohibitions against denying care or charging discriminatory, high premiums for people with pre-existing health conditions) established by a quasi-public, quasi-private agency. Preferably, it would include a public plan option as well that would compete with the private plans for enrollees.

.

People experiencing difficulties affording health coverage, but whose incomes render them ineligible for Medicaid or SCHIP, should be assisted with tax credits. To ensure that those tax credits provide realistic help, the credits should be refundable (thereby helping people with limited or no tax liabilities), substantial (so that they are not the economic equivalent of throwing a ten-foot rope for someone in a forty-foot hole), and advanceable (so that they help as premiums fall due, not on April 15 in the following year). To ensure proper targeting and that the tax credits truly make health coverage affordable, they should be offered on a sliding-scale basis.

Health reform should also seek to modernize the eligibility standards for Medicaid—the key public safety net system for people who can't get employer-sponsored health coverage and are too poor to pay for it on their own. Today's state-by-state eligibility standards for public coverage have their roots in the sixteenth-century Elizabethan Poor Laws of England and are based too little on need and too much on family status. A comparison of eligibility standards for three groups (children, the parents of those children, and non-parental adults) makes this clear.

In the overwhelming majority of states, children are eligible for public health coverage if they are in families with annual incomes below 200 percent of the federal poverty level ($34,340 for a family of three, $40,300 for a family of four).[22] However, the median income eligibility standard among the fifty states for the parents of these children is only approximately one-third of the standard for children (63 percent of the federal poverty level)[23]—and, as a result, the parents of children eligible for public coverage are often excluded from such coverage. For non-parental adults (singles and childless couples), the situation is even worse: In forty-two states, such adults can literally be penniless and yet they don't qualify for Medicaid.[24] Clearly, the eligibility standards need to be modernized and upgraded so they enable all low-income people to participate.

Additionally, health care reform should correct the injustice to legal immigrants that was enacted in 1996. As part of the welfare reform law, Congress prohibited legal immigrants from becoming eligible for public health coverage until they live in the country for five years.[25] Perhaps more significantly, at the end of those five years, the law authorized states to count the income of the immigration-sponsoring family as if it were available to the immigrant family—a fiction that wrongfully imputes that the immigrant family has "too much income" to qualify for Medicaid.[26] This injustice should be remedied.

Promoting Affordability and High-Quality Care

Expanding health coverage without moderating the skyrocketing costs of health care would be short-sighted. At best, it would provide a temporary fix to help the uninsured, but that fix would ultimately be undone if health care costs continue to escalate well beyond general inflation. Hence, real health care reform must moderate the unaffordable spiral of health care costs.

Some of the proposed "solutions" to the health care cost problem are a ruse and would exacerbate the affordability crisis for many millions of Americans. For example, some suggest that public policy should encourage the proliferation of high-deductible insurance policies, possibly coupled with Health Savings Accounts (HSAs). Those high-deductible policies—which, at this writing, can be as high as $10,500 per year for family coverage—would have a minimal impact on costs since the overwhelming majority of health care costs are for people needing expensive, specialized care.[27] The high-deductible policies, however, would deter the use of primary (and possibly preventive) care, which a good health care system should encourage, not discourage. Moreover, the coupling of high-deductible policies with HSAs would result in a very regressive tax benefit that would disproportionately help people in the highest tax brackets.[28]

Instead, an effective health cost strategy should seek to reduce unnecessary—indeed, often harmful—care. By some estimates, 30 percent of care is unneeded and does not comport with the best science.[29] Moreover, there are wide variations from one community to another in per-capita health care costs as well as the utilization of the most expensive health procedures.[30] Perhaps most importantly, the health care status and patient mortality in these high-cost, high-utilization communities are often worse than the results in less expensive communities.[31]

Health care reform, therefore, should include a significant investment in cost-effectiveness research guided by experts appointed by a quasi-public, quasi-private entity. The fruits of that research should be widely disseminated to physicians, hospitals, other health care providers and consumers. Additionally, payment systems devised by public and private payers of health care should be reformed so that they encourage evidence-based, cost-effective medical care.

For people with chronic health conditions or disabilities, thoughtful health care reform should encourage much better coordination of care, as the best practitioners of managed care have actually provided. Since people with chronic health conditions often suffer from multiple health problems, it is crucial that care be coordinated among different specialists, thereby ensuring that treatment of one problem does not exacerbate another. Increased reliance on so-called "medical homes," especially for people with chronic health conditions, would make abundant sense.

To further encourage good coordination of care, health care reform efforts should also encourage and invest in the creation of electronic medical records. This, of course, needs to be done with utmost sensitivity about patient privacy. We should also accelerate the availability and use of e-prescribing, thereby eliminating reliance on indecipherable physician scribbles that often lead to harmful and expensive medical errors.

Some other reforms, focused on unnecessary and extravagant costs in the Medicare program, should also be implemented. For starters, the windfall overpayments to private health insurance companies in the so-called "Medicare Advantage" program should be eliminated. The Medicare Payment Advisory Commission (MedPAC) estimates that these private plans are overpaid by 13 percent, for a current annual windfall of approximately $10 billion.[32] Even worse, the fastest-growing portion of "Medicare Advantage" is the private fee-for-service plans which MedPAC estimates are receiving 17 percent overpayments.[33] The only reason these plans are overpaid is because the Bush Administration and its Congressional allies have sought to privatize Medicare. This can and should be remedied.

Additionally, when the Bush Administration and Congress established Medicare Part D (the prescription drug benefit), the statute, at the behest of the pharmaceutical lobby, was written to prohibit Medicare from bargaining for cheaper drug prices. However, based on the experience of the Department of Veterans Affairs (VA), which does bargain for cheaper drug prices for veterans, a great deal of money could be saved if the Medicare bargaining prohibition were lifted. Among the top 20 drugs prescribed to seniors, the median difference between the lowest Part D plan price and the lowest VA price is 58 percent.[34] Congress should eliminate this costly extravagance that unnecessarily burdens Medicare beneficiaries and taxpayers.

Achieving Meaningful Health Care Reform

Now is the time to achieve meaningful health care reform. As past history shows, this will not be easy. However, with strong and timely leadership by our next President and Congress, the opportunities to succeed are much greater now than ever before. By building on what works today, and by remedying our health system's clearest weaknesses, we can establish a uniquely American health system that assures everyone will receive high-quality, affordable health care.

Resources

Alliance for Health Reform: www.allhealth.org
BenefitsCheckUp: www.benefitscheckup.org
The Center on Budget and Policy Priorities: www.cbpp.org
The Commonwealth Fund: www.cmwf.org
Community Catalyst: www.communitycatalyst.org
Consumer's Union: www.consumersunion.org
Cover the Uninsured Week: www.covertheuninsured.org
The Department of Health and Human Services: www.hhs.gov
The Employee Health Benefit Research Institute: www.ebri.org
Healthinsuranceinfo.net: www.healthinsuranceinfo.net

The Kaiser Family Foundation: www.kff.org
Medicare.gov: www.medicare.gov
The Medicare Rights Center: www.medicarerights.org
The National Conference of State Legislatures: www.ncsl.org
The National Partnership for Women and Families: www.nationalpartnership
.org

Notes

1. Kaiser Family Foundation, "Economy Tops List of Issues Voters Want Candidates to Discuss; Health Care Drops to Third Behind Iraq," *Kaiser Health Tracking Poll: Election 2008*, Issue 6, March 2008; Jackie Calmes and Michael M. Phillips, "Economy Moves to Fore as Issue for 2008 Voters," *The Wall Street Journal*, December 4, 2007; and Robin Toner and Janet Elder, "Most Support U.S. Guarantee of Health Care," *The New York Times*, March 2, 2007.

2. Business Roundtable, *Health Care Costs in America: A Call to Action for Covering the Uninsured* (Washington, D.C.: Business Roundtable, June 2007); and Jordan Rau, "Universal Healthcare Gains Unlikely Backer," *Los Angeles Times*, May 7, 2007.

3. Health Care Coverage Coalition for the Uninsured, *Expanding Health Care Coverage in the United States: A Historic Agreement* (Washington, D.C.: Health Care Coverage Coalition for the Uninsured, January 2007).

4. Kim Bailey, *Premiums Versus Paychecks: A Growing Burden for California's Workers* (Washington, D.C.: Families USA, September 2008).

5. Kim Bailey, *Premiums Versus Paychecks: A Growing Burden for Michigan's Workers* (Washington, D.C.: Families USA, September 2008).

6. Carmen DeNavas-Walt, Bernadette Proctor, and Jessica Smith, *Income, Poverty, and Health Insurance Coverage in the United States: 2007* (Washington, D.C.: U.S. Census Bureau, August 2008).

7. Calculations on file with Families USA.

8. Carmen DeNavas-Walt, Bernadette Proctor, and Jessica Smith, op cit.

9. Kim Bailey, *Wrong Direction: One Out of Three Americans Are Uninsured* (Washington, D.C.: Families USA, September 2007).

10. Ibid.

11. Ibid.

12. Kim Bailey and Beth Wikler, "Too Great a Burden: America's Families at Risk" (Washington, D.C.: Families USA, December 2007).

13. Ibid.

14. David Himmelstein, Elizabeth Warren, Deborah Thorne, and Steffie Woolhander, "Illness and Injury as Contributors to Bankruptcy," *Health Affairs*, Web Exclusive, February 2, 2005: W5-63–W5-73.

15. Steven Waldman, Bob Cohn, and Eleanor Clift, "The Lost Chance," *Newsweek* September 19, 1994 (Updated February 7, 2008).

16. Carmen DeNavas-Walt, Bernadette Proctor, and Jessica Smith, op cit.

17. Ibid.

18. James Robinson, "Reinvention of Health Insurance in the Consumer Era," *Journal of the American Medical Association* 291, no. 15, April 21, 2004: 1,880–1,886; See

also Cathy Schoen, Michelle Doty, Sara Collins, and Alyssa Holmgren, "Insured but Not Protected: How Many Adults Are Uninsured?" *Health Affairs* Web Exclusive, June 14, 2005: W5-289–W5-302.

19. Carmen DeNavas-Walt, Bernadette Proctor, and Jessica Smith, op cit.

20. Ruth Helman and Paul Fronstin, "2007 Health Confidence Survey: Rising Health Care Costs Are Changing the Ways Americans Use the Health Care System," *EBRI Notes,* Vol. 28, No. 11, November 2007.

21. Ella Hushagen and Cheryl Fish-Parcham, *Failing Grades: State Consumer Protections in the Individual Health Insurance Market* (Washington, D.C.: Families USA, June 2008).

22. Kaiser State Health Facts Online, "Income Eligibility Levels for Children's Separate SCHIP Programs by Annual Incomes and as a Percent of Federal Poverty Level, 2008," available at http://www.statehealthfacts.org/comparemaptable.jsp?ind=204&cat =4 (accessed on July 7, 2008).

23. Families USA calculations of the median income eligibility level for working parents in states that offer the standard Medicaid package or comparable coverage to working parents based on data from Kaiser State Health Facts Online, "Income Eligibility for Parents Applying for Medicaid by Annual Income as a Percent of Federal Poverty Level, 2008," available at http://www.statehealthfacts.org/comparetable.jsp?ind=205& cat=4 (accessed on July 7, 2008).

24. A list of states that provide some level of coverage to adults without children who do not qualify for disability-related coverage is on file with Families USA.

25. Kaiser Commission on Medicaid and the Uninsured, *Medicaid and SCHIP Eligibility for Immigrants* (Washington, D.C.: Kaiser Family Foundation, April 2006).

26. Ibid.

27. U.S. Department of the Treasury, *Health Savings Accounts* (Washington, D.C.: U.S. Department of the Treasury, January 2008), available at http://www.ustreas.gov/ offices/public-affairs/hsa/pdf/HSA-Tri-fold-english-07.pdf (accessed July 20, 2008).

28. Families USA, *HSAs: Missing the Target* (Washington, D.C.: Families USA, November 2006).

29. John Wennberg, Elliott Fisher, David Goodman, and Jonathan Skinner, *Tracking the Care of Patients with Severe Chronic Illness: The Dartmouth Atlas of Health Care 2008* (Lebanon, NH: The Dartmouth Institute for Health Policy and Clinical Practice, 2008).

30. John Wennberg, Elliott Fisher, and Jonathan Skinner, "Geography and the Debate Over Medicare Reform," *Health Affairs* Web Exclusive (February 13, 2002): W96– W114. See also Peter Orszag, *Opportunities to Increase Efficiency in Health Care, Statement at the Health Reform,* Summit of the Committee on Finance of the United States Senate, June 16, 2008.

31. John Wennberg, Elliott Fisher, David Goodman, and Jonathan Skinner, op cit.

32. Medicare Payment Advisory Commission, *Report to Congress: Medicare Payment Policy* (Washington, D.C.: Medicare Payment Advisory Commission, March 2008).

33. Ibid.

34. Marc Steinberg and Kim Bailey, *No Bargain: Medicare Drug Plans Deliver High Prices* (Washington, D.C.: Families USA, January 2007).

Chapter 4

The Education (Policy) We Need for the Citizens We Have

Gloria Ladson-Billings

POLICY PROPOSALS

- Re-invest in public education by increasing financial commitments and incentives to schools.
- Provide incentives and rewards for schools/districts that decrease the educational disparities between racial/ethnic groups and actively deseg-regate schools and within-school programming
- Encourage schools/districts to use rigorous and intellectually stimulating curricula without punishing those who initially post lower standardized test scores.
- Prepare and encourage qualified teachers by re-instituting a National Direct Student Loan–like program that forgives student loans of those who agree to teach in hard-to-staff schools/communities.
- Support the use of multiple assessments to determine student progress and achievement.
- Encourage innovation and re-invention rather than cookie-cutter school-ing experiences for all students.

* * * * * * * * * * * * * * *

Every four to eight years hope emerges on the American political landscape. U.S. citizens invariably believe that possibility for change and improvement exists through its political process. Whether that hope is naïve, misplaced or wrong-headed, it still exists. We want to believe that we can be better. With that prevailing worldview in place, I want to suggest that there are at least six important education policy stances that the incoming Administration must engage in in order to both engender our loyalty and sustain our hope.

Re-invest in Public Education

I could just as easily have termed this policy re-investing in the public, since the current trend in our nation is toward privatization. The strong emphasis on public services—transportation, housing, health and education—that blossomed in the Franklin Roosevelt Administration has evaporated in this era of neo-liberalism. Without sounding too nostalgic about a bygone era (after all, as an African American, little about the pre–civil rights era is to be fondly remembered), I want to remind us that that we depended upon these public services because they were safe, reliable, accessible and affordable. Working-class and poor people were able to live in clean and safe housing, take buses, trolleys and subways to the clinic to receive immunizations for their children who attended their local public schools. To no one's surprise, many middle-income people also accessed those same services.

In our current environment, we have retreated from the public sphere. Middle-income people want to live behind security gates, retain private health care services and send their children to private schools. In a democracy they have the right to do each of those things, but doing them should not mean that people pull away from the public discourse and interchange. When one's decision to seek private services means disdain and antagonism toward those who need public services, we find ourselves in a place where "public" becomes a dirty word.

Public education is one of the areas where the nation is beating a steady retreat. From the 1983 Commission on Excellence in Education Report, *A Nation at Risk*, to the passage of the Bush Administration's re-authorization of the Elementary and Secondary Education Act known as "No Child Left Behind" (NCLB), we have seen a combination of more federal intervention coupled with less federal (and as a consequence, public) support. This lack of support for public education is more acute in urban school districts serving large numbers of students of color, immigrant students, and working-class and poor students. Many of the predictions of doom and gloom about public schools focus on the twenty-five largest urban school districts. This is an interesting figure, since there are approximately 14,000 public school districts in the United States (NCES, 2001). Thus, the case against public education is being made based on those districts that generally are suffering from inadequate funding, deteriorating facilities and shrinking tax bases. The face of public education appears to us (much like the face of public transportation in many communities, and certainly the face of public housing), as a poor, often immigrant face of color. This is not a face middle-class America wants to see or acknowledge and certainly not a face with which it identifies.

For the past twenty-five years, public education has been under attack for failing to provide the kind of education Americans believe is needed for the changing work force. However, there is little discussion about the preparation of citizens for a highly complex, technology-driven, multicultural society. Educating citizens is the primary task of public education, and while that education must include knowledge of basic skills (i.e., mathematics, reading, writing), exposure to great thinkers and great ideas, and preparation for post-secondary education and the workforce, fundamentally the project of public education is to develop citizens who can and will engage with the democratic process. The very notion of civic capacity (Stone et al., 2001) relies heavily on building broad coalitions of citizens across political and social boundaries to pursue common goals.

The current calls for private school choice through publicly funded voucher programs move directly away from creating a civic culture that values its citizens regardless of their race, ethnicity or socioeconomic status. While the notion of giving individual families a voucher to be used as they choose appeals to the "freedom of choice" rhetoric, it ignores the notion of the public good that makes for a strong democracy. No voucher program can fully fund most private school education, but most proposals would provide enough money to allow middle-income families to supplement their choice. On the other hand, really poor families would not have enough to move into elite private schools and would find themselves permanently relegated to poorly funded schools lacking adequately prepared teachers, with inferior educational materials and supplies.

Create Equitable Education

We cannot claim to be re-investing in public education as long as we tolerate the inequitable outcomes that students experience in our schools. Two issues— school funding and school desegregation—are at the heart of those outcomes. According to Jonathan Kozol (2005), suburban school districts regularly spend thousands of dollars more per pupil than nearby urban counterparts. This funding disparity reflects a cumulative economic shortfall that did not always represent a divide between urban and suburban. Initially, the divide was between White schools and Black schools. In states that established two racially separate school districts, the majority of public resources went to White schools. Once the 1954 *Brown v. Board of Education* Supreme Court decision made public school segregation illegal, many White community members found ways to maintain all-White schools by moving beyond the city limits. Thus, the growing suburbs with their expanding tax bases were able to pay for newer schools, better equipment and fully qualified teachers. At the same time, urban schools were being left to poor and working-class students who were living in the midst of shrinking tax bases. Those wealthy families who remained in cities were able to opt out of public education while enjoying the benefits of city life. We will

never create equitable outcomes until we insist on equitable funding and real
school desegregation.

Provide a High-Quality Curriculum

In the 1983 Report of the Commission on Excellence in Education, *A Nation at
Risk,* the Commission reported that the cafeteria-style approach to the U.S. public school curriculum (in secondary schools) was ineffective in improving the
academic quality of our schools. The Commission report called for a core curriculum (four years of English, mathematics, science and social studies, with a
half year of computer literacy). What the Commission did not recognize was the
inter-related and complex way learning occurs and how that complexity demands knowledge of the arts and humanities as well as physical education.

A high-quality curriculum is not a stripped-down, barebones set of courses
that we push all students through. Rather, a high-quality curriculum provides
students with learning opportunities that help them link knowledge, skills and
information from a variety of disciplines. In 1978, when California voters chose
property tax relief over investment in the public good, the quality of the public
school curriculum suffered tremendously. Wealthy school districts were able to
supplement the loss of revenue by creating public school foundations that replaced the courses that school districts deemed "frills." And, in those cases
where foundation monies could not (or would not) supplement curriculum and
personnel, parents in these communities were able to purchase such services for
their individual students—e.g., music lessons, art lessons, dance lessons, sports
and athletic training opportunities.

The idea of an enriched curriculum is that engaged citizens first engage
their minds. Young people regularly rate courses and school activities such as
art, music, drama and sports as their favorite among all school offerings. The
call for enriched curriculum is not merely a response to popularity but rather an
understanding that the so-called "basic skills" of literacy and mathematics have
to be applied in broader, more meaningful contexts in order for students to understand how and why they are important to their overall development as human
beings. Courses in the arts and physical education help to humanize us in ways
rote learning of facts and figures can never do. To provide this kind of enrich-
ment only for those who can individually pay for it is to guarantee the continuation of a bifurcated society of haves and have-nots, of those with access to high
literacy (the ability to read critically across disciplines and produce knowledge)
and those relegated to low literacy (those who cannot make simple connections
and merely consume knowledge). A highly complex, highly technological society requires its citizens to comprehend, analyze, synthesize and evaluate large
bodies of information across multiple disciplines.

Prepare and Hire Qualified Teachers

Despite what policymakers and pundits argue, the place where educational improvement will take place is invariably the classroom. Thus, teachers are fundamental to the process of education change and improvement. However, teaching continues to be a poorly regarded (and poorly compensated) profession. Generations ago, sociologist Dan Lortie (1969) called teaching a "semi-profession" because it lacked the autonomy, authority and prestige of other professions like medicine, law, religion or architecture.

Since the early 1980s, teachers have received relentless criticism for failing to improve the educational outcomes of all students. Clearly, public school teachers have a major responsibility in teaching all students, but they must first be well-prepared to take on such a task. Demographic data suggest that while the complexion of the student population in large urban classrooms is increasingly non-white and non-English-speaking, the teachers who stand before these classrooms are just the opposite. Most students will experience learning under the tutelage of White, middle-class, monolingual English, female teachers, and in the case of urban students, these teachers are more likely to be people whose first choice was not to teach in the school and/or school district to which she was assigned. A study of urban teachers in Georgia (Freeman et al., 2002) indicated that White teachers regularly moved out of a school district as the number of African-American students increased.

Surveys of new teachers regularly report that the area that teachers feel least prepared in is "teaching diverse students" (National Comprehensive Center for Teacher Quality and Public Agenda, 2008). Because relatively few teachers want to teach in urban districts serving large numbers of poor children of color, these schools often find themselves without fully qualified teachers in crucial areas like mathematics, science, bilingual, and special education (National Partnership for Teaching in At-Risk Schools, 2005). The primary placements for teachers who receive their preparation in alternative programs such as Teach for America (TFA) are what the literature terms "hard to staff" schools (Foote, 2008). The desire to provide volunteer service for the nation's schools represents a noble calling on the part of the young people who apply to TFA and other alternative teacher preparation programs, but it reflects both the lack of regard our society has both for teaching as a profession (i.e., a belief that anybody can teach) and for the students who have the greatest need of high quality teachers.

Thus, we need to pay close attention to how we educate and prepare teachers for so-called hard-to-staff schools. I have deliberately differentiated between education and preparation. Teachers are entitled to broad educational experiences in the liberal arts and sciences (English, mathematics, science, social sciences, visual and performing arts) and deep educational knowledge in some area of study to make them well-versed in some discipline. Teachers also need the opportunity to learn how to teach their disciplines along with the requisite background knowledge in human development (child and adolescent) and the social, historical and cultural nature of schooling in a democratic society.

Finally, any serious effort toward recruiting and hiring qualified teachers for the nation's schools will require an adequate reward and compensation system. According to the National Education Association, the average annual salary for America's teachers is $47,605. Starting salaries vary greatly by states. On the low end, new teachers in Arkansas, Louisiana and Mississippi earn $29,725, $29,150 and $30,000, respectively, while new teachers in California, Connecticut and Massachusetts earn $37,645, $36,694 and $34,995, respectively. The National Association of Colleges and Employers indicates that the 2007 jobs outlook for new college graduates was: for accounting, $46,508; for business/management, $43,523; for computer sciences, $51,070; and for economics, $51,631. One can clearly see that we compensate new teachers at a far lower rate than these fields. A new Administration can help on the front end by reinvigorating the National Direct Student Loan program (now known as the Perkins Loan program) that will forgive student loans for those who elect to teach in hard-to-staff schools and communities. This would be different from the current iteration of the Perkins Loan program that focuses primarily on providing needs-based loans to applicants rather than encouraging a wider variety of students to go into teaching.

Promote Fair and Valid Assessments

Most of the education reforms of the last two decades have demanded accountability, and that accountability for the most part has fallen on the backs of students. The demand is for students to perform at higher levels in selected subject matter areas (e.g., English/reading, writing, mathematics and science), as measured by standardized tests. The open question is whether or not the current assessments are telling us what we need to know about student learning. Current federal legislation forces states and individual school districts to use testing as punishment rather than as important diagnostic tools. Right now the information we have about student assessment tells us the obvious—students living in poverty, attending poorly resourced schools, with inexperienced and/or less qualified teachers are more likely to post lower achievement test scores than their more affluent counterparts in wealthy, well-resourced school districts with experienced, well-qualified teachers.

Until we get better measures of student achievement (both the assessments and the interpretation of their results across contexts) we will continue to denigrate districts serving large numbers of poor students and chastise them for not performing at the same level as wealthier school districts. Thus, we need more robust measures of student achievement—performance-based or authentic tasks—to draw fuller pictures of what students know and are able to do. For example, West Philadelphia High School is rarely lauded for its academic achievement but regularly fields a team in its automotive technology program that wins (or competitively places) in the Tour de Sol hybrid and electric energy automotive competition. Current standardized tests cannot tell us much about the kind (and depth) of learning that took place in the experience of building the cars. Non-traditional learning programs throughout the country offer powerful learning experiences that we cannot capture on standardized tests. The idea is not to do away with standardized testing but to use them in more reasonable and fair ways to improve teaching and learning.

Encourage Innovation and Re-invention

Even the most ardent supporters of public education bemoan the fact that schools tend to be very bureaucratic and rarely allow for innovation among local administrators, teachers, community members or students. As a consequence, frustrated constituents look for ways to work outside of the system to get their needs for change met. The current charter school movement is evidence of the high degrees of dissatisfaction people are experiencing with the public schools. "Over one million students are enrolled in more than 3,500 schools in 40 states plus the District of Columbia and Puerto Rico this year" (http://www.uscharterschools.org/pub/uscs_docs/o/index.htm, retrieved electronically on June 13, 2008).

As we revisit the federal role in public education (via the re-authorization of the Elementary and Secondary Education Act), we must challenge ourselves to move creatively between autonomy and standardization. What are the fundamental aspects of educating students well that all schools must attend to (e.g., reading, writing, mathematics, science, preparation for post-secondary life), and what are the individual variations that schools must have the opportunities to pursue (e.g., attention to intellectual, community, cultural, etc. interests)? This is a delicate balancing act but one that American schools have always sought to manage. The very nature of our diversity means that we will have variation even when we think we are standardizing. New leadership will have to be courageous enough to say that what we need is not merely a public school system but rather systems of public schooling that foster, not thwart, innovation and change.

Although I am loath to adopt a business model, high-tech companies that thrive on innovation and variation from standard regimens fascinate me. Some rely on differentiated work groups. Others foster internal competition that is not divisive but stimulating. Still others allow workers great latitude in structuring their work day. Ultimately, such organizations keep an eye on meeting their goals rather than rigidly attending to the pathways for getting to those goals. For public education to be viable it will have to embrace notions of radical re-invention that serves democratic life. New leadership must be willing to embrace both vanguard (out-front) and grassroots (bottom-up) leadership to ensure this innovation.

Resources

U.S. Charter: http://www.uscharterschools.org/pub/uscs_docs/o/index.htm.

References

Commission on Excellence in Education. *A Nation At Risk: The Imperative for Educational Reform*. Washington, D.C.: Commission on Excellence in Education, 1983.

Foote, Donna. *Relentless Pursuit: A Year in the Trenches with Teach for America*. New York: Alfred Knopf, 2008.

Freeman, Catherine, Ben Scafidi, and David Sjoquist. *Racial Segregation in Georgia Public Schools, 1994-2001: Trends, Causes, and Impacts on Teacher Quality*. Report of the Andrew Young School of Policy Studies. Atlanta: Georgia State University, 2002.

Kozol, Jonathan. *The Shame of the Nation: The Restoration of Apartheid Schooling in America*. New York: Crown Publishers, 2005.

Lortie, Dan. "The Balance of Control and Autonomy in Elementary School Teaching." In *The Semi-Professions and Their Organizations*, ed. Amitai Etzioni. New York: The Free Press, 1969.

National Center for Education Statistics (NCES). "Revenue and Expenditures by Public School Districts: School Year 2001." *Education Statistics Quarterly* Vol. 6 (2005). http://nces.ed.gov/programs/quarterly/vol_6/1_2/4_3.asp accessed on 06/03/08 (accessed July 18, 2008).

National Comprehensive Center for Teacher Quality and Public Agenda. "Lessons Learned: New Teachers Talk About Their Jobs, Challenges, and Long Range Plans." Report 3 (2008).

National Partnership for Teaching in At-Risk Schools. *Qualified Teachers for At-Risk Schools: A National Imperative*. Report. Washington, DC: National Partnership for Teaching in At-Risk Schools, 2005.

Stone, Clarence, et al. *Building Civic Capacity: The Politics of Reforming Urban Schools*. Lawrence: University of Kansas Press, 2001.

Chapter 5

The Affordable Housing Crisis: It Is a Solvable Problem

Sheila Crowley

POLICY PROPOSALS

- Immediately implement National Housing Trust Fund and expand dedicated funding to at least $5 billion a year to meet goal of 1,500,000 units produced or preserved in ten years.
- Reform and revitalize HUD, starting with appointment of a Secretary who has demonstrated expertise in developing and operating good housing that is affordable for the lowest-income people and who is trusted and respected by the low-income housing community.
- Redistribute federal housing subsidies by reducing tax benefits to high-income people and funding federal housing programs at levels required to assure affordable and decent housing for all.
- Advance policies that will rebalance the nation's housing supply to meet current and future housing needs of all people; re-frame the meaning of housing from asset to home.
- Preserve and improve the federally assisted housing stock, protecting residents in good standing and preparing for its use for future generations.
- Expand the number of federal housing vouchers by at least 2,000,000 and maximize mobility opportunities that vouchers can provide.
- Enforce and strengthen the federal fair housing laws, including protection against discrimination on the basis of sources of income and fighting community opposition to the sitting of affordable housing.
- Commit to a full housing recovery of the Gulf Coast communities destroyed by Hurricanes Katrina and Rita.

■ **Remember to protect the hidden victims of the foreclosure crisis, low-income renters.**

* * * * * * * * * * * * * *

The majority of people in the United States have good housing in neighborhoods of their choosing at costs they can afford. But too many are poorly housed: Their homes are in inferior condition; too many people live in too small a space; they pay more than they reasonably afford to house themselves and their families; or their homes are in places that are dangerous or isolated from economic opportunities. The most desperate housing circumstances of all are faced by those who have no homes at all, the homeless. The housing problems of the poor are long-standing and have not been of enough concern to the larger population to warrant sufficient attention from policymakers.

But in 2008 housing problems hit the front page as mortgage foreclosures mounted and sent shock waves through the international economy. The crisis is a focusing event that is exposing the fault lines in U.S. housing policy and housing markets. There is plenty of blame to go around for the mortgage foreclosure crisis, including the thought purveyors and policymakers who have uncritically promoted homeownership as the idealized form of housing tenure in the United States and the path to the middle class for low-income people. The rhetoric on homeownership in America, equating it with worthiness and patriotism, in a political era that favored an unregulated market, created a fertile environment for risky and unscrupulous lending practices to flourish, while people who should have known better colluded or looked the other way.

A social environment saturated with messages that have propelled low-income people to seek homeownership at all costs has also delivered the corollary message that rental housing is inferior. And if rental housing is inferior, rental housing affordable for low-income people is downright undesirable. We need look no further than the diminished federal investment in low-income housing programs for evidence of the neglect of the rental housing sector. The virulent protests that erupt in communities across the country when proposals to build more low-income rental housing become public also demonstrate the degree to which rental housing is rejected as a necessary housing choice in a healthy community.

The interventions that the federal government has taken or will take to address the current foreclosure crisis should not be for the purpose of restoring the status quo. Rather, the opportunity should be seized to solve the larger problems in the U.S. housing market.

Housing affordability remains the single largest problem, but no more so than for the lowest-income renters.[1] Nowhere in the country can a full-time worker earning the minimum wage afford the rent in a modest one-bedroom home. In order to afford a two-bedroom rental home in Chicago, a household must earn $29,360 a year; in Phoenix, it is $24,360 a year.[2]

There is an acute shortage of rental housing that extremely low-income households (households in the bottom 30 percent of income in their areas) can afford. There are more than 9 million extremely low-income renters, 25 percent of all renters in the country. There are only 6.2 million rental housing units affordable to these households, based on the standard of affordability of no more than 30 percent of household income, for a shortage of over 2.8 million homes. Moreover, many of the units that are affordable to extremely low-income households are rented by higher-income people, such that the real shortage is 5.6 million units. Nationwide, there are just thirty-eight affordable and available rental units for every 100 extremely low-income households. Distributed across states, the ratio ranges from twenty-three in California to sixty-five in South Dakota.[3]

Due to this shortage, the majority of extremely low-income families pay substantially more for their homes than they can afford. Seventy-one percent of extremely low-income households pay more than half of their income for their homes, forcing them to forego other basic necessities and putting them at risk of eviction.[4] Extremely low-income households are those that are supported by people who toil in the low-wage workforce, performing jobs that are essential for everyone else to do their jobs, as well elderly and disabled people on fixed incomes. It is this shortage of housing affordable to this group that is the cause of homelessness. Under such conditions of scarcity, it is the people with the fewest resources, the weakest support systems and the most disabling conditions who are at greatest risk of losing their homes. No other income group comes close with regard to the percent of income consumed by housing.[5]

In 2009, it will be sixty years since Congress declared "the goal of a decent home and a suitable living environment for every American family."[6] The country can and should make good on this goal. It is well within the capacity of Americans to do so if we choose so. The incoming President should reaffirm this goal and pledge to achieve it during his Administration.

A National Housing Trust Fund

Legislation to establish a National Housing Trust Fund was signed into law on July 30, 2008. Implementation of the program should begin immediately. But that will be just the beginning. The legislation set up the framework of the program and provides for the first source of dedicated revenue, estimated to be about $300 million a year when fully phased in. This will produce about 3,000 homes. Much more will be needed to reach the goal of 1,500,000 homes in ten years.

National Housing Trust Fund advocates have examined several other possible sources of dedicated sources of revenue as well (see our other recommendation below). Given the huge federal deficit that the incoming President will inherit, new investments in housing of the scope needed to solve the shortage will necessarily rely on new sources of revenue. The incoming President should make a commitment to fully fund the National Housing Trust Fund.

Reform and Revitalize HUD

HUD has been decimated by the Bush Administration. Budget cuts and failed leadership have left the employees demoralized and the companies and citizens who do business with HUD barely interested in the agency's survival. The next Secretary faces a daunting task of rebuilding the HUD workforce and re-establishing confidence in the agency with Congress, the housing industry and citizens who rely on HUD programs. Political appointments to HUD in the incoming Administration must be of the highest caliber; HUD should never again be treated as an agency where political cronies are rewarded with jobs.

The next HUD Secretary must be a housing professional with proven leadership abilities who understands the intricacies of housing finance and the challenges of developing affordable housing. The first order of business of the new Secretary should be to recruit highly competent career staff to fill the many vacancies, with a program to attract the best and the brightest to public service. HUD cannot carry out its statutory responsibilities without having a staff that is right-sized with people with the right skill sets. The new HUD Secretary must reward outcome over process and seek the best possible outcomes for the intended beneficiaries of HUD programs—that is, low-income people in need of good housing.

The next HUD Secretary must be motivated by a commitment to social justice and be a champion for HUD programs within the Administration and with Congress.

Redistribute Federal Housing Subsidies

The total federal housing budget in 2006 was $199.5 billion: $160.2 billion tax expenditures and $39.2 billion in direct spending. Tax expenditures are primarily mortgage interest and property tax deductions, while direct spending is primarily HUD and USDA programs. The richest 20 percent of the U.S. population receives 81.5 percent of the total subsidies.[7]

Not only are tax expenditures regressive, the homeownership subsidies through the tax code are an entitlement—that is, all eligible recipients receive the benefit regardless of cost. However, direct housing assistance is not an entitlement and only a small fraction of those eligible for federal housing assistance actually receive it.

The mortgage interest deduction rewards excess and contributes to imbalance in the U.S. housing market. The interest on up to $1 million in mortgage debt, including mortgages on second and third homes, is deductible from one's taxable income base. The promise of a greater tax advantage has helped to fuel the building and buying of bigger and more expensive homes. However, the claims that the tax benefits of home ownership are necessary to achieve the high rate of homeownership for which the United States strives are not supported by the facts. Other countries have similar rates of homeownership without such a huge cost to their federal treasuries.[8]

The Congressional Budget Office (CBO) estimates that if the upper limit on mortgages eligible for tax subsidies was lowered from $1 million to $400,000, it would produce $4.2 billion in revenue in 2008 and $88.1 billion over ten years. Such a change in 2008 would have raised taxes for just 1.2 million people, those with the largest mortgages,[9] representing only 1 percent of all U.S. households.[10] Alternatively, CBO estimates that if the current mortgage interest tax deduction were replaced with a 15 percent tax credit on mortgages up to $400,000 for primary residences, revenue of $21.7 billion would be generated in 2008 alone, $418.5 billion between 2008 and 2017. Such an approach would benefit lower-income home-owners who do not itemize their taxes and thus get no housing subsidy, while creating a disincentive to over-invest in housing.[11]

The opposition to such a policy change from the building, real estate and lending sectors would be powerful. But an increasingly large number of housing experts and advocates are objecting to the continued subsidy of housing for the well-to-do while housing for the poor is so neglected.[12]

In order to answer the question of how to find dedicated revenue to fully fund the National Housing Trust Fund and to renew funding for other federal housing programs that help lower-income families, the incoming President need look no further than the mortgage interest deduction.

Advance Policies That Will Rebalance the Nation's Housing Supply

The U.S. housing market is in desperate need of re-balancing. Purchase prices need to make financial sense. Costs and incomes need to be more in sync. Homes need to be more reasonably sized and better for the environment. Communities need to make sure that their housing stock matches the needs of the people who live there, at each stage of the life cycle and at all income levels, with the right mix of rental and owner-occupied homes. Tax policy needs to reward moderation, not excess. Housing needs to be understood much more as the place where one is sheltered and carries out family life, and much less as a financial asset and a source of wealth-building. And housing should not be seen as privilege, but a right.

The housing bubble of the early years of twenty-first century has burst and the value of homes has fallen in most parts of the country, one of the primary causes of the rise in foreclosures. Yet in 40 out of 100 major cities in the United States, the cost of owning a home still far exceeds the cost of renting.[13] Public policy should encourage sound financial decision-making, not home ownership at all costs.

Public policy should also encourage moderation in the size of homes and green building practices so that homes are energy-efficient and environmentally friendly. [14]

Public policy should require local officials to engage in community planning and housing practices that makes room for all members of their communities. This means the right mix of single- and multi-family housing, attention to the housing needs and choices of singles, growing families, empty nesters and seniors. As much as possible, seniors should be allowed to age in place or live with family members, and avoid institutionalization.

The rhetoric about homeownership as the ticket to wealth-building needs to be altered. The ideal of owning a plot of land is deeply embedded in the American psyche, but the ideal needs to return to owning a home, not an asset to be gambled with. Home should be redefined as sanctuary and the center of family life. If we define our housing as a social good, not a market commodity, we will be closer to the day when America will declare housing to be a human right.

Preserve and Improve the Federally Assisted Housing Stock

There are approximately 3 million units of HUD-subsidized housing left today. Those that have a rent subsidy attached to them, including public housing and Section 8 project-based housing, provide some of the nation's poorest citizens with homes they can afford. Lack of funding, deferred maintenance, poor management and market forces threaten the loss of too many of these units. This valuable resource must be rescued and protected whenever possible, and replaced in those cases where loss of the units cannot be prevented.

The first tasks are to fully fund the operating and capital funds of public housing; to reform the HOPE VI public revitalization program along the lines H.R. 3524, passed by the U.S. House of Representatives in 2008; to fund Section 8 project-based assistance at levels needed to fully pay all contracts on time; and to pass legislation currently (as of July 2008) contemplated in the House to provide immediate protections to this stock.[15] Then the incoming Administration should set in motion a process to examine the future of the federally subsidized housing stock so as to improve and preserve it for use for the next fifty years.

Expand the Number of Federal Housing Vouchers and Maximize Mobility Opportunities

Approximately 2 million households are able to afford the homes they rent because they receive federal Housing Choice Vouchers. Millions more are on voucher waiting lists, most of which are years long. At one time, Congress was adding up to 100,000 new vouchers a year to meet the growing demand,[16] but the number of new vouchers has been a trickle since 1995. The new President should seek a renewed commitment to 200,000 new vouchers a year, with a goal of at least 2 million new vouchers in ten years.

A voucher offers a family fortunate enough to obtain one the flexibility to relocate if a better home becomes available in its community or to relocate to another community that offers better employment or educational opportunities. Policy and resources need to better support the ability of voucher holders to move to neighborhoods that offer them the best hope for their futures. The Section 8 Voucher Reform Act of 2007 (H.R. 1851) passed by the U.S. House of Representatives includes the full range of reforms needed to strengthen the program for years to come.

Enforce and Strengthen Federal Fair Housing Laws

Prohibition of discrimination on the basis of race, religion, ethnicity, disability and family status in all housing transactions has been the law of the land for many years, yet every day in our country people still are denied access to the housing of their choice because of illegal discrimination. Fair housing enforcement programs at HUD and the Department of Justice need to be re-invigorated.

HUD must take seriously its duty to see to it that all HUD grantees are "affirmatively furthering fair housing." This includes local officials who make land use and other decisions that dictate where new housing can be built and what can be done with existing buildings to change them to residential use. While land use is clearly the province of state and local governments, they should not be allowed to use federal dollars in a manner that discriminates as a result of succumbing to citizen opposition that may be based on racial animus or other illegal discrimination.

A prohibition against housing discrimination against people based on source of income should be added to the Fair Housing Act so as to improve access to housing for voucher holders and those who receive public assistance, and to eliminate the use of source of income as a proxy for another form of illegal discrimination.

Commit to a Full Housing Recovery of the Gulf Coast Communities Destroyed by Hurricanes Katrina and Rita

Seventy-one percent of the homes that were destroyed by Hurricane Katrina were affordable to low-income families.[17] Implementation of temporary housing assistance and programs to replace lost homes has been tragically flawed. Tens of thousands of low-income people remain displaced from their homes and communities three years after the storm. The incoming President has to meet our obligation to assure the complete recovery of Gulf Coast citizens, and to put policy and plans in place to assure that what happened there never happens again.

Protect the Hidden Victims of the Foreclosure Crisis, Low-Income Renters

A significant percentage of residential properties that too are being lost to foreclosure are not occupied by the homeowners, but by renters who have few rights and in most states are subject to quick eviction.[18] A federal standard is needed to allow renters reasonable time to relocate. H.R 5963 and S. 3034, introduced in the House and Senate in 2008, would create such a standard. In addition, federal resources are needed to prevent low income renters from becoming homeless due to foreclosure.

Resources

Alliance for Healthy Homes: www.afhh.org
American Association of Homes and Services for the Aging: www.aahsa.org
Catholic Charities USA: www.catholiccharitiesusa.org
Center on Budget and Policy and Priorities: www.cbpp.org
Center for Community Change Housing Trust Fund Project:
    www.communitychange.org
Center for Economic and Policy Research: www.cepr.net
Corporation for Supportive Housing: www.csh.org
Council of Large Public Housing Agencies: www.clpha.org
Enterprise Community Partners: www.enterprisecommunity.org
Housing Assistance Council: www.ruralhome.org
Joint Center for Housing Studies: www.jchs.harvard.edu
Lawyers Committee for Civil Rights under the Law:
    www.lawyerscommittee.org
Local Initiatives Support Corporation: www.lisc.org
Lutheran Services in America: www.lutheranservices.org

Mercy Housing: www.mercyhousing.org
National AIDS Housing Coalition: www.nationalaidshousing.org
National Alliance of HUD Tenants: www.saveourhomes.org
National Alliance to End Homelessness: www.endhomelessness.org
National Association of Housing and Redevelopment Officials: www.nahro.org
National Coalition for the Homeless: www.nch.org
National Council of State Housing Agencies: www.ncsha.org
National Fair Housing Alliance: www.nationalfairhousing.org
National Health Care for the Homeless Council: www.nhchc.org
National Housing Conference: www.nhc.org
National Housing Law Project: www.nhlp.org
National Housing Trust: www.nhtinc.org
National Law Center on Homelessness & Poverty: www.nlchp.org
National Low Income Housing Coalition: www.nlihc.org
National Policy and Advocacy Council on Homelessness: www.npach.org
Neighborworks America: www.nwa.org
OxfamAmerica: www.oxfamamerica.org
PolicyLink: www.policylink.org
Poverty and Race Research Action Council: www.prrac.org
Technical Assistance Collaborative: www.tacinc. org
Volunteers of America: www.voa.org

Notes

1. Joint Center for Housing Center for Housing Studies, *The State of the Nation's Housing 2008* (Cambridge, MA: Harvard University, 2008).

2. Danilo Pelletiere, Keith E. Wardrip, and Sheila Crowley, *Out of Reach 2007-2008* (Washington, D.C.: National Low Income Housing Coalition, 2008).

3. Danilo Pelletiere and Keith E. Wardrip, *Housing at the Half: A Mid-Decade Progress Report from the 2005 American Community Survey* (Washington, D.C: National Low Income Housing Coalition, 2008).

4. Ibid.

5. Ibid.

6. Housing Act of 1949, 42 U.S.C. 1441.

7. Gillian Reynolds, Federal Housing Subsidies: To Rent or Own? *Opportunity and Ownership Facts, No. 6* (Washington, D.C.: Urban Institute, 2007). Retrieved from www.urban.org/UploadedPDF/411592_housing_subsidies.pdf.

8. Congressional Budget Office, *Budget Options*. Washington, D.C.: Sheila Crowley, pp.267-268, 2007). Retrieved from http://www.cbo.gov/ftpdocs/78xx/doc7821/02-23-Budget Options.pdf. Other countries with comparable home ownership rates, without mortgage interest tax deductions, include United Kingdom, Canada and Australia.

9. Ibid.

10. Danilo Pelletiere and Keith E. Wardrip, *Housing at the Half.*

11. Congressional Budget Office, *Budget Options*. This proposal is based a recommendation from the 2005 report on the President's Advisory Panel on Federal Tax Reform.

12. Bart Harvey, *A Decent Home and Suitable Living Environment for All Americans: Rhetoric or Legitimate Goal?* The John T. Dunlop Lecture, Joint Center for Housing Studies, Harvard, 2006. Retrieved from http://www.jchs.harvard.edu/publications/m06-1_harvey.pdf.

13. Hye Jin Rho, Danilo Pelletiere and Dean Baker, *Ownership, Rental Costs and the Prospects of Building Home Equity An Analysis of 100 Metropolitan Areas.* (Washington, D.C.: National Low Income Housing Coalition and Center for Economic and Policy Research, 2008).

14. Enterprise Community Partners, *Green Communities Criteria 2008* (Columbia, MD: Sheila Crowley, 2008). Retrieved from http://www.greencommunitiesonline.org/tools/ criteria/GreenCriteria.pdf.

15. See testimony at June 19, 2008, hearing of House Financial Services Committee entitled "Affordable Housing Preservation and Protection of Tenants." Retrieved from http://www.house.gov/apps/list/hearing/financialsvcs_ dem/hr061908.shtml.

16. Jill Khadduri, *Housing Vouchers are Critical to Ending Family Homelessness* (Washington, D.C.: Sheila Crowley, 2008).

17. National Low Income Housing Coalition, *Hurricane Katrina's Impact on Low Income Housing Units Estimated 302,000 Units Lost or Damaged, 71% Low Income.* Research Note #05-02. Washington, D.C.: NLIHC, 2005).

18. See Keith E. Wardrip and Danilo Pelletiere, *Properties, Units, and Tenure in the Foreclosure Crisis: An Initial Analysis of Properties at the End of the Foreclosure Process in New England,* Research Note #08-01 (Washington, D.C.; National Low Income Housing Coalition and Keith E. Wardrip and Danilo Pelletiere, 2008); *Income and Tenure of Households Seeking Foreclosure Counseling: A Report from Recent Surveys,* Research Note #08-03 (Washington, D.C.: National Low Income Housing Coalition, 2008).

Chapter 6

Homelessness: Action to End and Prevent the Crisis*

Maria Foscarinis

POLICY PROPOSALS

- **Commit to end homelessness—now.** The incoming President should make an explicit, urgent commitment that no American should have to be homeless—and back it up with a specific national strategy to protect and promote homeless persons' human rights.
- **Expand, reauthorize and enforce the McKinney-Vento Act.** The McKinney-Vento Act, the primary federal law addressing homelessness, must be reauthorized, adequately funded and vigorously enforced.
- **Ensure decent, affordable housing.** The human right to housing should be implemented for all homeless people by increasing the availability of housing subsidies and production of affordable housing (through direct funding and/or incentives to private developers), preserving existing affordable housing, and enforcing and expanding fair housing laws.
- **Prevent people from losing their homes.** Poor renters and homeowners at risk of eviction or foreclosure, and domestic violence survivors, should be protected from losing their homes and becoming homeless. Poor people in danger of losing their homes due to eviction or foreclosure should be guaranteed free legal representation.

*I thank Adam Sparks for research assistance, Lana Tilley for administrative support and my colleagues in the Homeless Advocates Groups for their comments on an earlier draft of the proposals and their work on behalf of homeless Americans.

- **Ensure incomes adequate for housing. Ensure wage and public benefits levels are sufficient to afford housing and other basic necessities; ensure employment training; and ensure that homeless working people are able to claim the Earned Income Tax Credit.** Remove barriers and speed access to disability benefits for people unable to work. Eliminate stringent identification requirements that prevent homeless persons from obtaining public benefits, housing and jobs.
- **Ensure health care, education and supportive services.** Remove barriers and speed access to health (including mental health) care and addiction treatment, food stamps and temporary assistance. Ensure access to education for homeless children and youth, including special education, Head Start and higher education. Reauthorize and fund the Runaway and Homeless Youth Act.
- **Prevent discharge into homelessness.** Ensure that discharged military veterans have access to housing and support services, and ensure that people in institutions (including hospitals, mental health facilities, jails, prisons) and in foster care systems do not become homeless upon release, by expanding discharge planning to include housing.
- **Protect homeless people from discrimination.** Discourage communities from enacting and enforcing measures criminalizing homelessness and encourage constructive responses instead. Ensure homeless persons' right to vote. Protect homeless people from hate crimes and violence.

* * * * * * * * * * * * * * *

Homelessness in America is a crisis. At least 763,010 men, women and children are literally homeless on any given day.[1] Over the course of a year, 2.5–3.5 million Americans are literally homeless, including over 1.35 million children—living in public places, in shelters or other temporary housing for homeless people.[2] A broader definition of homelessness includes people living in hotels and motels or doubled up due to economic hardship; an estimated 4.5 million people fit this definition on any given night.[3]

Homelessness began exploding in the 1980s, and now affects a diverse group of people in urban, suburban and rural areas. About 34 percent are homeless as part of a family; about 32 percent are women; about 2 percent are children.[4] Homelessness disproportionately affects racial and ethnic minorities: African-Americans account for 12 percent of the general population, but represent about 40 percent of the homeless population. Another 11 percent are Latino, and 8 percent are Native American. About 23 percent of the homeless population are veterans.[5]

The McKinney-Vento Act, originally enacted in 1987, was the first and remains the only major federal response to homelessness. At the time this bipartisan legislation was passed, key sponsors—including then-Senator Al

Gore—stated that it was a first step only, to be followed by longer-term solutions. Those have yet to be enacted.

Homelessness is likely to worsen. The foreclosure crisis threatens low-income people—typically the targets of "subprime" loans—with loss of their homes. Thousands of Gulf War veterans are being discharged to face inadequate support and, sometimes, homelessness. Prisons and jails are releasing hundreds of thousands of indigent people, including among them a high proportion of formerly homeless people, without provision for housing or other basic needs.

Homelessness is costly financially. A 2004 nine-city study compared the cost of providing housing with supportive services versus doing nothing. Doing nothing produced increased emergency room and hospital use (in the absence of health care) and increased use of jail and prison. The study found that in almost all cases supportive housing was less expensive, in some cases by large margins, than doing nothing or merely providing shelter.[6]

Homelessness threatens America's standing in the world, as people from around the globe see and wonder at dire poverty in the midst of plenty. It undermines American democracy by marginalizing and shutting out its most vulnerable members. Homelessness in America is a human rights crisis—it should be confronted and addressed immediately.

Commit to End and Prevent Homelessness—Now

Strong White House leadership is needed to end the crisis. There is wide consensus among experts that solutions must be centered on affordable housing, supportive services for those who need them, and adequate incomes. In addition, recent public opinion polls show that 92 percent of Americans believe greater effort is needed nationally to address homelessness.[7] What has been lacking is the political will to put solutions into place.

The incoming President should convene a White House Summit of stakeholders to adopt a national strategy to end and prevent homelessness now. The U.S. Interagency Council on Homelessness, created by the McKinney-Vento Act to coordinate federal agency action to address homelessness, should be charged with implementing it.

A coalition of national organizations has developed a consensus statement of principles that should guide national policy on homelessness. The statement is now endorsed by over 20 national and local groups. The following points, drawn from that statement,[8] define the contours of a national strategy on homelessness.

Expand, Enforce and Reauthorize the McKinney-Vento Act

Funding for the Act, currently at about $1.6 billion per year, is not sufficient to meet the immediate needs of those now homeless: Approximately 45 percent of all homeless people are unsheltered.[9] Moreover, Title IV, the Act's housing programs, has not been reauthorized since 1992. HUD, the agency that administers this title, uses a very narrow definition of homelessness that limits aid and diverges from the definition used by the Department of Education, which administers Title VII of the Act, hampering the effectiveness of the programs and coordination among agencies.

The McKinney-Vento HUD programs must be reauthorized and funding increased. The definition of homelessness must be conformed across agencies to include those who are doubled-up due to economic need.

Ensure Decent, Affordable Housing

Federal funding for affordable housing has been slashed over the past thirty years. In 1978, 435,362 new units of low- and moderate-income housing were funded; in 2007, no new units were funded. In the private market, "gentrification" replaces inexpensive housing with luxury residential or commercial property, without provision for those displaced. Currently, in no U.S. county can a minimum-wage worker afford a one-bedroom apartment, according to federal affordability guidelines. In many cities, waiting lists for public housing and housing vouchers are years long.[10]

Housing must be ensured for all homeless people. Housing subsidies should be increased, affordable housing preserved, and production of affordable housing increased. The National Housing Trust Fund Act should be passed and funded. Incentives to private developers, such as inclusionary zoning laws, should be encouraged and supported. Vacant federal properties, including decommissioned military bases, should be converted to housing for homeless and at-risk people, by implementing and expanding Title V of the McKinney-Vento Act and the Base Closure and Homeless Assistance program. Enactment in 2003 by Scotland of legislation to ensure an enforceable right to housing for all homeless people in 10 years provides a valuable model.[11]

Efforts to develop affordable and supportive housing are often stymied by Not In My Back Yard (NIMBY) campaigns, often in violation of fair housing law. Further, in some communities, low income people who have been able to obtain housing vouchers are unable to use them because landlords will not accept them. Fair housing laws must be vigorously enforced, and expanded to include "source of income" discrimination, so that holders of housing subsidies can use them.

Prevent People from Losing Their Homes
and Becoming Homeless

Inability to pay the rent is the leading precipitating cause of homelessness; loss of a job closely follows. It is far less costly—in both human and financial terms—to prevent homelessness than to address the needs of people after they become homeless.

Currently, McKinney-Vento funds may be used for assistance with rental or mortgage arrears to avert homelessness, but they are insufficient. In addition, state revolving loan programs provide some assistance in selected areas. These efforts should be significantly expanded. Further, poor homeowners at risk of homelessness through foreclosure should be allowed to stay in their homes through purchase/leaseback programs.

For women and youth, domestic violence is a leading cause of homelessness. According to a twenty-three-city survey, 39 percent of cities cited domestic violence as the leading cause of homelessness for households with children.[12] The Violence Against Women Act, as reauthorized in January 2007, includes new housing protections for domestic violence survivors, but, as of July 2008, regulations to implement the law have not yet been promulgated. Further, at least 1.7 million youth run away or are expelled from their home each year due to severe family conflict, abuse or neglect. The Runaway and Homeless Youth Act provides critical assistance; its funding should be increased to meet the need.

Finally, according to a New York City study, in 2006, 76 percent of tenants facing eviction did not have legal representation.[13] Currently, there is no right to free legal representation for poor tenants, contributing to evictions—and homelessness—that possibly could have been avoided.

Ensure Incomes Adequate for Housing

In a given month, 44 percent of homeless people are employed, full or part-time, often as day laborers, but do not earn enough to pay for housing.[14] The Earned Income Tax Credit could help supplement low incomes, but homeless workers face barriers to claiming the credit: W2 forms may be lost, or not provided to day laborers. Low skills prevent homeless people from obtaining better-paying jobs.

Barriers that prevent homeless working people from claiming the Earned Income Tax Credit should be removed and levels raised for single individuals. Minimum wage levels must be sufficient to pay for housing and other basic necessities, consistent with federal affordability guidelines. The Workforce Investment Act should be reauthorized and amended to address the employment training needs of homeless people. The Temporary Assistance for Needy Families program should include a stronger commitment to meet families' housing needs.

Many homeless people are unable to work. Some 31 percent of homeless people experience mental illness, addiction or both in a year; some 45 percent report chronic health conditions, including diabetes, cancer and lost limbs.[15] Yet while many are eligible for disability benefits under the Supplemental Security Income (SSI) or Social Security Disability Income (SSDI) programs, only 11 percent receive SSI and only 8 percent receive SSDI benefits.[16]

Barriers include complex application processes; lack of access to doctors; and long delays, during which homeless applicants move and become "lost" to the system. To improve access, application assistance should be provided; applications for homeless people flagged for expedited processing; the types of medical professionals who can verify disability expanded; and automatic expedited benefits for persons with severe mental illness provided.

Moreover, measures enacted following 9/11, primarily the REAL ID Act, have made obtaining photo identification extremely difficult for homeless persons. As a result, they are unable to obtain benefits for which they are eligible or, in some cases, even to enter federal buildings to make application. The Act should be amended to allow alternative forms of identification for homeless persons, based on successful state models.

Ensure Health Care, Education and Supportive Services

Homeless people suffer from multiple health problems, yet 55 percent have no medical insurance; only 30 percent receive Medicaid, and only 7 percent receive medical care from the Department of Veterans Affairs.[17] Further, 40 percent of homeless people go without food for a day or longer over a thirty-day period because they cannot afford it, compared to 3 percent of all poor Americans; yet only 37 percent receive food stamps.[18] Barriers similar to those affecting the SSI and SSDI programs prevent eligible homeless people from receiving these benefits.

Clinics and other programs operated by the Health Care for the Homeless program provide crucial help; the program should be reauthorized. Similarly, the Program for Assistance in the Transition from Homelessness, the Treatment for Homeless Persons Program, and the Substance Abuse and Mental Health Services Administration Act provide crucial mental health and treatment resources; they should be reauthorized. All of these programs need increased funding, in the context of universal health care for all.

Homeless children and youth suffer particularly devastating harms. They are often denied enrollment in school, or forced to change school as their families are shuttled from shelter to shelter. Forty-seven percent suffer from anxiety, depression or withdrawal, compared to 18 percent of poor children; 21 percent repeat a grade, twice the rate of all children nationally.[19] Without an adequate education, they are less likely to acquire the skills they need to escape the cycle of homelessness. Indeed, childhood homelessness is a predictor of adult homelessness. Some 21 percent of homeless adults were homeless as children.[20]

The McKinney-Vento Education program protects homeless children's right to education, and gives their parents the right to keep them in their school of origin, if it is in the children's best interests. The program has resulted in considerable progress. But the law is still violated,[21] and the program is inadequately funded: currently, only 6 percent of all school districts receive program funding.[22] Barriers frequently prevent homeless children from gaining access to special education services for which they qualify. And while 49 percent of sheltered homeless children are under five years of age, only 15 percent are enrolled in early childhood education programs, compared to 53 percent of all children.[23]

The program should be vigorously monitored by the U.S. Department of Education, and funding increased so all school districts that need funding receive it. New amendments to the Individuals with Disabilities Education Act to ensure homeless children's access to special education should be implemented, and regulations to implement Part C of that Act—to identify and help homeless zero to three-year-olds—immediately issued. Pending amendments to the Higher Education Act, to open access for homeless students, should be enacted.

Prevent Discharge into Homelessness

Indigent people in hospitals, mental health institutions, prisons or jails with nowhere to go may be discharged to a shelter or even the street. Moreover, in many states, if such persons are institutionalized for longer than thirty days, any benefits they were receiving, such as food stamps or disability, are terminated.[24] Current federal law allows institutionalized persons to apply to for food stamps and SSI benefits prior to release, but this provision is optional, little known and little used. Moreover, it does not include housing. Discharge planning must include housing, and the pre-release program should be implemented widely and expanded to include housing.

Similarly, youth in foster care are at risk of becoming homeless as they "age out" of care, and foster care is a risk factor for homelessness: an estimated 19 percent of homeless people have been in foster care.[25] Plans must be in place before these youth age out to ensure their self-sufficiency, including planning for housing.

Finally, homeless veterans must be helped. In 1992, Congress established the HUD-Veterans Affairs Supportive Housing program; last year, 10,000 units were funded. But 20,000 more permanent and 10,000 more transitional housing units are needed, and funding should be increased from $75 million to $300 million to provide them. In addition, the Homeless Veterans Reintegration Program, which provides job training, should be reauthorized, and the Homes for Heroes Act enacted.

Protect Homeless People from Discrimination

Cities around the country have adopted laws and policies that make it a crime to sleep, sit, eat or beg in public places. These efforts to "criminalize" homelessness simply force people to move elsewhere; some have been struck down as unconstitutional. They are also counter-productive: With an arrest record, access to housing and jobs is more difficult or impossible. These measures also send a message that punishing homeless people for their status is acceptable, and may contribute to violence against homeless people. In 2007, 160 unprovoked assaults were committed against homeless persons, with twenty-eight of these resulting in death.[26]

More recently, some communities have adopted more constructive approaches. Portland, Oregon, is subsidizing permanent housing that outreach workers can immediately offer to people living on the streets for a predetermined length of time. In addition, some cities have adopted police protocols that prohibit arrests for sleeping in public when there is no shelter available. Localities receiving federal funds should be given incentives to adopt constructive policies. They should be discouraged from punitive responses through explicit policy directives from the Department of Justice (DoJ) and White House statements. Violence against homeless people should be deterred through expansion of federal hate crimes laws.

Homelessness undermines political rights: Voting is often difficult or impossible, The Federal Election Commission (FEC) has issued guidance to protect homeless persons' constitutional right to vote, but in practice it is often violated. The FEC and DoJ should work with state election officials to inform local officials, registration agencies, poll workers and homeless people of their rights.

Resources

Catholic Charities USA: www.catholiccharitiesusa.org
Corporation for Supportive Housing: www.csh.org
Family Promise: www.nihn.org
Give Us Your Poor: www.giveusyourpoor.org
Health Care for the Homeless, Inc.: www.hchmd.org
Institute on Homelessness and Trauma: www.nrchmi.samhsa.gov
Lutheran Services in America: www.lutheranservices.org
Mercy Housing: www.mercyhousing.org
National AIDS Housing Coalition: www.nationalaidshousing.org
National Alliance to End Homelessness: www.endhomelessness.org
National Center on Family Homelessness: www.familyhomelessness.org
National Coalition Against Domestic Violence: www.ncadv.org
National Coalition for the Homeless: www.nationalhomeless.org

National Coalition for Homeless Veterans: www.nchv.org
National Health Care for the Homeless Council: www.nhchc.org
National Housing Law Project: www.nhlp.org
National Law Center on Homelessness & Poverty: www.nlchp.org
National Low Income Housing Coalition: www.nlihc.org
National Network to End Domestic Violence: www.nnedv.org
National Network for Youth: www.nn4youth.org
National Policy and Advocacy Council on Homelessness: www.npach.org
Volunteers of America: www.voa.org

Notes

1. "The Annual Homeless Assessment Report to Congress," U.S. Department of Housing and Urban Development, February 2007: 24 n.6.

2. Martha Burt, "Homeless Families, Singles, and Others: Findings from the 1996 National Survey of Homeless Assistance Providers and Clients," *Housing Policy Debate* (2001): 737–80.

3. Mary Cunningham and Meghan Henry, "Data Snapshot: Doubled Up in the United States," Homelessness Research Institute, National Alliance to End Homelessness, March 2008.

4. U.S. Department of Housing and Urban Development (2007).

5. U.S. Department of Housing and Urban Development (2007).

6. The Lewin Group, for the Corporation for Supportive Housing, "Costs of Serving Homeless Individuals in Nine Cities," November 19, 2004.

7. Jennifer C. Kerr, Associated Press, "Poll: People Worry About Being Homeless," November 14, 2007.

8. The proposals presented here are not a verbatim recitation of the statement and thus they are not—as presented—endorsed by the coalition. The consensus statement and list of endorsing organizations are at McKinney20th.org.

9. U.S. Department of Housing and Urban Development (2007) at 23.

10. National Low Income Housing Coalition, *Out of Reach* (Washington, D.C.: National Low Income Housing Coalition, 2008), 5.

11. NLCHP: The Scotland Homeless Act: A Model for All (2007), available at http://www.nlchp.org/view_report.cfm?id=202.

12. U.S. Conference of Mayors, "A Status Report on Hunger and Homelessness in American's Cities" (2007), 12.

13. ActKnowledge and The Brennan Center for Justice, "Results from Three Surveys of Tenants Facing Eviction in New York City Housing Court," February 14, 2007.

14. Martha Burt, et al., The Urban Institute, "Homelessness: Programs and the People They Serve: Summary Report" (Interagency Council on the Homeless, December 1999), Table 2-6.

15. Ibid., 48.

16. Ibid., 5–6.

17. Ibid., 12.

18. Ibid., Table 5-4, 7-3.

19. The Institute for Children and Poverty, *Homeless in America: A Children's Story. Part One* (New York: The Institute for Children and Poverty, 1999).

20. Martha Burt, et al., "Homelessness," 22.

21. John Rather, "Agreement Near on Homeless Schooling," *New York Times*, Nov. 28, 2004. Susan Saulney, "Bouncing Among Shelters and Among City Schools," *New York Times,* Sept. 19, 2004.

22. National Center for Homeless Education, "Education for Homeless Children and Youth Program: Analysis of Data From the 2006-07 Federally Required State Data Collection for theMcKinney-Vento Education Assistance Improvements Act of 2001 and Comparison of the 2004-05, 2005-06, and 2006-07 Data Collections," July 2008, 3; J. Sable, N. Gaviola, and A. Garofano, "Documentation to the NCES Common Core of Data Local Education Agency Universe Survey: School Year 2005–06, Version 1a." (Washington, D.C.: U.S. Department of Education, National Center for Education Statistics, May 2007), 1.

23. The Institute for Children and Poverty (1999).

24. Steve Eiken and Sara Galantowicz, The Medstat Group, Inc., "Improving Medicaid Access for People Experiencing Chronic Homelessness: State Examples" (U.S. Department of Health and Human Services, Centers for Medicare and Medicaid Services, Disabled and Elderly Health Programs Division, 2004), 5–6, 10.

25. E. L. Bassuk, et al. "Homelessness in Female-Headed Families: Childhood and Adult Risk and Protective Factors," *American Journal of Public Health* 87(2), February 1997, 241-48.

26. The National Coalition for the Homeless and The National Law Center for Homelessness and Poverty, "Hate, Violence, and Death on Main Street USA: Report on Hate Crimes and Violence Against People Experiencing Homelessness in 2007," April 2008, 10. Amy Green, "Attacks on Homeless Rise, With Youths Mostly to Blame," *New York Times,* Feb. 15, 2008.

Chapter 7

A New Policy for Justice and Public Safety

Marc Mauer

POLICY PROPOSALS

- Eliminate the sentencing disparity between crack cocaine and powder cocaine.
- Fund the Second Chance Act to support prison and jail reentry programs that increase prospects for successful transition from prison to community.
- End federal bans on access to welfare benefits, public housing and student loans for people with felony drug convictions.
- Expand voting rights in federal elections for all non-incarcerated individuals.
- Adopt racial impact statement requirements for proposed sentencing policies in order to address racial disparities in criminal justice proactively.
- Provide federal seed funding for justice re-investment programs to support local initiatives for public safety.
- Endorse evidence-based approaches to enhancing public safety.

* * * * * * * * * * * * * * *

The incoming Administration and Congress have an opportunity to approach criminal justice issues at a critical moment for public policy. More than three decades of "get tough" policies have produced a world-record prison population, shocking racial disparities, a failed "war on drugs" and a skewed set of investments for addressing public safety. Yet at the same time, there are now openings for reform and reconsideration of the American approach to crime control that were not conceivable a decade ago, opportunities that suggest that a shift toward a more rational public policy is actually possible. This chapter examines the contours of the rise of mass incarceration and its impact on families and communities, and then outlines a plan for a progressive direction in promoting public safety.

The Rise of mass incarceration: In 1972, the U.S. prison and jail population stood at about 300,000. With only relatively modest fluctuations, the per-capita rate of incarceration in the U.S. had remained relatively stable since 1925, settling at about 160 per 100,000 by the early 1970s. Following that time, though, the prison and jail population has increased more than six-fold, now totaling 2.3 million people nationally. The U.S. rate of incarceration, 762 per 100,000, is the highest in the world, and some five to eight times that of other industrialized nations.

The reasons for this dramatic change are complex, but in broad terms they have been brought about by changes in policy, not changes in crime rates. These policy initiatives have predominantly focused on sentencing policies, legislative changes that have been designed to sentence more people to prison and to keep them incarcerated for longer periods of time. These have taken the form of mandatory sentencing laws that remove judicial discretion to consider the individual circumstances of offender and offense, "three strikes and you're out" laws that vastly expand the length of time offenders serve in prison, and the increasing tendency to return parolees to prison for technical violations of release conditions.

The most significant initiative during this period has been the set of policies enacted under the rubric of the "war on drugs," a concerted effort at all levels of government since the 1980s to use the apparatus of the criminal justice system in unprecedented ways to address a social problem. The war was initially conceived by the Reagan Administration, largely as a means of ramping up the federal profile in crime control, and launched with great fanfare and resources. Whereas most drug crimes had traditionally been treated as local offenses, the drastic federalization of even small-scale drug offenses resulted in the proportion of drug offenders in the federal prison system doubling from 25 percent in 1980 to 53 percent by 2008.

State and local governments were quick to join the war as well, culminating in a massive shift in incarceration resources toward housing drug offenders. Today, there are 500,000 persons in prison and jail awaiting trial or serving time for a drug offense, a 1,100 percent increase from the figure of 41,000 in 1980. Nearly two million drug arrests are made each year; more than 80 percent of these are for possession offenses and more than 40 percent are for marijuana charges. Despite these massive investments, there are few appreciable successes one can point to in the presumed objectives of the war, that of reducing supply, stopping drug abuse and increasing the price of illegal drugs.

The policy shift producing these outcomes has been both direct and intentional. In 1986 and again in 1988, Congress passed a host of mandatory sentencing laws, the most notorious of which were the harsh penalties adopted for crack cocaine offenses. Under these statutes *possession* of as little as five grams of crack warrants a five-year prison term, while for powder cocaine the same penalty is only triggered for *sales* of 500 grams of the drug. More than 80 percent of the persons charged with crack offenses have been African-American, while powder cocaine defendants are far more likely to be white or Latino.

Several years later, federal lawmakers continued their "get tough" campaign through the mechanism of the 1994 federal crime bill, a $30 billion package loaded with $8 billion in grants to the states for prison construction, much of it premised on the adoption of punitive "truth in sentencing" policies. Extending the drug war even further in the 1990s, Congress enacted a host of collateral sanctions for people convicted of a drug offense. These included restrictions on access to welfare benefits, residence in public housing and securing student loans for higher education.

People with felony convictions are also subject to the effects of felony disenfranchisement laws that restrict the right to vote for an estimated 5.3 million persons. These laws apply not only to people in prison, but in thirty-five states also to persons on probation and/or parole, and in eleven states, even for people who have completed their sentence. Of the total disenfranchised population, 4 million are living in the community; although they are working, paying taxes and raising families, they are excluded from the ballot box. Not surprisingly, the racial disparities of the criminal justice system translate onto disenfranchisement as well, with one in eight of all black males now ineligible to vote.

Effects of Mass Incarceration

The goal of producing a world-record prison population has presumably been to control crime, so we should assess the impact of incarceration in this regard over the past several decades. Supporters of current policies contend that since crime rates have declined significantly in recent years—victimization is now at a forty-year low—this is proof that "prison works." But the reality is far more complex.

First, while it is true that victimization rates have declined sharply, this only means that American rates of crime are finally *no worse* than the level they were at when there were only one-sixth as many people behind bars, despite the addition of nearly two million people to our prisons and jails. Second, these changes in crime have hardly been consistent over the thirty-five-year period. A decline in crime in the early 1980s was then followed by a steep seven-year rise in the late 1980s, which in turn was followed by a steady decline since the early 1990s. This suggests that the relationship between incarceration and crime is far more ambiguous than a simple "more prisons, less crime" correlation.

Leading criminologists have generally concluded that rising incarceration represents at best a relatively modest part of the explanation for declining crime rates, and needs to be assessed along with the impact of changes in the drug trade, community policing, economic conditions and community mobilization. Further, to the extent that imprisonment does have an effect on crime, this is now very much one of diminishing returns, as prisons are increasingly filled with low-level drug and property offenders. A substantial body of research also suggests that other social interventions, including pre-school education programs and high school dropout prevention initiatives, are more cost-effective than expanded incarceration in reducing crime.

At the scale of incarceration today, we now see that imprisonment exerts a host of collateral consequences on families and communities that are increasingly debilitating. Perhaps most prominent among these is the effect on children. There are now 1.7 million children who have a parent in prison, including one of every fourteen African-American children. These children suffer from the loss of emotional and financial support by having a parent behind bars, as well as carrying the stigma and shame that often accompanies these circumstances. These dynamics are exacerbated by the rapidly rising rates of incarceration for women, largely fueled by the drug war, that have further eroded family bonds.

To be fair, in recent years, policymakers at both the federal and state level have begun to reconsider some of these overly punitive approaches to public safety. Spurred on both by the rising costs of incarceration and the growing realization that public safety is best addressed by programs that are evidence-based, legislators have begun to consider new approaches to problems of reentry into the community after prison and expanding programs such as drug courts in an effort to address the underlying contributors to crime. While these are clearly steps in the direction of more rational policy, the scale of the change is still relatively modest and does not yet address the true crisis of mass imprisonment.

Directions for a New Policy

It is long past time for a new, and effective, national strategy for promoting public safety through approaches that strengthen the ability of communities to engage in solving problems while also promoting racial justice. In some cases, this can be accomplished through repeal or modification of statutes that run counter to the interest of promoting rational public policy. In other areas, we need to proactively employ resources and promote policies that provide communities with the tools they need to address the underlying contributors to crime. The incoming Administration can enact a variety of measures to begin shifting policy in these directions, including the following:

Eliminate the sentencing disparity between crack cocaine and powder cocaine: After more than twenty years and with broad support for reform across the political spectrum, there is finally significant momentum for reform of the federal mandatory penalties that apply to crack cocaine offenses. In 2007, the U.S. Sentencing Commission revised its sentencing guidelines for crack offenses and made the change retroactive, thus making 19,500 people eligible for a sentence reduction. But only Congress can change the harsh five- and ten-year mandatory penalties that apply to crack. Hearings were held in both the House and Senate in 2008 on reform legislation, but failed to move out of committee because of disagreement among policymakers over the best approach for reform. By eliminating the disparity in sentencing for these two forms of the same drug, Congress would refocus federal law enforcement efforts more appropriately on high-level traffickers while also addressing the profound racial inequities produced by these policies. Such a change would also lend support to the growing critique of mandatory sentencing broadly. These policies have unnecessarily applied a "one size fits all" approach to sentencing that restricts the longstanding ability of judges to make distinctions among various offenses and crime situations.

Fund Second Chance Act and reentry programming: In 2008, Congress passed the Second Chance Act, landmark legislation designed to establish model programs to enhance the reentry prospects for people returning to the community from prison and jail. While the act was passed with broad bipartisan support, due to budgetary constraints, it failed to have funds fully appropriated. Support for reentry initiatives at the federal level is critical to enhancing these efforts nationally. In the late 1990s, federal seed money provided to the states to establish reentry planning task forces was successful in helping to jump-start the reentry movement nationally. A decade into this process, federal support could help to stimulate the development of new programs and generate additional resources at the state and local level.

End federal bans on access to public benefits: Federal restrictions on access to welfare, public housing and student loans provide no demonstrable benefits to the public and in fact run counter to the community's interest in promoting public safety. Consider, for example, the case of a woman with a drug addiction who is sentenced to prison for two years for selling drugs. She successfully completes a treatment program in prison and gains employment upon release back to the community. But after six months of steady work, she is laid off because her company is not doing well financially. While looking for a new job she applies for welfare benefits, but is denied because of her prior drug conviction. To whom can she now turn? Such blanket denials of public benefits serve no rational purpose and should be repealed by Congress and state legislative bodies where appropriate.

Expand voting rights in federal elections for people with felony convictions: While the Constitution grants states the power to establish voting qualifications, Congress may set standards for federal elections. Currently, as a result of varying state policies, one's ability to vote for national leadership is dependent on the state of residence. Thus, we have the odd situation whereby an ex-felon in West Virginia can vote for President, but one in Virginia cannot. Such accidents of geography should not be used to determine national electoral outcomes. Companion legislation introduced in the House by Rep. John Conyers and in the Senate by Sen. Russ Feingold would permit anyone not incarcerated to vote in federal elections even if barred from voting in their state election. Such a policy would represent a significant step toward full democratic participation, as well as encouraging reform of state disenfranchisement policies. In addition, emerging research suggests that engagement in the electoral process can help to reduce recidivism among people with prior arrests.

Adopt racial impact statement requirements for proposed sentencing policies: Just as policymakers routinely require fiscal or environmental impact statements for proposed changes that may have unanticipated impacts, so too should lawmakers be required to prepare a racial/ethnic impact statement prior to the adoption of any legislation that might affect the size of the prison population. Such statements, developed by analyzing current crime and sentencing data, would project the relative racial/ethnic composition of new prison sentences. With hindsight, we can now see that Congress should have conducted such an analysis prior to considering the crack cocaine mandatory sentencing laws in 1986. Had it done so, perhaps documentation of the anticipated racial disparities might have caused lawmakers to consider alternative policies to accomplish the goal of addressing drug abuse without exacerbating existing racial disparities in incarceration. Both Iowa and Connecticut enacted racial impact statement requirements in 2008. Congress should now follow their lead for federal legislation as well.

Provide federal support for justice re-investment: A key problem with addressing crime and safety in low-income neighborhoods is not so much a lack of resources, but rather misdirected resources. Enormous investments are currently being made by taxpayers to support law enforcement and corrections systems that have combined to produce record numbers of arrests and prison terms. In some urban areas such as Brooklyn, New York, researchers have documented the presence of "million dollar blocks," neighborhoods where taxpayers collectively spend $1 million a year to incarcerate people just from a single block. At the same time, resources directed to other institutions in these communities—schools, health care facilities, treatment programs—are sorely inadequate to the community's needs.

The federal government can play a key role in enhancing public safety by providing resources and technical assistance to encourage the establishment of justice re-investment strategies. These would take the form of community-wide task forces comprised of criminal justice leadership, political officials, neighborhood leaders, and social service providers to come together to assess local crime problems and to develop comprehensive approaches to their resolution. Depending on the neighborhood, these might include community policing, school-based interventions to deal with disruptive behavior, transitional services for people coming home from prison, and job placement services. Such a framework would then be used in negotiations with political leadership on shifting resources from a disproportionately criminal justice approach to a more balanced set of investments.

Support evidence-based approaches to reducing crime: A key problem in addressing crime policy in recent decades is that far too often policy is driven by political "sound bites" rather than by an assessment of what works to reduce crime. One model that can be adopted and promoted by Congress is employed by Washington through its Washington State Institute for Public Policy. This non-partisan body is charged with reviewing research to provide lawmakers with an evidence-based assessment of the cost-effectiveness of various policy initiatives. In recent years, this has included evaluations of interventions to reduce juvenile violence, programs to address mentally ill offenders, and sentencing options for sex offenders. Congress should establish a similar body that could aid lawmakers in directing resources toward initiatives that are most likely to produce effective approaches to reducing crime.

Conclusion

The clear desire for "change" articulated in the 2008 election campaign suggests that a new approach to crime and public safety may now be possible. In recent years we have begun to see a reconsideration of "get tough" policies at the state level, with more than half the states having enacted various measures to divert drug offenders into treatment programs, reduce unnecessarily lengthy prison terms, and reform parole practices. These changes have been driven by both fiscal considerations and a growing interest in developing responses to crime that can produce measurable results. The new administration has an opportunity to build on these changes and to assert a more appropriate federal role in aiding local communities.

Resources

Critical Resistance: www.criticalresistance.org
Drug Policy Alliance: www.drugpolicyalliance.org
Families Against Mandatory Minimums: www.famm.org
The Fortune Society: www.fortunesociety.org
Justice Policy Institute: www.justicepolicy.org
The Sentencing Project: www.sentencingproject.org
Women's Prison Association: www.wpaonline.org

Chapter 8

A Road Map for Juvenile Justice Reform

Douglas W. Nelson and Bart Lubow

POLICY PROPOSALS

- Respect the well-established differences between youth and adults.
- End indiscriminate and wholesale incarceration of juveniles.
- Focus on the crucial role of families in resolving delinquency.
- Halt the increasing propensity to prosecute minor cases in the juvenile justice system.
- Rely on other systems for youth, rather than using the juvenile justice system as a dumping ground.
- End system policies and practices that allow unequal justice to persist.

* * * * * * * * * * * * * * *

Our nation's juvenile justice systems are poised for a fundamental, urgently needed transformation—and not a moment too soon.

Among all of the policy areas affecting vulnerable children and families, juvenile justice has probably suffered the most glaring gaps between best practice and common practice, between what we know and what we most often do. Perhaps because it serves an unpopular and powerless segment of our society—behaviorally troubled, primarily poor, mostly minority teenagers—juvenile justice policy has been too long shaped by misinformation, hyperbole and political prejudices.

The consequences have been both disturbing and costly: Our juvenile justice systems have become littered with poorly conceived strategies that often increase crime, endanger young people and damage their future prospects, waste billions of taxpayer dollars, and violate our deepest held principles about equal justice under the law.

71

These systems affect a wide swath of the U.S. youth population. Nationwide each year, police make 2.2 million juvenile arrests; 1.7 million cases are referred to juvenile courts; an estimated 400,000 youngsters cycle through juvenile detention centers; and on any given night nearly 100,000 youth are confined in juvenile jails, prisons, boot camps and other residential facilities. Young people who penetrate the systems deeply—those who end up confined in locked detention centers and training schools—suffer some of the worst odds of long-term success of any youth cohort in our nation. Over their lifetime, they will achieve less educationally, work less and for lower wages, fail more frequently to form enduring families, experience more chronic health problems (including addiction) and suffer more imprisonment.

That's the bad news. The good news is that over the past twenty years, a growing cadre of scholars, advocates and hands-on juvenile justice practitioners has vastly expanded our understanding of delinquency, as well as system reform. They've compiled powerful new evidence on what works in responding to delinquency, documented the harm and waste resulting from ill-informed juvenile justice practices, devised and tested new intervention strategies, and begun putting this new knowledge of what works into widespread use. Promising reforms are now under way and expanding in many jurisdictions, and the foundation for deeper and more systemic change has been firmly established.

There is now an increasingly clear route for moving juvenile justice away from counterproductive, dangerous, wasteful, but still commonplace, practices and toward a more effective, efficient and just approach to addressing adolescent crime. Given what we now know, and the terrible costs of retaining the status quo in juvenile justice, there no longer remains any reasonable excuse for inaction.

A Noble Idea, Unrealized

The first court of law dedicated exclusively to children was founded in 1899 in Cook County, Illinois, on Chicago's west side. Until then, children were tried in criminal courts just like adults. The new juvenile courts used closed and informal hearings to act in the best interests of the child. By 1915, most states had established their own juvenile courts, and today, all of the United States and most nations have separate justice systems for juveniles.

From the very beginning, however, the implementation and practice of juvenile justice fell far short of its lofty ideals. The courts relied heavily on "reformatories" where conditions were often more severe and discipline far harsher than their rehabilitative mission implied. Few jurisdictions devoted the proper staff, training or resources to deliver the intended care in an effective, meaningful way. Similarly, while the founding vision of the juvenile court revolved around a dedicated, specialized juvenile court system, in actual practice most juvenile judges spent a small fraction of their time on juvenile cases and hearings. They were granted extraordinary discretion, while few legal protections were given to youth, such as advance notice of charges, right to counsel and right to a jury trial.

This discretion and informality, which were intended to encourage flexible and creative responses, actually ended up producing enormous disparities and allowed many judges to heavily sanction youth accused of minor status offenses, including underage drinking, curfew violations and truancy.

In 1974, Congress enacted the Juvenile Justice and Delinquency Prevention Act, sharply curtailing detention and incarceration for status offenders. New federal guidelines also pushed states to desist from holding juveniles in adult jails. By the 1990s, however, the number of murders committed by youthful offenders nearly tripled, and the overall rate of juvenile violent crime nearly doubled. Combined with sensational media coverage and widely publicized (and ultimately inaccurate) predictions of a coming "tidal wave" of "juvenile super-predators," the spike in serious delinquency sparked a public policy panic. State legislatures enacted "get tough" juvenile policies at an unprecedented pace, expanding the classes of youth who could be tried as adults and requiring minimum periods of incarceration for specific crimes.

A Road Map for Reform

Virtually all of these "get tough" practices violate what we know about youth development and behavior, and all are producing worse, rather than better, outcomes for youth, communities and taxpayers. They have helped to create and perpetuate at least six pervasive challenges facing our juvenile justice systems. Fortunately, alternative policies, practices and programs have emerged that have the potential to fundamentally reform the system and greatly improve the odds of success for troubled youth. Moreover, most of these alternatives have already been implemented effectively, providing a clear and compelling road map for reform.

Trends in juvenile justice blur or ignore the well-established differences between youth and adults.

Key Facts
- Research clarifies that children and adolescents are far less able than adults to gauge risks and consequences, control impulses, handle stress and resist peer pressure. Strikingly, most youthful offenders will cease law-breaking as part of the normal maturation process.
- Every year, roughly 200,000 youth under age eighteen are tried in adult courts.
- During the 1990s, every state except Nebraska changed its laws to expand the number of youth tried in adult courts.

- According to several recent studies, youth tried in adult courts and punished in the adult corrections system go on to commit more subsequent crime—and more violent crime—than equivalent youth tried and punished in the juvenile system. Studies also show that adult-time-for-adult-crime laws do not deter youth from crime or lower youth offending rates.

Promising Solutions
- Connecticut increased the age of juvenile court jurisdiction from fifteen to seventeen, which will allow 8,000 more youth per year to receive juvenile court services and avoid a criminal record. Several other states have launched campaigns to pass similar legislation.
- In 2005, Illinois voted unanimously to repeal an adult-time-for-adult-crime law that required youth accused of drug crimes in or around public schools or housing projects to be transferred to the adult system. They did so after public hearings revealed that two-thirds of youth touched by the law were low-level offenders, and 97 percent were youth of color.
- States and localities should study and emulate the Children and Family Justice Center at Northwestern University Law School, the Neighborhood Defender Service of Harlem or Boston College Law School's Juvenile Rights Advocacy Project. These programs offer innovative, comprehensive representation for justice-involved youth.

Indiscriminate and wholesale incarceration of juveniles is proving expensive, abusive, and bad for public safety.

Key Facts
- According to the most recent data, just 24 percent of incarcerated youth nationwide are guilty of violent felonies; 45 percent are guilty only of probation violations, misdemeanors, or low-level charges unrelated to violence, weapons or drug trafficking.
- Recidivism studies show that 50–80 percent of youth released from juvenile correctional facilities are re-arrested within two to three years—even those who were not serious offenders prior to their commitment.
- Correctional confinement typically costs $200–300 per youth per day, far more than intensive home- and community-based treatment models that often show superior results in terms of recidivism.
- According to the Associated Press, 13,000 cases of abuse were reported in juvenile institutions nationwide from 2004 to 2007.
- The U.S. Justice Department has filed suit to protest conditions at juvenile facilities in eleven states, and public interest lawyers have litigated conditions in many others.

Promising Solutions

- Missouri's small, treatment-oriented juvenile correctional facilities demonstrate that there are better ways to address incarceration—the state has not been the subject of litigation over conditions of confinement for more than twenty-five years. Seventy percent of Missouri's former wards avoid recommitment to any correctional setting three years after discharge, far better than most states, even though its costs are low compared with other states.
- California has slashed the number of youth in state correctional facilities from more than 10,000 in the mid-1990s to 2,500 in 2007, and it's on track to reach 1,500 youth by 2010. In this period, California's youth crime rates have not increased either in absolute terms or relative to other states.
- In New York City, the Probation Department's Project Zero has enrolled more than 1,700 court-involved youth in new alternatives-to-incarceration programs since 2003. From 2004 to 2007, the number of incarcerated New York City youth declined 23 percent. Most youth in the new community supervision programs are remaining crime-free and avoiding subsequent placements, and city taxpayers have saved $11 million.
- The Annie E. Casey Foundation's Juvenile Detention Alternatives Initiative (JDAI) has also had a ripple effect on participating jurisdictions' overall use of confinement. For example, Cook County (Chicago), Illinois has reduced the number of youth committed to state confinement from more than 900 in 1996 to 400 in 2006, and it has slashed the population in group homes and other residential treatment centers from a monthly average of 426 youth in 1996 to just ten in 2007.
- Girls have needs different from boys in the system, and providing effective gender-specific services is an increasingly important challenge. Some promising models include PACE Center for Girls, Inc., a strength-based approach that stresses "understanding the relationship between victimization and female juvenile crime, then creating a safe, nurturing environment for these girls." San Francisco's Center for Young Women's Development is led entirely by young women and works extensively with detained and incarcerated girls.
- Effective community-based programming is also crucial for youth returning home following a correctional placement. One successful model, Family Integrated Transitions, serves youth offenders with substance abuse and mental health problems in six Washington State counties.

Juvenile justice systems too often ignore the crucial role of families in resolving delinquency.

Key Facts
- Of more than 600 models for preventing or treating youth violence reviewed by the Center for the Study and Prevention of Violence since 1996, the three to show significant positive results in repeated scientific trials work intensively with parents and other family members—not just with youth themselves.
  - o Two of the three "blueprint" models provide intensive family therapy following strict, research-driven protocols, and the other temporarily places youth with specially trained foster families while counseling their parents.
  - o All three blueprint models have dramatically lowered recidivism and future incarceration of treated youth in repeated trials.
  - o All three cost far less than incarceration, and all three return several dollars in benefits for every dollar spent delivering services.
- In a recent three-state survey of parents with court-involved children, many reported feeling blamed or looked down on by the juvenile justice systems. Specifically, surveyed parents complained about being excluded from legal decisions made on their children's behalf; alienated from the process by complex language and court procedures; frustrated by the failure of probation officers to reach out and keep them informed; and disappointed in the lack of support when youth re-integrate into the community following confinement.

Promising Solutions
- Nationwide, including both delinquent and non-delinquent teens, roughly 40,000 behaviorally troubled young people per year now participate in the family-focused blueprint model treatment programs.
- In Santa Cruz County, a JDAI site, the local probation agency is using family conferences to develop community-based disposition plans in its most serious cases. Probation leaders report that family-driven plans are more comprehensive and more likely to be implemented than staff-driven plans. Recently, Santa Cruz also began hiring Family Partners to help families navigate the juvenile court and probation systems. These family engagement strategies have helped Santa Cruz reduced state commitments and residential placements by 71 percent in recent years.
- In Louisiana, parents have organized a non-profit organization—Families and Friends of Louisiana's Incarcerated Children—initiated as part of the campaign to close the notoriously dangerous Tallulah Youth Corrections Center. They conduct outreach to families, investigate complaints about conditions of confinement, and serve as the collective voice of parents who otherwise are rarely heard by policymakers or system administrators.

The increasing propensity to prosecute minor cases in the juvenile justice system harms youth, with no benefit to public safety.

Key Facts
- From 1995 to 2004, the national juvenile arrest rate for serious property and violent crimes declined 45 percent, and the homicide arrest rate plummeted 70 percent. In this same period, the numbers of youth adjudicated delinquent, placed into secure detention, and sentenced to probation all grew nation-wide. For instance, more than twice as many youth were adjudicated for disorderly conduct in 2004 than in 1995.
- Many youth prosecuted for minor crimes are sentenced to probation, from which they can easily end up in a detention or corrections facility if they violate probation rules. One of every nine youth in corrections facilities nation-wide is committed for a technical (non-criminal) violation of probation rules.
- Thanks to the widespread adoption of "zero tolerance" policies in our nation's schools, many juvenile courts have experienced substantial increases in delinquency cases originating from schools—including many for fist-fights and other commonplace behaviors that were once handled within those schools.

Promising Solutions
- In Clayton County, Georgia, a JDAI site, school-originated delinquency cases increased tenfold (from fewer than 100 to approximately 1,100) from 1995 to 2003, as a result of "zero tolerance" policies. After the presiding juvenile court judge in 2004 documented for school officials this alarming growth, the County developed a School Referral Reduction Program. Since then, school referrals to Clayton County's delinquency court have decreased by more than 68 percent from record highs.
- In Multnomah County, Oregon, another JDAI site, law enforcement officers were bringing almost 1,400 low-level offenders per year in the 1990s to the local detention center simply because they had no other place to take them. To remedy the problem, the County established a Juvenile Reception Center where caseworkers, rather than court or probation personnel, could speak with the youth, reunite them with their families and refer them to appropriate services—sparing youth the trauma of locked detention and allowing police officers to quickly return to patrol duties.

Juvenile justice is too often used as a dumping ground for youth who should be served by other public systems.

Key Facts
- Over the past twenty years, in many states, juvenile justice has become the primary referral for youths with mental health disorders, due to the

collapse of public mental health services for children and adolescents. In just thirty large counties nationwide, 9,000 adolescents entered the juvenile justice system in 2001 for the sole purpose of securing mental health treatment, referred by their own parents.

- Child welfare agencies often terminate services to adolescents in foster care who get arrested or adjudicated delinquent, leading these youth to suffer harsher outcomes than other court-involved teens. For example, in New York City, a 1998 study found that following arrest, foster youth were more likely to be detained than other youth.
- A disproportionate share of public school students referred to juvenile justice under "zero tolerance" policies are youth with educational disabilities, suggesting that schools are opting to prosecute rather than educate many students with special needs.

Promising Solutions

- In the late 1990s, half the youth in detention in Bernalillo County (Albuquerque), New Mexico—including many low-level offenders who posed little threat to public safety—required psychotropic medications. In response, local leaders established the outpatient Children's Community Mental Health Clinic to serve these youth more appropriately. The clinic helped Bernalillo reduce its detention population by 45 percent from 2000 to 2006, and the money saved reducing detention populations has been reallocated to sustain the clinic.
- In five Washington counties, a legal advocacy project called TeamChild is reducing inappropriate referrals to juvenile justice. TeamChild staff document the mental health, special education and other needs of youth at risk of delinquency referrals and help break down any barriers preventing them from accessing services. An early evaluation of TeamChild found that participants were 20 percent less likely than a control group to be arrested for a felony by age twenty-five.
- After studies found that foster care youth in New York City were far more likely than other youth to be detained following arrest, the Vera Institute of Justice and the Administration for Children's Services launched Project Confirm to identify and seek alternative placements for foster care youth entering detention. Among those accused of less serious offenses, the project has eliminated the disparity in detention rates for foster care and other youth.

Systems policies and practices have allowed unequal justice to persist.

Key Facts

- Surveys show that, compared with white youth, African-American teens commit slightly more violent crime, about the same amount of property crime, and less drug crime. Yet African-American youth are arrested at dramatically higher rates than white youth for all types of crime.

- Whereas African Americans comprise just 16 percent of the total juvenile population nationwide, 38 percent of youth in juvenile correctional institutions and 58 percent of youth sentenced to prison are African-American.
- Once arrested, African-American teens are:
  o more likely to be detained than white youth;
  o more likely to be formally charged in juvenile court;
  o more likely to be placed into a locked correctional facility (and less likely to receive probation), once adjudicated;
  o more likely to be waived to adult court; and
  o more likely to be incarcerated in an adult prison, once waived to adult court.
- After reviewing more than 150 studies, D.M. Bishop, a leading juvenile justice scholar, found "incontrovertible" evidence of racial bias in the juvenile justice system. "The issue is no longer simply *whether* whites and youths of color are treated differently," she wrote. "Instead, the preeminent challenge for scholars is to explain *how* these differences come about."

Promising Solutions

- Before Multnomah County, Oregon entered JDAI, minority youth were about 30 percent more likely than white youth to be detained after arrest. By reviewing every decision point for underlying biases, increasing diversity among juvenile justice staff, and promoting new practices that equalized treatment, Multnomah completely eliminated this gap by 2000.
- In Santa Cruz County, California, at the outset of JDAI, Latino youth assigned to detention were spending many more days behind bars than white youth—mostly because the jurisdiction lacked culturally appropriate programming. Once the local probation department teamed with community-based organizations to developed new alternatives, lengths of stay began to equalize and disparities are being addressed. Today, the average number of Latino youth is half what it was in 1998.
- Efforts to combat racial inequalities in juvenile justice got a significant boost in 2002 when longtime juvenile justice advocate and civil rights attorney James Bell established the W. Haywood Burns Institute for Juvenile Justice Fairness and Equity, to help jurisdictions eliminate racial disparities in juvenile justice.

Conclusion

The case for reform is compelling, but where to begin? At the state and local levels, the crucial first ingredients are political will and leadership. Genuine progress requires real champions, as well as a broad commitment from multiple stakeholders and agencies. Otherwise, the narrow interests of individual bureaucracies and political partisanship are likely to prevent agreement on goals, strategies and results.

Next, leaders must identify a starting point for their efforts. The reforms presented here would be difficult to implement en masse. In participating jurisdictions, JDAI has demonstrated the power of an "entry point" strategy: Focus on a particular system problem or issue, whose solution requires the adoption of principles, policies and practices that can subsequently influence other components of the system.

Change also requires a strengthened focus on achieving results and on collecting and analyzing the data required to hold systems accountable for them. In too many jurisdictions, juvenile justice systems are not judged by the progress of their youth or the safety of communities. Funds and staff are provided even when youth recidivate at high rates, facilities remain unsafe or children encounter racially disparate treatment. A results focus requires investments in information technology and the analytical expertise necessary to use data to inform program improvement and innovation.

Though the reforms suggested here are ambitious and complex, they need not be costly. The real challenge in juvenile justice budgeting is not the size of the investments, but rather the quality. For instance, by redeploying existing resources in favor of more cost-effective strategies that produce better results, many JDAI sites have introduced multiple detention reforms without raising their total budgets. Many, in fact, have saved substantial sums.

Success in juvenile justice reform also requires focused efforts to strengthen the juvenile justice workforce. We cannot substantially improve outcomes for vulnerable children and families if we don't first take the steps needed to recruit, train and retain a qualified, motivated workforce.

While the "action" in juvenile justice occurs largely at the state and local levels, the federal government can and should make a crucial contribution. Many states and localities look to the federal government for guidance on how best to tackle juvenile justice challenges. In recent years, the federal government's role in juvenile justice has suffered from inattention and drift. Funding levels have dropped precipitously; many remaining resources have been allocated to pet projects, rather than innovative programs; and the output of meaningful new federally-funded research has slowed to a trickle.

Fortunately, the key federal law guiding juvenile justice policy—the Juvenile Justice and Delinquency Prevention Act (JJDPA)—is up for reauthorization.

Federal funding for juvenile justice should be substantially increased, and it should be targeted to support successful strategies and cost-effective programs.

In addition, the Act should require meaningful outcome measurements for all programs financed with federal dollars; ban the use of federal funds to support models that have been proven ineffective; support state and local research and evaluation efforts; and encourage all states to measure recidivism of youth released from correctional facilities in a consistent manner. The federal government should also study the feasibility of a uniform data collection system, which is essential to good planning and practice.

The federal government should also promote aggressive efforts to reverse the persistent injustice of disproportionate treatment of minority youth and to reduce the alarming levels of abuse in correctional custody. The core mandate in JJDPA for states to "address" disproportionate treatment should be strengthened and clarified, requiring states to analyze each stage of the juvenile court process and develop corrective action plans to reduce disparate outcomes.

Additionally, a strengthened federal juvenile justice act might require states to collect and report data on violent incidents inside youth corrections facilities, submit to outside monitoring, and adhere to performance-based standards.

Finally, Congress should reinforce its commitment to the original core protections of the JJDPA—deinstitutionalization of status offenders, separation of juveniles from adult offenders and adult facilities—and expand efforts to strengthen the juvenile justice workforce.

Whatever role the federal government plays in promoting reform, however, the ultimate responsibility lies with the state and local leaders who operate our nation's juvenile courts and corrections systems. Only they can put this wealth of information to use and finally, more than a century after the founding of the juvenile court, realize the court's noble vision as a place where youth receive a measure of justice worthy of the name.

Resources

Annie E. Casey Foundation: www.aecf.org
Campaign for Youth Justice: www.campaign4youthjustice.org
Census of Juveniles in Residential Placement Databook: www.ojjdp.ncjrs.org/ojstatbb/cjrp
Center for Children's Law and Policy: www.cclp.org.
Coalition for Juvenile Justice: http://www.juvjustice.org
Commonweal Juvenile Justice Program: http://www.commonweal.org
Families and Friends of Louisiana's Incarcerated Children: www.fflic.org.
Justice Policy Institute: www.justicepolicy.org
National Center for Juvenile Justice: http://www.ncjj.org
National Council of Juvenile & Family Court Judges: http://www.ncjfcj.org/
National Juvenile Defender Center: www.njdc.org.
National Partnership for Juvenile Services: http://www.npjs.org
Pretrial Justice Institute: www.jdaihelpdesk.org

Vera Institute of Justice: http://www.vera.org
W. Haywood Burns Institute: www.burnsintitute.org.
Youth Law Center: http://www.ylc.org

References

"A Road Map for Juvenile Justice Reform." The Annie E. Casey Foundation. *2008 Kids Count Data Book,* 2008.

"And Justice for Some: Differential Treatment of Youth of Color in the Justice System." Report. National Council on Crime and Delinquency, 2007.

Bishop, D.M. "The Role of Race and Ethnicity in Juvenile Justice Processing," in *Our Children, Their Children: Confronting Racial and Ethnic Differences in American Juvenile Justice*, D.F. Hawkins and K. Kempf-Leonard, eds. (Chicago, IL: University of Chicago Press, 2005).

Elliott, D. S., ed. *Blueprints for Violence Prevention (vols. 1-10).* Center for the Study & Prevention of Violence Boulder, CO: University of Colorado, 1998.

Feld, B. C. *Bad Kids: Race and the Transformation of the Juvenile Court.* New York: Oxford University Press, 1999.

Holman, B., and J. Zeidenberg. "The Dangers of Detention." Report. Justice Policy Institute, 2006.

Krisberg, B. *Juvenile Justice: Reclaiming our Children.* Thousand Oaks, CA: Sage Publications, 2005.

"Less Guilty by Reason of Adolescence." Issue Brief No. 3 Chicago, IL: MacArthur Foundation, 2006.

Pathways to Juvenile Detention Reform, vols 1-14. Report. The Annie E. Casey Foundation. Baltimore, MD, 1999-2007.

Rosenbeim, M.K., et al. *A Century of Juvenile Justice.* Chicago, IL: University of Chicago Press, 2002.

Second Chances: 100 Years of the Juvenile Court. Washington, D.C.: Justice Policy Institute and Children & Family Justice Center, 1999.

Chapter 9

Drug Policy Reform and Neutralizing the Third Rail of Politics

Sanho Tree

POLICY PROPOSALS

■ Reduce the potential harms caused by drug abuse.
  ▪ Make prevention a priority.
  ▪ Fully fund treatment on request.
  ▪ Promote evidence-based harm reduction strategies.
■ Reduce the harms caused by the "War on Drugs."
  ▪ Promote alternatives to incarceration for low-level nonviolent drug offenders.
  ▪ End major source country eradication programs.
  ▪ End over-reliance on counter-productive crackdown policies such as the Merida Initiative.
  ▪ Stop searching for easy answers.

* * * * * * * * * * * * * * *

Since President Richard Nixon first declared a "war on drugs" in 1971, the goal of a drug-free America is as remote as ever. Users who seek illicit drugs have little problem obtaining them cheaply, quickly and with ease. Indeed, the government's own major indicators of success (measuring the price, purity and availability of drugs) show dismal trends. In 1969, the Nixon Administration spent $65 million on the drug war at the federal level; in 1982, the Reagan Administration spent $1.65 billion; in 2000, the Clinton Administration spent more than $17 billion; and the Bush Administration is currently spending well over $20 billion per year. We have had ever-harsher sentencing, and more people are employed to wage the drug war than ever before. The problem is not that we are

83

under-spending or not being tough enough, but that drug war *politics* constantly gets in the way of sound, evidence-based *policy*. Not only can some drugs have very harmful results on physical and mental health, but the drug war itself is now causing as much (if not more) harm than the drugs themselves. This is not an acceptable substitute for an effective drug control policy.

The policy recommendations outlined above fall into two categories. The first reduces the potential harms caused by the drugs themselves and the second deals with minimizing the collateral damage caused by the war on drugs. These recommendations are hardly unique, but they are a bit like the weather: everybody talks about it but nobody ever does anything to change it. This chapter is unique in that it lays out for the first time a viable method for legislators to challenge current drug policy while minimizing their own political risk in the age of "swiftboating." Without this key component, there is little realistic hope for changing the status quo.

Reduce the Potential Harms Caused by Drug Abuse

Drug prevention efforts such as the DARE program have failed miserably. We teach our children from an early age not to "cry wolf" and exaggerate claims, but then we turn around and allow police officers to use precisely the same tactics to frighten kids away from using drugs. This has increased cynicism, and children often throw the baby out with the bathwater. Hyperbole about the dangers of marijuana can lead kids to dismiss the very important messages about the dangers of other drugs like methamphetamine and heroin. We must also include the dangers of tobacco and alcohol in such education programs, for these "legal drugs" kill about thirty times more Americans each year than all illicit and prescription drugs combined.

The incoming Administration should support expanded implementation of proven effective programs, such as those evaluated by the Substance Abuse and Mental Health Services Administration's own National Registry of Evidence-based Prevention Programs. Effective and honest prevention programs are, in addition, fiscally conservative investments.

Our nation's drug problems are driven by demand, yet the lion's share of federal funding has gone to supply reduction and law enforcement. It is time to re-order our priorities and funding patterns to match reality, instead of political posturing. It seems whenever "get tough" measures are requested, legislators have no problem finding money to appropriate, but when more effective demand reduction policies are requested, there never seems to be enough funding to go around. Those who champion prevention and treatment funding run the risk of being labeled "tax and spend liberals" who believe in throwing money at social problems. In fact, funding the "soft side" of drug policy is the fiscally conservative position.

A RAND Corporation study found that every additional dollar invested in substance abuse treatment saves taxpayers $7.46 in societal costs, and that additional domestic law enforcement efforts cost fifteen times as much as treatment to achieve the same reduction in societal costs. It makes little sense to squander billions on futile illicit crop eradication measures when addicts who actually want help cannot obtain it. Trying to constrict supply without reducing demand only makes drugs more valuable, thus drawing more actors into this illicit economy.

Funding syringe exchange programs to prevent the spread of communicable diseases, expanding methadone programs, and making overdose prevention antidotes available to addicts have all been shown to reduce mortality, disease and crime without increasing the number of drug users. Even Iran's "drug czar" has come around on syringe exchange and methadone programs. For a nation not known for tolerance, Iran has even installed vending machines in Tehran to sell cheap condoms and syringes to drug addicts. It is unfortunate that his U.S. counterpart still stubbornly rejects such measures—as though the "wages of sin" ought to be death.

Reduce the Harms Caused By the "War on Drugs"

At a time when the United States is falling behind in major global indicators of success, we are still number-one in one area. With less than one-twentieth of the planet's population, we have one-quarter of the planet's prisoners. Put another way, of the more than 9 million prisoners on earth, the United States has more than 2.3 million of them. Of those 2.3 million, nearly one-quarter of them are behind bars for drug offenses. These half million drug war prisoners (who are incarcerated solely for drug offenses and not violence) are greater than the entire U.S. prison and jail population in 1980. The draconian drug laws passed in the 1980s as a response to the spread of crack cocaine have mushroomed our prison population. In an effort to appear "tough on crime," legislators passed harsh mandatory minimum sentences, which left judges no discretion to consider mitigating factors. The most glaring inconsistency, however, is in the racially disproportionate application of our drug laws. African Americans and whites use and sell drugs at similar rates, but African Americans are ten times more likely than whites to be imprisoned for drug offenses.

In an era when we cannot even find a major political figure who can say he hasn't used illegal drugs (Bill Clinton, Al Gore, Newt Gingrich and George W. Bush to name but a few), we must ask a fundamental question of fairness: Would a good stiff prison sentence have helped them in their lives and careers? The same could be asked of the nearly one-third of all Americans who have used an illegal drug at least once in their lifetime. If the answer is no, then why is it such a good thing for all the poor people and people of color languishing in prison? The main casualty of our war on drugs has been the concept of equal justice under the law.

The main driver of illicit crop cultivation in places like Colombia and Afghanistan is poverty, lack of access to credit and the absence of infrastructure for getting alternative crops to markets. Our current policies, however, focus on crop eradication rather than asking why farmers continue to plant illicit crops. This is an unsustainable policy. Eradication may succeed temporarily squeezing down cultivation one area, but then it balloons in another area because global demand continues unabated. We have been playing Whack-a-Mole with illicit crop cultivation at tremendous human, environmental and financial cost.

The Administration should reframe the issue as less of an illicit crop problem and more of a surplus human problem. The peasant farmers who grow these crops are not "narco-terrorists," but rather, they are poor family farmers who lack economic alternatives. Like parents in any part of the world, they will do whatever it takes to feed their children. Since jobs in these rural regions are scarce and millions of people are already competing for limited relief aid, what do we expect these farmers to do once we eradicate their illicit crops? Do we simply expect this "human surplus" to melt away and disappear? Or are they replanting their fields or moving cultivation even deeper into remote areas? Moreover, our eradication policies have been driving many peasant farmers into the arms of our declared enemies like the FARC and the paramilitaries in Colombia and the Taliban in Afghanistan. To put it in the discourse of the Bush Administration, our policy seems to be creating "terrorists" faster than we can defeat them. We can eradicate for decades, but if we don't figure out how these farmers are going to feed their families, they will go right back to replanting or, worse, join the armed groups simply to earn some money so their families can survive.

Supply reduction programs also have another serious unintended consequence. As long as there is undiminished global demand for drugs, reducing the supply through eradication and interdiction creates an artificial shortage thus causing prices to skyrocket astronomically. In other words, our drug war policies create an unintended price support for these minimally processed agricultural commodities, which would otherwise have very little monetary value. With nearly two-thirds of all Colombians living below the official poverty line (which means surviving on about $2 per day), our fumigation planes are essentially giving a sort of crop subsidy to coca farmers because we try to make coca more scarce while there is still high demand. Given the widespread poverty in many drug-producing regions, we will never make these crops disappear by making them more valuable.

Of all the laws that governments can pass or repeal, the law of supply and demand is not one of them. Our planet has an inexhaustible reservoir of poor peasant farmers willing to risk growing illicit crops, and there is too much ungoverned territory in the world in which to cultivate these plants. Trying to destroy illicit crops at the source has been as effective as shoveling water.

While there is certainly a need for effective law enforcement, our over-reliance on militarized drug policies has backfired. Though it may seem counter-intuitive, decades of escalating the drug war have produced a perverse result. The drug trade evolves under Darwinian principles (i.e., survival of the fittest). Our response of constantly increasing law enforcement ensures that the clumsy and inefficient traffickers are weeded out while the smarter and more adaptable ones tend to avoid detection and capture. We cannot hope to win a war on drugs when our policies see to it that only the most efficient operations survive. Indeed, these survivors are richly rewarded because we have constricted the supply of drugs while the demand remains. This increases prices and profits for the surviving traffickers while "thinning out the herd" by eliminating their competition for them. Through this process of artificial selection, we have been unintentionally breeding "super traffickers" for decades. Time after time, these super traffickers have been helped by the very same foreign law enforcement personnel we have trained. If there is no way to guarantee their loyalty, then we must question the wisdom of training foreign forces that can make many times their low government salaries by working for the cartels.

Ultimately, there is no substitute for building a healthy society. The root causes of drug abuse and illicit drug cultivation (as well as many other societal problems) can be traced back to poverty, despair and alienation. While poverty is easy to identify, alienation and despair cut across class lines in powerful ways. In 1965, testifying before a House Subcommittee of the Committee on the Judiciary, Sen. Robert F. Kennedy tried to promote an enlightened drug policy before our country declared war on its own citizens. He told Congress:

> Now, more than at any other time in our history, the addict is a product of a society that has moved faster and further than it has allowed him to go, a society which in its complexity and its increasing material comfort has left him behind. In taking up the use of drugs, the addict is merely exhibiting the outermost aspects of a deep-seated alienation from this society, of a combination of personal problems having both psychological and sociological aspects. The fact that addiction is bound up with the hard core of the worst problems confronting us socially makes it discouraging at the outset to talk about "solving" it. "Solving" it really means solving poverty and broken homes, racial discrimination and inadequate education, slums and unemployment.

Forty-three years later, the preconditions contributing to drug abuse have changed little, but our response to the problem has become overwhelmingly punitive. The threat of harsh punishment, however, has done little to deter drug use. World Health Organization researchers, in a 2008 report on its just-completed mental health survey, concluded that "The U.S., which has been driving much of the world's drug research and drug policy agenda, stands out with higher levels of use of alcohol, cocaine, and cannabis, despite punitive illegal drug policies as well as (in many U.S. states), a higher minimum legal alcohol drinking age than many comparable developed countries. The Netherlands, with a less criminally punitive approach to cannabis use than the U.S., has experienced lower levels of use, particularly among younger adults."

Restoring our social safety net is a much-needed first step in that direction. If people believe that their best days are behind them, the tendency to self medicate will only increase. If we do not construct a society that gives average citizens reasons to look forward to tomorrow, then we will continue to pay a high social cost for that failure. The best path to building such a society is to adopt the other recommendations outlined in this book.

How to Cut the Gordian Knot

The Problem
The policy recommendations outlined above are neither new nor terribly controversial. Despite a chorus of legal, military, law enforcement and public health voices calling for fundamental reform of U.S. drug policies, their voices have largely fallen on deaf ears when it comes to elected officials. We do not need yet another blue ribbon commission or academic study to tell us our current policies are not working. Those who have worked on this issue know one of the most cynical secrets in Washington: many elected officials (if not an outright majority) are willing to acknowledge the fundamental failure of the drug war in private, but continue to vote in favor of it in public. Drug policy reform fails to get traction with elected officials because it is the quintessential "third rail"[1] political issue—thus, it is a subject to avoid unless one is declaring support for the status quo. As Jean-Claude Juncker, Prime Minister of Luxembourg, put it "We all know what to do, but we don't know how to get re-elected once we have done it." Although Juncker was referring to economic liberalization, the quote is even more applicable to the war on drugs. The following section offers a novel and counter-intuitive way out of this political dilemma and other third-rail controversies as well. Without such a solution, these recommendations will be as ineffectual as all the others that came before it.

The disconnect between private and public views of elected officials has to do with the difficulty in explaining why "get tough" measures sound attractive to voters but are often counter-productive. Politicians must hope that the voters will have some basic understanding of the economics of drug prohibition and how escalating the drug war only makes the drugs more valuable, thus attracting even more participants into the drug economy. This difficulty is compounded when political challengers can run negative smear ads relatively cheaply and repeatedly to decimate their opponent's poll numbers. Moreover, elected officials have to hope that the voters—who saw those "swiftboat-style" ads air repeatedly—will tune in to the local news to hear their own sixty-second defense of why they opposed further escalation of the drug war. Very few politicians are able to convey successfully such a paradigm shift in a soundbite. After all, if drugs are bad, why *not* wage a war against them?

Since Congress installed an electronic voting system in 1973, the number of recorded votes has soared. The reason so many votes were on record (as opposed to a voice vote or simple head count) is not so that average citizens can hold their representatives accountable for their votes. After all, the overwhelming majority of voters have never looked up their representative's voting record. Those recorded votes are for the benefit of the political parties so that they can put their adversary's votes on record to spotlight at a future time—usually during election season (e.g., "He voted for war funding before he voted against it"). Thus, legislators who dare to vote in dissent on third-rail issues expose themselves to possible attack ads when they run for reelection.

The degeneration of our political discourse and campaign tactics has made reforming the drug war synonymous with political suicide. In recent years, campaign strategists like Karl Rove have taken traditional wedge issues and refined them into what he calls "anger points"—third-rail issues that have complex and often counterintuitive solutions, but are extremely easy to take out of context and twist into an effective attack ad. While being smeared as soft on drugs or soft on "narco-terrorism" alone may not be enough to destroy a politician's career, few elected officials are willing to risk adding another political liability to their reelection campaign. In this way, reforming drug policy is analogous to placing a loaded pistol on the table and praying your political challenger will not shoot you with it.

The Solution

So how can politicians who care about getting re-elected make fundamental reforms without being electrocuted by the third rail? Just as the much-needed reforms of U.S. drug policy are counter-intuitive (where being tough is often the opposite of being effective), so too is the way out of this political stalemate. In order to get a more responsible legislature, it may be better to have less accountability—at least temporarily.

By utilizing a non-binding, anonymous straw poll, elected officials can express their true leanings without feeling the political backlash from myriad sources. While such a measure would have to be used as a "non-binding procedural aid" (the Constitution requires a *recorded* vote if one-fifth of the quorum requests it), an anonymous straw poll can produce surprising results and offer political cover during the debate over a binding recorded vote. Additionally, this temporary "veil of conscience" allows members of Congress to express their sentiments without crossing their party leadership, political donors, lobbyists and even their own electorate.

If the straw poll results show there is considerable dissension regarding a third-rail issue, then members who wish to vote against it can argue they represent the true majority of Congress. To be blunt, a great number of elected officials are essentially herd animals. When they detect significant movement, they often follow because there is political safety in numbers. In this way, anonymous straw polls potentially can become the catalyst for a stampede.

As long as one member votes in the minority, nobody can prove which way each member voted. The concept is not unlike a traditional firing squad where one shooter is randomly given a rifle with a blank cartridge. In anonymity, honesty can emerge long enough for elected officials to realize they are in fact in a "closeted" majority. This exercise in distributed responsibility could provide the solution for Congress to address other polarizing issues such as economic restructuring due to climate change, national health care or authorizations for war. It can also be used to quickly dispense with election-year gimmicks such as anti-flag burning amendments.

The Benefits

This process can be used to address a variety of third-rail issues besides the drug war. When significant appropriations, constituent jobs, campaign contributions or party loyalty are on the line, elected officials often cast votes that they know may not be in the best interest of the nation or their grandchildren's generation.

Every politician understands what is in his or her short-term interest. They know what the party leadership wants, what their campaign contributors want, and what lobbyists want. At what point does the long-term interest of the nation as a whole come into play? Who represents the interests of future generations? Short-sighted interests and market forces have hijacked our broken political system.

The straw poll can also be used for association meetings of mayors or chiefs of police. Such prominent figures often think they are the only one in the room who believes the drug war to be a counter-productive disaster. An anonymous straw poll taken at the beginning of such meetings can allow a silent majority to come out of the closet and thus begin a more rational debate.

An anonymous straw poll can create a temporary firewall separating sound public policy from partisan politics—or what Scott McClellan, Bush's former White House press secretary, calls the permanent campaign. Indeed, this may be the only viable way to undo the polarizing legacy of Karl Rove. With so many crises to address and such powerful interests opposing reforms, Washington cannot afford to play partisan games and conduct business as usual. Those who were elected based on a pledge of a "different kind of politics" in a year of "change" should consider this method of cutting the Gordian Knot and breaking the logjam in Washington.

Resources

The Criminal Justice Policy Foundation: http://www.cjpf.org
The Drug Policy Alliance: http://www.drugpolicy.org
Drug War Facts: http://www.drugwarfacts.org/index2.htm

Drug War Facts is the best resource for quick, footnoted information on most aspects of drug policy. It is updated regularly and cites mainly government-funded studies and professional journals.
The Effective National Drug Control Strategy, 1999: http://www.csdp.org/edcs/
Families Against Mandatory Minimums: http://www.famm.org
The Washington Office on Latin America: http://www.wola.org

Notes

1. The expression comes from the high-voltage third rail in a subway system and is used to refer to controversial issues that are thought to be political suicide for elected officials to engage. Other examples of third rail issues include U.S. aid to Israel, immigration reform, funding for law enforcement, gay marriage, military base closures, national health care, raising taxes, etc.

Chapter 10

Policies toward the Elderly: Strengthening Social Security and Medicare

Barbara B. Kennelly and Carroll L. Estes

POLICY PROPOSALS

Social Security
- Reject Social Security private accounts permanently.
- Improve Social Security's solvency without reducing benefits for current or future generations of retirees.
- Balance the federal budget, thus reducing fiscal pressure on both Social Security and Medicare.
- Enhance Social Security benefits.

Medicare
- Improve Medicare's finances by reducing the rate of health care inflation in general and across all insurance programs.
- Reverse the privatization of Medicare.
- Improve Medicare by adding a long term care benefit.

* * * * * * * * * * * * *

"We can never insure one hundred percent of the population against one hundred percent of the hazards and vicissitudes of life, but we have tried to frame a law which will give some measure of protection to the average citizen and to his family against the loss of a job and against poverty-ridden old age." – President Franklin D. Roosevelt upon signing the Social Security Act, 1935

Poverty-ridden old age. It is hard to imagine our not-so-distant past when many Americans faced old age without any income, assets or even the basic necessities of life. In 1935, over half of the nation's elderly were poverty-stricken. Today, this sad part of our history is gone. Far fewer American seniors live in poverty or are denied access to medical care, thanks to social insurance programs like Social Security and Medicare. Sadly, many conservatives and private-market advocates ridicule social insurance as an archaic system of government handouts. Yet, like other risk pools designed to insure individuals against physical and material losses, social insurance continues to provide income protection for workers and their families, retirees and the disabled.

Opponents of social insurance have, over the years, fomented intergenerational warfare, pitting the young against the old in an effort to erode support for Social Security and Medicare among those unfamiliar with the program's many virtues. In fact, the Social Security system reflects the ways in which the generations are interdependent. The system contributes to the well-being of Americans by providing a foundation of retirement income that permits seniors to live in dignity, while also relieving younger family members of direct financial costs for older parents and grandparents. In addition to retired worker and spouse benefits, wage-earners receive insurance protection for themselves and their families if they should become disabled or die.

Through economic crises, natural disasters and wartime, America's social insurance programs have remained reliable constants in a changing world. These are *not* the antiquated and archaic programs portrayed by those opposed to any government social insurance role. In fact, quite the contrary is true. Social insurance programs showcase the best of what government *can* do for its citizens, and create a lasting compact between our citizens and their government.

Private Accounts Cannot Be Part of the Debate

President George W. Bush announced immediately after his re-election that creating Social Security private accounts would be a key domestic priority for his Administration during his second term. He then embarked on a "Sixty Cities in Sixty Days" campaign to generate public support for his initiative. Fortunately, the more the American public learned about Social Security private accounts, the more their opposition grew. Americans quickly understood that private accounts funded with payroll taxes would dismantle Social Security and the protections it provides for retired and disabled workers and their families.

According to the National Committee to Preserve Social Security and Medicare, private accounts would worsen Social Security's long-term financing, reduce Social Security benefits for future retirees, trade Social Security guarantees for the volatility of the stock market and add trillions of dollars to the federal debt. They simply have no place in any discussion to strengthen the program's finances.

Strengthening Social Security's Finances Should Not Be Accomplished through Cutting Benefits

American seniors need Social Security. It's a simple truth often lost in the political and philosophical debates swirling around "entitlement reform." So much focus has been on long-term macro-economic projections that a top priority for progressive organizations in the coming decade will necessarily be protecting existing benefits from the budget-cutters' knife. To succeed, policymakers will need to understand the lack of income adequacy for tomorrow's retirees, along with the role Social Security must play as our older population grows.

Today's Social Security benefits are modest yet essential in providing an adequate retirement income for millions of American seniors. The average Social Security benefit is only about $1,000 a month. Today, it replaces about 40 percent of workers' average earnings, and once the retirement age increases to sixty-seven, that replacement rate will shrink further. For people who retire earlier than age sixty-five, Social Security benefits will replace even less of their income. Among thirty countries with advanced economies, the United States is fifth from the bottom in the generosity of its benefits for average earners, and single older women have the lowest income relative to married couples in cross-national comparisons of Western industrialized nations.

Retirees rely heavily on Social Security, and retirement income lost from cuts in Social Security benefits would not be easily replaced with other sources of income.
Of the dollars received by older people, four in ten come from Social Security. Women rely on the defined benefits of Social Security; without them, more than half of older women would be poor; 65 percent of African American older women would be poor. Only half of married couples and less than one-third of unmarried women have income from pensions or annuities. Only one in three elderly couples and one in six unmarried women receives $2,000 or more a year in income from assets.

Traditional pension plans have virtually disappeared from the workforce, eliminating a previous source of lifetime income in retirement. Their replacement by individual savings plans such as 401(k) plans both increases risk to individual workers and tends to result in lower amounts of income available in retirement.

Despite these realities, policymakers often consider deep cuts in Social Security benefits for future retirees. Some cuts, such as replacing Social Security's wage-indexing with various forms of price-indexing, would impose direct and deep cuts that are fairly apparent. Others, such as further increasing the retirement age at which Social Security benefits begin from the current sixty-seven to seventy, are more opaque. While made in the context of having retirement reflect increases in longevity, retirement age increases reflect a myopic view of the business climate and employer practices. Even in a tightening job market, few employers show interest in hiring workers in their late fifties, instead chasing younger entrants to the workforce. Unless employer hiring practices change, raising the retirement age merely dooms generations of older workers to retirements with smaller Social Security benefits and higher proportions of poor and near-poor, especially among minorities, women, and low- and middle-income wage workers.

Our Nation's Budget Deficits Must Be Brought under Control

The Bush Administration converted budget surpluses into deficits, through a combination of massive tax cuts, mostly directed toward the wealthy, and unprecedented military spending. These growing deficits have resulted in a $3 trillion national debt, and interest payments that represent the fastest growing component of our national budget. As a result of the 1983 Social Security Reform Amendments, Social Security has been running surpluses which have helped disguise the magnitude of the Administration's budget shortcomings. In the next decade, Social Security's surpluses will shrink and the program's bonds will begin to be redeemed.

Congress should seek to bring the short-term federal budget into balance *before* addressing Social Security's long-range funding gap. This will leave Congress free to take the modest steps necessary to address the projected shortfall in Social Security.

Social Security's Benefits Could Be Improved

Although the top priority of progressive organizations must be the preservation of Social Security's existing benefits, it is worth considering areas where the greatest need exists for benefit improvements. Three areas of greatest need are: providing a meaningful minimum benefit; improving survivor's benefits; and protecting the annual Cost of Living Adjustment.

Under current law, Social Security includes a Special Minimum Benefit intended to reduce poverty among retired lifetime low-wage workers. The Special Minimum Benefit targets modestly increased benefits at retirees with a low benefit based on a steady, long-time, low-wage work record. It accomplishes this goal by basing the benefit calculation on the number of years worked at a low level of earnings.

Unfortunately, the maximum benefit as currently calculated remains less than the official poverty level for aged persons. Moreover, because the benefit is indexed to price inflation rather than wage growth, it has provided a less generous benefit over time relative to the traditional wage-indexed Social Security benefit.

A newly designed minimum benefit could expand benefits for low earners across all demographic groups, including women, who are more likely than men to be at the bottom of the income distribution. All retirement benefits today are based on the expectation of thirty-five years of workforce participation, but the Special Minimum Benefit is calculated on thirty years of work. Counting five additional years of earnings would make this benefit method available to more low-wage workers and assure at least a poverty-level income to workers who spent a full worklife in the paid work force.

Additionally, if up to ten years spent caring for children or dependent adults are counted towards the Special Minimum Benefit, many women with work careers divided between home and the paid workforce would be eligible for higher worker benefits.

Among Social Security beneficiaries, widows are considered a particularly vulnerable group. In a one-earner family, when one spouse dies, the survivor receives two-thirds of the couple's combined benefits. In a two-earner family where each spouse has earned a worker benefit, the survivor receives the larger of the two benefits. This means that the survivor may receive a benefit which is half of the couple's combined benefit checks.

Studies show that elderly widows are the poorest category of Social Security beneficiaries. Once widowed, they receive one-half to one-third less in Social Security benefits. Moreover, they typically have less pension income and smaller savings. As they age, outliving their husbands by many years, their savings are further depleted.

One proposal to improve the living standard for elderly widows is to provide them with a benefit equal to 75 percent of the combined benefit they were receiving while their spouse was alive. Providing a widow three-quarters of the couple's combined benefit checks treats one-earner and two-earner couples more fairly and reduces the likelihood of leaving the survivor in poverty.

Social Security is one of the few retirement programs that helps seniors keep pace with inflation, through the use of an annual Cost-of-Living Adjustments (COLA). The annual COLA is calculated on the basis of general inflation, which has been outpaced by inflation in the health sector for many years. For this reason, Medicare premiums have been rising at a faster rate than Social Security benefits, thus eroding the ability of seniors to keep up with other increases in costs. While current law prevents net decreases in Social Security benefits resulting from increases in Part B premiums, it allows rising Part B premiums to consume a beneficiary's entire Social Security COLA. In addition, there is no such "hold-harmless" protection constraining the Part D premium, setting up a situation where seniors can lose ground each year as premiums for Part D increase at the rate of prescription drug cost inflation.

There are a number of options that could be considered to strengthen the ability of the COLA to protect seniors against the ravages of inflation. Two of the most effective options would be to limit cost increases in *both* Part B and Part D *combined* to no more than 25 percent of the increased Social Security benefit resulting from the Social Security COLA, and to create a new consumer price index that more accurately reflects the inflation rate of consumer spending among seniors.

Providing retirement income through Social Security is only one of the twin pillars of retirement security. Because health care costs consume increasing amounts of our retirement income, the future of Medicare is critical to a financially stable retirement. It is ironic that at a time when we are engaged in a Presidential debate about providing decent health care to our working population, the one universal, affordable health insurance program we do have—Medicare—is well on its way to becoming privatized.

Before Medicare was created, seniors were essentially on their own. Because older Americans are virtually guaranteed to draw higher health claims than any other segment of our population, they were mostly shunned by private health plans.

Prior to 1965, that left half of all seniors without insurance coverage.

Medicare changed all that. By creating a universal insurance pool, Medicare allowed the previously uninsurable senior population to share their risks, providing affordable coverage. Sharing risk over a broad population also allowed costs and benefits to be uniform, providing equity to seniors across a wide spectrum of health conditions. Although Medicare is not perfect, for millions of seniors it has been a godsend. It provides basic, affordable, universal health care to a population abandoned by private industry.

Slowing the Growth of Health Care Costs through Health Care Reform Will Improve Medicare's Finances

Although Medicare costs are rising for both beneficiaries and the federal government, the increases are not unique to Medicare. Because it is a health care program, it is subject to the same upward inflationary pressures that are forcing many employers to drop their policies, leaving their workers to join the ranks of America's 46 million uninsured. Due to Medicare's low administrative overhead and service efficiencies, the program's costs grow at roughly the same rate as insurance for the under-sixty-five population, despite seniors' higher need for services.

According to the Congressional Budget Office, the vast majority of Medicare's cost issues are not due to the aging of the population. They are the result of continued dramatic increases in the cost of health care generally. If the incoming Administration and Congress are successful in enacting health care reform that slows the rate of growth of health care costs so that they no longer grow faster than the rest of the economy, Medicare's long-range financial deficit could be cut by more than half.

Many who promote cuts in Medicare believe the erroneous caricature of older people spending golden years playing golf and traveling luxuriously. In fact, about 70 percent of Medicare beneficiaries have incomes under $25,000 and 85 percent have incomes under $40,000. Nearly two-thirds of older households have incomes under $20,000, and they are already spending 30–50 percent of their incomes on health care.

Arbitrarily cutting Medicare without getting at the root of the continuing upward trend of health care costs is a strategy for failure. It has real impacts on real people—most of whom have nowhere else to go for coverage and limited ability to pay higher medical costs, accounting for rising senior bankruptcies.

Reverse the Harm to Medicare Imposed by the Medicare Modernization Act

Rather than strengthening Medicare, this Administration and the previous Congress put it well on the road to privatization with the ill-named Medicare Modernization Act (MMA) of 2003. The MMA moves toward privatization by creating a Medicare drug benefit that may only be purchased through private insurance companies. The Part D program is confusing, and while individual seniors may have saved money because the government subsidizes part of their drug purchases, it prohibits federal Medicare price negotiations that could curb growing drug prices—increasing costs for seniors and taxpayers.

In addition, the MMA created what is now known as the Medicare Advantage program. Medicare Advantage is private health care being sold to seniors under the umbrella of the Medicare program. It is being subsidized by billions of dollars each year—with the federal government paying on average 13 percent more per beneficiary covered than it would pay if that beneficiary had stayed in traditional Medicare. Medicare Advantage plans are also designed to draw younger and healthier seniors, breaking up the universal risk pool that makes Medicare work. In time, the traditional program will no longer be affordable, and millions of seniors will again join the ranks of the uninsured.

The MMA not only created the privatized prescription drug benefit, it also included many long-term changes designed to privatize all of Medicare. Privatizing Medicare is just as likely to destroy the health care safety net for seniors as privatizing Social Security is to dismantle the foundation of income security for retirees, the disabled and survivors.

The new Administration and Congress must eliminate the private subsidies and incentives designed to privatize the Medicare program, and restore traditional Medicare to a level playing field. In addition, prescription drug benefits should be made more readily available to low-income beneficiaries by liberalizing the asset test for Part D's low-income subsidy.

The Growing Need for Long Term Care (LTC)

Nearly 10 million Americans, the majority of whom are elderly, rely on long-term care (LTC) services and supports to assist them with activities of daily living (ADLs). About 40 percent of those needing LTC are under age sixty-five. Because the United States lacks a comprehensive approach to financing LTC, many individuals forgo needed assistance, and 80 percent of LTC is provided, unpaid, by family, friends, and neighbors. As baby boomers age, rising demand for LTC will increase, straining more and more family caregivers as well as the only public program for LTC, Medicaid. This federal-state program primarily supports nursing home care, and it is the safety net for individuals who must first deplete their life savings (spending down to poverty).

For these reasons, the incoming Administration and Congress should create a universal comprehensive social insurance system in Medicare for LTC for Americans with significant functional limitations and eliminate the "institutional bias" in public financing for home- and community-based LTC, while standardizing and regulating private long-term care insurance. Paid care-givers employed through these systems should be provided fair pay and benefits.

The millions of unpaid caregivers (mostly women) who provide the majority of direct personal care for persons with ADL dependencies (or the need for constant supervision) receive no supportive health, financial or other assistance. Research consistently shows serious, financial, morbidity and mortality consequences for stressed care-givers. As the Coalition for the Continuum of Care recommended to the 2005 White House Conference on Aging, care-giver benefits must be integral to LTC policy: medical health insurance; public disability insurance; credit for work in calculation of Social Security benefits; inflation protection on the calculation of their peak earning years for Social Security; and a respite care benefit.

Resources

Administration on Aging: www.aoa.org
Alliance for Health Reform: www.allhealth.org
American Society on Aging: www.asaging.org
Center on Budget and Policy Priorities: www.cbpp.org
Center for Economic and Policy Research: www.cepr.net
Center for Medicare Advocacy: www.medicareadvocacy.org
Centers for Medicare and Medicaid Services (CMS): www.cms.hhs.gov

Commonwealth Fund: www.cmwf.org
Families USA: www.familiesusa.org
Institute for Women's Policy Research: www.iwpr.org
Kaiser Family Foundation: www.kff.org
Leadership Council on Aging Organizations: www.lcao.org
Medicare Rights Center: www.medicarerights.org
National Academy of Social Insurance: www.nasi.org
National Association of State Units on Aging: www.nasua.org
National Clearinghouse for Long Term Care: www.longtermcare.gov
National Committee to Preserve Social Security and Medicare (NCPSSM):
    www.ncpssm.org
National Council on Aging: www.ncoa.org
NCPSSM blog: www.entitledtoknow.blogspot.com
Older Women's League: www.owl-national.org
Social Security Administration: www.ssa.gov
Students for Social Security: www.studentsforsocialsecurity.org

Chapter 11

An Economic Justice Agenda

Dean Baker

POLICY PROPOSALS

■ Fix the health care system.
■ Mandate the Federal Reserve Board to combat financial bubbles.
■ Impose a modest financial transactions tax.
■ Change the rules of corporate governance so that shareholders must approve the compensation packages of top executives.
■ End patent monopoly financing of prescription drug research.
■ Mandate paid vacation for all workers.
■ Guarantee workers the right to join unions.
■ Lower the value of the dollar.

* * * * * * * * * * * * * *

Over the last three decades, the economy has been deliberately restructured in ways that ensure that the benefits from economic growth flow upward. As a result, the bulk of the population has seen little or no benefit from growth that has taken place over this period. The incoming President must look to rewire the economy to ensure that the benefits of economic growth are broadly shared.

Fix the Health Care System

There is no more important reform that the incoming President can implement than fixing the U.S. health care system and providing universal coverage. Almost 50 million people go without health insurance coverage year-round, and more than 80 million people are without coverage at some point in the year.

Even more important, those with coverage must fear that job loss, even if health-related, can place them among the uninsured.

In addition to the insecurity created by our health insurance system, it is also enormously expensive. We pay more than twice as much per person as the average in other wealthy countries, yet we rank near the bottom by most measures of health care outcomes, such as life expectancy. Furthermore, rapid cost growth is projected to make the U.S. health care system even less competitive in future decades. These projections of exploding health care costs will impose an enormous burden on the private sector if they actually come true. They are also the basis of the horror stories about the long-term budget or "entitlement" crisis featured prominently in the media.

The route to fixing the system is clear, even if the politics of getting there might be difficult. Creating a universal Medicare-type system can eliminate hundreds of billions of dollars of waste associated with the system of private insurance. It can also create a mechanism for restraining cost growth.

While it may be difficult to get to a universal Medicare system overnight, we can get there through a market process, since an efficient public system can easily out-compete private insurers. This fact has already been demonstrated within the Medicare system, where the traditional publicly run plan consistently wins out over private plans when they are placed on a level playing field.

The key to getting to a universal Medicare system is therefore to create a good publicly run health insurance plan that is open to everyone. This system will be able to undercut private insurers, since it won't have to waste money on marketing, high executive compensation and dividends to shareholders. It will also be able to use its market power to hold down the prices charged by providers. With a good publicly run system and generous subsidies for low- and moderate-income families, we can soon get to universal coverage at an affordable price.

Mandate the Federal Reserve Board
to Combat Financial Bubbles

At present, the Federal Reserve Board does not view preventing asset bubbles (unsustainable increases in price) like the stock bubble of the 1990s or the housing bubble in the current decade as part of its mandate. As a result, it allowed a $10 trillion stock bubble to grow unchecked at the end of the 1990s. In the current decade, it has allowed the housing bubble to grow to more than $8 trillion. This led to the creation of more than $110,000 of housing bubble wealth for every homeowner in the country.

The collapse of the housing bubble is now pushing the economy into a recession, just as the collapse of the stock bubble led to a recession seven years earlier. A recession inevitably means enormous hardship, as millions of workers will lose their jobs and families will lose their homes and their health care. In addition, tens of millions of middle class families will see most of their life's savings disappear, as their home plummets in value.

This disaster could have been prevented if the Fed had taken steps to stem the growth of the bubble. The Fed has a variety of tools to accomplish this goal, but the most obvious is simply information. If the Federal Reserve Board chairman had persistently laid out the evidence showing that there was a stock or housing bubble, and that its bursting would lead to enormous losses, it is likely that the bubbles never would have grown to such dangerous levels. The incoming President must appoint people to the Federal Reserve Board who take the problems created by financial bubbles seriously.

Impose a Modest Financial Transactions Tax

The financial sector is playing an ever- larger role in the U.S. economy. At the last cyclical profit peak in 2006, the financial sector accounted for more than 30 percent of all corporate profits. The financial sector is also one of the major sources of inequality, as top earners can take home more than $100 million a year, and in some cases more than $1 billion in a single year.

The financial sector serves an enormously important role in the economy by acting as an intermediary between savers and investors; therefore, it would be counter-productive to take steps that would hamper its operations. However, a large percentage of financial transactions are really just a form of gambling as investors buy and sell assets in the same day or even the same hour.

A modest tax on financial transactions—for example, 0.25 percent on the purchase or sale of a share of stock—could both raise an enormous sum of money and reduce the amount of speculative activity in the economy. A tax of this size could raise an amount of revenue equal to 1 percent of GDP ($150 billion a year). This sum could pay for extending health care coverage, green infrastructure or even a middle-class tax cut.

A tax of this size would also substantially reduce the amount of speculative trading in the financial sector. Even a modest tax would substantially increase the risk for traders who are hoping to profit from quickly buying and selling shares of stocks, currency or other assets.

At the same time, such a tax would have very little impact on the incentives facing long-term investors. In fact, since the cost of trading stock and other assets has plummeted in recent decades due to advances in computerization, a modest tax would simply be raising transaction costs back to where they were in the 1980s or 1990s. In effect, we would just be taxing gambling on Wall Street in the same way that we tax gambling in casinos or state lotteries.

Require Shareholder Approval for CEO Pay

The government currently sets down rules of corporate governance to prevent fraud and abuses by insiders. For example, there are requirements that corporate boards be voted on by shareholders at regular intervals and also rules that prohibit discrimination against minority shareholders.

These rules exist because it is possible for the insiders at corporations to take advantage of their situation and run the companies for their own benefit rather than the benefit of other stakeholders, including shareholders. This is exactly what is happening now as top executives frequently pay themselves salaries in the tens of millions, or even hundreds of millions of dollars.

These exorbitant salaries are not only a drain on the corporation, coming at the expense of workers' wages or shareholders' returns, they also set in place an extremely pernicious pay pattern in the economy. Top managers of other organizations, including universities, government agencies and even charities, compare their pay to the pay of CEOs at major corporations. This enshrines a pattern of inequality across the economy, with the top executives at many of these institutions now drawing salaries well into the hundreds of thousands, or in some cases even more than $1 million a year.

If corporations were required to send executive compensation packages to their shareholders for approval at regular intervals (with unreturned proxies not counted), it would likely impose a check on excessive CEO pay. Bringing CEO pay back down to more reasonable levels would eliminate one of the major causes of the growth of inequality over the last three decades.

End Patent Financing of Prescription Drug Research

Drugs are almost invariably cheap to produce, yet many life-saving drugs sell for hundreds or even thousands of dollars per prescription. The reason for the huge gap between the price of drugs and the cost of producing them is that the government grants drug companies patent monopolies. These legal monopolies allow the pharmaceutical industry to charge high prices, because people will be willing to pay almost anything to protect their health or life, or that of a family member.

Patent monopolies are justified by the high cost of researching and developing new drugs. However, there are far more efficient ways of financing biomedical research. For example, the federal government already spends $30 billion a year (approximately the same amount spent by the industry) on biomedical research, primarily through the National Institutes of Health (NIH).

While the NIH-funded research is primarily basic scientific research, there is no reason the government could not also pay for the development of new drugs and the clinical testing process. If the public paid for developing new drugs, then drugs could be sold in a competitive market, where the vast majority would cost just a few dollars per prescription. This would both make drugs more affordable and eliminate the incentives the industry now has to misrepresent the safety and effectiveness of its medicines. In short, publicly financed research would both save money and lead to better health outcomes.

Mandate Vacations for All Workers

The United States is the only wealthy country in the world in which workers are not guaranteed any time off from their jobs. In other countries, workers are guaranteed under the law four, five or even six weeks a year of paid time off. It would be an enormous improvement in the standard of living of tens of millions of workers in the United States if they could count on some paid time off from their jobs.

Paid time off could take a variety of forms. Tens of millions of workers have no right to paid, or even unpaid, sick leave from their jobs, leaving them at risk of losing their jobs if they don't go to work when they are sick. Similarly, most workers do not receive paid parental leave when they have a child. Here also many workers can lose their job if they take a few months off after having a baby. (Workers at larger employers are guaranteed unpaid time off under the Family and Medical Leave Act.) Mandates that required firms to provide paid sick days, paid parental leave, and/or paid vacation would bring the United States more in line with the rest of the world.

It is also worth noting that there are strong environmental reasons for encouraging workers to get more of the gains from productivity growth in the form of leisure time rather than income. There is a very solid relationship across countries between income per person and emissions of carbon dioxide per person. If workers took some of the benefits of productivity growth in the form of leisure, it would almost certainly lead to lower emissions of carbon dioxide, making this one of the easiest and most effective ways for combating global warming.

Guarantee Workers the Right to Join Unions

Under the law, workers are supposed to have the right to join a union, if they so choose. However, for practical purposes, this right does not exist due to current enforcement practices.

It has become standard practice for employers to fire workers who are engaged in an organizing drive. While it is illegal to fire a worker for trying to organize a union, the sanctions are very small. Therefore, many employers are willing to risk the penalties and simply fire all the workers who they think are involved in an organizing drive. According to a recent study by the Center for Economic and Policy Research, one in five workers involved in an organizing drive can expect to lose his or her job.

A measure that could change this situation is the Employee Free Choice Act (EFCA). EFCA would allow workers to file for recognition of a union once a majority of workers signed cards indicating their support for a union. At present, workers can organize a union through this route (rather than an election), but only at the discretion of the employer. The EFCA would allow workers the option to form a union by signing cards, even if the employer does not approve. This option would make it more difficult for employers to use firings and other illegal methods to prevent workers from organizing.

In addition to making workers better able to bargain for improved wages and working conditions, unions also provide workers with much greater security on the job. Since the government provides very few legal protections, most workers can be fired at any time for almost any reason. Union contracts typically require that employers have a reason for firing a worker. This protection would provide an enormous element of security to tens of millions of workers who do not have unions.

Lower the Value of the Dollar

The United States is currently running a trade deficit of more than $700 billion a year (4.7 percent of GDP). This deficit is unsustainable in the same way that a large budget deficit is unsustainable. The deficit can only be covered by borrowing, which leads to more interest payments in future years, which makes future deficits even larger. The main difference between the trade deficit and the budget deficit is that the United States has been running trade deficits that are far larger than its budget deficits.

The trade deficit is caused by an over-valued dollar. A high dollar effectively subsidizes imports and taxes exports. When the dollar is high, it means we can buy more euros or yuan with each dollar, making goods produced in Europe or China cheaper for people in the United States. As a result, we will purchase more cheap imports, instead of domestically produced goods. Similarly, if the dollar is high, it will cost more euros and yuan to buy a dollar. This will make exports from the United States more expensive to people living in Europe and China. Therefore, they will buy less of our exports.

If the dollar is pushed down through the actions of the Treasury and the Federal Reserve Board, it will bring our trade deficit down to a manageable level. The dollar will eventually fall in any case, as foreigners accumulate more dollars than they want, but it would be better if the government tried to ensure an orderly decline rather than waiting until market pressures finally push the dollar lower (which is already occurring to some extent).

There is also an important class element to the value of the dollar. The workers who most directly face international competition are less-educated workers in the manufacturing sector. By contrast, the most highly educated workers, such as doctors and lawyers, are largely protected from foreign competition. This means that a high dollar has the effect of putting downward pressure on the wages of less-educated workers by placing them at a competitive disadvantage relative to workers in other countries. By contrast, the highly educated workers who are not subject to international competition get to benefit from the high dollar by having access to cheap imports (or cheap trips to Europe).

This reality makes lowering the value of the dollar even more important. In addition to setting the trade deficit on a sustainable path, a lower valued dollar will also benefit less educated workers at the expense of highly educated workers who still enjoy protection from international competition. In fact, a lower dollar is likely to have a far greater impact than any foreseeable change in trade policy during the incoming Administration.

Resources

Bernard Schwartz Center for Economic Policy Analysis:
    http://www.newschool.edu/cepa/
Center for Economic and Policy Research: www.cepr.net
The Conservative Nanny State: www.conservativenannystate.org
Economic Policy Institute: www.epi.org
Levy Economics Institute of Bard: htpp://www.levy.org
Political Economy Research Institute: http://www.peri.umass.edu/

Chapter 12

Toward a Fair and Adequate Tax System

Chuck Collins

POLICY PROPOSALS

■ Eliminate corporate welfare and distortions to the corporate income tax.
  ▪ Create a corporate welfare reform commission to trim $50 billion in unneeded corporate welfare.
  ▪ Eliminate loopholes that make the corporate income tax porous and unfair.
■ Restore progressivity to federal personal taxes.
  ▪ Raise the cap on Social Security withholding.
  ▪ Increase the "No Tax Threshold."
  ▪ Expand the Child Care Credit and make it refundable.
  ▪ Tax capital gains as ordinary income.
  ▪ Institute a progressive estate tax.
■ Use the tax code to reduce pollution and global warming.
  ▪ Institute a progressive consumption tax.
  ▪ Create a "cap-and-dividend" system on carbon emissions.
■ Eliminate global tax havens that enable U.S. taxpayers to avoid their obligations.
  ▪ Institute the "Stop Tax Haven Abuse Act."

* * * * * * * * * * * * * * *

The incoming President and Congress will inherit several enormous challenges in relation to the U.S. system of taxation and revenue. These include the failed tax policies of the last decade and the deep deficits that make it difficult to make urgently needed investments in health care, energy and infrastructure. Challenges include:

111

- **The Gaming of the Tax Code**. Over the last decade, the tax code has been made more porous by powerful corporate interests seeking to extract subsidies and tax benefits. There is now an uneven playing field, as the tax code has different rules for different interest groups in the economy.
- **"Borrow and Squander Policies."** Since 2001, we've had annual federal deficits and a mushrooming national debt. As of June 2008, the cumulative national debt is $9.4 trillion, up from $5.7 trillion at the beginning of President George W. Bush's first term. There is nothing inherently wrong with federal borrowing, especially if funds are spent on investments that bolster future productivity, such as infrastructure and research. Unfortunately, the bulk of the $3.7 trillion in additional debt was squandered on war and tax cuts for the wealthy.
- **Urgent Investment Needs**. "Borrow and squander" policies have come at a cost, as the nation's infrastructure has suffered from lack of investment. According to the American Society of Civil Engineers, we should be spending $320 billion a year over the next five years—double the current outlay—just to bring up to par our existing infrastructure of roads, bridges, ports and rail facilities. At the same time, there are urgent needs for new investment to revamp the nation's energy system, expand health care coverage for the uninsured and other national priorities. While some of these funds could be raised through reduced spending and elimination of corporate tax loopholes, additional revenue will also be needed.

While past Presidents and Congresses have had to deal with deficits and short-sighted policies of their predecessors, the level of challenge facing incoming elected officials is unprecedented.

Progressive Tax Reform in 2009

The incoming President and Congress must grapple with the fiscal realities of our time and the need to make urgent new investments. The conventional wisdom is that Congress cannot reform the tax code, raise new revenue and encourage new behavior changes through the tax code at the same time. Past tax reforms, such as the 1986 effort, were "revenue-neutral"—raising the same amount of funds—with a focus on simplifying the rules. And efforts to reward or alter behavior—such as promote individual savings or adopt new energy systems and behaviors—typically add complexity to the tax system. Unfortunately, the legacy of the Bush Presidency will require urgent intervention in each area.

The key principles required to guide these changes include:

- Fairness: Are responsibilities shared fairly, based on capacity to pay?
- Simplicity: Is the system transparent and understandable?

- Adequacy: Does the system raise adequate revenue to meet our shared responsibilities?

Since the 1986 tax reform, trust in the tax system and the effectiveness of government has eroded. The 112th Congress, therefore, must rebuild the public trust both in how our funds are used as well our system of shared payment. The general public is aware that many corporations and the very wealthy are not paying their fair share, and this undermines faith in the entire system. To defend the commons, we need to address the systemic problems with our current tax and revenue system.

The following program is by no means comprehensive. But it identifies some of the important components of a fair and adequate tax system that is not overly complicated and open to manipulation.

Eliminate Corporate Welfare and Distortions to Corporate Income Taxation: The libertarian Cato Institute identified $92 billion in direct and indirect subsidies to businesses and private sector entities in the FY 2006 federal budget. The amount approaches $200 billion a year when special tax loopholes and preferences are included. For example:

- The current tax code showers $6 billion a year on the oil and gas industry, a mature sector of the economy that needs no government subsidies.[1]

- The federal Advanced Technology Programs have given direct subsidies to high-tech companies. Since 1991, the U.S. government has helped needy companies like IBM ($49 million), General Electric ($32.2 million), and Honeywell International ($29 million).

Much of this corporate welfare is entrenched in obscure provisions of the tax code and would require political leadership to expunge. The incoming President and Congress need to establish a "Corporate Welfare Reform Commission," similar to the military base closure commissions, to review a $50 billion package of recommendations for an up-or-down vote. Other subsidies are given away at the state and local level. See www.goodjobsfirst.org for information on eliminating local corporate welfare.

Restore Progressivity to Federal Personal Taxes

Raise Income Cap on Social Security Withholding: The current withholding tax is 12.4 percent, split between an individual and his/her employer, with self-employed workers paying the entire amount. For most Americans, the percentage of their income paid toward the withholding tax is greater than what they pay for income tax. It is one of the most regressive elements of the federal tax system. A CEO earning $10 million will be finished with his withholding tax on January 5th, while a nurse earning $65,000 will pay until December 31. This is because the amount of income subject to payroll taxes in 2008 is capped at $102,600. Raising the cap on earned income to $250,000 or eliminating it outright would allow Congress to lower the overall rate on 97 percent of employees.

Raise the No-Tax Threshold: Most working families with incomes over $50,000 pay a substantial amount of their income in state and local taxes, such as sales, property and state income taxes. These taxes tend to be quite regressive, shifting tax obligations onto those with the least capacity. The federal tax system could offset this regressivity and increase fairness by increasing the no-tax threshold for income taxes to $40,000 and adjusting that amount for inflation each year.

Expand the Child Tax Credit as a Means to Reducing Poverty: The Child Tax Credit of $1,000 per child should be increased and made refundable for lower income families. Under existing law, some 6 million children in working-poor families are barred from receiving the credit. Congress should permanently boost the amount of the credit to $2,000 per child and expand the opportunity for refundability to working-poor households.

Tax Capital Gains at the Same Rate as Work Wages: Over the last twenty years, wealthy Americans have succeeded in getting Congress to lower taxes on incomes from wealth—both capital gains and dividends. A capital gain is the profit from selling capital assets, such as stocks, real estate, bonds, artwork. The profit from selling your primary home is not subject to capital gains tax if it is under $250,000 for an individual and $500,000 for a couple.

These tax cuts overwhelmingly benefit the very richest Americans. Those with incomes over $500,000 (households in the top one-sixth of 1 percent) got 73.4 percent of the total tax reduction in 2005, an average saving of $81,204 per household in that income group. The super-rich (the one out of 1,000 households with incomes over $10 million) got 28.2 percent of total tax savings. Their average tax break was $1.87 million each. It is time to end the tax preference for capital gains and dividends that benefits the wealthy.

The tax law should be modified to treat all forms of income the same. Income from wages, corporate stock dividends or capital gains should be taxed with the same graduated rates that exist for ordinary earned income. Lower-income earners would pay at lower rates and higher income earners would pay at higher rates. This would greatly simplify the federal tax system and generate an estimated $100 billion a year.

Institute a Sensible Estate Tax: We should preserve and expand the federal estate tax, our nation's only levy on inherited wealth. A century ago, President Theodore Roosevelt advocated for the creation of a federal estate tax to slow the build-up of concentrated wealth in the hands of a few. The federal law was instituted in 1916 and has raised substantial revenue over the years from those most able to pay. Retaining and reforming the estate tax will preserve almost $1 trillion in revenue over the next decade, provide a powerful incentive for charitable giving, and reduce inequalities of wealth.

As Bill Gates Sr. said in a 2003 talk before San Francisco's Commonwealth Club, "The estate tax is a means by which wealthy people pay back the society and the commonwealth that has made their wealth possible." Eliminating or irresponsibly reforming the tax will shift tax obligations onto lower-income taxpayers or future generations.

Under the provisions of the Economic Growth and Tax Relief Reconciliation Act of 2001, the federal estate tax will be repealed in 2010. Unless Congress votes to make the 2001 tax cut permanent, the law "sunsets" and reverts back to its pre-2001 provisions. This would restore the estate tax to a $1 million wealth exemption per spouse and a 55 percent rate. Advocates of abolishing the tax have pressed for "permanent repeal" but have failed to win enough votes. All agree that Congressional action is required to allow for estate tax planning and predictability.

There are over a dozen proposals to reform the estate tax. Most are extremely costly and fail to restore some of the best provisions of the estate tax prior to 2001. The proposal introduced by Senator Jon Kyl would gut the law and lose $406 billion in revenue over the next ten years.

There is an urgent need for legislation that retains a robust estate tax that raises badly needed revenue in the face of deficits and puts a brake on concentrations of wealth. A sensible estate tax would set the amount of wealth exempted at $2 million ($4 million for a couple), index this to inflation, and institute progressively higher rates on estates over $5 million and $10 million.

Use the Tax Code to Reduce Pollution and Global Warming

In addition to eliminating corporate subsidies for fossil fuel industries, there are several other incentives that would help shift our economy toward less pollution.

Institute a Cap-and-Dividend System on Carbon Emissions: Climate activists are proposing a "cap-and-dividend" plan that would require fossil fuel companies to buy federal permits for the right to sell carbon-emitting fuel. Revenue from the permits would be distributed to U.S. citizens as equal dividends that could range from $1,200 to $6,000 a year. Consumers will pay higher prices for transportation, but users of the least efficient modes, such as Hummers and private jets, will pay proportionately more than those who buy fuel-efficient cars, take public transportation, cycle or walk. Since the dividend is equally divided among all citizens, there is a built-in incentive for consumers to choose more efficient modes of transportation.[2]

Institute a Progressive Consumption Tax: While a flat consumption tax—such as a sales tax—is regressive, a progressive consumption tax would charge steeper rates as an individual taxpayer's consumption rises. To calculate the tax, a taxpayer would report his or her income and savings for the year. The difference is consumption. After applying a standard exemption designed to render a basic standard of living tax-free, the taxpayer's remaining consumption would be taxed with a system of graduated brackets, as our current federal income tax system is designed. The higher a person's consumption, the higher marginal tax rate that person pays.

Eliminate Global Tax Havens that Enable U.S. Taxpayers to Avoid their Obligations

Institute the provisions of the "Stop Tax Haven Abuse Act" that has been introduced in both the U.S. Senate and the House. This would close loopholes that enable corporations and individuals to avoid U.S. tax law by shifting earnings and assets overseas.

A Fair Tax System Is Key to Progress

The U.S. public is moving past the reflexive anti-tax attitudes that have been promoted by advocates of limited government. There is a growing recognition that we have to make public investments to remain a healthy society that participates in the global economy. Key to making these investments will be a modern system of revenue that raises revenue from a wide variety of sources and types of taxes. A mix of fair and simple corporate and personal taxes will be the foundation of this system.

Resources

Citizens for Tax Justice: http://www.ctj.org
Good Jobs First: http://www.goodjobsfirst.org
Institute on Taxation and Economic Policy, "Tax Principles: Building Blocks of a Sound Tax System": http://www.itepnet.org/pb9princ.pdf
National Conference of State Legislatures, "Principles of a High Quality State Revenue System": http://www.ncsl.org/programs/

Tax Justice-USA: http://www.taxjustice-usa.org
Taxpayers for Common Sense: http://www.taxpayer.net
Tax Policy Center: http://www.taxpolicycenter.org
Working Group on Extreme Inequality: http://www.extremeinequality.org

References

Barlett, Donald, and James Steele. *The Great American Tax Dodge.* Boston: Little Brown, 2000.
Greenwood, Stephanie, ed. *Ten Excellent Reasons Not to Hate Taxes.* New York: The New Press, 2008.
Johnston, David Cay. *Free Lunch: How the Wealthiest Americans Enrich Themselves at Government Expense (and Stick You With the Bill).* New York: Portfolio, 2008.
———. *Perfectly Legal: The Covert Campaign to Rig Our Tax System to Benefit the Super Rich—and Cheat Everyone Else.* New York: Portfolio, 2003.
Gates, William Sr., and Chuck Collins. *Wealth and Our Commonwealth: Why America Should Tax Accumulated Fortunes.* Boston: Beacon, 2004.
Zepezauer, Mark. *Take the Rich Off Welfare.* Cambridge: South End Press, 2004.

Notes

1. Energy Program, "The Best Energy Bill Corporations Could Buy: Summary of Industry Giveaways in the 2005 Energy Bill," Public Citizen, available at http://www.citizen.org/cmep/energy_enviro_nuclear/electricity/energybill/2005/articles.cfm?ID=13980 (accessed July 16, 2008).

2. Marianne Lavelle, "A Climate Change Proposal with Cash," *U.S. News and World Report,* June 2, 2008.

Chapter 13

Ending Extreme Inequality:
The Need to Concentrate
on Concentrated Wealth

Sam Pizzigati, Sarah Anderson and Chuck Collins

POLICY PROPOSALS

- Stop rewarding unearned income.
  - End the preferential tax treatment of income from capital gains.
  - Limit the wealth the wealthy can pass on to their heirs.
- Leverage the power of the public purse.
  - Require companies that gain government contracts to fully disclose both how much they pay their top executives and the gap between executive and worker pay.
  - Cap the tax deductions corporations can take on executive compensation.
  - Deny government contracts and subsidies to corporations that pay their top executives excessively more than their workers.
- Restore serious progressivity to the federal tax system.
  - Double the top tax rate on income in the nation's highest tax bracket.
  - Subject the assets of the rich, not just the middle class, to taxation.

* * * * * * * * * * * * * *

A Deeply Divided Nation

How extremely unequal has the United States become? In 1982, the year *Forbes* started publishing an annual tally of America's 400 greatest fortunes, the magazine counted only thirteen individuals worth $1 billion or more. Just *entering* the *Forbes* 400 now takes $1.3 billion.

Together, America's 400 richest persons now hold as much wealth as the tens of millions of families that make up the entire bottom half of the U.S. wealth distribution.

But these super-rich don't just hold fantastically more wealth than average Americans. They hold fantastically more wealth than America's super-rich of a half-century ago.

The best measure of this rich then-and-now gap comes from the IRS. In 2005, America's top 400 averaged $174.9 million in after-tax income. Fifty years earlier, in 1955, the nation's top 400 averaged (in 2005 dollars) a mere $5.9 million.

In other words, after taxes, 2005's top 400 collectively had over $67 billion more take-home in their pockets than their counterparts in 1955. Add to this picture the annual income of the rest of America's current top 0.01 percent— that's basically everyone making over $10 million a year—and contemporary American politics suddenly starts to make sense.

Commentators regularly describe our contemporary politics as hopelessly "gridlocked." Lawmakers over recent decades, they note, haven't been able to do anything that significantly improves the well-being of average American families. But this famed gridlock magically evaporates whenever the wealthy and the corporations they run have a problem that needs fixing or an opportunity that needs seizing.

Examples abound. Average Americans, for instance, need lower prices on prescription drugs. They don't get them. Congress, instead, puts in place a prescription drug "benefit" bill that expressly forbids the federal government from bargaining for lower drug prices. Average Americans need lower credit card interest rates. Instead, Congress passes a bankruptcy "reform" that makes starting over—for families trapped in eternal credit card debt—next to impossible. Average Americans need affordable high-speed access to the Internet. Congress, in the name of "competition," deregulates the telecom industry and then winks at the resulting monopolization, a process that leaves working families paying more for Internet access—and getting slower service—than families in Europe and Asia.

Grand concentrations of private wealth don't just tilt the political deck against the interests of average families. Extreme inequality, researchers have documented, unleashes social dynamics that make life increasingly nasty, brutish and short. The more that wealth concentrates at the top, the less honest, trustful and compassionate the society. In deeply unequal societies, the research shows, people commute longer distances, spend more time at work and worry more about crime. Inequality, epidemiologists tell us, even kills: The more unequal a society, the shorter the lifespans of everyone in it—rich, poor, and middle alike.

Americans a century ago didn't need academic research to understand the dangers extreme inequality creates. They feared inequality and fought it—on two fronts. They battled to "level up" the bottom and "level down" the top. And they succeeded. By the 1950s, the United States had given birth to the first mass middle class in world history, and the mansions and estates of the original Gilded Age rich had been transformed into museums, libraries and college campuses.

That mass middle class, once so self-confident and forward-looking, now sits squeezed and frustrated by the economic and political power of a new American super-rich. What would the incoming Administration in the White House have to do to slice this super-rich down to democratic size? We offer a series of practical steps in three broadly related issue areas.

Stop Rewarding Unearned Income

Years ago, Americans carefully distinguished the income from an individual's actual labor ("earned" income) from the income that comes from control over assets ("unearned" income). Average families get the vast bulk of their incomes from work. The wealthy, by contrast, make money off money. The wealth they hold generates interest, dividends and rents. The wealth they sell generates capital gains.

No one in the United States is today making more money from money than the managers of hedge and private equity funds, the mammoth investment vehicles open only to deep-pocket investors. In 2007, the top fifty hedge fund managers each took home more than $210 million.

On these staggering incomes, hedge fund kingpins pay taxes at astoundingly low rates, mainly because current tax law lets them claim the bulk of their income as capital gains. The current tax rate on capital gains income is 15 percent, less than half the 35 percent tax rate that applies to multi-millions of ordinary income.

Closing this tax loophole for hedge fund managers, as many in Congress are urging, would make obvious sense. But merely defining hedge fund rewards as ordinary income would still leave the preferential 15 percent tax rate on normal capital gains income in place. That would be a mistake.

In a world that truly valued labor, people would pay taxes on unearned income at a higher rate than earned income. In the United States today, we have that backwards.

The wealthiest 1 percent of Americans annually receive between two-thirds and three-quarters of the nation's capital gains income. In 2005, the nation's richest 1 percent averaged nearly a quarter-million dollars each in capital gains income. If this top 1 percent had paid taxes on those gains at the current 35 percent top rate on ordinary income, the federal treasury would have collected over

$60 billion more in revenue, almost 50 percent more than the federal government spent that year on public elementary and secondary education.

The rich—to be more precise, the heirs of the rich—currently enjoy one other major source of unearned income: the assets they collect from the estates of wealthy dearly departeds whose genes they happen to share.

The federal government has been taxing these estates, to prevent wealth from concentrating across generations, ever since 1916. But in 2001 President George W. Bush gleefully signed into law a tax cut package that included an estate tax phase-out and repeal.

This repeal actually only applies to one year, 2010. After 2010, unless Congress acts, the estate tax rate on America's largest bequests will revert to pre-George W. levels. Estate tax opponents are lobbying desperately to make sure that doesn't happen. They're currently pushing "reforms" that would essentially gut the tax as an effective check on grand accumulations of private wealth.

Some leading Democrats, in response, want to freeze the top estate tax rate at the 2009 level, 45 percent. But this freeze would leave the estate tax a pale shadow of its former self. In the mid-twentieth century, bequests over $10 million faced a 77 percent top rate.

Instead of freezing the estate tax, we need to make it more progressive—by upping the tax rate on America's largest fortunes to a rate higher than 45 percent, as Representative Jim McDermott from Washington State is now proposing. If we don't move in McDermott's direction, the last three decades of CEO and Wall Street compensation excess will turn into a skyscraper-high foundation for a new American aristocracy. That aristocracy would have the wealth—and power—to frustrate progressive change in the United States for generations to come.

Leverage the Power of the Public Purse

The Securities and Exchange Commission, the federal watchdog agency over the stock market, currently requires publicly traded companies to reveal how much their top five executives are making. But privately held companies—like Blackwater, the global military security giant—face no such mandate, and last fall, Blackwater CEO Erik Prince refused to divulge how much he has personally pocketed from Blackwater's $1 billion in contracts since the war in Iraq started. One bill in the last Congress, the Government Contractor Accountability Act, aimed to force Blackwater and other private companies that receive federal contracts to disclose how lucrative these contracts can be for the executives who snare them.

That's just one small example of how lawmakers could leverage the power of the public purse to discourage the amassing of grand private fortunes. Another: Congress could require corporations to annually document not just pay at the top, but the gap between that pay and the wages that go to a company's lowest-paid employees.

This pay gap disclosure proposal appears in the Income Equity Act, a bill introduced last year by Rep. Barbara Lee from California. This same legislation proposes an even more direct challenge to overpaid corporate executives. The Lee bill would override the U.S. tax code clause that actually encourages excessive CEO pay.

Here's how: Corporations can currently deduct, as a "reasonable" business expense, all those bloated pay packages they hand their top executives. Indeed, the more corporations shell out in executive pay, the less they owe in taxes, so long as they label their executive payouts rewards for "performance."

Average Americans, in effect, are subsidizing the pay of executives who routinely make more in a day than workers take home in a year. Rep. Lee's Income Equity Act, if enacted, would cap the amount of executive compensation corporations can deduct at twenty-five times the pay of a company's lowest-paid workers, about the gap between CEO and worker pay that existed back a half-century ago. Our present-day CEOs can routinely make over 400 times what workers take home.

The Income Equity Act points towards an even more potent antidote to executive excess. Our governments at the local, state and national levels annually pump hundreds of billions of dollars into the private sector. They procure goods and services from private businesses. They hand out subsidies, development grants and tax breaks. They bestow upon private business licenses and leases that let them turn nature, at little or no cost, into lush profit-making opportunities.

This state of economic affairs actually gives the public sector enormous potential leverage over private-sector behavior. On some equality-related fronts, we're already exercising this leverage. We deny government contracts, for instance, to companies whose employment practices discriminate by race or gender. Our tax dollars, we as a society now agree, should simply not go to companies that increase racial or gender inequality. So why should we let our tax dollars go to companies that increase—through top-heavy reward structures—economic inequality?

Federal procurement law does already limit the amount of pay that a company with a government contract can bill the government for executive compensation. But this "cap" only applies to direct federal dollars. A corporation with a share price that soars after landing a federal contract can pay its top execs whatever the company pleases. What could we do to prevent this executive profiteering? One approach: We could deny federal contracts or subsidies to companies that pay their top executives over twenty-five (or fifty) times what their lowest-paid workers receive.

Some lawmakers in Congress have taken a step in this direction by signing on to legislation known as the "Patriot Corporation of America" Act, a bill that would extend tax breaks and federal contracting preferences to companies that reject outsourcing, provide decent health care and pension benefits, and comply with federal worker, consumer and environmental protection regulations. To quality for "Patriot" status, a company would also have to not compensate any executive at a rate that "exceeds 10,000 percent" of—the equivalent of 100 times—the pay of that company's lowest full-time employee.

Imagine if progressive lawmakers began introducing a 100-times—or twenty-five-times—rider into every corporate bailout or subsidy or budget bill that hit the legislative floor. What better way to help Americans understand how our tax dollars are making some among us fabulously rich?

Restore Genuine Progressivity to the Federal Tax System

A half-century ago, in Eisenhower America, income over $400,000—the equivalent of a bit less than $3 million today—faced a top marginal tax rate of 91 percent.

Wealthy taxpayers, of course, don't pay taxes at the top marginal rate, either then or now. The wealthy actually pay, after exploiting loopholes, far less of their total incomes in taxes than marginal tax rate schedules would suggest. But back in the 1950s, even with loopholes, America's wealthiest paid far more of their total incomes in federal income tax than they do today.

How much more? In 2004, taxpayers who took home over $5 million paid an average 21.9 percent of their incomes in federal tax. Back in 1954, the federal tax bite—on taxpayers who made comparable incomes, after adjusting for inflation—averaged 54.5 percent.

The Institute on Taxation and Economic Policy has run the numbers on how much new revenue would be raised by a significant tax hike on America's 50,000 highest incomes, a group that makes up less than one-tenth of 1 percent of the nation's taxpayers. If the top marginal federal income tax rate were raised to 50 percent on all income between $5 million and $10 million and 70 percent on all annual income above $10 million, federal revenues in 2008 would increase by a stunning $105 billion—and the nation's rich would still be paying less in taxes than they did under Ike.

Higher tax rates on income in the top tax brackets would help restore progressivity to our tax system. So would overhauling how we tax property.

Homeowners in America currently pay a levy called the "property tax." For typical American families, this property tax amounts to a tax on wealth, since typical families have little net worth outside the value of their residences. But that's not the case for the super-wealthy, even those with multiple homes. The bulk of the wealth of the super-wealthy sits in stocks and bonds and other financial investments. The upshot of this difference? Average Americans pay a tax on their wealth. Rich Americans don't.

About a dozen European nations have a broader approach to taxing wealth. They levy a small annual tax on all wealth holdings, and New York University economist Edward Wolff has proposed a similar initiative for the United States. A wealth tax that exempted the first $250,000 of household wealth, then imposed a series of tax rates that rose by wealth level and topped off at 0.8 percent on wealth over $5 million would raise, Wolff calculated a few years ago, about $60 billion a year—with 80 percent of families paying no tax at all and 95 percent paying less than $1,000.

The Equality Imperative

This past May, a *Financial Times*/Harris poll revealed that over three-quarters of Americans—78 percent—feel that the gap between rich and poor in the United States has grown "too wide." But Americans, the same poll found, also don't see much hope for narrowing that gap. Fifteen percent expect that gap to stay even over the next five years. Seventy-four percent expect the gap to widen.

Our incoming President will clearly face enormous resistance from the rich and powerful, should he make a serious move to reverse our national slide into extreme inequality. The good news? Our incoming President won't have to hope for the support of the American people. He will have it.

Resources

AFL-CIO: http://www.aflcio.org
Behind the Buyouts: Inside the World of Private Equity: http://www.behindthebuyouts.org/
Center on Budget and Policy Priorities: www.cbpp.org
Center for Corporate Policy: http://www.corporatepolicy.org
Citizens for Tax Justice: http://www.ctj.org
Class Action: http://www.classism.org/
Executive Pay Watch: http://www.aflcio.org/corporatewatch/paywatch/
Inequality.org: www.inequality.org
Poverty & Race Research Action Council: http://www.prrac.org
Responsible Wealth: http://www.responsiblewealth.org/commonwealth
Tax Policy Center: http://www.taxpolicycenter.org
Too Much: http://www.toomuchonline.org
United for a Fair Economy: http://www.faireconomy.org
War on Greed: http://warongreed.org/
Working Group on Extreme Inequality: http://www.extremeinequality.org

References

Bernstein, Jared. *Crunch: Why Do I Feel So Squeezed?* San Francisco: Berrett-Koehler, 2008.

Collins, Chuck, and Felice Yeskel. *Economic Apartheid in America: A Primer on Economic Inequality and Insecurity.* New York: New Press, 2005.

Collins, Chuck et al., eds. *The Wealth Inequality Reader.* Boston: Dollars and Sense, 2008.

Frank, Robert. *Richistan: A Journey Through the American Wealth Boom and the Lies of the New Rich.* New York: Crown, 2007.

Ehrenreich, Barbara. *This Land is Their Land: Reports from a Divided Nation.* New York: Henry Holt & Company, 2008.

Frank, Robert H. *Falling Behind: How Rising Inequality Harms the Middle Class.* Berkeley: University of California Press, 2006.

Greenhouse, Stephen. *The Big Squeeze: Tough Times for the American Worker.* New York: Random House, 2008.

Kuttner, Bob. *The Squandering of America: How the Failure of Our Politics Undermines Our Prosperity.* New York: Random House, 2007.

Lardner, James, ed. *Inequality Matters: The Growing Economic Divide in America and its Poisonous Consequences.* New York: New Press, 2006.

Lui, Meizhu, et al. *The Color of Wealth: The Story Behind the U.S. Racial Wealth Divide.* New York: New Press, 2006.

Pizzigati, Sam. *Greed and Good: Understanding and Overcoming the Inequality that Limits Our Lives.* New York: Apex Press, 2004.

Chapter 14

Re-establishing a
Workers' Rights Agenda

Kate Bronfenbrenner and Dorian Warren

POLICY PROPOSALS

■ Restore the right to organize, bargain collectively, and strike for all workers.
■ Expand the definition of *employee* under labor law to cover all workers.
■ Establish and enforce a worker- and community-centered global trade and investment policy.
■ Return the Department of Labor to one whose mission is to represent and protect the interests of working people in the United States.
■ Increase funding, regulatory authority, and enforcement capacity to all workers' rights agencies.
■ Provide incentives and sanctions for coordinated efforts at enforcing all labor and employment laws, particularly those protecting the most vulnerable workers, such as immigrants, from willful, serious and/or repeat violations.

* * * * * * * * * * * * * *

Workers in the United States live and work in the richest country in the world. Yet, while the nation's Gross Domestic Product leapt from $4,739.5 billion in 1987 to $13,841.3 billion in 2007,[1] for the last two decades workers have witnessed the steady erosion of their economic security and workplace rights. In every aspect of basic labor and employment law, employer violations are increasing while agency enforcement is on the decline. Unless Congress moves quickly to make significant, substantive changes in workers' rights policies, employers will be increasingly emboldened to put workers lives and livelihoods at risk.

127

Restoring the Right to Organize, Bargain and Strike

From the moment the 1935 National Labor Relations Act (NLRA—The Wagner Act) was ruled constitutional two years after its passage,[2] the right to organize, the right to collective bargaining and the right to strike have each been under attack and severely curtailed by capital and the political Right. Employers fought for and won several significant victories from the 1940s to the present, from legislative reforms encoding their frontal attack on workers' rights which constrained the power of unions (1947 Taft-Hartley and 1959 Landrum-Griffin bills), to successful attempts to block progressive labor law reforms. Over the past three decades, employers have become increasingly aggressive at violating workers' rights to organize under a much less protective labor law regime which, contrary to the intent of the NLRA, provides incentives for employers to break the law. It is no surprise that union density is at its lowest rate while income and wealth inequality are at their highest rates since the cusp of the Great Depression.[3] Extreme inequality is the handmaiden to the lack of workers' rights.

Dozens of research studies confirm what workers and union organizers have known for decades: American employers continue to be exceptionally hostile to workers' rights and unions. This hostility is revealed in the arsenal of legal and illegal anti-union tactics management routinely uses whenever workers try to organize, including but not limited to interrogation, threats, discharges, surveillance, bribes, promises of improvements, captive audience meetings and supervisor one-on-ones with workers.[4] In one in four campaigns workers are fired for union activity, employers use plant closing threats in more than half, and 92 percent of employers require employees to attend captive audience meetings during worker hours, and 78 percent had their supervisors regularly talk to workers one-on-one about the union campaign, with a focus on threats of plant closings, strikes, wage and benefit cuts, and job loss. In fact, the interrogation and harassment in these meetings is so effective that there is no longer any such thing as a "secret ballot" in the National Labor Relations Board (NLRB) election process. Workers may mark their ballots in secret, but by the time of the election both the union and the employer can be very certain about which way each worker is planning to vote. Although many of these actions, such as discharges, threats, bribes and interrogation are illegal, the penalties are minimal. There are no punitive damages, criminal charges and no large fines. And even when workers prevail over employer opposition to win union recognition, they still face enormous obstacles to securing a first contract.

Compounding the ineffectiveness of the gutted New Deal labor relations regime is the development of a different domain of workplace regulations rooted in Title VI of the 1964 Civil Rights Act targeting race- and sex-based discrimination.[5] Even though the 1964 Civil Rights Act's comparable federal agency—the Equal Employment Opportunity Commission (EEOC)—has weak enforcement power similar to the National Labor Relations Board, Title VI does provide better mechanisms and incentives for private remedies and sanctions through the courts, acting as a stronger curb against flagrant employer violations. Indeed, the financial incentives of plaintiffs' fees, punitive and compensatory damages, and back pay combined with stronger court enforcement should be tools used across the multiple workers' rights domains.[6]

We argue here for reclaiming the true intent of the Wagner Act and the entire New Deal workers' rights regime, while also modifying it to govern workers in our current and radically changed political and economic era. Policy reforms would include repealing several of the provisions of the Taft-Hartley and Landrum-Griffin Acts; expanding coverage of categories of workers excluded from the original NLRA (as well as the Social Security Act and Fair Labor Standards Act) because of racism; increasing penalties and sanctions on employers who violate the law; providing adequate funding for monitoring and enforcement capacity of all labor-related federal agencies; and expanding some of the strongest provisions of Title VI. Fundamental to restoring workers' rights in a global economy is a focus on re-shifting the unequal balance of power between workers and capital.

The following specific policy recommendations would tilt the playing field back to workers and undermine employers' continuing erosions of workers' rights:

The first is putting into law the Employee Free Choice Act (EFCA), which has already passed in the House.[7] Under EFCA, the NLRB would be required to automatically certify the union as their representative if the majority of employees in the unit signed authorization cards designating the union as their bargaining representative. It would also establish a process for thirty days of mediation and then binding arbitration if the parties cannot reach a first contract within ninety days of bargaining.

EFCA would also establish stronger penalties for labor law violations during organizing and first campaigns. These include requiring the NLRB to seek federal court injunctions for discharges, discrimination, threats and other interference with workers rights during organizing and first-contract campaigns. It also triples back-pay awards and provides for civil fines of up to $20,000 per violation for willful or repeat violations.

In addition to EFCA, there are several other key policy changes needed to restore workers' rights to organize, bargain and strike. These include: reversing the *Lechmere, Inc. v. NLRB* decision to allow union organizers access to company premises; allowing union organizers equal time and access to communicate with workers; providing injunctive relief for all employer unfair labor practices, not just in organizing and first-contract campaigns; restoring the right to strike though the banning of employer use of permanent replacements during strikes and temporary replacements during lockouts; repealing the ban on most forms of secondary activity; and strengthening union rights to engage in concerted activity inside and outside the workplace. Finally, policy changes must ensure that all rights attained for workers under the NLRA are also expanded to cover workers under the Railway Labor Act.

Expand Coverage of Labor Laws

Every worker in the public and private sector in the U.S. should have the protection of labor and employment laws. Historically, domestic workers and agricultural workers were excluded from the Wagner Act because they were disproportionately Southern African Americans.[8] More recently, several key groups of workers have been excluded under public- and private-sector labor law, thanks to the joint efforts of employers and state and federal labor boards; these exclusions affect graduate student employees, welfare-to-work and workfare recipients, supervisors and low-level managers, and workers in Homeland Security. One of the most serious issues is the increasing tendency of employers to misclassify employees as independent contractors, thereby exempting them from minimum wage, overtime, workers compensation, discrimination, and collective bargaining requirements under both federal and state legislation.[9] These workers not only lose their right to organize, but also are denied access to other employment benefits and workplace protections.

Yet many of these same employees—supervisors, managers and graduate students—are organizing and bargaining in the public sector with no apparent problems. In California, there is a functioning agricultural labor law. Therefore the NLRA, Social Security Act and Fair Labor Standards Act should all be amended to have the definition of employee be the most expansive definition possible, adding in agricultural, domestic, supervisory and low-level managers, graduate students, workfare employees, all public employees. In the case of independent contractors and others where employers want to question their status, the labor boards should assume employee status and put the burden on employers to prove otherwise. Section 2 (11) of the NLRA should be amended to define supervisors as those with the authority to both direct and discipline others, and the Act should be amended to provide full coverage to immigrant workers by reversing the Supreme Court's *Hoffman Plastics* decision.[10] Finally, labor law coverage should be expanded to cover all workers at the local, state and federal levels, including workfare and welfare-to-work recipients.

Worker Rights and Global Trade and Investment Policy

As flawed and open to employer abuse as our organizing and representation process may be, the single greatest barrier to exercising any and all employment rights—whether organizing, collective bargaining or simply asking for a raise—continues to be the economic insecurity created by living and working in a rapidly changing global economy. Employers, in concert with government policy-makers, have quickly learned to use that insecurity to their advantage, using trade policy and the inherent threat of job loss to crush organizing campaigns, avoid first contracts, break strikes, hold down wage demands, gain major concessions, and keep workers from filing health and safety and other employment law claims.[11]

It is no coincidence that capital mobility and threats of capital mobility increased during the same period that the United States became the leading force promoting the neo-liberal agenda. Successive Administrations have utilized the World Trade Organization (WTO), International Monetary Fund (IMF) and World Bank through a combination of regional free trade agreements, deregulation, privatization, debt agreements and global outsourcing. The underlying agenda, while not made public, has been clear and straightforward: promote the interests of Northern investors, intellectual property rights and the world's largest multinationals, at the expense of workers, unions, communities, the environment, and national sovereignty.

Initially, these agreements were sold to the U.S. public as a means for creating new high-paying export-related jobs. But the reality was something quite different. Even Robert Cassidy, the principal negotiator of China's 2001 entry into the WTO, agrees that the primary beneficiaries of these agreements have been the corporations that have shifted production and the financial institutions that have financed those investments, trade flows and deficits. As Cassidy explained: "It is doubtful that the U.S. economy or its workers are better off" since China joined the WTO. "Wages have been stagnant and real disposable income for three-quarters of U.S. households has been stable or declining. Only the top quartile of families has seen significant increases in real disposable income."[12]

But if the promise of "free trade" has failed in the United States, it has been even worse in countries in the Southern Hemisphere which partnered with the United States in these trade agreements. By almost every economic measure, conditions have worsened: Income gaps are wider, debt has increased, economic growth has slowed, the inequality index is up and overall economic insecurity has increased.[13] Because it is the United States that has the greatest influence over bodies such as the WTO, IMF and World Bank, and has been promoting NAFTA-style pacts, it is up to the incoming Administration to develop new criteria by which every new trade policy must be measured before going forward.

First, all current and future trade and investment agreements must include enforceable labor and environmental rights, while not undermining strong national health and safety, and other core standards. They should exclude any mandatory privatization or deregulation requirements, protections for patents that restrict access to medications, or any special rights for foreign investors.

Second, the fast-track trade negotiation process needs to be put back in the hands of elected Congressional representatives by requiring that Congress establish a review process to ensure that all agreements (including those negotiated under Fast Track that have not yet been finalized) meet the fair trade criteria and are voted on by Congress before they are signed.

Third, the Trade Adjustment Assistance Act (TAA) and other worker training programs must be fully funded and expanded to ensure more adequate income, education, training and health care for all workers whose jobs are directly or indirectly lost due to shifts in trade and investment policy, including white collar, service and public sector workers, as well as production workers. The WARN Act should be amended to apply to all workers and to provide at least six months notice before layoff.

Fourth, U.S. participation within the WTO, IMF and World Bank should be contingent on those bodies making their decisions based on what is in the interest of the broader global economic community, rather than just investor and corporate interests, and doing so with the utmost democracy, transparency and accountability. This should include advocating for sustainable, equitable and democratic development that includes generous aid, reform of international financial institutions, and 100 percent debt relief for the poorest indebted countries that are working to actively improve and respect human rights conditions in their country.

Fifth, in order to better understand the extent of the impact of current trade policy on workers, wages, unions and communities, we must have better data. Therefore, the government must develop a monitoring and tracking system that requires companies to report production shifts out of the country and to adequately label the source of all goods coming into the country. Moreover, as new trade legislation by Sen. Sherrod Brown (D-Ohio) proposes, some effort must be made to account for specific trade agreements' impact on trade deficits and job loss in trading sectors.[14]

Make the Department of Labor
a Department for Workers Again

When a weak and poorly enforced system of organizing and collective bargaining rights is combined with an investor-driven trade and investment policy, the race to the bottom becomes most acute in day-to-day conditions in the workplace, particularly in the largest corporations. Under our current law and policy, the Department of Labor (DOL), through the Occupational Safety and Health Administration (OSHA), Mine Safety and Health Administration (MSHA), and the Wage and Hour Division (WHD), have neither the resources nor the enforcement power to protect U.S. workers from death, injury or illness in the workplace or from being forced to work unreasonable hours, denied pay or denied basic employment rights. These agencies are grossly underfunded and understaffed. Just in the last six years, enforcement staffing for OSHA has declined by 6.26 percent to 1,542, while in WHD it has dropped by 9.73 percent, down to

1,336 staff, each serving more than 100 million workers in more than 7 million establishments.[15] OSHA capacity is so low that that state and federal inspectors combined can inspect workplaces only once in every ninety-two years. Despite a series of deadly mine disasters, MSHA has followed a similar pattern.[16]

The costs to workers are staggering. On the health and safety front, on average, each day, sixteen workers die from workplace injuries, and tens of thousands more are injured, while as many as 130 daily are estimated to lose their lives from workplace-related disease.[17] OSHA penalties for employers involve little more than a slap on the wrist. Serious violations involving deaths are subject to maximum penalties of $7,000, while willful and repeated violations carry a maximum penalty of $70,000, and willfully and knowingly ordering employees to do something that kills them or puts them at risk of death or serious injury is, at most, a Class B misdemeanor, with a six-month maximum jail sentence.

There is a similar crisis in enforcing work standards. As noted above, misclassification of employees as independent contractors has been one of the most effective tools used by employers to exempt workers from all labor and employment legislation, including wage-and-hour laws. In addition to misclassification, the failure to follow basic wage-and-hour laws has become an escalating problem, particularly among low-wage immigrant workers such as day laborers.[18] But the problem is not just among our most marginalized workers. Some the nation's largest and most profitable companies[19] and industries are out of compliance with wage-and-hour laws, most notably 60 percent of nursing homes, a majority of restaurants in New York City, 100 percent of the poultry processing industry, and 50 percent of garment manufacturing.[20]

The solution for both health and safety and wage-and-hour laws is a combination of increased funding and strengthening enforcement powers that bring the DOL back to its mission of representing the rights and interests of U.S. workers.

OSHA Policy Solutions

The first priority is passing the Protecting America's Workers Act (PAWA) which includes several key components. First, expand OSHA coverage to include public sector and transportation workers. Second, increase the minimum penalty to $50,000 for a death caused by a willful safety violation and the maximum criminal penalty for killing or seriously injuring a worker to ten years in prison. Third, provide whistle-blower protection to all workers who speak up about unsafe conditions on the job bringing the law into line with other federal whistle-blower statutes. Finally, require OSHA to investigate every case where a worker is killed or seriously injured and give family members better access to OSHA fatality investigations.

However, PAWA simply sets the floor. In addition to changes recommended by the Act, all well documented hazards should be re-examined, starting with the Ergonomics Program Standard. A broader, corporate-wide investigation, enforcement and penalty process should be established in partnership with the Justice Department for large corporations that are multiple offenders of OSHA and MSHA. Lastly, large corporations should be subject to criminal felony charges under worker endangerment standards when they knowingly commit violations that put workers at risk of serious injury, death or illness. Even greater penalties should be assessed if the employer knows he is acting in violation of the law.

Policies to Enforce Labor Standards

For the Department of Labor to be effective in enforcing fair labor standards, it will need to not only have adequate funding and staffing but also become an affirmative agency that takes the investigation to the sectors and industries where the problems are concentrated and takes the burden of solving the problem off the workers who have been suffering the consequences. This can be best accomplished if the DOL creates a presumption of employee status, putting a burden on the employer to prove the worker is not an employee. Also, there needs to be a change in the legislation to allow unions and community organizations to file claims on behalf of workers, as well as allow an option to file anonymous claims to protect workers from retribution or deportation and establish strong whistle-blower protections to ensure there will be no retaliation. This includes creating and strengthening the firewall between DOL and Immigration and Customs Enforcement.

The DOL and the WHD should target those companies and industries where there has been an egregious pattern of repeat violations. In the case of large corporations, claims need to move to a corporate-based level, so that employers with multi-site violations can be held to a higher penalty standard. Equally important, these agencies need to develop a more comprehensive data collection and compliance monitoring strategy with increased staff for monitoring and surprise inspections, and which tracks data on all workers, including those classified as independent contractors.

Clearly in order to reach a higher enforcement standard for all DOL activities, there needs to be more intra- and inter-agency cooperation in data collection and enforcement, and more partnering with unions and community organizations for assistance in monitoring compliance, public education and encouraging workers to come forward, particularly in sectors where violations are most concentrated. But that will not be enough. The evidence from the NLRA, OSHA, FLSA, EEOC and trade side-agreements combined suggests that employers do not take DOL sanctions seriously. Employers should be subject to criminal and civil penalties and sanctions for violating workers rights under every labor and employment law. This should include civil and criminal contempt sanctions for violations of OSHA, FSLA and Sections 8(a)3 and 8(a)5 of the NLRA. And it should make employers subject to attorney's fees and court costs in addition to economic, compensatory, and punitive damages. Finally, the DOL needs to integrate the entire workers' rights regime to make all workplace violations under all major labor and employment laws subject to punitive and compensatory damages. Only then will the Department of Labor begins working to represent the interests of the nation's most vulnerable workers rather than the nations' most egregious labor and employment law violators.

Resources

America Rights at Work: http://www.americanrightsatwork.org/
Global Trade Watch: http://www.citizen.org/trade/

References

Bronfenbrenner, Kate. *Uneasy Terrain: The Impact of Capital Mobility on Workers, Wages, and Union Organizing.* Report submitted to the U.S. Trade Deficit Review Commission, September 6, 2000. http://digitalcommons.ilr.cornell.edu/reports/3/ (accessed July 16 2008); and *Part II, First contract supplement,* March 2001 http://digitalcommons.ilr.cornell.edu/reports/1/ (accessed July 16, 2008).

Frumin, Eric. Testimony. "Serious OSHA Violations: Strategies for Breaking Dangerous Patterns Tuesday." Senate Hearing, April 1, 2008. http://help. senate.gov/Hearings/2008_04_01/2008_04_01.html (accessed July 19, 2008).

Human Rights Watch. *Unfair Advantage: Workers' Freedom of Association in the United States under International Human Rights Standards.* New York: Human Rights Watch 2000. http://www.hrw.org/reports/2000/uslabor/ (accessed July 16, 2008).

Lafer, Gordon "Neither Free Nor Fair: The Subversion of Democracy under National Labor Relations Board Elections," America Rights at Work Report (2007). pp 1-75, http://www.americanrightsatwork.org/resources/neither_free_exec_su.cfm (accessed July 16, 2008).

National Employment Law Project. *Holding the Wage Floor: Enforcement of Wage and Hour Standards for Low-Wage Workers in an Era of Government Inaction and Employer Unaccountability.* Immigrant & Nonstandard Worker Project Policy Update. Advocating for the Working Poor and the Unemployed, October 2006. http://www.immigrant-nonstandard.org/.

Seminario, Peg, and David Uhlmann. "When a Worker is Killed: Do OSHA Penalties Enhance Workplace Safety?" Senate Hearing, April 29, 2008. http://help.senate.gov/Hearings/2008_04_29/2008_04_29.html (accessed July 19, 2008).

Notes

1. Bureau of Economic Analysis, "National Income and Product Accounts Table 1.1.5 Gross Domestic Product," http://www.bea.gov/national/nipaweb/ (accessed July 9, 2008).

2. *NLRB v. Jones & Laughlin Steel Corp,* 301 U.S. 1 (1937).

3. Bradford Plummer, "A Democracy—For The Wealthy The New Republic: Swelling Gap In Wealth Is Worrisome For Equality," *The New Republic,* January, 31, 2007.

4. For the catalogue of anti-union employer campaign tactics and their effects on union organizing and first-contract campaigns, see Kate Bronfenbrenner, "Employer behavior in certification elections and first-contract campaigns: Implications for labor law reform," in *Restoring the Promise of American Labor Law,* S. Friedman, R. Hurd, R. Oswald, and R. Seeber, eds. (pp. 75-89), (Ithaca N.Y.: ILR Press, 2001. http:// digital-commons.ilr.cornell.edu/articles/18; Kate Bronfenbrenner, *Uneasy Terrain: The Impact of Capital Mobility on Workers, Wages, and Union Organizing,* Commissioned Research Paper and Supplement to The US Trade Deficit: Causes, Consequences, and Recommendations for Action (Washington, D.C.: US Trade Deficit Review Commission, September, 2000); http://digitalcommons.ilr.cornell.edu/reports/3/ (accessed July 20, 2008); and *Part II: First Contract Supplement,* March 2001, http://digitalcommons.ilr.cornell.edu/reports/1/ (accessed July 20, 2008).

5. Nelson Lichtenstein, *State of the Union: A Century of American Labor (Politics and Society in Twentieth Century America)* (Princeton: Princeton University Press, 2002).

6. This includes violations of OHSA, FLSA and other violations of individual and collective workers' rights.

7. H.R. 800, "Employee Free Choice Act of 2007," TheMiddleClass.org, http://the middleclass.org/bill/employee-free-choice-act-2007 (accessed July 19, 2008).

8. See Ira Katznelson, *When Affirmative Action Was White: An Untold History of Racial Inequality in Twentieth-Century America* (New York: W.W. Norton & Company, 2005); Paul Frymer, *Black and Blue: African Americans, the Labor Movement, and the Decline of the Democratic Party* (Princeton, NJ: Princeton University Press, 2008).

9. "Immigrant & Nonstandard Worker Project Policy Update: Advocating for the Working Poor and the Unemployed," National Employment Law Project, 2005, www.nelp.org (accessed July 18, 2008).

10. *Hoffman Plastic Compounds, Inc. v. NLRB,* 535 U.S. 137 (2002).

11. See Bronfenbrenner *Uneasy Terrain*; Kate Bronfenbrenner and Stephanie Luce, *The Changing Nature of Corporate Global Restructuring: The Impact of Production Shifts on Jobs in the US, China, and Around the Globe* (Washington, DC: US-China Economic and Security Review Commission, October 2005), http://digitalcommons.ilr.cornell.edu/cbpubs/16 (accessed July 18, 2008).

12. Robert Cassidy, "The Failed Expectations of US Trade Policy," *Foreign Policy in Focus,* June 4, 2008, http://www.fpif.org/fpiftxt/5274 (accessed July 18, 2008).

13. Josh L. Bivens, "Reclaiming an Economic Future Through Democracy: A New Direction for Economic Policy in the Americas," EPI Issue Brief #217, October, 25, 2005, http://www.epi.org/content.cfm/ib217 (accessed July 18, 2008). However, as Mark Weisbrot from the Center for Economic Policy Research argues, there is a new trend in Latin America among countries that have not yet signed trade agreements with the United States, such as Bolivia, Argentina, Brazil and Venezuela, which have made themselves less vulnerable to the IMF, World Bank's, and U.S. influence in part because of combina-

tion of "the availability of alternative sources of finance, most importantly from the reserves of the Venezuelan government . . . [and] the increasing assertion of national control over natural resources." Mark Weisbrot, "The End of an Era," *International Journal of Health Services,* Vol. 27, No. 3 (2006), p. 1.

14. Public Citizen, "June 4 - Public Citizen Supports Landmark Trade Expansion Legislation, June 4, 2007," http://www.citizen.org/hot_issues/issue.cfm?ID=1922 (accessed July 18, 2008).

15. Fiscal Year 2007 Congressional Budget Justification OSHA, page 25. Employment Standards Administration (Wage and Hour Division), page 14. Fiscal Year 2008 Congressional Budget Justification—OSHA, p. 21. Employment Standards Administration (Wage and Hour Division), page 19.

16. Steven Greenhouse, "Report Cites Mine-Safety Agency Failures," *New York Times,* November 18, 2007.

17. Bureau of Labor Statistics (BLS). Census of Fatal Occupational Injuries (CFOI) 2006, http://www.bls.gov/iif/oshcfoi1.htm (accessed July 18, 2008). Centers for Disease Control and Prevention (CDC). National Occupational Research Agenda, *Morbidity and Mortality Weekly Report,* Vol. 45 (1990) 445-446, http://www.healthypeople.gov/ (accessed July 18, 2008).

18. Abel Valenzuela Jr. and Nik Theodore et al., "On the Corner: Day Labor in the United States," http://www.sscnet.ucla.edu/issr/csup/index.php (accessed July 18, 2008).

19. Alison Frankel, "Wal-Mart loses $6.5 Million Wage-and-Hour Class Action," *The American Lawyer,* July, 2, 2008. p. 1. Human Rights Watch. "Discounting Rights: Wal-Mart's Violation of US Workers, Right to Freedom of Association" (New York: Human Rights Watch, May 2001), http://hrw.org/reports/2007/us0507/ (accessed July 18, 2008).

20. Catherine Ruckelshaus, "Adequacy of Labor Law Enforcement in New Orleans," Testimony. United States Congress House of Representatives Committee on Oversight and Government Reform, June 26, 2007, http://domesticpolicy.oversight. house.gov/ story.asp?ID=1377 (accessed July 19, 2008).

Chapter 15

Will the Incoming Administration Cut the Racial Trip Wire?*

Bill Fletcher, Jr.

POLICY PROPOSALS

■ Create a new race initiative.
■ Institute reparations and a "Marshall Plan" for the cities.
■ De-monopolize farms; strengthen the family farmer; defend Black, Native American and Chicano land rights.
■ Create a just immigration policy/end attacks on immigrants.
■ Implement a democratic foreign policy.
■ Re-do our post-Katrina efforts.
■ Initiate a United Nations-supervised plebiscite on the future of Puerto Rico.

* * * * * * * * * * * * * *

The trip wire of U.S. political and social movement activity remains race. No matter how much one may wish to avoid it, step around it or jump over it, it snags the feet of the movement. Only by cutting it can we actually address it, but the wire is so sharp, so barbed and so rusty that we fear it will snap back and severely lacerate us.

Given all of this, we then find the irony of the 2008 Presidential race. An African-American candidate emerged who, despite a background in community organizing, chose to advance a non-racial, or, better put, *post-racial* campaign in the interest of building a broad, winning coalition. But, ironically, while he succeeded in building such a coalition, he was compelled by events to articulate the most eloquent, though admittedly mainstream, analysis of race in the United States ever delivered to millions of Americans.

*I thank IPS intern Daniel Scheer for his research help in preparing this chapter.

Attempts to ignore race in the United States, or to collapse it into economics, almost always fail because such efforts fail to factor in the nation's racial construction, going back to the colonial era. Race is not an add-on to a list of various ills, nor is it an appendix to an otherwise complete and total system. Race, as a socio-political construction, is as integral to the U.S. system as are lungs in a human. But, as opposed to lungs, which help one live, race and racism function more as a tumor which, while organic and part of the system, nevertheless ultimately strain to kill the body it inhabits.

Efforts aimed at defeating racial injustice are regularly symbolic, or in many cases, anemic. Part of this results from an inaccurate analysis of the problem itself. Part of it results from the pushback from right-wing social movements. And, it must be admitted, part of this results from a lack of political will within many Administrations. For these reasons, any approach toward racial justice reforms needs to begin, at a minimum, with a debate focusing on developing a common point of reference. In that context, the specific reform efforts not only take shape, but can be better understood.

The Problem

Race does not exist as a genetic category except and insofar as one is referring to the human race. It does exist, however, as a *socio-political category*, a category developed first with the English invasion of Ireland and later with the European invasion of the Western Hemisphere. With regard to the latter, the construction of race as a means of classifying segments of the population largely by color became an important instrument in the operation of social control over the entire working population. Race became an arbitrary category in the entire Western Hemisphere, but certainly within the British North American colonies (and later the United States). The definition of someone being Black, for instance, was based on their possessing even a tiny portion of "African blood," irrespective of the rest of their heritage.

What the system of racial slavery and later racist oppression accomplished was the creation of relevant and irrelevant populations, and correspondingly, relevant and irrelevant experiences. Africans or Blacks, for instance, not only under slavery had no rights a white person was bound to expect, but they had no experiences and history that white people were—compelled to acknowledge. They had no pain that white people were compelled to address. And they had no work that white people felt compelled to compensate.

Despite continuous efforts to put the slavery experience behind us—on the part of white America—the impact of racial slavery cannot be overstated. Not only did it represent the removal of peoples from their respective histories in Africa and the creation of a new people in North America, but it was aimed at destroying their humanity. In so doing, it destroyed the humanity of so-called whites because it placed them in a space where they had to entirely block out any senses or any feeling. It would be the equivalent of numbing one's sense of touch or smell or sight.

In general, race and racist oppression permitted life to operate on different planes—that for those in the category called white, and that for those in the categories eventually known as "other." With regard to slavery, the pain and suffering of the African slave could, for so long, be ignored or in some cases justified because the Africans were not seen as quite or entirely human. In that sense, the millions who died in slavery or in the slave trade could not, for many whites, amount to a holocaust because a holocaust—as a term—must be reserved for those who are considered white.

Race, however, was not about a Black/white dichotomy. The racial construction of the United States meant layers and it meant nuance. From the standpoint of social control, priority went towards establishing a "white bloc" to which rights and privileges were entitled. Native Americans/First Nations were viewed as an exotic, and simultaneously redundant, population that stood in the way of progress. Contrary to the Latin-American experience, Europeans in North America never attempted to mix with Native Americans on any scale, nor was there any attempt at creating a North American mestizo population. Native Americans were to be removed and/or exterminated.

Race played itself out in a very complicated fashion with the various Latino populations that inhabited what would become the United States or those who were absorbed into the United States. Mexicans north of the Rio Grande River were annexed as a result of the U.S. War with Mexico (1846–1848). With the Treaty of Guadalupe Hidalgo, the Mexicans who were seized at this time were classified as "white." The irony, however, is that they gained neither the rights and privileges of the white bloc, but instead the status of the post-Civil War African American, living in conditions that were the equivalent of *de facto* Jim Crow segregation. They were subject to the theft of their lands, much as were the Native Americans, and the failure to recognize the legitimacy of their language.

The experiences of other Latinos, most especially the Puerto Ricans, were quite distinct. Puerto Rico, which had a significant African influence, was seized in the Spanish-American War and never released from a colonial status (despite the nuance of the term "commonwealth" used to describe its political existence). During the course of the twentieth century, Puerto Ricans increasingly migrated North as a result of the economic destruction of their island into conditions greatly resembling (and often linked to) African Americans.

Asian nationalities came to the United States in the nineteenth century as migrants seeking freedom from feudal oppression. They were encouraged to come to the United States as cheap labor by U.S. capitalists. They were among the first migrants who not only faced intense discrimination, but a consistent racial demonization and bombardment. They were blamed for illnesses and joblessness among whites, and were ultimately restricted in their ability to migrate altogether. While certain exceptions were made for Filipinos after the United

States seized the Philippines in the Spanish-American War, their conditions as well started to mirror much of the experience of the African American.

There are several points that are critical to remember when considering race in the current situation:

- As becomes clear anytime a matter of race and racist oppression is raised, most of white America would rather forget about the crimes of the past. There is a typically "American" frame of reference that is used, whereby many white Americans will assert that they do not wish to focus on the past, but rather look to the future. While this may sound optimistic, the net impact of it is to ignore the actual reality of race today—on whites and non-whites—that has resulted from years of systemic oppression.

- Race in the United States is not about someone else; it concerns the manner in which the United States was constructed and remains organized. A great deal of the difficulty with the Race Initiative launched by President Bill Clinton in the late 1990s is that it was perceived as being about someone else—i.e., it was about "colored people." A discussion of race involves the totality of the population. It involves the manner in which the country functions such that disasters can take place (e.g., Katrina), and the fate of hundreds of thousands of human beings can be treated as unfortunate but not critical. It also means that actions taken that are identified as affecting an irrelevant population—that is, a racially suppressed group—can be ignored even if such actions can and will have an impact on whites. The fact that the actions first and disproportionately hit people of color results in those actions being either misunderstood or not seen at all.

- Following from this, it must be understood that a *racialization* of issues takes place on a regular basis, "coloring" the way they are understood. In the contemporary world, there are four examples that illustrate this problem, one of which has already been noted.
  - *War against terrorism:* Terrorism, as a phenomenon, has come to be identified with a particular religion (Islam) and a group of people (Arabs and Central Asians). This identification preceded the Bush Administration and, to a great extent, goes back to the early twentieth century with the caricaturization of Arabs that followed World War I and coincided with the rise of films. The removal of Arab and non-Arab Muslims and their imprisonment without trial could only happen as a result of a demonization. When the Oklahoma City bombing took place in the 1990s, the immediate assumption was that this was carried out by Muslim terrorists. The discovery of Timothy McVeigh and Terry Nichols brought with it social and psychological confusion for many white Americans who could not grasp the roots of terrorism within the soil of the United States.
  - *Katrina:* As noted, the now famous contrast between white and Black survivors attempting to secure food, water and other supplies, where

the Black was characterized as a looter reinforced every stereotype concerning African Americans. The refusal to allow evacuees to enter nearby cities, but rather condemning them to their fate demonstrated the manner in which the Katrina disaster had been racialized, portraying it as a black disaster. While the Katrina disaster integrates race and class, race permits the larger society to ignore the impact, be it for Black evacuees or Native Americans in Louisiana who have literally disappeared.

o *Health Care:* While Michael Moore's much-discussed film *Sicko* captured the problem of the partially insured and the fates that can befall them, the health care calamity in the United States has its racial aspect. The most dramatic is that in every income category, there is a health care discrepancy between those who are white vs. those who are Black. Irrespective of income. In other words, people of the same income group are treated differently when it comes to health care (and have different life expectancies and health care treatment), depending on whether they are white or Black.

o *Immigration:* Little can be as startling as the racialization of immigration. Whereas the 1980s brought with it significant numbers of documented and undocumented Irish immigrating to the United States, little attention, and even less demonization, accompanied it. This could be contrasted with immigration from Haiti, the Dominican Republic and Central America and, during the 1990s, other parts of Latin America, most especially Mexico. At the same time that undocumented Irish were seeking work in the construction industries of Boston and New York, Haitian immigrants were being taunted as being one of the major sources of HIV/AIDS. Massive numbers of Eastern and Central European immigrants came to the United States following the collapse of the Soviet Union, yet the workers who were described as the threat to the livelihood of U.S. (read: mainly white U.S.) workers, were those from Latin America.

None of this is to ignore injustices other than race. It is to say that this society has a great deal of difficulty coming to grips with race and its implications for the present. Rather than looking at it as something that can be forgotten or something that is only a matter of the past, it would be better to recognize it as a chronic ailment that disables, if not ultimately kills, the patient.

With this as background, the specific policy proposals outlined above (not in order of importance) for the incoming Administration provide direction for coming to grips with the history and current reality of race in the United States.

A New Race Initiative

The Bill Clinton Race Initiative failed entirely. After beginning with great fanfare, it accomplished nothing. The findings of the Advisory Committee have been all but forgotten. We must begin again.

A Race Initiative should be understood as an "anti-racism initiative." In other words, the objective is to develop a more in-depth understanding of racism in the United States and develop means and methods to combat it. Such an initiative must, from the beginning, recognize that race and racism is not represented by a Black/white dichotomy, but that race and racism are experienced both independently and jointly by various peoples of color. Race and racism, as noted above, also have an impact on the dehumanization of whites.

A Race Initiative must involve local meetings, as well as significant research. It should aim to produce specific policy recommendations that go to the roots of the problem. Such recommendations would need to involve whites in what might in effect be a U.S. variant of a "truth & reconciliation commission."

Reparations and a "Marshall Plan" for the Cities

A race dialogue/initiative lays the foundation for a discussion of reparations—i.e., repairing the damage done by slavery; Jim Crow oppression; and *de facto* race discrimination for African Americans, but needing to be expanded to address the legacy of the seizure of Northern Mexico, the removal of Native Americans and the oppression of Asian Americans. It is not enough to look at this in rhetorical terms. Any discussion of reparations must recognize it to be part of a larger discussion concerning structural reforms that address the vast disparity of wealth and resources in U.S. society. Reparations, however, speaks specifically to recognizing and addressing the conditions faced by people of color within this larger context and most directly the African-American and Native-American experiences in North America.

Most immediately, a massive effort must be undertaken to address the urban crisis, a crisis that disproportionately affects people of color. The National Urban League has sounded the call over many years for a "Marshall Plan"-like approach to addressing the crisis of the cities over a host of issues.[1] Such an approach would need to include the rebuilding of the infrastructure of the United States—e.g., bridges, tunnels, sewers, as well as the upgrading of public education and health care. None of this can or will happen as long as the United States ignores the cities; ignores the question of race; and continues illegal and immoral wars and occupations.

De-monopolize Farms; Strengthen the Family Farmer; Defend Black, Native American and Chicano Land Rights

The tendency over the twentieth century has been toward the growth of mega agri-businesses. Family farmers have decreased significantly as a percentage of farmers. This phenomenon was dramatized during the 1980s both as a result of right-wing populist agitating (e.g., Posse Comitatus), and, to the left, the work of groups such as the North American Farm Alliance (and the coverage brought about by the Rev. Jesse Jackson's campaign during his 1988 bid for the White House).

Yet the Black farmer has all but disappeared. From a high in 1910 of between 16 and 19 million acres, Black farmers by 1997 were down to owning approximately 1.5 million acres.[2] Black land has been stolen over the years through a variety of means, including partition sales and tax fraud. In addition, the very real phenomenon of family loss of interest has contributed to the ability of others to seize the land.

A Congressional commission on the family farm, with subpoena powers, is necessary, to investigate the crisis and establish recommendations. Legal action needs to be taken to specifically address illegal and questionable means that have been undertaken to expropriate land possessed by Black farmers in the South, Chicano farmers in the Southwest, and Native American land generally.

Additionally, a program should be instituted that promotes farming, both in rural areas as well as urban farming. Farming cooperatives should receive special assistance, including tax incentives. Farming programs should be established closer to major metropolitan areas in order to cut down on transportation costs, as well as to be an incentive for urban youth to consider farming as an occupation.

Finally, not only are farms under assault, but the territory occupied by African Americans, Native Americans and Chicanos, in general, has been subject to seizure and abuse by outsiders. This includes annexation, threats to water rights, destructive mining and toxic waste disposal. Immediate steps need to be taken by government, including demands upon companies that abused land, to compensate the owners (and those affected) for damages. Annexations of land historically occupied by populations which have been subject to racist discrimination should be halted, including through support for autonomous incorporation (where a territory is unincorporated). The people on such lands should have a right to determine their own futures.

Create a Just Immigration Policy/End Attacks on Immigrants

There are immediate tasks that need to take place with regard to immigration. What must be first understood is that the bulk of immigration to the United

States comes from countries that have been directly affected by the foreign policies—economic, political, military—of the United States. This is fundamentally different from the immigration waves of the nineteenth and early twentieth century that were not directly related to the policies of the United States. The larger context is that the forces of neo-liberal globalization are generating a massive migration internationally which tends toward the movement of peoples within either the sphere of influence of a greater power or to the former colonizer (e.g., migration from the Caribbean to Britain).

The second feature of this period is the racialization of migration, as noted above. Thus, the focus on migrants from Latin America (particularly), Asia and Africa, with little attention on the impact of immigrants from Canada or Europe. The immigrant, particularly the undocumented immigrant, is painted "brown" and is charged with disrupting the lives of non-immigrants in the United States.

The third feature is the demonization and persecution of immigrants both from Latin America as well as from the Middle East and Central Asia. With the so-called War against Terrorism, immigrants and the children of immigrants from the Middle East and Central Asia have become subject to special attention, including detention and deportation. Racial profiling has become commonplace in this new period.

Specific steps that need to be taken include:

- Amnesty for undocumented workers who have no criminal record. Permanent residency status.
- Priority on family reunification.
- Revised application process that gives priority to refugees from political conflicts where the United States has been historically involved.
- No guest worker programs. Investigation of programs that already exist and their impact on domestic workers as well as the foreign-born.
- The right to unionize for all workers who exist inside the borders of the United States irrespective of their immigration status.
- No detention without charges and a fair trial.
- An end to racial profiling.

Implement a Democratic Foreign Policy

U.S. foreign policy is very arbitrary when it comes to matters of human rights, sovereignty and democracy. This has always been the case. What is noteworthy is that race permeates the determinations of U.S. foreign policy. U.S. attitudes towards Haiti, for instance, historically have been arrogant and contemptuous. During the Bush years, Haitian refugees were subject to horrendous treatment, assumed to be what were euphemistically termed "economic refugees," as opposed to refugees from Cuba who were termed "political refugees." As a result, they were regularly detained and deported, irrespective of whether they faced torture and/or death upon returning. This was compounded by the destabilization policies aimed at ousting the legitimately elected President of Haiti, Jean-Bertrand Aristide.

U.S. foreign policy must address repairing the damage that has been created by past actions. This is particularly focused on the conditions in the so-called Global South. Foreign assistance can, therefore, not be determined based on the willingness of a country to conform to the U.S.-imposed economic model, but must instead reflect efforts to (a) correct damage done by prior U.S. policies, and (b) promote sustainable economic development based on the needs and objectives of the people of that country.

Re-do Our Post-Katrina Efforts

Katrina was not fundamentally a natural disaster, but a political and economic disaster brought on by a hurricane. The African American Leadership Project of New Orleans, along with many other groups has developed demands that should be acted upon immediately by the incoming Administration. These include, but are not limited to:

- The right of return for all evacuees.
- The right of all displaced people to citizenship in the city.
- The right to shape and envision the future of the city (and the Gulf Region).
- The right to participate in the rebuilding of the city and the Gulf Region.
- The right to quality goods and services based on equity and equality.
- The right to affordable neighborhoods.
- The right to a living wage.
- The right to increase economic benefits and ownership.
- Preferential treatment in clean-up, construction and operational work associated with rebuilding.
- Contracting preference to community development collaboratives, community- and faith-based corporations/organizations, and businesses that partner with nonprofit service providers and people of color.
- Making the city and Gulf hurricane-safe.
- The right to preservation of the rich and diverse cultural traditions of the city and the Gulf.[3]

Initiate a United Nations-Supervised Plebiscite on the Future of Puerto Rico

Puerto Rico is one of the few remaining colonies of the United States. Votes have been taken in the past on the status of Puerto Rico (independence, commonwealth or statehood) that have resulted in Puerto Rico remaining a commonwealth. Yet these votes have not been internationally supervised and have been subject to the influence of outside forces. It also does not help that there are U.S. military operations situated in Puerto Rico. Therefore, in order for the Puerto Rican people to be able to decide their own future, they must be guaranteed a United Nations plebiscite free and clear of any and all intimidation. The results of such a plebiscite, assuming that it passes international standards for a free and fair vote, should be certified and supported by the United Nations and its members irrespective of the outcome.

Resources

Economic Policy Institute: www.epi.org
Federation of Southern Cooperatives Land Assistance Fund:
www.federationsoutherncoop.com
Joint Center for Political and Economic Studies: www.jointcenter.org
Las Culturas: www.lasculturas.com
National Black Farmers Association: www.blackfarmers.org
National Coalition of Blacks for Reparations in America: www.ncobra.com
Tulsa Reparations Coalition: www.tulsareparations.org

References

Fletcher, Bill, and Fenando Gapasin. *Solidarity Divided: The Crisis in Organized Labor and a New Path toward Social Justice.* Berkeley: University of California Press, 2008.

Notes

1. See, for example, www.nul.org/PressReleases/2007/2007PR417.html (accessed July 19, 2008).

2. Thomas Mitchell, "Destabilizing the Normalization of Rural Black Land Loss: A Critical Role for Legal Empiricism," *Wisconsin Law Review* (2005), 557.

3. Based upon a memo dated 9/22/05 to the Congressional Black Caucus, Attn: U.S. Rep. Sheila Jackson-Lee, Re: AALP Prespective on the Rebuilding of the City. I expanded this to cover not only the city of New Orleans, but the Gulf Coast region. That was consistent with the thrust of this memo, but the authors of the memo were not consulted in the modifications found in this chapter.

Chapter 16

Turning King's Dream into Reality

Dedrick Muhammad

POLICY PROPOSALS

■ Create Individual Development Accounts and Kid Saving Accounts for poor and middle-class Americans throughout the country.

■ Provide and fund financial education and counseling to all Americans participating in government-subsidized wealth development, including homeownership.

■ Tie federal housing aid to states to a mandate requiring all new construction and/or major renovations to have a minimum percentage of affordable low-income housing.

■ Enact stronger and broader national standards and regulations in home-buying.

■ Lower the ceiling for the mortgage interest deduction to no more than $415,000, as opposed to the current over $1 million cap.

■ Make public education a joint federal and state responsibility.

■ Create an Urban Infrastructure and Job Development Fund.

* * * * * * * * * * * * * * *

Over forty years since the assassination of Dr. Martin Luther King, the United States of America is still plagued by what King called America's three sins: militarism, materialism and racism. Militarism is seen in the "war against terrorism," where thousands upon thousands of U.S. soldiers and hundreds of billions of dollars are invested in a war that too many around the globe view as a war *of* terrorism. The materialism of this nation has turned its people into owners of the symbols of wealth but devoid of the substance of wealth. The United States is a nation full of the most luxurious consumer goods but has an economy where the average American lacks savings and job security, is too often under-insured if

149

they even have health insurance, and where 10 percent of the population controls 70 percent of the wealth. Finally, despite the proclamation of a post-racial America, the United States still stands as a nation marked by separate and unequal communities. A 2002 Census Bureau report titled "Beyond Black and White" concludes that African Americans are still the most segregated racial group in the United States. The report, "40 Years Later: The Unrealized American Dream," highlights that African Americans make 57 cents for every dollar that white Americans receive in income and have only 10 percent of the savings of white Americans.

Rev. Martin Luther King Jr.'s words tragically speak to our current reality. "The majority of white Americans consider themselves sincerely committed to justice for the Negro," he wrote in his 1967 book, *Where Do We Go From Here: Chaos or Community?* "They [the majority of whites] believe that American society is essentially hospitable to fair play and to steady growth toward a middle-class Utopia embodying racial harmony. But unfortunately this is a fantasy of deception and comfortable vanity."

Dr. King recognized that the next phase in the quest for civil rights and equality would focus on the economic divide. He understood that this next step would not just require non-violent action and the blood of civil rights martyrs, but also billions of dollars of investment. King proposed bold initiatives such as the Bill of Rights for the Disadvantaged and supported the proposed Freedom Budget of 1966. These proposals called for mass federal investment in the poor and working class of America to secure jobs, housing, and the opportunity to build wealth for all Americans.

It is time to turn King's Dream into a reality. The following are contemporary policy actions that could, if implemented, bridge the racial divide and the class divide that still prevent King's vision of social justice and equality from becoming more than just a dream.

Development/Saving Accounts, Low-Cost Credit, Financial Education

A growing amount of sociological research reveals that wealth is a key indicator for educational success, the ability to save and invest, and better health conditions. The net worth of one generation also contributes significantly to the wealth prospects of the next generation. Asset development assistance is essential to developing greater equality for African Americans who disproportionately hold few or no assets. Wealth development aimed at marginalized people of color would fulfill the next phase of the U.S. Civil Rights Movement, socioeconomic inequality. The implementation of asset-building policies that are racially/ethnically inclusive will strengthen the social fabric and bridge the racial wealth divide for future generations.

Individual Development Accounts and Kids Savings Accounts

Individual Development Accounts (IDAs) and Kids Saving Accounts are savings accounts with matching funds to give additional incentive to lower-income families to build wealth. Similar to the way that upper-income Americans receive matching funds from their employer into a 401(k), lower- and middle-income Americans would be eligible to receive matching funds through partnerships between various community-based organizations, government programs and sometimes the private sector.

Currently, there are small IDA programs across the country that provide insight into the greater possibilities of a mass wealth development program. The 2002 Millennial Housing Commission reported that "[IDA] Demonstration program results show very-low-income families actually save at a higher rate than the less-poor, with an average savings of $900 annually. . . . Recent proposals have been levied suggesting a 100 percent tax credit to financial institutions to provide 1:1 matches of up to $500 annually per qualified individual saving in an IDA."

Kids Saving Accounts began in 2003 in Britain, where the government established government-financed trust funds for each newborn in the country. Thomas Shapiro and Melvin Oliver in *Black Wealth/White Wealth* suggest that a Kids Saving Account be developed so that low- to moderate-income youth will have some starting capital with which they can enter their adult life. These funds, like IDA's, could be utilized only for particular wealth-building investments like higher education, job training or homeownership.

Strengthen Programs Providing Low-Cost Credit

Providing high-cost loans to low- to moderate-income individuals with less than perfect credit can too often, as shown by our current subprime economic crisis, lead to unsustainable lending agreements. Low-interest mortgage loans are required for more low- to moderate-income Americans. Vehicles such as low-interest tax-free Mortgage Revenue Bonds that are sold to investors need to be advanced so that low-interest loans are more available to first-time homebuyers with low-to-moderate-incomes.

A Wealth Program Tied to Financial Education

With wealth development programs must come education and counseling as to how to best utilize these programs. The 2002 Millennial Housing Commission reports that face-to-face counseling reduces defaults on home mortgages by up to 34 percent. This reports also points out that financial education programs for low-income people are drastically inadequate. The Housing Commission report finds only 120,000 to 150,000 individuals out of the approximately 1 million lower-income first-time homebuyers received pre-purchase education through HUD-related programs. Creating mass wealth-building programs provides a massive network that can require participation in wealth education before people receive the benefits of these government programs. These wealth education programs will strengthen individuals' economies as well as the national economy. Saving and wealth development must become a national mission, and those historically marginalized must be placed at the forefront of this mission.

Restructure Home-Buying Subsidies

Homeownership is the number-one source of wealth for Americans. In 2006, white Americans had a homeownership rate of 75.8 percent, while Black homeownership rate was only 48.4 percent (Wolf). This disparity partially accounts for Blacks having only 10 percent of the median household wealth of white Americans (Muhammad).

Today, two of the greatest challenges facing all working-class Americans in becoming homeowners are finding affordable housing and navigating through the technical legal documents involved in purchasing a home. Historically, the federal government has offered mass federal subsidies to working-class Americans to assist them in becoming owners of property. Whether it was the Homestead Act of the 1800s, the GI Bill of the 1940s or the ongoing mortgage insurance programs by the federal government, government subsidies and regulation have been necessary components for making homeownership achievable for more Americans. As in the past, the federal government can play an important role in strengthening this important wealth building opportunity for Middle America.

Affordable Housing

The private market's quest for greater and greater profits has limited the private market opportunities for the non-wealthy, particularly as it relates to housing. The higher profit margins that come with building expensive homes have made the affordable housing market less attractive for private home development companies. In many communities throughout the country, local government mandates that a certain amount of all new construction is affordable housing. The federal government should tie federal housing aid given to states with a mandate requiring a percentage of all new construction and/or major renovations go towards affordable or low-income housing. The federal government provides billions of dollars in incentives for homeownership, particular via the mortgage interest tax deduction. These incentives and tax deductions lower the costs to the homebuyer, providing greater incentive for homeownership, and thus serve as an indirect subsidy to housing developers. This mandate would ensure that housing developers across the country pay back in part some of the public funding that helps fuel their industry.

Simplify the Home-Buying Process

There needs to be a stronger national standard in homebuying instead of the current complicated patch-quilt system of state and local regulations. Years before our current subprime crisis, the 2000 "Curbing Predatory Home Mortgage Lending" report recommended simplifying the Real Estate Settlement Procedures Act (RESPA) and the Truth in Lending Act (TILA) forms. In other words, simplify the paperwork for homeownership and lending so it is clear as to how large a mortgage loan one is taking out and what the monthly payments will be throughout the loan. The federal government should also strengthen the Home Ownership Equity Protection Act (HOEPA), which would better regulate the securitization of subprime loans. As the nation faces the fall-out of the mass securitization of bad subprime loans, the need for greater regulation of the mortgage-lending industry is all too apparent. HOEPA should be also be expanded to include contractors, appraisers and other actors in real estate transactions.

End the Housing Subsidy for the Wealthiest Americans

In 2005, President Bush's advisory commission on tax reform recommended lowering the mortgage ceiling amount for the mortgage interest deduction. The commission recommended that the mortgage ceiling for tax deduction be placed on a sliding scale related to the area's real estate market. In 2005, the recommended ceiling was $415,000 in the most expensive areas, as opposed to the $1.1 million ceiling then in effect. This would prevent the American public from subsidizing more than the interest on a $415,000 loan. Since the median home price in the nation was in the low $200,000s, this would cover the overwhelming majority of homes in the United States. Bush's advisory group also recommended making the mortgage interest deduction a tax credit instead of a tax deduction. Only one-third of taxpayers—usually the richest third—find it to their benefit to itemize their taxes so they can use tax deductions. A tax credit assists all taxpayers, not just those with high-enough incomes to itemize their tax deductions.

Federalize Education, Privilege Multi-class/
Multi-cultural Schooling

The Civil Rights Movement and Dr. King understood that an essential part of Black advancement was to strengthen public education for African Americans. African Americans since the end of slavery have worked hard to overcome the educational deficit imposed on them. In the last forty years, Blacks have increased their high school education rate by 214 percent and their college graduation rate by almost 400 percent (Muhammad).

Despite these advances, Black youth are still disproportionately ill-served by the nation's education system. Over fifty years after *Brown vs. Board of Education*, Blacks are still segregated into inferior schools with unequal resources and investment. As the UN Committee on the Elimination of Racial Discrimination has stated, there is "the persistence of de facto segregation in public schools," where Blacks are segregated into schools with a high concentration of lower-performing and poorer students. Jonathan Kozol has highlighted how racial segregation has in fact remained a contemporary reality. Kozol points out that in 2005 the proportion of Black students at majority white schools was at "a level lower than in any year since 1968" (Kozol).

Evidence of the unequal government investment in the education of Black youth can be found in the Urban League's "State of Black America 2007," which reports that Black students receive only 82 percent of what is spent per white student and that twice as many teachers have less than three years' teaching experience in majority-Black districts as compared to majority-white districts.

Professor Edmund W. Gordon, in "Establishing a System of Public Education," notes that various forms of capital or resources are required to enable a student to take best advantage of public education. Due to their overall weak socio-economic condition, African Americans are lacking in the forms of capital for effective education (Smiley). Gordon identifies the different forms of effective education capital as: health, financial, human, social, polity, personal, institutional and pedagogical. So Black youth, with already deficient effective education capital, have less financial capital invested in them.

Professor Gordon writes that "the most direct approach to the solution of the problem of maldistribution would involve the redistribution of income, wealth and related resources." But continues: "It is not reasonable to expect that such a radical solution will resonate with a twenty-first century America (Smiley)." Such a radical solution is necessary if we hope to end the 400-year legacy of racial Apartheid, particularly as it relates to education. The policy solutions that help redistribute wealth to the economically disenfranchised will be of major assistance to bridging the educational gap between African Americans and whites.

To truly make sure that "no child is left behind," federal funds must be attached to levels of representation of under-achieving racial/ethnic groups in the context of the demographics of the school system. Federal aid should be further weighed to low-income, low-achieving schools that have less spending per pupil than a national average. Public education must become a national priority, not in just election rhetoric but in federal spending.

Congressman Jesse Jackson Jr., in his important book, *A More Perfect Union: Advancing New American Rights,* argues that an educated citizenry is of such importance that a constitutional amendment is required to make the federal government accountable for universal high-quality education. Congressman Jackson rightfully articulates that a patchwork of local school systems with minimal federal contribution to its improvement and oversight is not sufficient in the twenty-first century.

Finally, the federal government should guarantee debt-free higher education to first-generation and low-income college students up to the associate degree level. Income should not be an obstacle to those historically disenfranchised from higher education.

An Urban Infrastructure and Job Development Fund

The Urban League, in their Opportunity Act of 2007, proposes an Urban Infrastructure Bank that would fund the repair and development of our schools, water systems, parks, roads, bridges and community centers. This would also provide employment opportunities that should go to those from chronically unemployed areas.

The old saying goes that in crisis one finds opportunity. This is helpful to remember as we look at the rising cost of oil along with the rising concern of the environmental effect our economy is having on the world. Out of this high energy cost and environmental crisis, groups like Green For All have developed an agenda to create mass employment as we as a nation scale back our energy use and become more environmentally responsible. African-American unemployment over the last thirty years has been twice the rate of white unemployment and in some communities Black male unemployment has been estimated to be as high as 50 percent (Levitan). A mass federal investment could create a new form of industrial jobs that could help replace some of those jobs that have been exported to other nations.

An urban infrastructure and green jobs investment will of course benefit the economy as a whole, increasing the spending power of the consumer whose dollars run two-thirds of the economy (Gongloff). The report "Alternative Spending: Effects on Job Creation" notes that federal spending in construction and home weatherization is much more effective in the economic stimulus of job creation than the standard conservative measure of tax cuts or military spending. The crisis of Black unemployment, the need for a new green economy, and the crisis of stimulating a middle-class economy have produced an opportunity to create an infrastructure and job development fund program that could address all three issues.

Conclusion

2009 promises to be a year of great national political change. There is a mood of national discontent that encompasses foreign policy, economics and the political status quo as a whole. To change the Black/white race divide in this nation will require a national commitment followed by a mass national investment in America that will benefit all nations and invest specifically in those who have been and continue to be disenfranchised. Dr. King said over forty years ago that the United States had the means to end poverty but the question was, does it have the will? Today, we clearly have the means to bridge the Black/white divide. The question is as it was over forty years ago: Do we have the will? Do we have the will to dedicate the wealth of this country to the development of a broad-based, racially inclusive wealth?

Resources

Demos: www.demos.org
Economic Policy Institute: http://www.epi.org
Inequality and the Common Good Project: www.extremeinequality.org
Inequality.org: www.inequality.org
United For A Fair Economy: www.faireconomy.org

References

Gongloff, Mark. "Consumer Confidence Falls." CNN, March 25, 2003.
Kozol, Jonathan. "Overcoming Apartheid." *The Nation*, December 19, 2005.
Levitan, Mark. "A Crisis of Black Male Employment." Report. Community Service Society, February 2004.
Muhammad, Dedrick. "40 years later: The Unrealized American Dream." Report. Institute for Policy Studies (April 2008).
Smiley, Tavis. *The Covenant with Black America*. Chicago: Third World Press, 2006.
Wolf, Edward. "Recent Trends in Household Wealth in the US." The Levy Economics Institute of Bard College Working Paper Collection (June 2007). http://www.levy.org/pubs/wp_502.pdf (accessed July 21, 2008).

Chapter 17

Climate and Energy Solutions for a Secure, Equitable and Sustainable Future

Betsy Taylor

POLICY PROPOSALS

- Set a national goal for reducing greenhouse gases and engage all sectors in moving beyond rhetoric to action.
- Urge Congress to enact comprehensive climate legislation that puts a price on carbon and global warming pollution. Make carbon polluters pay for their CO2 emissions and redirect a majority of the revenue to protect Americans from rising energy prices to ensure a just and equitable transition to a low-carbon future. Use executive branch authority to regulate CO2.
- Place an immediate moratorium on all new coal-fired plants that emit global warming gases.[1]
- Conserve at least 20 percent of the nation's energy by 2015 and stimulate the creation of at least 5 million new public- and private-sector jobs by making America the world's most energy-efficient country.
- Promote clean and renewable energy. Generate all electricity from renewable energy sources within ten years.
- Invest in opportunity: Establish a youth Clean Energy Corps, green jobs training programs, and retooling for workers making the transition to a new energy economy.
- Strengthen local economies by promoting smart growth, regional planning and an array of local infrastructure programs.
- Establish a bipartisan commission to examine and report back on the root causes of global warming and ecological collapse and with recommendations for addressing these causes at a systemic level.
- Rally the nation to action.

* * * * * * * * * * * * * * *

The most renowned climate scientist in the United States claims that he is 99.9 percent sure that we have already exceeded the safe limit for greenhouse gas emissions. NASA's Dr. James Hansen testified before Congress in June 2008 that the United States and other nations have already put enough carbon pollution in the atmosphere to cause cataclysmic disaster in this century—perhaps in the next few decades. We are coming to the end of the fossil fuel era. The only question is how quickly we can reduce carbon pollution and pivot to a clean energy future. The incoming President will either go down in human history as a champion of human progress or as a tragic figure who failed to seize the moment. We are out of time.

There is a huge chasm between what scientists are reporting about climate change and how human societies are responding. Consider just a few facts:

- Before the industrial revolution the atmosphere held 280 parts per million (ppm) of carbon dioxide (CO_2). Scientists at the Mauna Loa observatory in Hawaii reported in May 2008 that CO_2 levels in the atmosphere now stand at 387 ppm, up almost 40 percent since the industrial revolution and the highest for at least the last 650,000 years.[2] This figure does not include the additional greenhouse gases such as methane and nitrous oxide.
- Carbon dioxide has an atmospheric lifetime of 50 to 200 years. Consequently, carbon dioxide emitted into the atmosphere today will cause global warming for up to two centuries to come.
- In 1970, we imported 24 percent of our oil. Today, it's nearly 70 percent and growing. As imports grow and world prices rise, the amount of money we send to foreign nations every year is soaring. At current oil prices, we will send $700 billion out of the country in 2008 alone—that's four times the annual cost of the Iraq war.[3]

The climate is snapping, but despite lots of talk, little is being done to actually transform our fossil fuel-dependent lifestyles and economy. The great ice sheets of Greenland and Antarctica are melting, and if Greenland goes, sea levels will rise to levels that would restructure the world's coastlines and displace hundreds of millions of people. Everyone will be affected, but according to the UN it is the poor who will suffer the most. "It is the poorest of the poor in the world, and this includes poor people even in prosperous societies, who are going to be the worst hit," according to Intergovernmental Panel on Climate Change (IPCC) Chairman Rajendra Pachauri.[4] The incoming President and Congress must respond to the threat of climate disruption at a speed and scale that must eclipse even the great mobilization for the Marshall Plan or the Apollo Project. Scientists from IPCC say we have only seven years to halt all growth in emissions world-wide, which means the highly-developed nations must cut deeply. Americans must come together to do whatever it takes to preserve the legacy left to us by our parents, and ensure the future we owe to our children and grandchildren. The incoming President must act boldly and decisively.

Set a national goal for reducing greenhouse gases and engage all sectors in moving beyond rhetoric to action:

- Commit to mandatory reductions in carbon emissions that meet the demands of science. Reduce CO2 at least 25–40 percent by 2020[5] and work to achieve zero emissions as fast as humanly possible, no later than 2050.
- Require all state governments, sectors and businesses to quantify their current emissions levels and then challenge mayors, governors, university presidents, non-profit leaders, business executives and patriotic citizens to do their part to meet this challenge.
- Create a Climate Solutions block grant program earmarked for states that submit concrete, results-driven plans for helping achieve the national goal at the state level.
- Establish a Cabinet-level position to engage all government departments in the implementation of solutions. Charge this inter-agency Secretary with action now and an aggressive search for new technologies and solutions.

Urge Congress to enact comprehensive climate legislation that puts a price on carbon and global warming pollution. Make carbon polluters pay for their CO2 emissions and redirect the revenue to protect Americans from rising energy prices to ensure a just and equitable transition to a low-carbon future. Use Executive Branch authority to regulate CO2:

- Carbon pollution is invisible and currently unregulated at the federal level. As a result, there are few incentives to stop heating up the atmosphere. Urge Congress to enact a comprehensive cap on greenhouse gas emissions and require carbon polluters to pay for 100 percent of their pollution through a cap-and-tax and/or cap-and-auction program. Redirect the estimated $50–$300 billion in revenue to protect Americans from rising energy prices.[6] According to a July 2008 AP-Yahoo poll, 90 percent of Americans expect rising gas prices to pose a financial hardship in the immediate future.[7] Return at least 70 percent of the revenue from corporate polluter payments back to American households in the form of monthly checks to offset the rising cost of heating, transport and food.[8]
- Use a portion of revenue from the sale of pollution permits to protect the most vulnerable with a mix of programs, including home energy assistance and weatherization programs, as well as direct benefit transfers for low-income senior citizens and families on fixed income in the bottom fifth of all households.[9]
- Help developing nations with adaptation plans and programs to help those being displaced by droughts, fires and water shortages that have resulted largely from the disproportionate share of global warming emissions generated by the United States.

- Use a portion of the polluter payments to invest in energy efficiency and renewable energy programs that rapidly cut carbon emissions while generating new green jobs.
- Demand that the Environmental Protection Agency regulate carbon; don't wait for Congress to pass legislation before moving to regulate CO2 through the Executive Branch.

Place an immediate moratorium on all new coal-fired plants that emit global warming gases:[10]

If we don't do this, we lose. Coal is responsible for 40 percent of the nation's greenhouse gas emissions. If we hope to avert a permanent carbon economy, we must stop building new coal plants unless or until all emissions can be safely and permanently sequestered and stored. The coal industry is underwriting a multi-million dollar PR campaign to promote "clean coal," but carbon sequestration and storage is generally considered to be either a pipe-dream or a solution too far in the future to apply to current plants. Coal causes severe public health effects, including lung, kidney and heart disease and other ailments blamed for premature deaths and illness.[11] Mountain-top removal in the Southeast and other coal-mining practices in the West have devastated local communities and natural habitats. Coal miners will need buy-outs and transition support.

Conserve at least 20 percent of the nation's energy by 2015 and stimulate the creation of at least 5 million new public- and private-sector jobs by making America the world's most energy-efficient country:

- Pass a national efficiency standard for all utilities operating power plants. Require utilities to promote energy conservation and installation of energy-efficient technologies in homes and businesses. De-couple utility profits from production.
- Enact efficiency standards for all new buildings and appliances, and make retrofitting of all old buildings mandatory. Set a national goal of making all buildings carbon-neutral by 2030.[12]
- Do the simple stuff and do it now: Turn lights off in all industrial and commercial buildings at night (excluding security lighting); make high-efficiency LED lights the new lighting standard and see they get mass-produced to bring the price of the new best technology down; require mandatory energy-saving thermostats in all residential and commercial buildings.
- Pass new fuel efficiency standards, including a low-carbon standard and CAFÉ standards of 50 mpg.
- Promote a new generation of vehicles, including advanced hybrids and electric vehicles. Place recharging stations at conveniently located grocery stores and shopping areas.

Promote clean and renewable energy:

- Shift subsidies such as loan guarantees and investment and consumer tax credits to wind, solar, geothermal and biomass and away from coal, nuclear and oil.
- Redirect R&D funds and government procurement to trigger a rapid deployment of technologies aimed at zero carbon emissions. Imagine small 5W–10W wind turbines on every telephone pole and clip-on solar water heaters for apartment buildings and homes. Promote open-source solutions so all companies can make products that are compatible. A consumer might have roof voltaic sections from one source and water heating from another and air heating from a third, but with all of them making a single functioning easy-to install roof.
- Require all utility companies to produce all electric power from renewable sources by 2020. It can be done. A 2005 Stanford University study found that there is enough wind power worldwide to satisfy global demand seven times over—even if only 20 percent of wind power could be captured.[13]
- Redirect federal subsidies for corn-based ethanol and other biofuels away from food stocks and high carbon-emitting sources to high-yield, non-food sources such as agricultural wastes and low-quality trees and brush cleared from forests for habitat management and restoration.[14]

Invest in Opportunity:

- Expand AmeriCorps to create a Clean Energy Corps that trains and employs youth to weatherize homes in low-income communities and install energy-efficient water heaters, insulation and lighting.
- Create green pathways out of poverty for America's most economically disenfranchised populations. Invest in green-collar job-training and education programs with grants to community colleges, non-profits and local small businesses.
- Provide transition assistance for workers laid off by the fossil fuel sector.
- Redirect a portion of foreign aid to assist developing nations with adaptation for vulnerable communities and ecosystems.

Rebuild Communities and Strengthen Local Economies:

- Redirect billions of taxpayer dollars from expanding roads and highways to promote smart growth, mass transit systems, and zero carbon residential and commercial buildings next to transit hubs.
- Establish a Livable Communities program to promote best practices among cities and towns that implement innovative programs to enhance quality of life, save energy, generate jobs and reduce carbon emissions. Imagine free mass transportation for all students; no-idling rules for buses; walking and biking paths connected to cafes for commuters; liv-

ing-wage jobs to build mass transit systems, rooftop gardens, and upgraded bus and subway systems.
- Create an Executive Order charging all state governments and all federal
  agencies to incorporate local sourcing of food and other products into
  procurement guidelines. Work through the Small Business Administration to help women- and minority-owned businesses bid on these contracts. Local sourcing reduces carbon emissions, generates more jobs and
  increases community benefits from business and government activities.

**Establish a Bipartisan Commission to examine and report back on the root
causes of global warming and ecological collapse and with recommendations for addressing these causes at a systemic level:**
We are failing to address the root causes of global warming and many other ecological ills. The human species and other life on the planet will not survive in an
economic system premised on rising growth, consumption, materialism and
ever-expanding physical infrastructure. We rarely even talk about these causes
of collapse because the field of economics doesn't have the necessary language
or tools. Furthermore, all of us are dependent on growth and consumption for
our short-term security. Criticism of consumption and growth is consistently
dismissed as naïve or driven by ideology when in fact it is science-based. Most
of the ecological systems that sustain life are in jeopardy and our blind global
march toward material progress as we have defined it must be confronted. No
doubt billions of humans need increased material security but don't let this obvious truth prevent a deeper conversation about the forces that are taking us off a
cliff. As our leaders work to stabilize and restructure the global economic system, they should catalyze local, sustainable economies that will anchor unpre-
dictable global markets in resilient, community-based systems of commerce,
agriculture and energy production. Our current economic structures bind everyone into a collective action problem. We urgently need a fundamental rethinking of global capitalism and excessive materialism. Political and economic
leaders have resisted this conversation since *The Limits to Growth* was published in 1972. We can no longer put ideological taboos in front of common
sense. Create a Bipartisan Commission of visionary yet pragmatic economists,
local elected officials, farmers, energy-producers and business leaders to rethink
the global economic systems that are jeopardizing our future.

Rally the nation to action:
- Article II, Section 3 of the U.S. Constitution gives the President the
  power to convene a special session of both houses of Congress. This is
  rarely used, since Congress is almost continuously in session. Demonstrate seriousness of purpose; harness this power to speak to the entire nation and announce that the nation is going to war—not against a foreign
  power but against greenhouse gas emissions and in support of solutions
  that protect American households from rising energy prices and depend-

ence on fossil fuels. Avoid pandering and politically expedient descriptions of reality. There is no short-term fix for rising gasoline prices. There is no clean coal. But there are solutions to climate change and fossil fuel dependence. Help American citizens understand the unprecedented threats posed by carbon emissions and rising energy prices while inspiring hope in the limitless potential of a clean energy future.

- Convene a high-level summit of innovative leaders from every sector of society, inviting those who have already demonstrated positive action on clean energy solutions. Issue an "all hands on deck" challenge with a specific set of proposals—those above—that will catalyze a race for results. Focus on programs that simultaneously cut carbon, improve quality of life, and foster economic security and opportunity, especially for low- and middle-income households. Encourage novel approaches, such as the Utah Governor's June 2008 announcement of a four-day work week to conserve energy and improve family life or the repainting of roads and roofs white to reflect heat.

There is still time to avert catastrophe, but only if far more Americans push for bold action. The incoming President will need to throw the fossil fuel moneychangers out of Congress and urge the citizens to rise up to reclaim our government. If we do this, we will be part of one of the most extraordinary turnings in human history.

Resources

1Sky: http://www.1sky.org
350: http://www.350.org
Climate Action Project: http://www.climateactionproject.com
Green for All: http://www.greenforall.org

References

Barnes, Peter. *Climate Solutions: What Works, What Doesn't, and Why: A Citizen's Guide*. White River Junction: Chelsea Green Publishing, 2008.

Inslee, Jay, and Bracken Hendricks. *Apollo's Fire: Igniting America's Clean Energy Economy*. Washington, D.C.: Island Press, 2007.

McKibben, Bill. *Deep Economy: The Wealth of Communities and the Durable Future*. New York: Times Books, 2007.

Notes

1. James Hansen, "The Need for an International Moratorium on Coal Power," *Bulletin of the Atomic Scientists* (January 21, 2008), http://www.thebulletin.org/web-edition/features/the-need-international-moratorium-coal-power (accessed July 16, 2008).

2. David Adam, "World CO2 Levels at Record High, Scientists Warn," *The Guardian* (May 12, 2008), www.guardian.co.uk/environment/2008/may/ 12/climatechange.car bonemissions (accessed July 16, 2008).

3. T. Boone Pickens, *Pickens Plan,* http://www.pickensplan.com/theplan/ (accessed July 18, 2008).

4. Environmental News Service, "UN Climate Change Impact Report: Poor Will Suffer Most," April 6, 2007, http://www.ens-newswire.com/ens/apr2007/ 2007-04-06-01.asp (accessed July 18, 2008).

5. The Intergovernmental Panel on Climate Change issued a report prior to the United Nations Framework Convention on Climate Change in Bali, December 2007. This report included a chart indicating that if developed nations reduce greenhouse gases 25-40 percent by 2020, the world will have a 50 percent chance of avoiding global temperatures from rising 2 degrees C (based on 450 ppm emissions rather than the 350 recommended by James Hansen of NASA). This national goal is the bare minimum for avoiding disaster.

6. There is a robust debate about whether a cap-and-trade versus a cap-and-carbon tax or fee will be more or less effective in reducing emissions. The incoming President should be prepared to move with both instruments in case one is gamed or distorted by industry lobbying corporate give-aways. The debate over how best to redirect the revenue from an auction or tax to ensure economic protection and opportunity is equally lively. See list of resources for details.

7. Nelson D. Schwartz, "American Energy Policy: Asleep at the Spigot," *New York Times*, July 6, 2008.

8. The best way to return auction revenue to consumers is via monthly rebates. This makes the program popular and will sustain long-term support for a cap, despite rising energy prices. The tighter the cap, the bigger the rebate. This also is the best defense against the offense being paid for by big oil and coal—that a cap-and-trade with auction will hurt average Americans.

9. Center on Budget and Policy Priorities, "Climate-Change Policies Can Treat Poor Families Fairly and Be Fiscally Responsible," Center on Budget & Policy Priorities website, http://www.cbpp.org/pubs/climate-brochure.htm (accessed July 18, 2008).

10. See James Hansen, "The Need for an International Moratorium on Coal Power," *Bulletin of the Atomic Scientists*, January 21, 2008, http://www.thebulletin.org/web-edition/features/the-need-international-moratorium-coal-power (accessed July 18, 2008).

11. "WVU Researchers Say Coal Mining Endangers Public Health," Associated Press, March 25, 2008.

12. Edward Mazria and Kristina Kershner, "The 2030 Blueprint: Solving Climate Change Saves Billions," *Architecture 2030*, April 7, 2008.

13. "New Global Wind Map May Lead to Cheaper Power Supply," *Stanford News Service*, May 20, 2005, http://news-service.stanford.edu/news/2005/may25/wind-052505.html (accessed July 18, 2008).

14. Carol Werner, "Resolving the Biofuels Dilemma," *Solar Today*, July/August 2008.

Chapter 18

Green Jobs in a Sustainable Economy

Jon Rynn

POLICY PROPOSALS

- Establish an Infrastructure Capital Development Bank to provide long-term funding, worker training and business services for sustainable economy projects.
- Create an electric high-speed rail network that can provide inter-city transportation.
- Create an expanded subway, light rail, bus rapid transit, electrified commuter rail system and electric cars that can provide transportation within urban areas.
- Create programs that allow buildings to heat and cool themselves, and provide much of their own electricity.
- Establish local electricity authorities that can create and maintain wind and solar energy farms for a metropolitan area.
- Establish a national electric authority to rebuild the national electric grid and construct and maintain large-scale wind and solar installations.
- Establish an Urban Gardening Corps to create and maintain urban gardens and small, local organic farms in urban areas.
- Create programs to encourage the manufacturing of the equipment and materials needed for a green economy, thus creating blue-green-collar jobs.

* * * * * * * * * * * * * *

We face several simultaneous crises—global warming, high oil prices, a brittle agricultural system and a major economic slowdown—all of which can be addressed at the same time by embarking on a program of creating millions of high-quality green collar jobs.

A green-collar jobs program can help create an environmentally and economically sustainable society that: drastically reduces its greenhouse gas emissions; encourages energy independence from oil; eliminates the worry of heating and cooling one's home; and increases food security, all while providing millions of high-quality, well-paying, long-term jobs, thus bringing millions of people into a stable middle class.

The following eight initiatives could result in transportation, energy, building construction, agricultural and manufacturing sectors that would have very low carbon emissions, would be economically and ecologically sustainable for the foreseeable future, and whose workers and employees would all be green-collar.

First, the infrastructure of the United States is crumbling,[1] which means that there is plenty of work to do even without worries about global warming, oil and food. We should build a *sustainable* infrastructure, not just maintain the one that we have.

Senators Chris Dodd and Chuck Hagel introduced a bill in 2007, the National Infrastructure Bank Act,[2] which is a good starting point for a discussion about how to rebuild the country's infrastructure. Infrastructure funding has been inadequate for decades, and we need an institution that can provide long-term stability of funding.

However, the federal government should go even further and create a bank that also develops *human* capital. The bank could be called an Infrastructure Capital Development Bank, one that would, in addition to providing funding for infrastructure construction, run a network of Training Institutes that would train the millions of people we need in order to build a sustainable economy. Green-collar jobs need green-collar job classes.

In addition, the Bank could help businesses start up or expand their green-collar activities, with financial help and/or by providing technical assistance. If desired, the Bank could help these firms become employee-owned-and-operated, thus increasing efficiency and insuring that jobs stay in the United States.

Second, our transportation industries are in trouble because the era of cheap oil is over, and at the same time we need to drastically cut our carbon emissions. For inter-city travel, our infrastructure has been built around airplanes, cars and trucks. In much of the world, however, trains of various kinds fulfill the roles of intercity passenger and freight transportation. In the United States, the incoming Administration has a chance to jump-start the construction of a national network of electrified high-speed passenger and freight trains.

At least initially, foreign companies will be the only ones with the expertise to produce high-speed trains. If domestic content legislation was passed, these companies and the hundreds of subcontractors that would be needed for such systems could employ a whole new generation of high-skill blue-collar, or blue-green-collar workers.

High-speed rail is the cutting edge of transportation technology, having been developed even more recently than air travel, much less the 100-year-plus old technology of the internal combustion engine. There are already several federally recognized high-speed rail networks "in waiting," around Chicago, Ohio, Texas, Florida and California, in addition to the one between Boston and Washington, D.C., which could certainly be expanded.[3]

A national system of high-speed rail could do in the twenty-first century what the Interstate Highway System did for the United States after World War II: create the infrastructure for a period of high-speed economic growth. In addition, if the rail system was powered by solar and wind-generated electricity, the United States would have the first carbon-free inter-city transportation system in the world.

Third, as oil prices increase, so does the demand for public transportation. Subways and light rail can be run on renewable electricity, and commuter rail systems can be expanded and electrified. In addition, many cities are contemplating bus rapid transit, pioneered in Curitaba, Colombia, which allow buses to move much faster and more comfortably.

Currently, as in the case of high-speed rail, there are no domestic primary contractors for subway construction, but in the case of New York State, domestic content laws have led to the establishment of many subway construction factories, and the same could be mandated across the country. Again, these are blue-green-collar jobs, jobs in industry that will help us move toward a zero carbon emission economy, while making us energy independent and more secure.

Another advantage to public transit is that it will encourage the development of dense, "mixed-use" city and town areas, that is, areas that are composed of apartment buildings, stores, offices and other kinds of buildings. Christopher Leinberger of the Brookings Institution calls for the construction of "walkable urbanism" that is, "the development approach that creates pedestrian-oriented, mixed-use and mixed-income places."[4] When there are fixed subway or light rail stops, then developers, prospective residents and store owners can be confident that there will be fast and easy transportation to any residence or store.

The construction of dense, mixed use buildings near transit stops will bring about a construction boom for decades to come. Building construction or reconstruction, not normally considered "green," should be so categorized if new construction takes place near transit stops. There are two ways to make buildings "green"—make them energy efficient, and place them in dense areas next to transit stops.

Thus, public transit decreases carbon emissions, helps us achieve energy independence, and lays the groundwork for walkable communities. In addition, staffing, maintaining and building public transit will provide millions of high-quality jobs all across the country. Since the transit and construction jobs will be in urban areas, low-income neighborhoods can be targeted for recruitment into training and apprenticeship programs.

While government can directly create networks of rail and transit, it can also indirectly encourage the replacement of gasoline-only automobiles and trucks with plug-in hybrids and all-electric vehicles. The first step in this process would be to mandate that all federal cars and trucks be plug-ins or all-electric by 2020. Eventually, if the entire transportation sector can run on renewable electricity, then all jobs in the transportation sector will be green-collar.

Fourth, in the United States today, about two-thirds of our electricity and one-third of our natural gas is used within residential and commercial buildings. Heating and cooling accounts for almost all of the natural gas use in commercial and residential buildings, and accounts for 30 percent of all electrical use in the country. And those natural gas and electric bills are going up, threatening to make life miserable for tens of millions of households in winters or summers.

Decreasing the heating and cooling needs of buildings would therefore lead to significant reductions in carbon emissions and lower energy bills. Thus, retrofitting old buildings, making them more energy-efficient, and constructing sustainable buildings will be essential occupations in a green society.

If buildings were able to heat and cool themselves, enough electric generation could be eliminated, and enough natural gas could be diverted into electricity generation, that all coal plants could be shut down.[5] This could be achieved in a number of ways: first, by installing geothermal heat pumps under buildings in order to take care of heating and cooling needs; second, by installing solar photovoltaic systems, for direct electrical heating and cooling, or in order to power the geothermal heat pumps; third, by installing solar thermal units for heating needs; or some combination of the three, which would probably involve battery storage in the building. In other words, to a significant extent, buildings can become energy self-reliant.

Millions of green-collar jobs would be needed for these programs. Within metropolitan areas, low-income neighborhoods can provide much of the labor for turning urban buildings into carbon-neutral structures, as has been mandated in the Green Collar Jobs Bill, which will create a Pathways out of Poverty program.[6] For too long, people from outside low-income areas have been the beneficiaries of construction there, so it is imperative that labor pools hired to create sustainable buildings in low-income areas be filled by the residents of those neighborhoods.

The two roadblocks to self-reliant buildings are financing and skilled labor. An Infrastructure Bank could help overcome both problems. It could follow the lead of the City of Berkeley, which offers loans to homeowners to install solar photovoltaic panels, paying back the loan with the savings from lower electricity bills. The Bank could overcome the second problem by overseeing training institutes for green-collar jobs. Eventually, as in transportation, all building construction jobs could be green-collar jobs.

Fifth, while buildings could provide much of the energy for their own needs, in order to green the energy sector we would need wind- and solar-based electricity generated at the metropolitan level in order to help minimize the use of coal and natural gas. Local electric authorities could establish region-based, medium-sized renewable electrical systems.

Many metropolitan areas have been creating a *community choice aggregation*, or CCA. In a CCA, the metropolitan government uses its power to control the electrical distribution in its territory to contract out the generation of electricity to an energy-service provider (ESP), who is usually required to provide a certain percentage of electricity from solar and wind energy, as well as from conservation. For example, San Francisco is requiring its ESP to provide 103 MW (megawatts) from distributed renewables, mostly PV (solar voltaics) on buildings; 150 MW from a wind farm; and 107 MW from conservation and efficiency. That should constitute 51 percent of San Francisco's electricity needs.[7]

If CCAs or other kinds of urban electric authorities (such as municipal utilities) spread throughout the country, it would create a perfect opportunity to use labor trained in the metropolitan area to install and maintain the energy systems.

Note that conservation and efficiency can be considered a part of the energy mix, creating a great potential for local employment. A local government could hire thousands of energy auditors to help building owners maximize the energy potential of their buildings. In addition, a "smart grid" can be installed in each region, allowing the local ESP to rationally run or shut down appliances within a building depending on the price of electricity at particular points in time; this will require more service personnel to make sure that the system lives up to its potential.

Sixth, even with building- and metropolitan-based energy systems, the needs of an electrified transportation system would require a national system of solar and wind facilities; in addition, the capability to access electricity from anywhere in the country helps insure that everybody will always have electricity, even if the local sun is not shining or the wind is not blowing. A National Electric Authority could be established with two main responsibilities: rebuild the national electric grid, and help create large, long-distance concentrated solar power (CSP) and wind farms.

The current national electric grid, which moves electricity from power plants to the industrial, commercial and residential buildings were the electricity is used, is in desperate need of repair.[8] Each piece is owned by a different utility, and the regulatory environment is such that there is little incentive to maintain it, much less upgrade it to the level that will be required to add rich sources of wind and solar energy. In addition, an authority would need to build a system of high-voltage direct current (HVDC) lines, which would be a more efficient way to move electricity from large-scale renewable energy sources to the rest of the country.

The American Southwest contains enough solar energy potential to supply all of the electricity for the entire country. The Great Plains, such as North Dakota or parts of Texas, likewise contains enough wind power potential to fill all of our current electrical needs, and then some.[9] A National Electric Authority could oversee the construction of large-scale CSP, wind farms and the upgrading of the national grid.

The labor trained by the Institutes could help to install and maintain these large-scale systems. The creation of a continent-wide, high-tech electric grid, fed by carbon-free energy sources, would create millions of high-skilled green jobs. In combination with the building and metropolitan energy systems, the energy sector could be transformed from an environmentally damaging industry into a completely green-collar one.

Seventh, the global agricultural system is coming unglued. The days of transporting food over thousands of miles, of dousing soils with pesticides and artificial fertilizers, and of growing thousands of acres of the same crop, will soon draw to a close. Millions of new urban gardening jobs could be created within cities and suburbs in order to produce most of our fruits and vegetables, and most grain could be grown close to urban areas. This kind of agriculture will build up the soil, which is the natural capital of our farming system, instead of letting it be destroyed and washed away (two examples of sustainable agricultural practices are permaculture and bio-intensive gardening).

A soil-enhancing, pesticide- and artificial fertilizer-free agriculture would be much more labor-intensive than the current system. Industrial agriculture is only productive because of the indiscriminate use of greenhouse gas-emitting fossil fuels. Organic, intensive agriculture is more productive in terms of land, but requires high skill levels and more labor.

Training Institutes could help new gardener/farmers to produce healthy, sustainable food, and the Bank could be used to help them set up a new garden/farm. The American agricultural workforce could balloon from the current 1 million to many millions, making it one of the most effective green-collar jobs possible.

Agriculture, like transportation, building construction and energy, could stop being a source of crisis and start becoming a source of sustainability.

Eighth, our economy teeters on the edge of a cliff, at least partly caused by the decline of the manufacturing sector. But the various programs advocated in this chapter all rely on a healthy manufacturing sector to produce the trains, wind turbines, solar panels, zero emission buildings, organic gardens and more that are needed to decrease carbon emissions and avoid the wholesale destruction of the biosphere. Thus, in order to create a sustainable society and guarantee our economic well-being, it is imperative that the federal government act to support the revival of the manufacturing sector.

The Infrastructure Capital Development Bank could include a national system of manufacturing extension services, which would help start and expand manufacturing firms to provide the sinews of the green economy. The extension services could also start an epochal shift, from manufacturing which uses up the Earth's resources and pollutes our ecosystems, to a manufacturing system that is "cradle to cradle"[10]—that is, that uses recycled materials and creates zero pollution. If this shift happens, all manufacturing, for the first time in human history, could be sustainable and all manufacturing workers would be blue-green-collar.

Manufacturing is not simply a source of jobs, it is a critical part of any prosperous society. Even the capacity to trade for manufactured goods requires a thriving manufacturing sector. According to the WTO, only 20 percent of the trade among the regions of the world is in services; the rest is in merchandise. So, even though 65 percent of the U.S. economy is part of the nongovernmental service economy, most of that output cannot be traded for foreign manufacturing goods.[11] Indeed, the U.S. trade deficit that threatens the value of the dollar cannot be closed unless manufacturing activity is increased.

This imbalance occurs because services usually involve the act of *using* manufactured goods, which can only be done on-site. Thus, a solar panel is installed and maintained by service personnel; a salesperson might sell the panel to the homeowner after he/she saw an advertisement; a trucker might bring the panel to the home after various office services such as accounting have been involved. All of these services added together might yield many more jobs and much more economic activity than the manufacture of the solar panels in the first place. But the services are all dependent on the manufactured solar panels, and technological advances in the manufacture of the solar panels can have large effects on the employment possibilities of the industry.

Manufacturing the solar panels also brings about the need for services at various stages of the production process, such as in research, design and marketing. Most importantly, however, the solar panels themselves are built with parts that have been produced using industrial machinery. These various kinds of industrial machinery, such as machine tools or silicon-purification equipment, have their own "ecosystems" of services and manufacturing attached to them. And this industrial machinery has a unique aspect: It can be used for all manufacturing industries, which in their turn spawn the rest of the services that make up the economy.

Thus, manufacturing solar panels not only makes the various service jobs such as installation possible, it also provides a market for the very core of the economic ecosystem: The various industrial machineries that in turn are used to produce the goods and services that power the entire economy.

Now consider how this process takes place when making wind turbines, trains, building materials, geothermal heat pumps or gardening tools. Not only are the millions of service jobs associated with these technologies expanded as green industries grow, the entire industrial machinery core of the system could be rebuilt in the United States. This provides a short-term boost to the economy, but more importantly, it creates the long-term foundation of economic reconstruction that can help rebuild the middle class, move people out of poverty and create a prosperous society for the foreseeable future.[12]

In sum, a green-collar jobs program can achieve a carbon-free inter-city and intra-city transportation system supported by walkable urbanism, a carbon-free energy system based on buildings, metropolitan areas and a national grid, and a sustainable agricultural and manufacturing system. New federal policies can move us, now, in the direction of a society in which *all* jobs are green-collar.

Resources

Apollo Alliance: http://www.apolloalliance.org
Architecture 2030: http://www.architecture2030.org
BlueGreen Alliance: http://www.bluegreenalliance.org
Center for a New Urbanism: http://www.cnu.org
Earth Policy Institute: http://www.earth-policy.org
Ella Baker Center for Human Rights: http://www.ellabakercenter.org
Energy Bulletin: http://www.EnergyBulletin.net
Green for all: http://www.greenforall.org
Grist Magazine: http://www.grist.org
Institute for Food and Development Policy: http://www.foodfirst.org
Light Rail Now: http://www.lightrailnow.org
Local Power: http://www.localpower.com
The Oil Drum: http://www.theoildrum.com
Sustainable South Bronx: http://www.ssbx.org/
World Changing: http://www.worldchanging.com

References

Brown, Lester R. *Plan B 3.0: Mobilizing to Save Civilization.* Third ed. New York: W.W. Norton, 2008.
Jones, Van. *The Future's Getting Restless.* Forthcoming, 2008.
Lipow, Gar W. *Cooling it! No Hair Shirt Solutions to Global Warming.* Self-published at: *http://www.nohairshirts.com/chap0.php* (accessed July 19, 2008).

Notes

1. "Report Card for America's Infrastructure," American Society of Civil Engineers, http://www.asce.org/reportcard/2005/index.cfm (accessed July 20, 2008). Infrastructure refers to large systems in society that support the rest of the economy, such as highways, rails, sewage systems, bridges, electric grids, ports, airports, drinking water, and schools.

2. Infrastructure Packet from Senator Chris Dodd, http://dodd.senate.gov/multimedia/2007/080107_InfrastructurePacket.pdf (accessed July 20, 2008).

3. Allison L. C. de Cerreño, Daniel M. Evans, and Howard Permut, "High-Speed Rail Projects in the United States: Identifying the Elements for Success," Mineta Transportation Institute, College of Business, San José State University, (October 2005) Report 05-01.

4. See the many Walkable Urbanism Reports at the Brookings Institution: http://www.brookings.edu/topics/walkable-urbanism.aspx (accessed July 20, 2008).

5. I show how this can be done with geothermal heat pumps and rooftop solar photovoltaics in the promotional issue of CitiesGoGreen.com, "How Cities Can Elimi-

nate Coal-Based Electricity in the U.S.," http://www.nxtbook.com/nxtbooks/verde/cities-gogreen_promo/ (accessed July 20, 2008); "Let Buildings Heat and Cool Themselves," *Grist Magazine,* http://gristmill.grist.org/story/2008/2/18/212538/864 (accessed July 21, 2008). Gar Lipow discusses how to do this with just rooftop solar panels in "Power from Rooftops Could Replace Coal," *Grist Magazine,* http://gristmill.grist.org/story/2008/6/29/ 132129/715 (accessed July 20, 2008); Lester R. Brown discusses the potential of solar thermal energy in *Plan B 3.0: Mobilizing to save civilization.* Third ed. (New York: W.W. Norton, 2008).

6. Van Jones, "Green-Collar Jobs: Energy Bill Includes Christmas Present for Nation's Job Seekers," HuffingtonPost.com, December 21, 2007, http://www.huffington-post.com/van-jones/greencollar-jobs-energy_b_77934.html (accessed July 20, 2008).

7. See Jon Rynn's post: "Oh Say Can I See a CCA," *Grist Magazine,* http://grist-mill.grist.org/story/2008/5/4/16740/63167. For an explanation from the founder of the concept of CCA, see Paul Fenn, "Community Choice Aggregation: A Huge New Opportunity for Energy Sustainability, Security and Competition in an Otherwise Volatile and Polluting Energy Market," http://www.local.org/commchoi.html (accessed July 21, 2008).

8. Gail Tverberg, "The U.S. Electric Grid: Will It Be Our Undoing?" TheOil-Drum.com, May 11, 2008, http://www.theoildrum.com/node/3934 (accessed July 20, 2008); Jason Makansi, *Lights Out: The Electricity Crisis, the Global Economy, and What It Means to You* (New York: Wiley, 2007).

9. For solar, see: "A Solar Grand Plan," *Scientific American,* December 2007, http://www.sciam.com/article.cfm?id=a-solar-grand-plan&page=1 (accessed July 20, 2008). For wind, see the American Wind Energy Association's website, http://www. awea.org/faq/wwt_potential.html (accessed July 20, 2008).

10. William McDonough and Michael Braungart, *Cradle to Cradle: Remaking the Way We Make Things* (New York: North Point Press, 2002).

11. For WTO figures, see "World Trade in Review, 2005," page 21, at http:// www.wto.org/english/res_e/statis_e/its2006_e/its06_overview_e.pdf (accessed July 21, 2008). For services as a percentage of the economy, see "Annual Industry Accounts," Survey of Current Business, February 2008, Table 2.

12. For more on the importance of manufacturing and machinery, see Jon Rynn's articles: "Grow Locally, Manufacture Locally," *Grist,* http://gristmill.grist.org/story/ 2007/10/29/193440/07 (accessed July 22, 2008); "Growing Pains: Why Ecology Explains Growth, and Economists Don't," *Grist,* http://gristmill.grist.org/story/2007/12/12/ 204059/42 (accessed July 21, 2008); "Rebuild the Economy by Building Green Industries: The Economy is an Ecosystem," *Grist,* http://gristmill.grist.org/story/2007/12/2/ 172147/145 (accessed July 21, 2008).

Chapter 19

Advancing Women's Equality

Kim Gandy

POLICY PROPOSALS

■ Increase the economic advancement of women through policies promoting workplace equality and educational opportunity.

■ Secure economic justice for poor and other vulnerable and underserved women; repair the safety net and give women a clear path to lift themselves and their families out of poverty.

■ Guarantee full access to reproductive health care services that include prenatal care, maternal health care, birth control, emergency contraception and abortion.

■ Move the United States to a leadership position in the effort to end violence against women and girls; increase anti-violence funding, and hold public and private leaders accountable for enforcing zero tolerance for violence.

■ Validate women's civil and human right to be free from discrimination based on gender, race, ethnicity, religion, disability, sexual orientation or identity; ensure a judiciary that will protect these rights.

■ Initiate a major campaign to change societal attitudes that stereotype and constrain women and girls, denouncing the "soft hate speech" on the airwaves, in classrooms and workplaces, and on city streets, that targets and demeans women.

* * * * * * * * * * * * * * *

Over the past century, the role and status of women in the United States and around the world has changed dramatically. Women won the right to vote and secured other legal rights (such as the right to own property and make contracts) that seem unquestionable now. Women's reproductive autonomy was asserted through Supreme Court decisions *Griswold v. Connecticut* in 1965 and *Roe v. Wade* in 1973. Violence against women, including domestic violence and marital rape, were exposed as the serious crimes they are. Sexual harassment and other forms of workplace discrimination were identified as forms of injustice.

A greater proportion of women attended college, earned advanced degrees, joined the paid labor force and entered fields traditionally reserved for men. More women now serve in the U.S. Congress than ever before, and Speaker of the House Rep. Nancy Pelosi is currently the top elected woman in U.S. history. The glass ceiling of the U.S. Presidency has yet to be broken, but this year Sen. Hillary Rodham Clinton came closer to winning a major party nomination for President than any woman candidate before her.

Despite this undeniable progress, gender inequality remains. And, in some cases, the United States has taken steps backward. The George W. Bush Administration has been a disaster for women. So, in addition to looking forward, we must undo the harm of the past eight years.

As we do so, we must keep in mind that sex-based discrimination is compounded by other forms of discrimination against women of color; poor and low-income women; lesbian, bisexual and transgender women; women with disabilities; immigrant women; older women; and even girls, who have fewer rights but nonetheless need protection. Equality must reach all women and girls.

End the Discrimination that Limits Women's Advancement

Women in the United States are still paid only 77 cents for every dollar paid to men, and progress in closing the gender wage gap has slowed considerably since 1990.[1] Women of color are short-changed even more, with African-American women paid only 72 cents and Latinas just 60 cents for every dollar aid to men.[2] This pay disparity affects women from the day they enter the workforce straight through to retirement, with the average woman losing hundreds of thousands of dollars in wages and benefits during her lifetime. Unequal pay hurts women's ability to save for a home, for medical emergencies, for their children's education and for retirement.

Outright discrimination plays a large part in this gap. Even after controlling for experience, training, hours, occupation, parenthood and other factors commonly associated with pay, college-educated women still earn less than their male peers, and this gap may worsen over time.[3]

The incoming U.S. President can tackle this issue head-on by urging Congress to re-introduce legislation such as the Lilly Ledbetter Fair Pay Restoration Act and the Harkin-Norton Fair Pay Act, designed to prevent and remedy pay discrimination. With a President poised to sign such legislation into law, we could witness real progress in this area.

The incoming Administration can promote a family-friendly workplace with legislation expanding the Family and Medical Leave Act, and promoting paid sick days; flexible work schedules; proportional pay and benefits for part-time and seasonal workers; affordable, quality child care; and high-quality, universal pre-K, kindergarten and after-school programs.

We need more effective enforcement of Title VII and other laws prohibiting sexual harassment, discrimination in hiring and promotion, pregnancy discrimination, and "maternal profiling" or family responsibility discrimination. Increased funding, not privatization, is needed for the EEOC and other agencies charged with enforcing those laws.

The Bush Administration's war on Title IX equal education laws, and regulatory changes advancing sex segregation in public schools must be halted and reversed. Finally, women are lagging far behind men in the lucrative STEM fields (science, technology, engineering and math), earning only 20–25 percent of degrees in physics, computer sciences and engineering, and the culture in STEM fields continues to isolate and exclude girls and women.[4] A President who understands both discrimination and the need for international competitiveness will tackle this challenge.

Remove the Roadblocks to Economic Security for Women

With the wage gap, pregnancy discrimination, job segregation, challenges of work/family balance and other roadblocks to economic security for women, it makes sense that the face of U.S. poverty is disproportionately female: More than 20 million women live in poverty, compared with 16 million males.[5] Female-headed households with no spouse present experience a far higher poverty rate than married-couple or male-headed households.

Twenty-eight percent of families headed by women, more than 4 million, are living in poverty, and they struggle to get by. Poverty rates for people of color also are notably higher than the average,[6] and so women of color are doubly-burdened. A family illness, disability, job loss or retirement can push a woman even further into economic peril. These women are hanging on to the edges of society, with a shredded safety net beneath them.

The incoming President must do all he can to help women make ends meet and eventually lift their families out of poverty. For families on public assistance, the incoming Administration should endorse subsidized child care for women transitioning to education, job training and employment; realistic work expectations in light of available child care; expanded housing, transportation and nutritional assistance; and much more.

If we are to have economic justice, passage of a true "living wage" must be on the table, as well as universal health care and recognition of the unpaid caregiving that is so necessary to many of our families. The demonizing of poor women must stop, starting with genuinely compassionate leadership from the top.

Reproductive Health Care is Essential to Women's Lives

The single most important thing the incoming President could do is ensure that every person in the United States has comprehensive health care, which must cover all reproductive services for women, including contraceptives, abortion, maternity care and birthing options. A single-payer system is the ideal way to accomplish this goal; the incoming President should work to gain public and Congressional support for such a plan.

Just as any other safe and effective medical procedure, treatment or drug, reproductive services should be available and affordable to all of the 61 million U.S. women who are of child-bearing age.[7] Reproductive health should be a national priority, and health care that is first-rate must not put limits on the safe medical options of the woman or her doctor.

The Supreme Court said in *Planned Parenthood v. Casey*: "The ability of women to participate equally in the economic and social life of the Nation has been facilitated by their ability to control their reproductive lives."[8] Indeed, the ability to plan one's family—deciding whether and when to have children—is at the very heart of women's autonomy and ultimate equality. Each year, more than 6 million women become pregnant in the United States.[9] Close to half of those pregnancies are unintended, with 1.21 million resulting in abortions.[10]

Reproductive self-determination, or the lack thereof, plays a large role in women's economic security and promise. While pregnancy and motherhood don't always or entirely derail women's efforts to seek education, training and job advancement, they negatively impact women's earning potential,[11] while parenthood has a negligible effect on men's earnings.

Globally, an estimated 230 million women do not have information about or access to safe and reliable contraception, contributing to the more than 80 million annual unplanned pregnancies worldwide.[12] Real women make up these statistics, and the Bush Administration has undercut them at every turn. Just as George W. Bush signed a global gag rule into effect on his first full day in office, denying family planning funds to any overseas clinic that provides abortion or even information about abortion (even if they use separate, locally-raised funds), the incoming President should reverse it at once, restoring these life-saving funds to programs around the world. Similarly, the president should immediately reinstate U.S. contributions to the United Nations Population Fund (UNFPA).

Other steps the incoming Administration could take would be to swiftly restore affordable birth control in the United States by issuing a regulation that would correct the pricing problem created by the Deficit Reduction Act; and to help position the United States as a leader in reproductive justice for women by: signaling its support for the Freedom of Choice Act; ending funding for abstinence-only education in public schools; urging the Food and Drug Administration to remove age barriers on over-the-counter access to emergency contraception; working to eliminate pharmacist refusal clauses regarding contraception;

restoring previously cut Medicaid funds; and pushing for repeal of the Hyde Amendment , which routinely denies access to safe and legal abortion to women disproportionately women of color who depend on government health coverage.

Violence Continues to Limit Women's Lives and Opportunities

Violence against women and girls takes many forms, including: partner violence, rape, trafficking, child marriage, "honor" killings, sexual violence as a weapon of war, femicide, forced sterilization, sexual harassment, stalking, emotional abuse and more.[13]

The statistics paint a grim picture. The National Violence Against Women Survey found that violence against women in the United States is primarily intimate partner violence: 64 percent of the women who reported being raped, physically assaulted, and/or stalked since age eighteen were victimized by a current or former husband, co-habiting partner, boyfriend or date. More than half (54 percent) of female survivors were younger than age eighteen when they experienced their first attempted or completed rape.[14]

Breaking the cycle of violence will be a critical mission of the incoming Administration. Since its enactment in 1994, the Violence Against Women Act (VAWA) has had a notable impact on domestic violence, rape and killings by intimate partners.[15] However, VAWA's full potential remains unmet. The incoming President should call for full funding and enhancement of the Act.

Violence against women in the military, particularly rape, sexual assault and gender-based harassment, is a growing problem.[16] Bringing our troops home from Iraq should be a first priority of the incoming President, but that will not repair a military culture built on dominance above all. Military women must be able to report these crimes without fear of reprisal, and with the knowledge that swift and just action will be taken. This directive must come from the Commander-in-Chief who must insist on zero tolerance.

The incoming President should also push for Congress to add the categories of gender (actual or perceived), sexual orientation, disability and gender identity to those already protected under hate crimes legislation.

There is so much more that an Administration genuinely committed to ending violence against women and girls could do, including working diplomatically with our allies around the globe to put a stop to sex trafficking, femicide, "honor" killings, child marriage, forced marriage and mass rape as a weapon in armed conflict.

Our Country Must Recognize Women's
Civil and Human Rights

Validating women's civil and human rights would be a major step in demonstrating to the world that the United States is moving in the right direction after eight regressive years.

CEDAW—the United Nations Convention on the Elimination of All Forms of Discrimination Against Women—is an international treaty that was adopted by the United Nations in 1979.[17] The United States is the world's only developed nation that has not ratified the treaty, and women worldwide say that U.S. failure to ratify is an impediment to their own use of the treaty. The incoming President should work with the Senate leadership to move CEDAW to the front of its agenda and schedule a vote for ratification.

The incoming Administration should also take the lead in advancing Constitutional equality for women—most commonly referred to as the Equal Rights Amendment or Women's Equality Amendment. Many people are not aware that women's equal rights under the law are not fully guaranteed in the U.S. Constitution, and a sizeable number believe the ERA was ratified years ago (which it was not, despite a spirited and valiant effort by women's rights supporters).

With a President willing to stand up to the opponents of Constitutional equality, disregarding their irrational arguments based on ignorance and fear, the United States could at last move forward on this most essential element of women's equality.

Formally validating women's civil and human rights will not happen overnight, nor will it be enough. The incoming President also must be committed to selecting judicial nominees who will recognize women's right to equality and autonomy.

Societal Attitudes, Bolstered by Media, Hold Women Back

Even in the twenty-first century, we cannot escape embedded societal notions—with their sex-based stereotypes and traditional gender roles—conventions that tell us what women can or can't do, should or shouldn't do. Many assumptions and expectations about the sexes remain, and they are re-inforced through custom, habit and fear of change, as well as by those with an interest in perpetuating the status quo.

In this case the tools are the media and popular culture, and the message is one of "soft hate speech" directed at women and girls, people of color, immigrants, people with disabilities anyone who is supposedly different from the norm. And the norm, around which all "others" pivot, continues to be white and male—preferably young, macho and on the hunt for sexual conquest.

Some might argue that these informal, more subtle forms of oppression are of minor importance. But the media and pop culture may in fact be the most insidious delivery systems and breeding grounds for sexism because of their ubiquity and shrewd marketing.

The incoming President could make an unprecedented impact on this issue, and on generations of women and girls. The country is ripe for a dialogue on sexism, racism, homophobia and the other -isms that separate people and hold them back. The President should address this issue in his first State of the Union address, and speak out in no uncertain terms against: hateful bigots on talk radio; the exploitation of women in all genres of music; violence against women on TV and in the movies; a male sports culture that often trades on slurs against women; advertising that promotes unrealistic and unhealthy beauty standards for girls and women; and a patriarchal system that is built on selling women a concept of "femininity" that it simultaneously defines as demeaning.

There's So Much More to Do

The six issues addressed in this chapter and the policy proposals covered within each issue are critical to advancing women's equality. But they do not represent the complete picture. Women's empowerment is a complex and expansive issue that could fill volumes. We can only recommend that the incoming Administration take women into account when implementing any and all of the proposals put forth in the other chapters of this book.

References

Abortion and Reproductive Rights, National Organization for Women subject index: http://www.now.org/issues/abortion/

American Association of University Women Educational Foundation, "Behind the Pay Gap," April 2007: http://www.aauw.org/research/behindPayGap.cfm

Convention on the Elimination of All Forms of Discrimination against Women (CEDAW), Office of the United Nations High Commissioner for Human Rights: http://www2.ohchr.org/english/law/cedaw.htm

Education and Title IX, National Organization for Women, subject index: http://www.now.org/issues/title_ix/index.html

Guttmacher Institute, "An Overview of Abortion in the United States," January 2008: http://www.guttmacher.org/media/presskits/2005/06/28/abortionoverview.html

Institute for Women's Policy Research, "The Gender Wage Ratio: Women's and Men's Earnings," February 2008: http://www.iwpr.org/pdf/C350.pdf

Media Activism, National Organization for Women: http://www.now.org/issues/
    media/index.html
National Abortion Federation, "United Nations Population Fund": https://www.
    prochoice.org/policy/international/unfpa.html
National Campaign To Prevent Teen and Unplanned Pregnancy, "Teen Preg-
    nancy—So What?" October 2006: http://www.teenpregnancy.org/whycare/
    sowhat.asp
National Coalition for Women and Girls in Education. "Title IX at 35: Beyond
    the Headlines," January 2008: http://www.ncwge.org/PDF/TitleIXat35.pdf
National Institute of Justice, Office of Justice Programs, U.S. Department of
    Justice and the Centers for Disease Control and Prevention, "Full Report of
    the Prevalence, Incidence, and Consequences of Violence Against Women;
    Findings From the National Violence Against Women Survey," November
    2000: http://www.ncjrs.gov/pdffiles1/nij/183781.pdf
NOW and Economic Justice, National Organization for Women, subject index:
    http://www.now.org/issues/economic/
NOW and Violence Against Women, National Organization for Women, subject
    index: http://www.now.org/issues/title_ix/index.html
*Sex, Stereotypes and Beauty: The ABCs and Ds of Commercial Images of
    Women,* NOW Foundation: http://www.nowfoundation.org/sexbeauty
United Nations Population Fund, "Can You Name 16 Forms of Gender-Based
    Violence?": http://www.unfpa.org/16days/

Notes

1. Institute for Women's Policy Research, "The Gender Wage Ratio: Women's and
Men's Earnings," February 2008. http://www.iwpr.org/pdf/C350.pdf (accessed July 19,
2008).
    2. "It's Time for Working Women to Earn Equal Pay," AFL-CIO, 2007, http://
www.aflcio.org/issues/jobseconomy/women/equalpay/ (accessed July 19, 2008).
    3. "Behind the Pay Gap," American Association of University Women Educational
Foundation, April 2007, http://www.aauw.org/research/behindPayGap.cfm (accessed July
19, 2008).
    4. National Coalition for Women and Girls in Education, "Title IX at 35: Beyond the
Headlines," January 2008, http://www.ncwge.org/PDF/TitleIXat35.pdf (accessed July 19,
2008).
    5. U.S. Bureau of the Census, Current Population Survey, Annual Social and Eco-
nomic Supplements, "Historical Poverty Tables - Table 7," 2006, http://www.census.gov/
hhes/www/poverty/histpov/hstpov7.html (accessed July 19, 2008).
    6. Carmen DeNavas-Walt, et al., "Income, Poverty, and Health Insurance Coverage
in the United States: 2006," U.S. Census Bureau, Current Population Reports, http://
www.census.gov/prod/2007pubs/p60-233.pdf (accessed July 19, 2008).
    7. U.S. Department of Commerce, Economics and Statistics Administration, U.S.
Census Bureau, "Fertility of American Women: June 2004," December 2005, http://
www.census.gov/prod/2005pubs/p20-555.pdf (accessed July 19, 2008).

8. Planned Parenthood of Southeastern Pa. v. Casey, 505 U.S. 833 (1992).

9. U.S. Department of Health and Human Services, CDC National Center for Health Statistics, "Estimated Pregnancy Rates by Outcome for the United States, 1990-2004," http://www.cdc.gov/nchs/pressroom/08newsreleases/pregnancydrop.htm (accessed July 19, 2008).

10. Guttmacher Institute, "An Overview of Abortion in the United States," January 2008, http://www.guttmacher.org/media/presskits/2005/06/28/abortionoverview.html (accessed July 19, 2008).

11. The National Campaign To Prevent Teen and Unplanned Pregnancy, "Teen Pregnancy—So What?" October 2006, http://www.teenpregnancy.org/whycare/sowhat.asp (accessed July 19, 2008).

12. National Abortion Federation, "United Nations Population Fund," https://www.prochoice.org/policy/international/unfpa.html (accessed July 19, 2008).

13. United Nations Population Fund, "Can You Name 16 Forms of Gender-Based Violence?" http://www.unfpa.org/16days/ (accessed July 19, 2008).

14. National Institute of Justice, Office of Justice Programs, U.S. Department of Justice and the Centers for Disease Control and Prevention, "Full Report of the Prevalence, Incidence, and Consequences of Violence Against Women. Findings From the National Violence Against Women Survey," November 2000, http://www.ncjrs.gov/pdffiles1/nij/183781.pdf (accessed July 19, 2008).

15. U.S. Senator for Delaware Joe Biden, "Domestic Violence," http://biden.senate.gov/issues/issue/?id=975b0cf4-ce25-42cc-b63d-072fb81e8618 (accessed July 19, 2008).

16. USA Today, "Mental Toll of War Hitting Female Servicemembers," January 2008, http://www.usatoday.com/news/nation/2008-01-01-womenvets_N.htm (accessed July 19, 2008).

17. Office of the United Nations High Commissioner for Human Rights, "Convention on the Elimination of All Forms of Discrimination against Women," http://www2.ohchr.org/english/law/cedaw.htm (accessed July 19, 2008).

Chapter 20

Strengthening Families and Creating Pathways to Opportunity

Alan W. Houseman

POLICY PROPOSALS

- Create a guarantee for child care for all families at or below 200 percent of poverty and include substantial new funds to help states improve the quality of child care and to remove barriers to access for underserved families.
- Reverse funding cut to the Child Support Program and require distribution of all child support collected to families and children.
- Adopt realistic child support policies for low-income, non-custodial fathers and expand assistance to low-income fathers to strengthen families.
- Improve Temporary Assistance for Needy Families Program (TANF) and other safety-net programs so that all families have necessary works supports and TANF focuses on positive outcomes for families and reducing poverty.
- Improve the child welfare system so that we do as much to prevent child abuse and neglect as we do to ameliorate the harm of such maltreatment.
- Transform and fund at a scale comparable to the GI Bill workforce education and training programs to help low-skill, low-income individuals advance economically, increase our nation's productivity and secure a better future for children.
- Provide government leadership to improve job quality in terms of wages, benefits, paid leave, and predictable and responsive schedules so that workers can meet both work and family responsibilities and advance to new challenges.

■ **Invest in building the youth service delivery capacity in communities of
high youth distress to reconnect disconnected youth.**

*   *   *   *   *   *   *   *   *   *   *   *   *   *   *

The incoming Administration and Congress will face three major policy challenges as they consider how to improve the lives of low-income families.

First, our safety net is not working. It is a patchwork of outmoded, uncoor-
dinated policies that leave out too many vulnerable people. It often fails to meet
basic needs, reward work, or strengthen families and communities. It is crisis-
driven rather than prevention-focused. We need a strong and modernized safety
net that includes a system of benefits that are easy to access, unstigmatized, responsive to economic hardship, open to immigrants, and fully funded; and we
need a continuum of preventive family-support services that reduce the need for
more intensive services. Such a safety net leads to adults who can contribute to
society and the economy, and children and youth who are equipped to learn and
achieve their full potential—bolstering individuals and families who face
heightened risk in a global economy.

Second, far too many children are not safe and well cared for, and far too
many live in areas of concentrated, persistent poverty. Far too many families
lack the basic supports they need to help their children grow up healthy, secure
and prepared to succeed. It is time to make an increased investment in proven
programs that concretely help children, youth and families thrive.

Third, prosperity is fragile and not permanent for too many working families. Today's job market is filled with poor-quality jobs, many offering little
opportunity for advancement. Our nation is not equipping people with skills to
succeed or to serve the needs of employers in a changing economy. It is time to
build supportive pathways to good jobs that sustain families and communities,
and to ensure that better jobs are available for everyone seeking work. We need
to improve the skills and incomes of low-income youth and adults, and build
pathways to reconnect our more vulnerable and disconnected individuals—high
school dropouts, people leaving prison, returning veterans, low-skilled immigrants. In addition, we need to create more equitable labor markets, not only
with respect to wages but also with respect to job schedule, sick pay and work
leave.

The family policy of the incoming Administration can address these three
fundamental policy challenges by improving key family-support programs.

Improving Child Care

With four out of ten children under age six living in low-income households
(under 200 percent of poverty) and facing multiple risk factors that affect their

chances for success in later life, investments in young children are increasingly important. Decades of research confirm that high-quality child care and early education can improve outcomes for children, particularly low-income children. High-quality early learning experiences, which support the full range of children's development, promote child well-being and help build solid foundations for future learning and success in life. Parents also benefit when they have access to reliable, affordable, quality child care that allows them to work to support their families. Research shows that investments in child care assistance make a significant difference in the economic health and security of families by helping families move out of poverty, sustain their participation in the workforce, and limit instability in care arrangements that can impact work.

Across the country, business leaders, economists, neuroscientists, researchers and policy experts alike have championed the importance of investing in quality early childhood programs for our nation's youngest children. From longitudinal studies showing positive outcomes for children into adulthood, to economic impact studies, a broad consensus of support for early investments has emerged. Yet few children have access to the help they need: Only one in seven federally-eligible children receives child care assistance; approximately half of eligible children are receiving Head Start services; and only 3 percent of eligible children participate in Early Head Start. Current rules in states make it difficult for families to get and keep child care assistance—some studies suggest that many families maintain their assistance for as few as three months at a time. Yet even when families get help paying for child care, there is very little high-quality care available, especially for infants and toddlers, children with special needs, families in rural areas and those living in very poor communities.

Using the reauthorization of the Child Care and Development Block Grant as a vehicle for change, Congress and the incoming Administration should act to create a guarantee for child care assistance to all working families at or below 200 percent of the federal poverty level. This will guarantee a stable funding stream for states and will eliminate long waiting lists in many states, as well as eliminate the many different eligibility rules and requirements that exist. It will also make it easier for families to access and maintain the child care assistance they need to work.

At the same time, federal policymakers can signal a real commitment to supporting the healthy development of young children by helping states expand their investments in quality initiatives, such as those that increase training, education and compensation for all care-givers; expand licensing requirements and increase monitoring to ensure that all children in care are safe; increase access to screening and developmental assessments; and target assistance to children and providers who are limited English proficient.

Improving Child Support

The child support program is an essential family support program intended to ensure families' self-sufficiency by making child support a more reliable source of income. Child support both reduces child poverty and is the backbone of family budgets of poor families. The program serves 17 million children and collects $25 billion every year in support paid for children by their non-custodial parents. The program secures more cash to more working families than almost any other family assistance program—of the $25 billion collected, $23 billion in private child support payments goes to working families every year. However, the effectiveness of the child support program is jeopardized by a 20 percent cut in federal funds included in the Deficit Reduction Act (DRA) of 2005. If these cuts continue, the Congressional Budget Office projects that $11 billion in support will go uncollected over the next ten years. Therefore it is critical that the incoming Administration leads the effort to repeal the 20 percent DRA child support funding cut and instead increase child support program funding.

Originally, the child support program was established to recover state and federal welfare costs, and the state continues to withhold $2 billion in support payments owed to current and former TANF families. *All* collected child support should go to families and children. The incentive to pay child support is greater when non-custodial parents know that their payment is going to their child, rather than being retained by the state. To be a truly effective family support program, the incoming Administration and other federal policymakers should mandate full family distribution and eliminate cost recovery policies in the federal TANF and foster care programs.

Assisting Low-Income Fathers

Compliance with support orders is strongly linked to ability to pay. Yet, because of state policies and practices, low-income fathers, including those who leave prison, often have child support orders that do not reflect their ability to pay. Parents who cannot keep up with their child support obligations fall deeply into debt. Fathers who see no end in sight to their child support debt have fewer reasons to maintain steady employment in the formal economy, to comply with such orders in the future, or to cooperate with the child support system—particularly when their children will not see the money. Parents who comply with realistic child support obligations are more likely to remain employed and have stronger family relationships. Therefore, the incoming Administration should lead the effort to adopt realistic child support policies for the lowest income fathers that will help make work pay, including early intervention processes; fair orders; more reasonable income-withholding levels; more effective modification procedures; and debt reduction policies.

We simply have failed to set up effective systems for delivery of services to low-income fathers in the communities in which they reside. Low-income fathers have limited access to EITC, TANF and publicly-funded health coverage; are often disconnected from domestic violence and marriage programs; and are not engaged in child welfare placement decisions. Therefore, the incoming Administration should expand funding to programs that help low-income men get jobs to support themselves and their children; expand community-based service delivery capacity to assist low-income fathers; build a network of work supports for low-income fathers, including expanding access to and increasing the benefits under the EITC; and integrate family assistance programs to make benefits and services available to fathers as well as mothers.

Improving TANF and Work Supports

From 1996, the year TANF replaced AFDC, to 2004, the share of eligible families receiving assistance from the program fell by half, from 84 percent to 42 percent. Over that same period, the real value of the basic TANF block grant has declined 28 percent due to inflation. The share of single mothers who are employed has increased dramatically, but they have joined a labor market full of low-wage jobs that do not provide enough income to make ends meet and that often force workers to choose between their jobs and their responsibilities as parents. Work supports help bridge the gap between labor market income and basic needs, but too many working families are denied assistance due to funding limitations or barriers to participation, or lose benefits before their paychecks are enough to cover their needs. At the same time, the share of low-income single mothers who neither work nor receive cash assistance has grown steadily, and is now more than 20 percent.

The incoming President should appoint a commission to evaluate the full range of work-support/safety-net programs, identify the gaps and ways to improve them. Because many of the "disconnected" appear to be falling in the gap between a work-focused TANF program and the requirement that individuals be completely and permanently unable to work in order to qualify for SSI, a subgroup should focus on the specific needs of individuals with disabilities.

TANF will need to be reauthorized in 2010. The last reauthorization, part of the Deficit Reduction Act, forced states to focus almost exclusively on meeting a strict work participation requirement for families receiving assistance. The Bush Administration has used both regulations and subregulatory guidance to further restrict state flexibility. In particular, these policies have made it hard for states to allow recipients to participate in education and training, or to make appropriate accommodations for individuals with disabilities, as required under the Americans with Disabilities Act.

Therefore, the incoming Administration should lead an effort as part of TANF reauthorization to give states more flexibility to develop welfare-to-work programs that meet the needs of a diverse group of recipients; engage participants in skill-building activities; and shift the focus from work participation rates to outcomes and poverty reduction. The incoming Administration should solicit both written feedback and participation at town meetings or listening sessions, with explicit and visible invitations to states and advocates to participate, leading up to development of principles and a vision for reauthorization.

Improving the Child Welfare System

Prevention is the best way to accomplish the sometimes conflicting goals of keeping children safe and avoiding the trauma of being separated from one's parents, but the nation's child welfare system has traditionally focused much more on intervening after maltreatment occurs. The bulk of federal funds pay for foster care room and board as well as adoption subsidies for the small fraction of children removed from their homes—about one-fifth of the substantiated victims. Almost 40 percent of children whom we know to be abused and neglected get no help at all, not foster care, not counseling, nothing. Even for those in foster care, federal support is inadequate. Only about half of such children are eligible for federal foster care payments. Only one-quarter of children in foster care receive mental health services. Many grandparents and other relatives are willing to provide a loving home for struggling children, but these relatives frequently need help to meet the children's needs, and too often federal policies prevent them from accessing assistance. There are many dedicated child welfare staffers, but they lack adequate training and experience—less than two years on average—and juggle too large caseloads that prevent them from spending the necessary time with the children and families in their charge. Even when families' needs are identified, caseworkers are often unable to connect them with services because the services simply do not exist.

The incoming Administration and Congress must better target the use of federal child welfare funds and significantly increase investments in child welfare services. Only then can the nation reduce the incidence of maltreatment; reduce the trauma to children who do experience abuse or neglect; empower parents to care for their children when possible and provide alternative, loving homes for children whose parents cannot care for them. We must develop and sustain a continuum of services and supports and must ensure coordinated and integrated service provision across programs and systems. In addition to room and board, federal foster care funds should be available to provide needed prevention programs, treatment services and aftercare supports. These funds should be available to support all maltreated children, regardless of the income of their abusive or neglectful parents. Federal adoption assistance funds should also be available for guardianship subsidies so that more children can live permanently with relatives for whom adoption is not an appropriate option. Indian tribes should have direct access to federal foster care and adoption assistance funds to care for children in their charge. The training and casework of all child welfare staff, including those in private agencies, should be supported by federal and state governments. Finally, child welfare agencies and officials should be more accountable—both for how they utilize federal child welfare funds and for the outcomes children and families experience.

Improving Workforce Education and Training Programs

A strong workforce and education system is critical to ensuring that low-income individuals are able to secure stable employment in jobs that pay family support-ing wages, and that American businesses have access to workers with the skills they need in order to compete in the global economy. Unfortunately, the current system is too fragmented and underfunded to accomplish these goals. The in-coming Administration and Congress should align adult education, job training and higher education policies to create pathways to the post-secondary educa-tional credentials that are increasingly the door to the middle class, and stable employment in jobs that pay family-sustaining wages. Workforce development, economic development and community development should also be aligned to ensure that low-income populations benefit from the engines of economic growth and share in our nation's prosperity.

Through reauthorization of the Workforce Investment Act, English as a Second Language (ESL) and GED-oriented adult education programs should be refocused on promoting transitions to post-secondary education and training; and workforce investment programs that currently emphasize rapid labor market attachment should be refocused on developing education and training pathways from low-wage to high-skilled jobs and implementing transitional jobs programs that help individuals address barriers to employment and get connected to jobs. Federal policies should enhance the capacity of institutions and providers to foster community partnerships and to promote connections to necessary income and other supports that enable low-income youth and adults to succeed in educa-tion, training and work.

Program transformation should be coupled with vastly increased investment in reauthorized workforce and education programs. The incoming Administra-tion and Congress should put adult education funding on a long-term path that substantially expands capacity to meet growing need, especially for ESL ser-vices; and increase funding for the Pell Grant program to more fully cover col-lege costs and living expenses for the lowest-income students. In addition, the federal government should dedicate a portion of new federal investments in in-frastructure, transportation, the environment and health care to creating training opportunities for low-income populations so that they are prepared to access the newly created jobs.

Improving Job Quality

While skills development is essential for advancing the prospects of low-skill individuals, by itself it is insufficient to expand economic opportunity for low-wage workers and their families. We need to complement efforts to provide education and training so individuals can access better jobs with efforts to overcome discrimination in the labor market, improve bad jobs, and expand the number of good jobs that provide workers with decent wages, benefits, working conditions, a safe and healthy environment, opportunities for advancement and work-life balance. Currently, too many jobs in America pay low wages, offer little opportunity for advancement, and lack benefits and workplace flexibility. The prevalence of poor-quality jobs is a critical issue that deserves government attention.

The incoming Administration should make it a top priority to improve the quality of work for all workers, with a special focus on low-wage workers, since poor-quality jobs are especially prevalent in the low-wage labor market. In 2005, one in four workers was working in poverty-level jobs. The incoming Administration should use the bully pulpit to talk about job quality as important to the American dream, and a complement to a high-road economic growth strategy that will keep America competitive. It should also offer a legislative package aimed at improving jobs, which would include a minimum labor standard that mandates paid sick days, paid family and medical leave, expansions of the Family Medical Leave Act to include employers with fewer than fifty employees, and expand the purposes for which paid leave may be used. The Administration should support enactment of the Employee Free Choice Act, and index the minimum wage to median wages. In addition, jobs created through federal investment in infrastructure, the environment and other areas should meet certain job-quality standards and be subject to targeted hiring requirements. The incoming Administration should also establish a Presidential commission aimed at ensuring equitable treatment of part-time workers regarding pay, benefits and advancement, workplace flexibility and improving low-wage work. Finally, the Administration should create a "Job Quality Czar" at the Department of Labor whose responsibility it will be to work across agencies to improve job quality; make recommendations to policymakers about further legislative action to improve job quality; and report to Congress and the Administration about progress made.

Reconnecting Disconnected Youth

The cycle of intergenerational poverty is perpetuated by the continued challenge of millions of youth who are dropping out of high school and disconnecting from the education and labor market mainstreams, with many falling into harm's way. One in three youth—and more than 50 percent of minority youth—who start high school will not graduate four years later. Each year, nearly a half million youth dropout and join the approximately 3.8 million young people between the ages of sixteen and twenty-four who are out of school and out of work. This problem disproportionately impacts low-income minority communities where youth unemployment is extremely high, where gang participation and youth violence is on the rise, and where approximately one-third of all young black men are involved with the criminal justice system. In past decades there was substantial investment in the youth delivery system that provided opportunities for education credentialing, training, work experience and support for these youth to help them get back on track. The federal youth programs and supports have been all but dismantled over the past ten years through the withdrawal of federal funding and support. There are thus very few pathways that will reconnect these youth to the education, training, and support they will need to become engaged citizens, responsible parents and skilled workers.

A signal from the incoming President and Administration about the importance of re-engaging these youth who are being left behind in the economy can provide visibility and urgency to this issue, and can serve to rally all levels of government and sectors of the community to actively engage in outreach efforts aimed at reconnecting disconnected youth. Changing the landscape for the millions of disconnected youth will require substantially increased federal investment. There are specific actions an incoming Administration and Congress can take to elevate priority and expand investment in programming for this population.

First, Congress should re-establish the Federal Youth Development Council, which was created in federal statute but was never implemented; have it report to a White House Director of Youth Policy; and charge it with the responsibility of advancing strategies for solving the problems that disconnected youth face in the context of our emerging global economy. Second, the Administration, working with Congress, should provide federal funding to help build in a youth service delivery capacity in communities of high youth distress. Similar to the Youth Opportunity Grant Program established under the Workforce Investment Act, this effort should help communities align their education and youth-serving systems and put programs in place, at scale, that connect youth to alternative education, training, work experience, post-secondary school opportunities and jobs. Third, federal investment should be greatly expanded to support opportunities for work experience, internship and civic engagement. This should include funding to local and regional partnerships that engage business, workforce and education systems in creating pathways and bridge programs to prepare out-of-school youth for high-skill, high-wage career opportunities.

Resources

The Center for Law and Social Policy: http://www.clasp.org

References

Albelda, Randy, et al. *Bridging the Gaps: A Picture of How Work Supports Work in Ten States*: http://www.bridgingthegaps.org/publications/national-report.pdf.

Blank, Rebecca M., and Brian K. Kovak. *Helping Disconnected Single Mothers.* National Poverty Center: http://www.npc.umich.edu/publications/policy briefs/ brief10/.

Recommendations of the Partnership to Protect Children and Strengthen Families. Center for Law and Social Policy: http://www.clasp.org/publications/changes_cw_law.pdf.

Strawn, Julie. *Policies to Promote Adult Education and Postsecondary Alignment, prepared for the National Commission on Adult Literacy*. Center for Law and Social Policy (October 2007): http://www.nationalcommissionon adultliteracy.org/content/strawnbriefrev101807.pdf.pdf.

Chapter 21

The "Homosexual Agenda," Revisited

Jaime Grant and Rebecca Sawyer

POLICY PROPOSALS

- **Protect our families.**
  - Create a federal safety net that does not privilege marriage and does not penalize single people.
  - Ensure that the tax code is fair for LGBT individuals and families.
  - Repeal the Defense of Marriage Act; ensure federal recognition and support for LGBT marriages.
  - Promote "permanent partners" legislation and other reform legislation allowing same-sex couples the rights of married opposite-sex couples with respect to immigration of partners/spouses.
  - Remove barriers to granting asylum for LGBT people and those living with HIV.
- **Support our families.**
  - Provide equal access to and coverage of fertility treatments.
  - Provide equal access to adoption and foster care.
  - Through the Family Medical Leave Act, recognize LGBT families and provide funding for leave.
- **Care for our youth.**
  - Stop funding proven failures in sexuality education, especially those that stigmatize and defame LGBT youth, such as abstinence-only approaches.
  - Ensure that LGBT youth have access to supportive, appropriate sexual literacy and education.
  - Create holistic approaches and provide funding to combat the epidemic of LGBT youth homelessness.

195

■ Care for our elders.
  ▪ Extend federal benefits associated with relationship recognition to same-sex couples, ensuring equality in Social Security and Medicare regulations.
  ▪ Allow same-sex couples equal access to shared bedroom facilities and housing in federal- and state-funded housing programs and facilities.
  ▪ Include grandparents who are LGBT or whose children are LGBT in the National Family Caregivers Support Act.
  ▪ Ensure that the federal Older Americans Act and the Administration on Aging include LGBT people as a part of the recognized "Vulnerable Senior Constituencies and Identities" and as those with "Greatest Social Need."
  ▪ Legally ensure that sexual orientation and gender identity categories are included as a designated and mandated component of federally funded aging research and data collection.
  ▪ Officially recognize the impact of HIV and AIDS on all older communities, including its special impact on older adults in the LGBT communities and their care-givers.
■ Increase our economic security.
  ▪ Support affirmative action.
■ Promote an Employment Non-Discrimination Act that covers sexual orientation and gender identity/expression.
  ▪ Create fair policies for LGBT federal employees around employment benefits through the Domestic Partnership Benefits and Obligations Act or similar legislation.
  ▪ Repeal "don't ask, don't tell," providing equal access to the military as an employer for LGBT people.
  ▪ Repeal the Solomon Amendment and allow colleges and universities access to federal funding regardless of their stance on military recruiters on campus.
  ▪ Ensure that job-training is safe and accessible to LGBT people.
  ▪ Provide increased federal funding to make college accessible to poor, working-class and middle-class students.
  ▪ Support "safe schools" legislation and make anti-bullying and anti-hate work in the schools more visible.
■ Protect our health.
  ▪ Every American must have access to health care.
  ▪ Health care parity for mental illness is essential to the health of all citizens.
  ▪ Transgender people must have access to federal, state and private health care programs/insurance for their gender-related health needs, as recommended by the American Medical Association.

- Reproductive justice is central to the well-being of women, men and their families. This entails not only the right to choose parenthood, but the material, social and legal conditions essential to having a breadth of options in creating one's family of choice.
- Internationally, the United States should end its global gag rule on the United States AID Population Program and allow funding for critical reproductive health services, including abortion services and abortion law reform.[1]
- Funding for HIV research, prevention and treatment must be increased; interventions and support for communities hardest hit by the epidemic must be researched, created and widely deployed.

■ Protect our privacy.
  - Social Security records and other federal documents need to be updated to reflect the way people self-identify and express their gender.
  - Repeal the REAL ID Act, which would regulate requirements for state-issued identification cards and mandate that states share their databases.

■ Improve the justice system.
  - Develop a comprehensive program of education and enforcement to end sexual assault and rape of prisoners by staff personnel and other prisoners.
  - House transgender prisoners with their stated gender identity.
  - Enact comprehensive federal hate crimes legislation.

* * * * * * * * * * * * *

Political and legal debates around lesbian, gay, bisexual and transgender (LGBT) rights often center on the two political footballs of the last fifteen years: marriage and the military. However, the issues facing LGBT people extend well beyond the right to marry and the right to serve in our armed forces. From protecting our health to safeguarding our economic security, the vulnerabilities faced by LGBT people involve challenges universal to all Americans, but with the added, specific jeopardy of a people stigmatized and targeted for discrimination because of our sexual orientation and gender identity/expression.

We offer a broad overview of pressing issues for the incoming Administration to review and resolve. Our concerns are as varied and as diverse as our communities, and include universal health care, equitable treatment of LGBT prisoners, affirmative action, reproductive justice, employment non-discrimination, addressing the challenges of aging as an LGBT person, and the creation of a federal safety net that does not privilege married couples over other kinship structures.

We hope to spark not only rich, provocative discussions about the depth and breadth of today's "homosexual agenda," but to lead the way to critical changes, improving the lives of all Americans, regardless of sexual orientation or gender identity/expression.

Our Communities

The religious Right paints a picture of LGBT America as white, male, affluent and sex-obsessed. The scant federal data collected on our community offer a strikingly different portrait. A study on African-American same-sex couples reveals that Black female same-sex couples earn $10,000 less than Black married couples.[2] A similar study on Hispanic and Latino same-sex couples indicates that over half of Hispanic female same-sex couples are raising a child.[3] However, these two studies, based on data from Census 2000, provide limited information on the realities of life as a LGBT Black or Latino person; these studies do not include important information on the economic and social well-being of single LGBT Black and Latino people. Correspondingly, federal health surveys are not inclusive of the health needs of transgender people, while a limited few collect data on the physical and mental health needs of lesbian and bisexual women.

Until LGBT people can build a case for justice via the gold-standard data sets that other communities routinely draw upon to demonstrate their vulnerabilities, the very real harms caused by homophobic, biphobic and transphobic discrimination will continue to be discounted, distorted, and ignored.

How many LGBT individuals are there in the United States? How many LGBT elders lack access to health care? How many of us are homeless and preyed on in the streets? How many transgender Americans face employment discrimination? What set of forces converge to create high rates of HIV infection among Black gay men? What are the social, emotional and material consequences of being targeted as "other" and defined as "less than" by religious figures, policymakers and—in the case of aggressive anti-LGBT ballot measures—a majority of our neighbors and colleagues?

A first, essential step in uncovering and understanding the complexities of LGBT life—including our work lives, health needs, diverse family and kinship structures, racial and cultural legacies, and the outcomes of being targeted for discrimination and public abuse—must be the inclusion of LGBT check-offs and signifiers on key federal survey instruments. Housing, labor statistics, family and social surveys, and health surveys (to name just a few) all offer critical data collection opportunities for the grossly understudied LGBT communities.

Our Families

There appears to be no way to create an LGBT life and escape the profile of depravity and despair defined by politically powerful, moneyed interests in this country. When we choose single life, LGBT singles are portrayed as lonely, depressed and addicted. Making the choice to couple, LGBT partners are seen as either "failing" at commitment, or in the event of undeniably long-term relationships, undeserving of state recognition and support. Finally, LGBT parents are pronounced inherently unfit—a threat to our children and all other children in our midst.

These attitudes seem out of date and even laughable alongside the truth of our rich, varied, thriving contributions to American life. The harsh reality is that current public policy much more closely reflects these dangerous, outrageous prejudices about LGBT people than the widely acknowledged, significant value of our talents and efforts as LGBT workers, neighbors and family members.

As a result, the various ways that LGBT people partner, build communities and build families remain unrecognized and in exile from the benefits and legal rights afforded heterosexual marriage. As a community that has long built our families against all odds, LGBT people have a history of moving beyond a couples-only, nuclear family framework in our kinship structures. Our families take many forms, including:

- a lesbian and a gay male couple raising a child together;
- three same-sex friends and a same-sex couple raising foster children;
- a transgender couple serving as grandparents for a gay man's children;
- two lesbian friends joining forces to help raise one of the women's teenage siblings;
- a lesbian adopting her bisexual partner's child from a former relationship.

U.S. Census findings tell us that a majority of people, regardless of their sexual orientation or gender identity, no longer live in traditional nuclear families. We need to create new forms of legal recognition that address the complexity of our diverse family configurations.

Our Economic Security

Like all people, the foundation of our sense of safety and security lies in our ability to "pursue happiness," including employment in our chosen fields. Economic security for LGBT people requires that we are not thwarted by discrimination in securing the education we need to pursue our dreams, and that the fields we wish to contribute to be open to us.

Our Health

The World Health Organization defines health as not merely the "absence of infirmity and disease, but also a state of physical, mental and social well-being."[4] Thus, ensuring the physical, mental and social well-being of our communities requires access to LGBT-affirming and -inclusive health care. We ground our health approach within the reproductive justice framework, where "reproductive justice exists when all people have the economic, social and political power and resources to make healthy decisions about our gender, bodies and sexuality for ourselves, our families and our communities."[5]

Our Freedoms

Ensuring fundamental freedoms enshrined in the Bill of Rights for all Americans requires laws and policies that recognize and protect freedoms of expression, assembly and religion in the public spheres. Of special meaning in the lives of LGBT people is the enumerated right to privacy, whether in our bedrooms and homes, in transitional shelters or in prison cells. Equally important are privacy rights with regards to transitions of gender, identity and expression.

As recently as 1986, the U.S. Supreme Court in *Bowers v. Hardwick* found no right of privacy to engage in adult, consensual, private homosexual behavior. The Court's decision, while widely scorned in the media as socially out-of-touch, nonetheless upheld state laws that criminalized same-sex sexual behaviors, as well as sexual behaviors enjoyed by hundreds of millions of heterosexual Americans. In upholding these laws, the Court also gave license to the ongoing attacks on LGBT people, through denials of child custody to lesbian mothers and gay male fathers, the refusal to publicly fund AIDS prevention education material, and the denial of recognition to LGBT student groups on college campuses. In 2003, the U.S. Supreme Court reversed its decision in *Bowers v. Hardwick*, striking down anti-sodomy laws and declaring that a Texas law classifying homosexual intercourse as illegal sodomy violated the privacy and liberty of adults to engage in private intimate conduct under the 14th Amendment.

All Americans, but especially LGBT Americans, must have security in fundamental freedoms, but also must live free of hate speech, religious-based persecutions and abuses within the justice system, specifically as it relates to prisoners' rights.

Speech
The incoming Administration should protect LGBT communities from hate speech by speaking out against all campaigns that target LGBT persons for defamation, discrimination, violence and isolation.

Religion
The incoming Administration should recognize that freedom *of* religion necessarily includes freedom *from* religion. Therefore, LGBT exclusions from anti-discrimination practices in hiring for faith-based groups and programs should be halted.

Resources

COLAGE: Children of Lesbians and Gays Everywhere: http://www.colage.org

The Family Equality Council: http://www.familyequality.org

Gay and Lesbian Leadership Institute's Presidential Appointments Project: http://www.glli.org/presidential

Immigration Equality: http://www.immigrationequality.org

International Gay and Lesbian Human Rights Commission: http://www.iglhrc.org

Lambda Legal Defense and Education Fund: www.lambdalegal.org

The National Center for Lesbian Rights: http://www.nclrights.org

The National Center for Transgender Equality: http://www.nctequality.org

The National Gay and Lesbian Task Force: http://www.thetaskforce.org

Queers for Economic Justice: http://qej.tripod.org/qej2

Services and Advocacy for GLBT Elders (SAGE): http://www.sageusa.org

Southerners on New Ground: http://www.southernersonnewground.org

Task Force Policy Institute Reports: http://www.thetaskforce.org/reports_and_research

The Transgender Law and Policy Institute: http://www.transgenderlaw.org

The Williams Institute at UCLA: http://www.law.ucla.edu/williamsinstitute

Notes

1. *The Bush Global Gag Rule: Endangering Women's Health, Free Speech and Democracy*, Retrieved July 8, 2008, from the Center for Reproductive Rights, http://www.reproductiverights.org/pub_fac_ggrbush.html.

2. A. Dang and S. Frazer, *Black Same-Sex Households in the United States: A Report from the 2000 Census* (New York: National Gay and Lesbian Task Force Policy Institute and the National Black Justice Coalition, 2004), p. 16.

3. J. Cianciotto, *Hispanic and Latino Same-Sex Couple Households in the United States: A Report from the 2000 Census* (New York: National Gay and Lesbian Task Force Policy Institute and the National Latino/a Coalition for Justice, 2005), p. 4.

4. *WHO Definition of Health*, Retrieved July 8, 2008, from World Health Organization, http://www.who.int/about/definition/en/print.html.

5. *Welcome!*, Retrieved July 8, 2008, from Asian Communities for Reproductive Justice, http://www.reproductivejustice.org/.

Chapter 22

Promoting Full Participation of People with Disabilities

Nancy Starnes

POLICY PROPOSALS

■ Uphold the Congressional intent of the Americans with Disabilities Act.
■ Staff the U.S. Department of Justice at levels that lead to increased capacity for forceful investigation of discrimination claims.
■ Elevate the focus of the U.S. Commission on Civil Rights to study disability discrimination.
■ Eliminate the "in-home" rule.
■ Provide options for health care and long-term care that support independent living.
■ Fund a program to promote financial literacy for people with disabilities.
■ Eliminate the "cash cliff" that discourages people from seeking paid employment rather than relying on government benefits.
■ Establish new hiring goals for all departments of the U.S. government.
■ Simplify the online application process for government jobs.
■ Promote and fund financial literacy programs for persons with disabilities.
■ Sign the U.S. on to the UN Convention on the Rights of Persons with Disabilities.

* * * * * * * * * * * * * * *

The Americans with Disabilities Act of 1990 (ADA) is the foundation for removing barriers to the contribution of 54 million men, women and children with disabilities who want to play a role in the economic, social and cultural vitality of our nation. The U.S. Department of Justice, Civil Rights Division, is responsible for enforcing the ADA and other federal laws related to discrimination.

The enforcement of civil rights and other laws protecting opportunities for persons with disabilities in employment, housing, education, voting, technology and transportation can minimize the growing number of instances where persons knowingly or unknowingly violate our nation's laws. Department of Justice staffing should include the most talented and knowledgeable career lawyers who will influence these important decisions.

One study highlighted the affronts to civil rights violations in the area of employment. The study showed that plaintiffs with disabilities who took their case to court lost 97 percent of their employment discrimination suits, mostly on the grounds that they do not meet the definition of "disability." Many of the plaintiffs had medical conditions that are clearly covered by the ADA, but they were never even given the chance to demonstrate their ability. A September 2007 U.S. House oversight hearing described the record in this area as "dismal" and "inexcusable."

Elevating the U.S. Commission on Civil Rights to its former level of importance could ensure that enforcement of anti-discrimination laws will be a priority on behalf of all people, including those with disabilities. The Commission's insightful collection and study of data on disability in America today could be both eye-opening and introduce opportunities for corrective action.

Health Care

People with disabilities should have access to affordable, quality health care now and for the future. This includes professional medical services, prescription drugs, physical therapy, mental health services, durable medical equipment and long-term care that maximizes the individual's capacity for independent living.

Preventative measures that promote the highest level of heath and wellness for people with disabilities will pay big dividends for future generations. Promoting personal responsibility for diet and exercise, coupled with clinical knowledge provided by health care professionals, should be one of our top national priorities. The National Center on Physical Activity and Disability (NCPAD) promotes the health benefits that can be gained from participating in regular physical activity. They provide information and resources that encourage *Exercise for EVERY body* and help people with disabilities to become as physically active as they choose to be.

Requiring an individual to remain within the walls of his or her home setting in order to receive benefits and services is an affront to the American dream for people with disabilities and a needless waste of productivity. The opportunities leading to full- or part-time employment, volunteer opportunities or education should not be pitted against one's health or financial well-being.

Medicaid should continue to be a safety net to protect the health of people with disabilities. State Medicaid programs vary in their list of optional services that are tied to matching rates based on per capita personal income. Flexibility in Medicaid benefit packages will help to ensure all participants the most productive lifestyle possible.

Medicare's "in home" rule restricts coverage of mobility devices to those needed for assistance with meal preparation or personal care activities. If the individual needs a mobility device outside of the home for work, school, doctor visits or any other community activity, Medicare determines them ineligible for services. This restriction is inconsistent with initiatives that support independent living in a community setting—i.e., the Olmstead Act, the Ticket-to-Work Program, the New Freedom Initiative and the Americans with Disabilities Act.

Medicare's two-year waiting period for eligibility should be lifted. The cap on therapy services should be lifted. Mobile technology must be accessible and should expand health care into communities and neighborhoods.

There seems to be a bias in our country toward institutional placement of people with disabilities. Last year, 155,272 persons were admitted directly from their home or apartments to a medical institution for long-term care without exploring the independent living option of home health services. They were not admitted as a result of any determination by an acute care hospital, a rehabilitation hospital, another nursing home or an assisted living facility. The average cost of a private nursing home room is $75,000 per year. The cost of a full-time home health aide is $39,500 per year. The potential savings to the state and federal government could foster expanded health care services and the elimination of waiting lists that often are years-long for many individuals. For some, the wait is simply too long, and they are forced to resort to the less desirable institutional setting.

Financial Independence

Americans of all abilities should be supplied with the necessary tools to help manage their current and future financial needs. Resources that promote financial literacy are key to successful planning now and for the future.

The Volunteer Income Tax Assistance (VITA) Program and the Tax Counseling for the Elderly (TCE) Program are funded by the IRS to provide free tax help to low-moderate income people and people age sixty and over. This model should be expanded to help people with disabilities develop, implement and make adjustments as needed to a lifetime financial plan.

People with disabilities who are employed full time should be encouraged to develop a comprehensive financial plan for their eventual retirement. Social Security will no longer be the sole source of income available to meet all of their future needs. Retirement planning for persons with disabilities should begin as early as possible and include a forecast of special needs expenses, such as personal care attendants, home-delivered meals, medical equipment, transportation and private insurance.

Individuals who are unable to work because of their disability and are receiving disability benefits should be counseled on managing fixed incomes.

Employment

Employment is the key to the security and prosperity we all seek. Having a job opens doors to health care, transportation, education, socialization and the full range of issues that currently separate people with and without disabilities. Americans with disabilities can, and want to, work.

Throughout the past twenty years, the National Organization on Disability has tracked this country's progress in closing what it terms the "participation gaps" that exist between our citizens with and without disabilities. Notable progress has been made in seeing that many of the barriers to an inclusive society are coming down. The Americans with Disabilities Act brought about positive changes in physical accessibility to buildings, transportation systems and information systems. It also brought with it the promise to eliminate discrimination in the pursuit of employment, requiring in essence that employers look not at the disability of a person, but at the more important abilities and skills each person brings to the job. There are curb cuts in our city streets that allow people in wheelchairs to participate, and yet the figures on the employment of people with disabilities remain the most intransigent of the participation gaps we follow.

A mere half of one percent of the people receiving disability-related benefits ever return to work. Improving this number should be seen as a paramount concern to the nation as a new Administration enters government.

The NOD/Harris Survey of Americans with Disabilities reports a 43 percentage point gap in the rates of employment for people with disabilities compared to those without. Some two-thirds of that population want to work. Their non-participation in the workforce represents a great cost to our country. Between 1990 and 1999, the federal outlay for public benefits for people with disabilities grew from $3.21 billion to $5.85 billion each month.

The incoming Administration will be faced with a demographically aging population quick to retire en masse, creating a need for 10–15 million new workers for the American economy. Tapping into the vast latent resource of people with disabilities is a most logical response to this societal trend. Telecommuting and assistive technology should be leveraged to support the work life potential of people with disabilities.

Unfortunately, the current system carries with it many outdated policy components that create disincentives, erecting barriers in the way of job-seekers with disabilities. The fear of losing valuable health care benefits, for example, forces many to worry that they must gamble their health if they choose to pursue work. A range of faulty policies, including Medicare's "in-home" restrictions, and policies originating across various levels of governmental bureaucracy must address this problem.

The incoming Administration has a chance to see that everyone has an opportunity for work with a sustainable wage. The result would be greater prosperity for all.

UN Convention on the Rights of Persons with Disabilities

The UN Convention on the Rights of Persons with Disabilities is the international community's first human rights treaty of the twenty-first century. It is also remarkable as having been the fastest-negotiated human rights treaty in UN's history.

As of today, the treaty, which enshrines in international law the right of people with disabilities to be free of discrimination, and to be granted equal access to all facets of their society's public life, has legal force. That the United States, whose Americans with Disabilities Act became a guiding beacon to the international disability community in their efforts to secure similar rights, has resigned its leadership position on this issue is troubling.

The United States should sign the UN Convention and signal our support for international recognition of the world-wide scale of disability and its impact on the world's economy.

The reticence by the United States to join with other world leaders by signing the Convention further signals a weakening of our own commitment to people with disabilities in this country.

Resources

Arc/UCP Disability Policy Collaborative www.ucpa.org
American Association of People with Disabilities: http://www.aapd.com
American Association of Retired People: http://www.aarp.org
Center for Medicare Advocacy: http://www.medicareadvocacy.org
Consortium for Citizens with Disabilities: http://www.c-c-d.org
Disability Rights Education and Defense Fund: http://www.dredf.org
National Council on Independent Living: www.ncil.org
National Disability Rights Network: www.napas.org
National Organization on Disability: www.nod.org

Chapter 23

A Budget Is a Statement of Values

Miriam Pemberton

POLICY PROPOSALS

- Renounce the "Global War on Terror."
- Make ending the Iraq War the lead item in a list of cuts in military spending.
- Repeal twenty-first century tax cuts for the rich.
- Use some of the resulting dividend to re-invest in non-military forms of engagement with the rest of the world.
- Use the remainder to re-invest in neglected domestic needs.
- Build much of that re-investment around an agenda to save the planet form climate catastrophe.

* * * * * * * * * * * * * *

The precursor to this book, *Winning America: Ideas and Leadership for the 1990s* (1988), came out as the Reagan military build-up was winding up its full run. Many of that book's contributors detailed its ravages on the foundations of the American Dream. None of them could have foreseen that the build-up's Cold War underpinnings were about to be knocked clear out from under it.

We have arrived again at a similar moment. The post-9/11 military build-up has been piled even higher than the Reagan Administration dared to send it. This time, though, its porous foundations are visible for all to see. As is clear to most citizens, our militarized foreign policy, sold to us as a Global War on Terror, has, perversely, made us less safe. Our own intelligence agencies have declared that its centerpiece War on Iraq has created more terrorists than it has killed or captured. For many months, opposition to this war has hovered around 70 percent.

And within a few years, U.S. military-led power projection has generated higher levels of anti-American sentiment around the world than at any time since such attitudes began to be systematically measured.

The Administration that sold the public on war with Iraq as effective anti-terrorism also used 9/11-inspired fear and war fever as a pretext to launch the most ambitious expansion of executive power in U.S. history. At the same time, it has used the military blank checks Congress has been issuing year after year to begin fulfilling the political right wing's objective of "starving the beast." The beast in question, of course, is public spending on almost everything except military contracts and operations.

Between 2001 and 2008, according to the Center on Budget and Policy Priorities, defense programs have grown *twenty-seven times faster* than domestic "discretionary" programs (that is, the programs Congress votes on every year). And much of this money is going into the "regular" defense budget, as distinct from the "emergency" budgets funding the wars. Much of this "regular" budget is keeping production lines churning out things like exotic fighter jets that are useless for either the wars in Iraq and Afghanistan or the so-called "War on Terror." This "regular" budget has grown at an average inflation-adjusted annual rate of 4.8 percent, substantially higher than Social Security, Medicare and Medicaid (Richard Kogan, "Federal Spending, 2001-2008," March 6, 2008).

The President's budget for FY2009 proposed to spend $20 billion less on domestic discretionary programs, excluding homeland security, than the previous year. These cuts would further diminish programs that had already been starved by his previous budgets. This budget would reduce K–12 education funds, the lifeblood of his signature No Child Left Behind program, by nearly 9 percent below their FY2004 level. In a year of soaring energy prices, this budget would cut funding to help low-income Americans pay their heating bills by 22 percent. It would give the Environmental Protection Agency 26 percent less money to do its job than it had in 2001 (http://www.cbpp.org/2-20-08bud.pdf).

Meanwhile, the evidence of accelerating climate change continues to mount, as do the extreme weather events that give us a small taste of what is to come without immediate, concerted action to severely curtail greenhouse gas emissions. The U.S. military is beginning to map out for itself the massive security problems arising from climate change-induced food and water shortages that its weapons and forces will be powerless to control. In addition to obstructing the regulations on emissions that must drive the necessary transition, the current Administration has declined to put any but the most meager resources into addressing the problem. Its current budget allocates $88 to the military for every $1 it invests in climate change. $20 is being allocated to developing new weapons for every $1 spent on developing clean energy technologies. And $50 is going to seeding the world with U.S.-made weapons for every $1 spent on helping the rest of the world make its needed transition to clean energy (http://www.fpif.org/pdf/reports/0801milvclimate.pdf).

The other major starving device has been the successive waves of tax cuts that have been awarded to the richest Americans. If made permanent, they will deprive the Treasury of funds to invest in the public good as a whole during the next ten years to the tune of $2.4 trillion. Three-quarters of this money will be donated to the one-fifth of the population that already has the most. The top 1 percent will get an average of $60,000 more to spend per year ("The President's Budget: More for Tax Cuts and War; Failure to Invest in America's Future," National Priorities Project, March 2008).

According to the Center on Budget and Policy Priorities, tax cuts enacted in 2001 and 2003 have shrunk the funds available for public purposes by 1.3 percent of Gross Domestic Product. Add in the surge of military spending, and the resulting deterioration in the budget amounts to 3.3 percent of GDP.

Turning the Page

The list of necessary repairs to a damaged country is long. But the task does have a focal point, which is our federal budget. A country's budget is (or should be) an expression of what it values. Ours has prioritized militarism: fear over hope. This is the moment to reclaim the lost post-Cold War possibility of reversing these priorities. Here are the major pieces of a program to do so.

Renounce the "Global War on Terror"

The highly militarized response to the 9/11 attacks has created terrorists where they didn't exist, and converted the sympathy toward the United States of millions around the world into antipathy.

Countering terrorism involves military forces, but is not primarily a task to be pursued by military means. Effective opposition to al Qaeda has involved a range of methods, including small-scale search-and-capture operations; international cooperation to shut down financial flows to terrorist networks; airline and port security-tightening measures; international cooperation to secure and dismantle nuclear stockpiles in the former Soviet Union.

Make Ending the Iraq War the Lead Item in a List of Cuts in Military Spending

Next in importance on the list will be shrinking the global network of U.S. military bases that speak to the world of imperial ambitions and occupation. It's pretty simple: Countries don't want to be occupied. We currently spend more than $130 billion annually to maintain bases on every continent and in the liquid spaces in between. The largest base ever is now under construction in Iraq. Let the shrinkage start there.

We'll also need to finally go to work on the array of big-ticket weapons systems that have more to do with the interests of military contractors and their amply rewarded Congressional champions than with Constitution's mandate to provide for the common defense. "A Unified Security Budget for the United States" lists the systems to start with and the reasons we don't need them (http://www.fpif.org/pdf/reports/0704unifiedsecuritybudget.pdf).

Other ways to bring military spending under some control: Resume cutting the nuclear arsenal. Cut "foreign military financing" programs; all too often, they fuel conflicts rather than suppressing them and strengthen military control in the recipient countries, at the expense of civil society. Fix Pentagon procurement and business operations, whose proliferating accounting systems, combined with a shrinking corps of auditors to monitor them, allowed an estimated $15 billion to be hidden in 2,822 "earmarks" in 2007 (Jeffrey M. Tebbs, "Pruning the Defense Budget," Brookings Institution, January 2007).

Repeal Twenty-First Century Tax Cuts for the Rich
In addition to shifting the scales of the budget heavily toward finance for a militarized foreign policy, funding for non-military priorities has been starved by means of a Grand Bargain of tax cutting. The proposition is certainly simple, and seductive: You will be richer because we will give you money. Beyond the audacity of targeting these donations to the very rich is the damage they have done to the idea of common purposes beyond shoring up fortress America and making offense into defense.

Use Some of the Resulting Dividend to Invest in Non-Military Forms of Engagement with the Rest of the World
Our country has a massive international relations repair job ahead of it in the post-Bush years. This is the moment to show the rest of the world that we are ready to engage our fellow planetary citizens differently. This task will involve recommitting, politically and financially, to the post-war project of building international institutions and the structures of international agreements to control the world-destroying power of the nuclear age and to keep the peace among nations.

Repairing the damage also entails shifting more of our security spending toward such non-military security tools as foreign aid, crafted in partnership with its recipients. As we increase this budget, we will also need to redirect it to where it will do the most good. Foreign "assistance" now devoted to supplying other countries, most of them ruled by dictators, with U.S.-made weapons must be redirected to such purposes as training and equipping 4 million new public health workers to address the burgeoning health crises in the developing world, and to building a clean energy infrastructure there. (See the report "Just Security" (http://www.ips-dc.org/reports/070608-justsecurity.pdf). These purposes must not be subordinated to military objectives.

Negotiating trade agreements that institutionalize fair labor and environmental standards, and give fair access to international markets to developing countries, are also crucial elements of a new era of demilitarized U.S. global engagement. So is a strengthened diplomacy mission that promotes our country as a partner in, rather than a director, or policer, of world affairs.

Underscoring that partnership will be a commitment to invest new resources in international organizations—the United Nations, international peacekeeping forces, the International Atomic Energy Agency, the World Health Organization, and the Food and Agriculture Organization among them. The "Unified Security Budget for the United States" outlines a dollar-for-dollar reinvestment of money saved from unneeded weapons systems into such purposes. It's a beginning.

Use the Remainder to Invest in Neglected Domestic Needs

A society fearful for its economic health needs to target investments that will provide for its most vulnerable citizens while lifting all boats by boosting its economy's productivity.

No less likely a source than Wall Street's favorite Federal Reserve chairman, Alan Greenspan, has tied this objective to constrained military spending. Funding for the military is like a family's insurance policies, he said. Families should only buy as much insurance as they need to safeguard themselves against ruin, because this is money they cannot be spending to improve their standard of living.

So a government, he said, should spend what it needs, and only what it needs, to defend its citizens from attack, but devote as much as possible to investing in their economic well-being. As we seize this opportunity to demilitarize our foreign policy, we have to invest the savings in such priorities as health care and education: An economy can't function without a healthy and well-educated workforce. If we stopped spending $400 million a day on the Iraq War, we could fund universal health care (John Broder, "Views on Money for Iraq War, and What Else Could Be Done With It," *New York Times*, April 14, 2008).

The other principal investment yielding great dividends in our productivity must be our decaying infrastructure: Moving goods and people around quickly, cleanly and efficiently is an economy's lifeblood. The lack of efficient mass transit and freight rail in most areas of the country clogs our economic arteries. According to the annual Urban Mobility Report from Texas A&M, traffic congestion cost our economy $78 billion in 2005, while wasting 4.2 billion hours of time and 2.9 billion gallons of gas.

Each year, the American Society of Civil Engineers issues a report card on the state of U.S. infrastructure, and what it will cost to repair it. Each year we get lower grades, because investments are deferred for "lack of funds"—which is to say, for other purposes, like a massive military build-up that has made us less safe, and tax cutting. The ASCE's 2005 report card estimated the bill for needed repairs at $1.6 trillion. The bill has now grown larger, and the bridge collapses and disastrous levee failures since then are only the most visible results.

Build Much of that Re-investment around an Agenda to Save the Planet from Climate Catastrophe

A national program of infrastructure repair can dovetail perfectly with a commitment, finally, to the most serious challenge to human survival we have ever faced. Drastically reducing global greenhouse gas emissions will require wholly redesigned energy and transportation systems, as well as retrofitted residential and commercial structures, for efficiency. We can—we must—re-build our infrastructure to be cleaner and more efficient and therefore to become a better economic foundation, all at the same time.

Investing in mass transit in particular has a few added benefits directly related to a demilitarized foreign policy. First, it will create more American jobs. A 2007 study by University of Massachusetts economists found that $1 billion of federal money invested in the military created an average of 8,500 jobs; the same amount invested in mass transit created more than twice as many: 19,500. Second, these investments will revive a sector of the U.S. manufacturing base that atrophied as Cold War-era military budgets lured more and more manufacturers into military production. Public financing for mass transit will provide American manufacturers with the incentive to get back into a market now dominated by the Europeans and the Japanese. It is also a market in which military contractors, when they put their hearts and minds to it and are willing to learn from their mistakes, have a proven track record of success. It is, in other words, a key domain where the conversion of swords into plowshares can take place.

The knock on these investments has long been that the American love affair with car travel, and the home and work sprawl thereby created, put an unraisable ceiling on American mass transit use. That conventional wisdom has been decisively dislodged. Soaring gas prices, it turns out, have gotten people out of their cars and into buses and trains in a hurry. The biggest surprise is that the biggest surges in ridership are occurring in cities of the South and West, where the "driving culture" is strongest. A much-strengthened argument for serious investment in mass transit thus has been born, since these are the regions where this service mostly doesn't now exist (Clifford Krauss, "Gas Prices Send Surge of Riders to Mass Transit, *New York Times*, May 10, 2008, p. A1).

Conclusion

Re-aligning and demilitarizing federal budget priorities won't be easy. After the end of the Cold War, U.S. military contractors successfully mobilized to send military spending climbing again, even though the rationale for this build-up had disappeared. If members of Congress now show signs of responding to a war-weary, economically strained public by crafting a budget more in line with the actual interests of their constituents, these contractors will pull out all the stops to thwart them.

Last spring, news reports drew back the curtain revealing the collusion of Administration officials, contractors and the "independent" retired military media commentators to gin up support for the Iraq War. These same collaborators, joined by key members of the Joint Chiefs of Staff, having been pushing hard on the notion that military spending should be tied to the size of the total U.S. economy. This sleight of hand labors to obscure the fact that military spending is higher, in real terms, than it has been at any time since World War II.

But there are signs of push-back. In crafting its Budget Resolution outlining spending for 2009, the House of Representatives for the first time rejected this odd measuring stick. Military spending, it said, should be tied to what is needed to address the threats we face, not to some arbitrary proportion of private as well as public national wealth.

And guns vs. butter has begun to make a modest comeback in the debate over national priorities. In speeches in their districts and on the House floor at the beginning of 2008 numerous members of Congress pitted funding for the war against funding for "SCHIP," the children's health insurance program. And in their legislation providing massive gun funding to continue the war, they added a shipment of butter: money for such domestic priorities as improved GI education funding, extended unemployment benefits, and new levee construction to prevent another Katrina disaster.

Let these tentative steps begin a movement to bring our budget into line with our values.

Resources

Center for Budget and Policy Priorities: http://www.cbpp.org
National Priorities Project: http://www.nationalpriorities.org

References

"ASCE's Report Card for America's Infrastructure 2005." American Society of Civil Engineers, 2005. http://www.asce.org/reportcard/2005/page.cfm?id= 103 (accessed July 18, 2008).
Foreign Policy in Focus. "Just Security: An Alternative Foreign Policy Framework." Institute for Policy Studies, 2007. http://www.ips-dc.org/reports/070608-justsecurity.pdf (accessed July 18, 2008).
Foreign Policy in Focus. "Report of the Task Force on a Unified Security Budget for the United States, FY 2008." Institute for Policy Studies, 2007. http://www.fpif.org/pdf/reports/0704unifiedsecuritybudget.pdf (accessed July 18, 2008).

Pollin, Robert, and Heidi Garrett-Peltier. "The U.S. Employment Effects of Military and Domestic Spending Priorities." Political Economy Research Institute, University of Massachusetts, 2007.

Chapter 24

A Food System We Can Believe In

Ben Lilliston and Jim Harkness

POLICY PROPOSALS

- Establish a strategic grain reserve—a well-constructed grain reserve would lessen the volatility of food prices and reduce the need for subsidies.
- Launch a new Farmers Corps—a series of government loans, grants and training would make land and equipment more accessible and help prepare a new generation of farmers using sustainable practices.
- Support healthy food for all—by shifting the emphasis of government programs, like school meals and food assistance, to encourage the purchase of healthier food.
- Expand green farming—the new Conservation Stewardship Program, which supports farmers who adopt sustainable practices, can be the basis for a new era of green farming.
- Restore market competition—stepped-up enforcement of existing laws along with greater market transparency would restore fair competition throughout the food system.
- Control speculation—the government must restore its proper role in protecting consumers against speculation in food markets.
- Bolster food safety—the government must reassert control of food safety from the big food companies through greater testing and inspection.
- Nurture sustainable bioenergy—we must shift government support from unsustainable to sustainable forms of bioenergy.
- Initiate a new research agenda—a new agricultural research agenda would include public health concerns and a climate-friendly agriculture that uses less energy, fewer inputs and reduces water use.

* * * * * * * * * * * * * * *

The Food Crisis: A Symptom of Deeper Problems

In the last year, Americans witnessed two disturbing shocks to our food system. First, food prices shot up by over 6 percent in just one year, with the cost of staples like bread, eggs and milk rising even higher.[1] Second, a steady string of food contamination recalls shook public confidence in the safety of the food supply. These shocks are hitting all Americans, but particularly those struggling just to put food on the table.

Rising food prices and recalls get the headlines, but there are a number of equally alarming signs that our food system is not working. From the record-sized dead zone in the Gulf of Mexico, to air and water pollution from factory farms, to the rise in obesity and diet-related diseases, to the loss of family farmers—the signs of a breaking food system are everywhere.

The cause of this breakdown is not a mystery: In the name of Free Markets vs. Big Government, we have deregulated the food and farm economy at the expense of our farmers, our health, the environment and rural communities—and to the benefit of big agribusiness and food companies.

An incoming Administration that recognizes the importance of a strong food system can get us back on track. Like education and health care, a thriving food system benefits all Americans.

Food Is Different

Our food system is more fundamentally important to our national well-being than other sectors of the economy. Food production has a profound effect on our environment and on public health. Over 930 million acres in the United States are used for agricultural production,[2] and the way land is used directly affects our water systems, air quality, wildlife and climate. The type of food we produce and the way we produce it also has major effects on public health, from the working conditions of farm laborers to the national epidemic of childhood obesity, which has been fuelled partially by an abundance of cheap, unhealthy food.

More fundamentally, unlike iPods or SUVs, food is a basic necessity of life, and a secure food supply is essential to our national security. America's farmers have been so successful at providing us with abundant food that it is easy to forget this basic fact. But the way we have managed our food and farming in the past several decades has reduced our food security, devastated rural communities and undermined both public health and the environment.

A Food System in Trouble

The incoming Administration must take on some major cracks in our fragile food system. Here are the key challenges they will face:

Price Volatility—Food prices are projected to jump another 9 percent this year, and farm commodity prices have risen even faster. The price of corn has shot up from $4.50 a bushel to a record-high $7 a bushel in the last six months. Soybean and wheat prices have also seen record highs.

Why the recent extreme volatility in prices? We used to have a food reserve program that worked with a price floor and ceiling to help manage prices in the agricultural marketplace for both farmers and consumers—and did so at little cost to taxpayers. The 1996 Farm Bill wiped out the last vestiges of that system to stabilize prices. In its place, we have a system that pays out huge government subsidies, ($24.5 billion in 2005) when prices are low, and causes pain for consumers, particularly those on fixed incomes, when prices spike.

The deregulation of commodity futures trading that led to the Enron disaster also removed a significant barrier to speculation in food markets. This means the prices we see in the market are pushed up artificially by Wall Street index and derivative traders, and are not just a reflection of an imbalance in supply and demand.[3]

Price volatility in the United States wreaks havoc around the world. When prices were low, U.S. agribusiness companies routinely dumped major commodity crops onto international markets at well below the cost of production, effectively pushing farmers in countries like Mexico off the land.[4] Now that food prices have surged, many poor countries that have become reliant on cheap food imports are experiencing widespread hunger.

Obesity and Diet-Related Health Effects—In the United States, nearly two-thirds (65 percent) of adults and more than one-third (34 percent) of children and adolescents are overweight and obese, increasing their risk for heart disease, type-2 diabetes and other diseases. The direct and indirect health costs associated with obesity are estimated at $117 billion per year nationwide.[5] Farm policy has facilitated this public health crisis: while the real prices of fruits and vegetables have risen nearly 40 percent over the last twenty years, the costs of unhealthy soft drinks, sweets and fats and oil (often based on ingredients from subsidized corn and soybeans) have dropped considerably.[6] Access to healthy food has been a challenge for many low-income communities, which often find themselves within "food deserts"—regions without supermarkets carrying fresh, healthy food.[7]

Environmental Threats—Industrial agriculture, with its heavy dependence on fossil fuels, use of toxic chemicals and high water consumption, is a major threat to the environment. The row crop dominated landscape of the Upper Midwest, geared largely toward animal feed and exports, correlates with high rates of soil erosion, overabundance of nutrients in waters and a loss of biodiversity. The oxygen-deprived dead zone at the mouth of the Mississippi River, created in large part by fertilizer runoff upstream, is projected to extend a record 10,000 square miles this year.[8] In 2001 (the last year the EPA published data), 675 million pounds of chemical pesticides were used in agriculture.[9] Pesticides are now in 97 percent of U.S. streams in both agricultural and urban areas, often exceeding water quality benchmarks for aquatic life.[10]

Confined Animal Feeding Operations (CAFOs) pose another series of immediate environmental threats. These facilities dump huge quantities of animal waste into the water and air. Air in and around CAFOs contains toxic gases, odorous substances and particulates that carry human pathogens.[11] These factory farms are economically viable only because they exploit immigrant labor, obtain exemptions from environmental laws and have access to cheap animal feed. An analysis from Tufts University found that below-cost feed saved CAFOs $35 billion from 1997 to 2005.[12]

Work in industrial agriculture production, whether inside a CAFO or in pesticide-soaked fields, is some of the lowest-paid and most dangerous in America, and exposes farmers and farmworkers to a host of illnesses.[13]

Biofuel Boom—U.S. biofuels programs were originally conceived as a way for farmers to add value to crops when grain prices were low, and many first-wave ethanol plants were locally-owned engines for community growth.[14] But with rising oil prices, biofuels have been falsely touted as a cure-all for import dependence and climate change, and the biofuels agenda has been hijacked by corporate interests and turned into a global investment bubble that could threaten communities, the environment and even food production.

Corporate Power vs. Fair Competition—Economists believe if the top four companies in any sector control 40 percent of the market, competitiveness declines and the risk of collusion increases. Currently, the top four companies exceed the 40 percent threshold in the beef, pork, poultry, flour-milling and soybean-crushing sectors.[15] While the industry has concentrated, government anti-trust enforcement has lagged. The USDA Office of Inspector General found that USDA administrators prevented its employees from investigating anti-competitive behavior and artificially inflated the number of investigations conducted. Previous government audits found that poor coordination among USDA agencies severely undermined enforcement of the anti-trust Packers and Stockyards Act.[16]

Food Safety Breakdown—The Centers for Disease Control and Prevention estimates that 300,000 Americans are hospitalized each year, and 5,000 die, because of food-borne illnesses.[17] In 2007, there were nineteen recalls of E. coli-contaminated beef products, more than in any year in our history.[18] This modern wave of food contamination follows successful efforts to deregulate food safety under the guise of the USDA's Hazard Analysis Critical Control Point program. The program relies largely on the food industry to police itself, while government inspection and testing has been slashed.

A New Food and Agriculture Program for America

In the realm of food and farming, as in so many other areas, the Bush Administration has abdicated the government's proper role of helping markets work efficiently and supporting widely-held societal goals such as fairness and environmental sustainability. To restore a healthy food system for America and stop undermining food security abroad, the incoming Administration will need to make public welfare and not corporate profit the guiding principle of farm and food policies. In some cases, this requires no more than full enforcement of existing laws and regulations. In others, the harmful effects of years of corporate welfare, perverse incentives and misplaced priorities will need to be undone through new initiatives. Taken together, these measures will help restore hope to rural America, heal our ailing planet and make healthy food available to all Americans.

Establish a Strategic Grain Reserve. *Goals: 1) Stabilize volatile food prices. 2) Strengthen food security.*
The incoming Administration should establish a new national grain reserve and initiate a global dialogue on building a network of reserves around the world to stabilize global prices.[19] The mechanics of an effective reserve program are fairly simple. The government sets a price floor and ceiling for commodities that would ensure farmers and consumers a fair price. When market prices dip below the price floor, the government accepts commodities at the set price as payment for a government loan, and builds the reserve. When prices rise above the set ceiling, the government releases grain from the reserve. This system needs to be coupled with border protections to ensure that prices aren't destabilized by a flood of cheap imports. The result is a balance of supply and demand, more stable prices and a major drop in controversial farm subsidies. Stable markets would reduce the rampant commodity speculation fueling the current food crisis[20] and would eliminate export dumping, which undermines food security in other countries.

Launch a New Farmers Corps. *Goal: Provide truly green jobs to a new generation of farmers.*
To meet a variety of environmental, health and food security goals, we need more people—especially younger people—farming in a sustainable manner. The average age of a U.S. farmer is fifty-five years. The high costs of land and equipment block most people not from farm families from considering farming.

Federal loan, grant and training programs for new farmers should be expanded and tied to greener farming practices. And the government should provide more support for new and existing farmers who want to convert conventional farmland to organic.

Support Healthy Food for All. *Goal: To make healthy food accessible to all Americans.*
Wages, income supports and nutrition assistance programs like food stamps must be made adequate for families to have the resources needed to purchase healthy foods. Public health goals must be integrated into agriculture policy and food assistance programs like the National School Lunch and School Breakfast programs. All foods in schools, whether or not federally-reimbursed, and whether available in the cafeteria, in vending machines, or otherwise, should meet the federal Dietary Guidelines for Americans. Programs that increase access to fresh, healthy food in low-income communities and bring fresh farm products into schools should be expanded. Government programs should also help support the infrastructure necessary to increase the production, processing, distribution and retail of local, healthy foods.

Expand Green Farming. *Goals: 1) More farmland utilizing conservation practices. 2) Better regulation of CAFO operations.*
The new Conservation Stewardship Program in the Farm Bill should be fully implemented, and special emphasis within CSP should be placed on "carbon farming" to support farmers who increase the organic matter in their soil and utilize carbon sequestration methods to counter global warming. The incoming Administration should promote environmental service markets to give new income sources to farmers who use sustainable farming practices. Confined Animal Feeding Operations should be regulated as industrial operations, and should not be exempted from the Comprehensive Environmental Response, Compensation, and Liability Act (CERCLA), the Clean Water Act, the Clean Air Act or any other environmental laws. Owners of CAFOs should be required to pay for the clean-up of their animal waste, including water and air pollution. Resources from the Environmental Quality and Incentives Program should be targeted to family farmers to encourage environmentally sound farming practices, not to subsidize the environmentally destructive practices of CAFOs.

Restore Market Competition. *Goals: 1) Greater enforcement of existing anti-trust provisions. 2) Greater price transparency in markets.*
At the last minute, the 2008 Farm Bill stripped away funding for a new Special Counsel for Competition to improve enforcement of the Packers and Stockyards Act and the Agricultural Fair Practices Act. This new position needs to be established and should work to better coordinate with the Justice Department's anti-trust division. The USDA should also propose rules to require public bidding on all contracts with meat and poultry producers, and to prohibit direct

ownership of livestock by meatpacking corporations. This would re-establish price transparency and competitive bidding among packers, and help independent feeders get a fairer price.

Control Speculation. *Goal: Restore the government's role in protecting consumers against speculation in food markets.*
The incoming Administration must undo the damage caused by the Commodity Futures Modernization Act of 2000 and strengthen the Commodity Futures Trading Commission's authority and capacity to control speculation, especially by non-commercial investors.

Bolster Food Safety: *Goals: 1) Ensure food is produced in a way that avoids unnecessary health threats. 2) Ensure that food entering the food supply is subject to strong, independent inspection.*
The incoming Administration should: ban the use of non-therapeutic antibiotics, arsenic and growth promoters in food animal production; restore the Office of Pesticide Monitoring and make the pesticide poisoning database public; ban food packaging that includes plastics containing known carcinogens and heavy metals. In addition, the incoming Administration should: increase resources for food inspection and new detection technology; modernize inspection and testing on food imports; give the FDA authority to recall tainted food; and allow private companies to test beef for BSE (Mad Cow Disease), which customers are demanding.

Nurture Sustainable Bioenergy: *Goals: 1) Shift government support from unsustainable to sustainable forms of bioenergy. 2) Support farmer- and community-owned facilities.*
The incoming Administration should phase out biofuel subsidies for feedstocks that do not demonstrate environmental and climate benefits, and provide more incentives for use of sustainable biomass for heat and power generation. In addition, the incoming Administration should support farmer-owned facilities through community planning and financial assistance, and the establishment of purchasing, grant, licensing and loan preferences for locally-owned facilities.

Initiate a New Research Agenda. *Goal: Strengthen government support for an agricultural research agenda that prioritizes public health and environmental sustainability.*
The government's agriculture research should emphasize food's relationship to disease prevention and how healthier food could be grown more effectively, and promote the necessary shift toward an agriculture that emits fewer greenhouse gases, relies on fewer fossil fuel inputs and uses less water. Finally, government and land grant research needs to be kept in the public domain and made available to farmers and rural communities.

Resources

Agricultural Policy Analysis Center: http://www.agpolicy.org
The Ethicurean: http://www.ethicurean.com/
FarmPolicy.com: http://www.farmpolicy.com/
Global Development and Environment Institute: http://ase.tufts.edu/gdae/
Institute for Agriculture and Trade Policy: http://www.iatp.org
National Family Farm Coalition: http://www.nffc.net
Sustainable Agriculture Coalition: http://www.msawg.org/

References

De la Torre Ugarte, Daniel. "The Contributions and Challenges of Supply Management in a New Institutional Agricultural Trade Framework." Eco Fair Trade Dialogue. March 2007. http://www.ecofair-trade.org/pics/en/EcoFair_Trade_Paper_No6_Torre_Ugarte_new.pdf.
Hendrickson, Mary, and William Heffernan. "Concentration of Agricultural Markets." National Farmers Union. 2007. http://www.nfu.org/wp-content/2007-heffernanreport.pdf.
Kleinschmit, Jim. "Biofueling Rural Development." The Carsey Institute. Policy Brief 5. Winter 2007. http://www.agobservatory.org/library.cfm?RefID=96834.
Marlow, Scott. "A Non-Wonk Guide to Understanding Federal Commodity Payments." RAFI-USA. May 2005. http://www.rafiusa.org/pubs/nonwonk guide.
Pew Commission on Industrial Farm Animal Production. "Putting Meat on the Table: Industrial Farm Animal Production in America." April 29, 2008. http://www.ncifap.org/_images/PCIFAPFin.pdf.
Pollan, Michael. *In Defense of Food: An Eater's Manifesto*. New York: Penguin Press. 2008. http://www.michaelpollan.com/indefense.php.
Ray, Darryl, and Daniel De La Ugarte Torre, "Rethinking U.S. Agricultural Policy: Changing Course to Secure Farmer Livelihoods Worldwide." Agriculture Policy Analysis Center, University of Tennessee. 2003. http://agpolicy.org/ blueprint.html.
Roberts, Paul. *The End of Food*, Electronically Published, 2008. http://www.theendoffood.com/.
Schoonover, Heather, and Mark Muller. "Food Without Thought: How U.S. Farm Policy Contributes to Obesity." Institute for Agriculture and Trade Policy. March 2006. http://www.iatp.org/iatp/publications.cfm?accountID=258&refID=80627.
Starmer, Elanor, and Timothy Wise. "Feeding at the Trough: Industrial Livestock Firms Save $35 Billion from Low Feed Prices." Global

Development and Environment Institute, Tufts University. December 2007.
http://www.ase.tufts.edu/gdae/Pubs/rp/PB07-3FeedingAtTroughDec07.pdf.

Notes

1. U.S. Department of Agriculture, "Changes in Food Price Indexes, 2004-2008," http://www.ers.usda.gov/Briefing/CPIFoodAndExpenditures/Data/cpiforecasts.htm (accessed June 12, 2008).

2. U.S. Department of Agriculture, "2002 Census on Agriculture," http://www.ers.usda.gov/StateFacts/US.htm (accessed June 12, 2008).

3. Ed Wallace, "ICE, ICE, Baby: Conclusion," Star-Telegram.com, http://www.star-telegram.com/ed_wallace/story/659081.html (posted May 22, 2008).

4. Sophia Murphy, Ben Lilliston, and Mary Beth Lake, "The WTO Agreement on Agriculture: A Decade of Dumping," Institute for Agriculture and Trade Policy, February 2005. http://www.iatp.org/iatp/publications.cfm?accounted=451&refID=48532 (accessed July 19, 2008).

5. Institute for Agriculture and Trade Policy, "Wingspread Conference on Childhood Obesity, Healthy Eating and Agricultural Policy—Conference Summary," March 2007, http://www.healthyeatingresearch.org/uploads/1Wing spreadSummary.pdf (accessed July 19, 2008).

6. Heather Schoonover and Mark Muller, "Food Without Thought: How U.S. Farm Policy Contributes to Obesity," Institute for Agriculture and Trade Policy, March 2006, http://www.iatp.org/iatp/publications.cfm?accountID =258 &refID=80627 (accessed July 19, 2008).

7. Mary Gallagher Research and Consulting Group, "Food Deserts and Public Health," http://marigallagher.com/projects/ (accessed July 19, 2008).

8. Louisiana Universities Marine Consortium, "Dead Zone Present and Growing, Record Year Predicted," June 10, 2008, http://www.gulfhypoxia.net/news/default.asp?XMLFilename=200806091535.xml (accessed July 19, 2008).

9. Center for Food Safety, "Agricultural Pesticide Use in U.S. Agriculture," May 2008, http://www.centerforfoodsafety.org/pubs/USDA%20NASS%20Backgrounder-final.pdf (accessed July 19, 2008).

10. Robert Gilliom, "Pesticides in U.S. Streams and Groundwater," U.S. Geological Survey. Environmental Science and Technology, May 15, 2007, http://water.usgs.gov/nawqa/pnsp/pubs/files/051507.ESTfeature_gilliom.pdf (accessed July 19, 2008).

11. Pew Commission on Industrial Farm Animal Production, "Putting Meat on the Table: Industrial Farm Animal Production in America," April 29, 2008, http://www.ncifap.org/_images/PCIFAPFin.pdf (accessed July 19, 2008).

12. Elanor Starmer and Timothy Wise, "Feeding at the Trough: Industrial Livestock Firms Save $35 Billion from Low Feed Prices," Global Development and Environment Institute, Tufts University, December 2007, http://www.ase.tufts.edu/gdae/Pubs/rp/ PB07-03FeedingAtTroughDec07.pdf (accessed July 19, 2008).

13. Steven Kirkhorn and Marc Schenker, "Human Health Effects of Agriculture: Physical Disease and Illness," National Agriculture Safety Database, 2001, http://www.cdc.gov/nasd/docs/d001701-d001800/d001772/ d001772. html (accessed July 19, 2008).

14. Jim Kleinschmit, "Biofueling Rural Development," The Carsey Institute, Policy Brief 5, Winter 2007, http://www.agobservatory.org/library.cfm?RefID=96834 (accessed July 19, 2008).

15. Mary Hendrickson and William Heffernan, "Concentration of Agricultural Markets," National Farmers Union, 2007, http://www.nfu.org/wp-content/2007-heffernan report.pdf (accessed July 19, 2008).

16. Institute for Agriculture and Trade Policy, "A Fair Farm Bill for Competitive Markets," May 2007, http://www.agobservatory.org/library.cfm? refid=98445 (accessed July 19, 2008).

17. Michael Doyle, "Food Safety on Back Burner," *McClatchy Newspapers*, June 11, 2008, http://www.sacbee.com/103/story/1004306.html (accessed July 19, 2008).

18. Rod Leonard and Steve Suppan, "Losing Control of U.S. Food Safety," Institute for Agriculture and Trade Policy, November 2007, http://www.iatp.org/iatp/publications. cfm?accountID=421&refID=100754 (accessed July 19, 2008).

19. Daniel De la Torre Ugarte, "The Contributions and Challenges of Supply Management in a New Institutional Agricultural Trade Framework," Eco Fair Trade Dialogue, March 2007, http://www.ecofair-trade.org/pics/en/EcoFair_Trade_Paper_ No6 _Torre_Ugarte_new.pdf (accessed July 19, 2008).

20. Sinclair Steward and Paul Waldie, "Feeding Frenzy," *Toronto Globe and Mail*, May 31, 2008, http://www.reportonbusiness.com/servlet/story/LAC.20080531.RCOVER 31/TPStory/Business/?pageRequested=all (accessed July 19, 2008).

Chapter 25

Transforming U.S. Transportation

Michael A. Replogle

POLICY PROPOSALS

- Issue an Executive Order on climate change and NEPA.
- Enact an economy-wide cap-and-trade law, which should include goals for state and local agencies to reduce greenhouse gases related to transportation and land use.
- Adopt a low-carbon fuel standard (LCFS).
- Issue an executive order on transportation equity.
- Extend motor vehicle emission standards adopted in California and a dozen other states into a U.S. national framework.
- Establish in the next federal transportation bill:
  - Clear objectives for federal transportation programs and funding.
  - Accountability to these federal objectives by state, regional and local agencies, with a growing share of funds tied to performance.
  - Modal neutrality policy in transportation funding for capital-intensive investments, with requirement to consider cost-effectiveness of better managing, pricing and operating existing systems in lieu of more capacity.
  - Adoption of a national complete streets policy.
  - Promotion of an equitable re-pricing of transportation, removing barriers to tolling, pay-as-you-drive insurance, parking cashout, ride-sharing.
  - Expand efforts to spur equal access to jobs and public facilities for all.
  - Fostering of integrated transportation and smart growth land use planning by states, regions and local governments.
  - Fostering of fast-track approval of financially viable, cost-effective public transportation and non-motorized transportation projects.

- A program for direct federal transportation funding to larger cities.
- Fostering national transportation planning and investment.
- Accelerate transition to emission- and distance-based national road user fees with new standards, pilot-testing, research and planning.
- Remove regulatory and market barriers to increased coastal shipping and rail investment.

* * * * * * * * * * * * * *

The current system of U.S. transportation financing is broke, broken and adrift with only vague purpose. The Highway Trust Fund will be bankrupt in 2009, the Transit Trust Fund shortly thereafter. The incoming President and Congress should help define the purpose of federal transportation programs and provide new funding sources to states, regions and cities that pursue transportation plans and programs advancing those purposes. Federal transportation funds should reward and incentivize performance and innovation, cut traffic growth and greenhouse gas (GHG) pollution, and enhance equity of access to jobs and public facilities, spurring innovation. The era of growing transportation earmarks should end. New standards should be adopted for traffic management and road-pricing, cleaner vehicles and fuels, data collection and institutional capacity-building.

America's transportation sector is at a transition point like 1956, when the Interstate Highway Act was passed, and like 1991, when a new intermodal transportation law was enacted. The next federal transportation bill will be considered in 2009 concurrently with path-breaking climate legislation. With the decades-old gas-tax model for financing transportation running out of steam as oil prices hit record levels, U.S. transportation is poised for major reform.

Climate Change

The next transportation bill should set the nation on a new path, supporting smart growth, smart system management, expanded travel choices and a greening of the transportation industry. It should lay the foundation for a shift to mileage- and emission-based road-user fees to finance and manage U.S. transportation over the next decade, cooperating with the European Union in developing vehicle-infrastructure-communications standards. This will help America manage traffic growth and adapt its economy to a climate-constrained world.

This should include the allocation of sufficient funds from carbon allowance auctions to provide strong incentives and resources for timely local and state action. Transportation GHG emissions from oil-well-to-wheel-to-disposal are roughly 40 percent of America's total, so it makes sense for a significant portion of cap-and-trade allowance proceeds to be invested in ways that will reduce transportation GHGs.

The incoming President should start by issuing an Executive Order in early 2009 to require all federal agencies to assess and disclose the greenhouse gas emissions and global warming vulnerabilities associated with federal actions, exercising authority under the National Environmental Policy Act (NEPA). These assessments should include a quantitative analysis of a federal action's direct and indirect contributions to greenhouse gas emissions, an evaluation of the consequences of changing climatic conditions for a federal action, and consideration of alternative actions and mitigation measures that could reduce greenhouse gas emissions and climatic vulnerability.[1]

Transportation Equity

State and regional transportation plans and programs and new financing approaches should contribute to timely progress in ensuring equal access, without undue time and cost burdens, to jobs and public facilities for all, including those without cars, exercising authority under Title VI of the Civil Rights Act.

Require evaluation of the distribution of benefits and burdens of transportation and land use plans and programs, including new pricing and management strategies. Expand financing tools and incentives to create affordable housing units near transit and jobs, and incentives for local governments to revise zoning to encourage creation of accessory apartments in existing homes near transit and job centers, with technical and financing support for creation of these almost invisible, affordable, in-fill housing units.

Vehicle Fuel Efficiency

The incoming President should ensure an increase in vehicle fuel efficiency for improving fuel economy and reducing air pollution, while proposing to further strengthen fuel-conserving goals out to 2040 and beyond, using authority under the Clean Air Act and other statutes. Congress should expand research and development of plug-in hybrid and electric vehicles and other promising technologies for low-carbon transportation vehicles and fuels.

The Next Federal Transportation Bill

The incoming President should work with Congress to ensure that when the current federal transportation law expires in September 2009, the new law lays a foundation for sweeping reforms to enhance mobility, U.S. economic competitiveness, and equity of access to jobs and public facilities, while reducing transportation's environmental footprint. This will happen only by tying transportation funding and contracting to performance, expanding accountability in planning and decision-making, and ensuring transparency as private capital increasingly complements public investment. This is consistent with final or interim recommendations from several recent national transportation commissions established by Congress.[2, 3]

Specifically, the law should:

- Include timely action to reduce greenhouse gas emissions, protect public health, boost equitable access to jobs and public facilities for all, expand travel alternatives to reduce vehicle miles traveled, and support equitable economic and community development.
- Make a substantial portion of federal transportation funds available as: (i) incentives for agencies to develop state and local plans and programs aimed at making timely progress towards these objectives; (ii) rewards for demonstrated performance; (iii) to build institutional capacity needed for such efforts; (iv) to fund local innovations (modeled on the UK Innovation Fund and the recent U.S. Urban Partnerships Program).
- Initiate, for new capacity development for highways and for public transportation, a federal share of 50 percent, which would need to be matched with state, local or private funding. Currently, highways get 80 percent and transit projects typically get only 50 percent, due to intense competition for scarce transit capital funding. Proposed new transportation capacity investments and alternatives to these projects should be evaluated for their user benefits and cost-effectiveness, considering indirect, secondary, cumulative and induced development impacts. Funding for new roadway capacity should be administered separately from infrastructure maintenance and operations funding, and made contingent on demonstrating that roadways and bridges are being kept in a good state of repair.
- Take other initiatives to ensure timely action to improve the safety of walking and cycling, including retaining higher federal matching shares (80 percent or greater) where such projects or investments improve bicycle and pedestrian safety and access to schools, public transportation and activity centers; improve safety and public health; and reduce greenhouse gas emissions. Double funding for walking and cycling.
- Enact measures to remove all state barriers to pay-as-you-drive (PAYD) insurance, ensure equality in commuter benefits and eliminate remaining barriers to tolling Interstate highways. Lay a foundation for a rapid transition to a national system of emission and distance-based road-user vehicle miles traveled (VMT) fees over the next decade, starting with multistate pilot programs, a national architecture for automated toll collection and GPS, and vehicle-intelligent infrastructure standards for new cars sold in the United States.

- Reduce federal matching share for new capital investment in road projects to 25 percent or less for regions that do not have in place regional and state plans that are designed to reduce by at least 10 percent per-capita vehicle miles traveled by 2020 from the level in 2010. Provide incentives for regions and states to adopt indirect source rules like the San Joaquin, CA program, targeting GHG reductions as well as criteria pollutants.

- Foster fast-track approval of public transportation and non-motorized transportation projects where these are demonstrated to reduce regional gasoline use and to support transit-oriented development. Such approvals should routinely consider the potential for high- quality bus rapid transit, flexible transit and innovative ride-sharing options to deliver equal or better mobility improvement compared to fixed rail, giving a higher federal match ratio for more cost-effective options, while not proscribing community choices. A new federal infrastructure bond program should provide low-cost financing of transit expansions tied to transit-oriented development and establishment of congestion pricing on existing roadways to fund substantial expansion of transit, enabling front-loaded transit investments. The economic development benefits of transit investment and related transportation pricing strategies should be fully recognized in transit financial appraisal and planning. Boost federal transit funding by at least a factor of two, so cities do not face a twelve-year wait for New Starts Program applications.

- Enable a direct aid relationship between U.S. DOT and city transportation agencies in order to help streamline project delivery. State transportation agencies often add little or no value to urban projects but do delay them. Cities with demonstrated institutional capacity and interest should be able to opt-in to become direct federal funding recipients, taking on a delegated function of roles ascribed to states for matters related to city transportation decision-making and planning.

- Create a National Infrastructure Commission to develop a new national freight and passenger transport strategy, aimed at improving productivity and reducing adverse environmental and health impacts of freight and passenger transportation. It should engage regional, state, federal and private sector interests in developing new regional freight and passenger management and investment initiatives, especially in high-speed rail and coastal shipping, considering cost-effectiveness, externalities and ways of better pricing and managing existing resources.

- Focus on how to enhance freight and inter-city transportation through strategic planning, investment, public-private partnerships and new regulations aimed at ensuring economic competitiveness, improved environmental performance and fair labor policies. Shifting a portion of trucking traffic from the nation's highways to rail or coastal ships could cut GHG emissions and congestion, as well as public health problems related to diesel truck pollution. But this will require reform of many regulatory and statutory barriers, with new incentives and rules to ensure expanded choices for shippers, smart pricing incentives and new fair protections for labor. To help address concerns of the trucking industry, road pricing strategies should be designed to enable truckers to readily pass the cost of road-user fees to their customers through smart bills of lading, much like the new Los Angeles/Long Beach port container fee is assigned to the shipper, rather than the trucker.

- Support new approaches to planning, investment and regulation of inter-city passenger travel. High-quality inter-city rail and bus services need to play a bigger role, connecting airports and central cities across America. These can help the airline industry adapt to high fuel prices, help communities losing air services by offering new connections to other airports and cities for travel markets of up to several hundred miles. Excess airline capacity offered at low prices is not good for climate change. Neither is inadequate rail system capacity, which causes delays and unreliability for passenger rail and enables freight railroads, which own the lines, to charge higher rates that force much freight traffic onto the nation's highways, where related diesel air pollution harms the health of people living close to major highways. New approaches to public-private cooperation and investment are needed.

Coastal Shipping and Rail Investment

Consider reforms to the Jones Act, which impedes development of coastal shipping. Expand private-public partnerships to spur investment in new rail capacity in corridors that warrant it, especially serving congested trade gateways, considering anti-trust or Surface Transportation Board intervention if necessary to influence markets where monopolies or near-monopolies are inhibiting investments needed for effective provision of lower-carbon freight services needed by shippers. Promote rapid expansion of clean rail and shipping fuels and equipment to protect the health of people living near shipping centers and corridors. Adopt emission-based truck tolls and urban low-emission zones, starting with state pilot-projects adapted from the German model, to finance freight system investment and replacement of old, inefficient equipment with clean, low-carbon vehicles, fuels and intermodal systems.

Low-Carbon Fuel Standard (LCFS)

Congress should establish a standard that ensures that biofuels do not worsen greenhouse gas emissions, and replace subsidies for conventional corn-based ethanol (which worsen GHGs) with incentives for development of second-generation low-carbon bio-fuels. LCFS programs have been adopted in California, the European Union, British Columbia and Ontario. Unlike a Renewable Fuel Standard, which may favor specific biofuels, a LCFS can support development of added technologies like plug-in hybrids or natural gas, and help prevent high-carbon fuels, like tar sands, liquid coal and oil shale, from undermining the carbon savings from Renewable Fuel Standards. Removing U.S. tariffs on sugar-based ethanol would expand the market for GHG-reducing biofuels.

Repricing Transportation, Reallocating Street Space

Today's transportation pricing and subsidy systems encourage driving and sprawl. These need to be replaced by such measures as pay-as-you-drive insurance, parking-cash-out, equalization of commuter benefits, and congestion pricing and other road-user charges designed to support better transit and traffic performance. Organizing new bus rapid transit systems can free buses now stuck in traffic, yielding productivity gains. A national Complete Streets policy can ensure safer walking and cycling everywhere, and ensure that transportation investments better serve the one-quarter of all U.S. trips that are less than one mile in length. New incentives, leadership and marketing can make real-time ride-sharing and flexible transit services more socially desirable and attractive as means of mobility in places where conventional transit services don't go. New rail and high-speed rail investments can free up crowded highway space in key gateway corridors. New bicycle parking facilities at transit stops and activity centers can expand the market area for public transportation. These services need to be incorporated into regional planning for improved equity of access to jobs and public facilities.

PAYD insurance pricing is based on traditional rating factors, but is charged by the mile instead of by the month—the less you drive (and in some cases, the more calmly you drive), the more you save. A recent Brookings Institution study[4] estimated such a system could cut GHG emissions and VMT by 8 percent while saving two-thirds of U.S. households money on car insurance, with $270/vehicle average savings for these households. Several companies, such as GMAC Insurance and Progressive, have introduced PAYD products in states where it is not barred, offering mileage-based discounts of 40 percent or more. Congress should require all states to identify and eliminate regulatory barriers that now inhibit PAYD insurance, and ensure that all Americans are offered the option of buying PAYD policies by 2012, with additional incentives to spur insurance companies to offer strong PAYD pricing incentives in their rate plans.

Renovating Governance, Operations and Planning

Reforms to federal funding and programs need to remove barriers to innovation, such as prohibitions on tolling Interstate highways and state insurance regulations that limit PAYD insurance. Federal policy should be reformed so metropolitan planning organizations give much fairer representation to their central city and inner suburban areas, with state DOTs as cooperating, not dominating, partners. MPOs should be given authority to decide on capital investments and management systems in their regions. Cities and counties that have the institutional capacity should be given the option of gaining direct access to federal funds consistent with MPO plans without going through state DOTs, thus eliminating a source of delay in project delivery. Federal performance-based funding should encourage wider application of information technology and private investment in new mobility services. The often fragmented environmental reviews for transportation projects should be made more effective by ensuring that regional and state plans consider alternatives to minimize or avoid adverse impacts, with appropriate notice and public comment, enabling project-level reviews to focus on more detailed elements of project design. Planning and project reviews should consider ways that system management could reduce the need for capacity expansion.

Mobilizing New Public and Private Capital and Initiatives for Superior Performance

The incoming President and Congress should make greater use of performance-based contracting and performance-based funding to protect communities, public health and environmental resources, as well as to ensure more cost-effective service delivery. These approaches, administered through public-public or public-private partnerships, could, for example, reward public or private infrastructure operators with increased funding if they exceed environmental compliance goals and penalize them financially if they fall short. In the event of persistent failure to meet environmental or system performance goals, infrastructure operating entities could go into default and face loss of their authority to continue to operate a facility, which might be re-tendered to another public or private operator under a new performance contract. Enforceable, transparent, auditable performance-based agreements could become the basis for expedited environmental approval of programs and projects. Public-private partnerships should be explored where they might deliver superior results for the public in terms of better environmental and system performance and cost-effectiveness, and in partnership with labor, as has been done in the UK and recently in Chicago. But transparency and timely stakeholder consultation are vital.

Harmonizing Transportation and Environmental Goals

The incoming President needs to renew enforcement of the Clean Air Act and other environmental laws with respect to transportation and other matters, reversing the Bush Administration's persistent efforts to undermine these laws. The incoming Administration should take prompt action to approve a federal waiver for California and a dozen other states to adopt more stringent motor vehicle fuel economy standards to reduce GHGs. To protect public health, the President should instruct EPA to issue new guidance that ensures states will establish new PM 2.5 fine soot monitors near major highways, ports, rail yards, trucking and bus depots, in urban street canyons, and near other likely pollution hot-spot locations, rather than deliberately locating such monitors in places designed to cover up the degree to which people are exposed to harmful pollution concentrations. The incoming President should also ensure that federal agencies in the planning and project review process better account for near-road and near-transportation facility elevated concentrations of mobile-source air toxics which harm public health The incoming President should ask EPA to revisit recent rules and rules-in-progress for sufficiency, given the frequency with which senior Bush Administration officials have overruled EPA staff and scientific advisory panels to the detriment of the environment.

Financing

U.S. infrastructure is in need of significant added investment to restore it to good repair, meet growing mobility demands, improve travel choices, mitigate or remediate adverse impacts of mobility on public health and the environment, and enhance system productivity and service to customers. A short-term funding fix will be required in 2009 as the Highway Trust Fund goes into deficit before the SAFETEA-LU transportation authorization expires in September 2009.

Congress could start by repealing $35 billion in subsidies to the oil industry; expanding the gas-guzzler tax to apply to light trucks (SUVs, minivans, pickups); repealing the remaining $25,000 federal tax credit now available to businesses that purchase the largest SUVs or other gas-guzzling vehicles; removing the remaining restrictions tolling Interstate highways to finance transit and other mobility improvements; and ensuring that the billions of dollars spent on roads and transit go into the most cost-effective transportation investments, whether these be better system management, new roads or new transit.

Congress should lay the foundations for a transition over the next decade to a national system of mileage-based road-user fees to replace or augment the gas tax, which produces shrinking revenues each year. The federal gas tax has not been increased since 1993. Public opinion increasingly sees gas tax increases as among the least desirable ways to finance transportation, preferring direct user fees, such as tolls. Some states have turned to sales taxes to finance transportation, but these are regressive taxes, especially when used to pay for road investments. Because the number of miles driven rises proportionally with income, road-user charges can be a quite equitable means of financing transportation, particularly if the revenues are used to expand travel options, not just to build more roads faster.

The incoming President and Congress should lay a foundation for a new transportation financing system to augment or replace the gas tax, consistent with recommendations of the National Surface Transportation Policy and Revenue Study Commission and the preliminary findings of the National Surface Transportation Finance Commission. Done properly, this will enable state and regional authorities to gain operational control of transportation networks for much higher performance, as well as putting transportation financing on a sound foundation.

The next transportation bill should ensure funding in a number of states of additional larger-scale pilot projects of emission- and mileage-based fees, building on the experience of just-completed Oregon and Washington State pilot projects. These might start with emission-based truck tolls in several states, modeled after Germany's successful experience. There, such tolls have cut GHG emissions by 7 percent and raise over $5 billion per year for road, rail and water transport investments. Because old, dirty trucks pay a 50 percent toll premium, the German trucking industry has supported the tolls, as it helps them compete with truckers from Southern and Eastern Europe. Metropolitan area congestion pricing that is tied to substantial transit system improvement, smart growth planning and bicycle/pedestrian improvements should also be fostered through dedicated innovations grant funding. States should be encouraged to toll existing Interstate highways to pay for reconstruction, maintenance and upgrades.

The United States should transition to emission-based VMT fees over the next decade, following the lead of countries like The Netherlands. To achieve this, the United States should establish national toll technology standards, coordinating with the EU and existing U.S. toll authorities, and ensure rapid development of GPS satellite-based tolling. This will require coordination with car makers, high technology companies, telecommunication companies and companies capable of handling the anticipated volume of toll transactions.

The Oregon VMT pilot program showed how this kind of pricing can be accomplished in an automated manner, with payment at the gas pump, with full privacy protection for individuals who wish to have zero information about their movement patterns available to the government.[5] The Puget Sound VMT pilot showed that more sophisticated billing systems can offer greater system benefits.[6]

Pilot-testing will reveal more about public attitudes and options for full-scale deployment of these new technologies for traffic management and transportation finance. These pilot programs should further explore distributional impacts and benefits and how these might be affected by different approaches to revenue allocation. Means-tested mobility tax credits might ensure positive equity benefits for lower-income households, who will otherwise face diminished mobility under area-wide pricing in areas where public transportation services are poor.[7]

All of these changes will transform how we finance, manage and deliver transportation over the coming decade and lead to transportation services that better meet societal, environmental and economic development goals. Labor, community, environmental justice, business and civic interests all have a stake in the definition of these new mobility system frameworks.

Resources

America Bikes: http://www.americabikes.org/default.asp

American Public Transportation Association: http://www.apta.com/

Association for Commuter Transportation: http://www.actweb.org/mc/page.do?sitePageId=60181&orgId=asct

Bi Partisan Policy Center: http://www.bipartisanpolicy.org/ht/d/sp/i/599/pid/599

Brookings Institution Hamilton Project: http://www.brookings.edu/PROJECTS/HAMILTON PROJECT.ASPX

Brookings Institution Metropolitan Project: http://www.brookings.edu/ METRO.ASPX

Cascadia Institute: http://www.discovery.org/cascadia/

Center for American Progress: http://www.americanprogress.org/

Congestion Pricing Websites at FHWA: http://www.fhwa.dot.gov/congestion/toolbox/pricing.htm, http://www.fhwa.dot.gov/policy/otps/valuepricing.htm

Environmental Defense Fund: www.edf.org

Intelligent Transportation Society of America: www.itsa.org

International Bridge, Tunnel and Turnpike Association: www.ibtta.org

Institute for Transportation and Development Policy: www.itdp.org

League of American Bicyclists: http://www.bikeleague.org/

National Center for Walking and Bicycling: http://www.bikewalk.org

National Housing Conference and the Center for Housing Policy: http://www.nhc.org/

National Surface Transportation Finance Commission: http://financecommission.dot.gov/

National Surface Transportation Policy and Revenue Study Commission: http://www.transportationfortomorrow.org/

Rails to Trails Conservancy: http://www.railtrails.org/index.html

Regional Plan Association: http://www.rpa.org/

T4America: http://t4america.org

Transportation Alternatives: http://www.transalt.org/

Notes

1. Christopher Pyke, Kit Batten, *Full Disclosure: An Executive Order to Require Consideration of Global Warming Under the National Environmental Policy Act,* May 5, 2008, Center for American Progress, http://www.american progress.org/issues/2008/05/pdf/nepa.pdf.

2. National Surface Transportation Policy and Revenue Study Commission. *Transportation for Tomorrow,* January 2008, Washington, D.C.

3. National Surface Transportation Infrastructure Financing Commission, *The Path Forward: Funding and Financing our Surface Transportation System, Interim Report,* February 2008, Washington, D.C., http://financecommission.dot.gov/Documents/Interim %20Report%20-%20The%20Path%20Forward.pdf.

4. Jason E. Bordoff, Jason E. and Pascal Noel, *Pay-As-You-Drive Auto Insurance: A Simple Way to Reduce Driving-Related Harms and Increase Equity,*Washington, D.C, July 2008.

5. James M. Whitty, *Oregon's Mileage Fee Concept and Road User Fee Pilot Program,* Oregon Department of Transportation, Final Report, Salem, OR, November 2007.

6. Puget Sound Regional Council, *Traffic Choices Study—Summary Report: A Global Positioning System Based Pricing Pilot Project: Evaluating Traveler Response to Variable Road Tolling Through a Sample of Volunteer Participants,* April 2008, Seattle, WA.

7. David Lewis, *America's Traffic Congestion Problem: Toward a Framework for Nationwide Reform,* Brookings Institution Hamilton Project, April 2008, Washington, D.C.

Chapter 26

Rebuilding and Renewing America: A National Infrastructure Plan for the Twenty-first Century

Earl Blumenauer

POLICY PROPOSALS

- Establish a National Infrastructure Commission to identify current and future infrastructure needs and challenges in the areas of transportation; water supplies, treatment and delivery systems; and power distribution systems.
- Develop a national transportation policy that addresses public health outcomes, land uses, energy consumption, carbon emissions and local needs; supports a range of transportation options; and identifies sustainable funding.
- Create a water trust fund to provide a deficit-neutral, consistent and sustainable source of revenue to support the nation's water supply and wastewater treatment infrastructure.
- Reinstate the Superfund Tax to clean up abandoned toxic sites.
- Craft a comprehensive national disaster policy that focuses on prevention instead of recovery.
- Reform the relationship between the federal government and its partners.

* * * * * * * * * * * * * * *

Our nation is falling apart.

American communities of all sizes are suffering from failing infrastructure: deteriorating roads and bridges; crumbling water lines; overburdened water treatment plants; and an energy distribution system incapable of serving new energy sources and growing demands.

This crisis is so bad that the American Society of Civil Engineers has given our nation's infrastructure a grade of D-minus, estimating that it will cost $1.6 trillion over the next five years just to repair it.

- The National Surface Transportation Policy and Revenue Study Commission calculated that maintaining our existing transportation system will cost $225 billion annually for the next fifty years. Yet the Highway Trust Fund, the most reliable source of federal transportation dollars since the Great Depression, will be broke by 2009.
- Our water infrastructure is also showing its age. More than 72,000 miles of municipal water and sewer pipe are more than eighty years old, threatening the health, environment and economy of communities large and small. Yet the federal government contribution to total clean water spending has shrunk dramatically in the past thirty years, from 78 percent to a mere 3 percent. Today, we need to spend $300–$500 billion more, just to make sure our aging water infrastructure doesn't collapse. The GAO, the Environmental Protection Agency, the Congressional Budget Office and the Water Infrastructure Network all estimate a growing water infrastructure funding gap.

Sadly, our federal government is investing less in our infrastructure than we have for the last fifty years—a mere two-thirds of 1 percent of our GDP. Meanwhile, other nations are not only planning, but investing heavily in their future. China, for example, is currently investing 8 percent of its GDP for the next twenty years in building 18,000 miles of railroad, a 53,000-mile highway system and nearly 100 new airports.

This disparity between our neglect and others' investments places our international leadership at risk. We simply cannot leave it to our communities alone to respond to the growing challenges of rising energy prices, unstable world events and increasingly competitive global marketplaces. The federal government must be a visionary leader and partner, committing both resources and political will to repairing and maintaining our national infrastructure.

We've seen what happens when a nation can no longer compete in the global economy; the Soviet Union collapsed in the 1990s not because of superior American military might, but because the USSR no longer had the governmental and economic structure to be efficient and competitive. If we lose our capacity to provide the critical transportation, communication and energy systems needed for our nation and our communities to thrive and prosper, we run the same risk of economic and international irrelevance.

We are also facing the greatest crisis of our civilization: global warming. Already, we have witnessed the impact of extreme weather events on our roads, bridges, levees, water systems and communications networks—and there is more to come. To avoid the worst effects of climate change, we must reduce our carbon emissions by 80 percent below 1990 levels by 2050. We have no time to waste. To reach this goal, we need to take action within the next thirty months.

The good news is that millions of Americans are not waiting for the federal government, but are taking action now to address these challenges. In churches and synagogues, in colleges and universities and high schools and grade schools, in new business start-ups and established international corporations, Americans are changing individual behaviors and moving towards more sustainable practices. Over 850 cities in all fifty states have signed on to the Mayors' Climate Change Agreement to conserve energy and reduce their greenhouse gas emissions, some already with spectacular results. Several states are adopting their own fuel emission standards; Americans are driving less and taking transit more; Americans are moving to urban areas with convenient services and transportation options. People are eagerly taking action to support their local economies, reduce energy use and protect their communities from climate change.

The federal government must take responsibility for its leadership role in addressing global climate change—and it needs to do this with all possible haste. If we delay, we run an increasing risk of becoming irrelevant. Our nation has much to offer the international community in terms of creativity, technical knowledge and innovation, but we are quickly losing the opportunity to capitalize on our contributions, and to limit the impacts of global climate change.

Unfortunately, our existing patterns of government leave us remarkably ill-suited to meet these challenges. Federal agencies, Congressional committees and the federal budget are organized into narrow issue areas that stymie big-picture approaches and collaboration; turf battles between federal and state and local jurisdictions favor constrained projects and short-term fixes over comprehensive policies and creative partnerships, while special interests continue to protect the status quo.

We certainly do not lack the knowledge or even the wisdom to meet these challenges; we have plenty of experts in finance, science, design and construction who are eager to help us tackle these problems. What we lack, however, is the political will to weave these answers into comprehensive solutions that will address our past neglect and create the twenty-first century transportation and water systems we need.

If we are bold enough, we can craft collaborative and sustainable solutions to life in a carbon-constrained economy. We can ensure adequate supplies of clean water to strengthen our communities, nurture our environment, improve public health and improve food security for all Americans. With increased investments in renewable energy, we can decrease the impacts of global climate change, reduce our reliance on foreign oil, strengthen our national security and lay the groundwork for a more sustainable economy.

The Precedent

Presidential leadership to tackle critical infrastructure problems is nothing new. The challenges of creating a new nation in the nineteenth century and ensuring its economic survival one hundred years later were just as immense and over-whelming in their days as our investment shortfalls and global warming are to-day.

In 1808, President Thomas Jefferson commissioned Secretary of the Treas-ury Albert Gallatin to create a transportation and financing plan to knit a ragtag bunch of colonies along the eastern seaboard into a nation that spanned an entire continent. The Gallatin Plan built on George Washington's vision of roads and canals to connect interior settlements to the East Coast, defined the Homestead Act and established the public-private partnerships that built the first transconti-nental railroad and the Erie Canal.

One hundred years later, President Theodore Roosevelt invited governors, Cabinet and Congressional members, and business leaders to develop a plan for American twentieth-century infrastructure needs. The report from this White House Conference protected natural resources through improved farming and soil conservation methods, established federal policies to curtail the excesses of the industrial revolution, and created the National Park System. It also laid the groundwork for the massive hydropower projects that provided water and elec-tric power to rural America and jump-started the nation's recovery from the Great Depression.

Today, it is our turn to build upon the American tradition of bold and suc-cessful plans, by crafting a National Infrastructure Plan to Rebuild and Renew America.

The challenges of the twenty-first century—crumbling infrastructure, soar-ing energy prices, global warming and rapid population growth—provide us with a unique opportunity to strengthen our communities and national economy. By optimizing our existing investments and employing sustainable technologies and processes that increase our energy independence, we can address our infra-structure needs while we generate hundreds of thousands of skilled, family-wage jobs that support local businesses and establish a new direction for sustainable economic growth.

We need to start with a new approach to today's problems. Increased infra-structure investments must reflect our understanding of this century's global climate changes, economic shifts and energy uncertainties. If we are to capture the most value from each dollar invested, we need to start with a vision that sup-ports these priorities with strong commitments to implement the needed changes. Why should we pay more, for example, for short-term, high-tech solu-tions when less-intrusive, greener solutions are often cheaper? Rethinking the purpose and priorities of our investments is a critical component of Rebuilding and Renewing America.

This new approach will also require a strong political message, one that builds public trust and support and overcomes partisan politics. We can no longer allow critical issues and immediate actions to fall prey to destructive par-tisan politics. Instead, we must craft solutions that encourage investments in and benefits for people from the full range of political thought. We need to express solutions in terms that people understand, reward rather than penalize risk-takers, and capture value from our investments.

Establish a National Infrastructure Commission

This Commission would conduct national public hearings and develop a vision and a set of principles that optimize our existing investments, address the impacts of global warming, and support local economies. I have introduced HR 5976, The U.S. Commission on Rebuilding America, to do just that.

Develop a National Transportation Policy

The authorization of the federal transportation legislation in 2009 provides a significant opportunity to put national infrastructure values and principles into practice. Our new transportation policy should:
- Maximize existing investments; capture value from future investments.
- Create a transportation system that provides a range of choices and strong links among all modes, including highway, rail, air, public transit, walking and biking.
- Reduce greenhouse gas emissions.
- Provide a mode-neutral match ratio for federal funds.
- Support the economies and desired land uses of rural communities as well as metropolitan regions.
- Protect public and environmental health.

Create a Water Trust Fund

This fund would:
- Ensure sustainable funding for water conservation and re-use, through sources such as container fees; taxes on flushable products, and agricultural chemicals and practices; and certain pharmaceuticals.
- Provide authority to states to establish priorities; deliver funds directly to municipalities.
- Provide additional funding programs for research and development, green infrastructure, small water systems and other priorities.
- Prohibit funding for systems that contribute to sprawling development.

Reinstate the Superfund Tax

The Superfund Program has expired, yet the remaining pollution at these sites poses a significant and ongoing risk to public and environmental health.

Craft a Comprehensive National Disaster Policy

The federal government has a responsibility to help communities prepare for natural events, yet our longstanding policies provide a false sense of security by focusing on guaranteed relief efforts instead of preventive measures. Because our cities, counties, states, private companies, and citizens have come to expect the federal government to bail them out after disaster strkes, they have no incentive to take precautions that would minimize damage.

The Disaster Policy also needs to be fiscally honest. Currently, disaster relief funds are not accounted for in the usual budgeting process, so are seen as "free money" by policymakers, while funds for "prevention" must submit to the rigors and politics of the Congressional appropriations process. Addressing this obvious inequity is a first step to focusing on policies and measures that can save lives, property and scarce taxpayer dollars.

A National Disaster Policy can correct these problems and do a better job of saving lives and property by:

- Shifting the focus of federal investments from recovery to prevention and protection, and by conditioning relief funds on precautionary and mitigating measures.
- Providing technical assistance to local jurisdictions to support mitigation efforts, such as hazard mapping, land use planning, and building and design codes that limit the loss of life and property.
- Optimizing the ability of natural features such as wetlands, forests and watersheds to reduce the impact of devastating and predictable natural events.
- Investing in evacuation plans that serve all citizens.
- Refusing to favor funding for disaster relief over funding for disaster prevention.

Reform the Relationship Between the Federal Government and Its Partners

The premise that the federal government is immune from the regulations and restrictions imposed upon state and local governments and the private sector destroys Americans' belief in the credibility in their federal government. Our efforts to renew and rebuild America will not be successful unless we can replace this dynamic with a new ethic that requires the federal government to lead by example. Some such examples:

- Locate federal buildings near transit; require them to be highly energy-efficient.
- Increase the fuel efficiency of federal auto fleets.
- Require the U.S. military to provide affordable and energy-efficient housing.
- Require the U.S. military to speed up its cleanup of left-behind pollutants and unexploded ordnance (UXO).
- Require federal policies that reduce global warming, reward energy conservation and invest in alternative energy sources.

Central to this vision is a new relationship in which the federal government plays a constructive and reliable role with its partners. It should make uniform investments in projects and activities where there is a federal interest, instead of selecting winners and losers by lavishly supporting some projects and giving little or nothing to others.

Conclusion

Our ability to maintain our leadership in a rapidly changing world depends on our ability to re-invest in our own infrastructure to support our economy, strengthen our communities and address the growing impacts of global warming. But this investment will not be successful if it continues to rely on outmoded funding sources and antiquated assumptions about the role of the federal government. Rebuilding and Renewing America provides us with an opportunity to not just shape the next twenty years, but to embark on a new century of American leadership at home and abroad.

Resources

America2050: www.america2050.org
American Association of State Highway and Transportation Officials: www.transportation.org
American Institute of Architects: www.aia.org
American Planning Association: www.planning.org
American Society of Civil Engineers: www.asce.org
American Water Works Association Research Foundation: www.awwarf.org
Association of Metropolitan Water Agencies: www.amwa.net
Association of State Floodplain Managers: www.floods.org

Brookings Institution: www.brookings.edu
Center for Neighborhood Technology: www.cnt.org
Clean Water America: http://www.cleanwateramerica.org/
Environment America: http://www.environmentamerica.org/stop-toxic-pollution
Environmental Protection Agency: http://www.epa.gov/superfund/
Food and Water Watch: http://www.fwwatch.org
Institute for Business and Home Safety: www.disastersafety.org
League of American Bicyclists: http://www.bikeleague.org
Lincoln Land Institute: http://www.lincolnlandinst.edu
National Association of Clean Water Agencies: http://www.nacwa.org
National Surface Transportation Policy and Revenue Study Commission:
    http://www.transportationfortomorrow.org
Partners for Disaster Resistance and Resilience: http://www.oregonshowcase.org
Public Entity Risk Institute: http://www.riskinstitute.org
Smart Growth America: www.smartgrowthamerica.com
Surface Transportation Policy Partnership: http://www.transact.org
Transportation for America: http://www.t4america.org
US Mayors Climate Protection Agreement:
    http://www.usmayors.org/climateprotection/agreement.htm
US Public Interest Research Group (PIRG): http://www.uspirg.org
Water Environment Federation: http://www.wef.org
Water Environment Research Foundation: http://www.werf.org
Water Infrastructure Network: http://www.win-water.org

References

Abramovitz, Janet. *Unnatural Disasters: Worldwatch Paper 158.* World Watch
    Institute (October 1, 2001).
Evaluation of Erosion Hazards. Report by The Heinz Center for the Federal
    Emergency Management Association (FEMA), April 2000.
*Higher Ground: A Report on Voluntary Property Buyouts in the Nation's
    Floodplains.* Report by National Wildlife Federation, July 1998.
Kunreuther, Howard, and Richard J. Roth Sr., eds. *Paying the Price: The Status
    and Role of Insurance Against Natural Disasters in the United States.*
    Washington, D.C.: Joseph Henry Press, 1998.
Mileti, Dennis. *Disasters by Design: A Reassessment of Natural Hazards in the
    United States.* Boulder: University of Colorado Press, 1999.
Sharing the Challenge: Floodplain Management into the 21ˢᵗ Century. Report of
    the Interagency Floodplain Management Review Committee to the Admini-
    stration Floodplain Management Task Force, 1994.

Chapter 27

Katrina: A Chance to Do It Right

William Quigley

POLICY PROPOSALS

- Establish an independent bipartisan Katrina Inquiry Commission to prepare a full and complete account of the circumstances surrounding the Katrina disaster, including preparedness for and the immediate response to the disaster. Mandate the Commission to provide recommendations designed to guard against future attacks.
- Appoint a special prosecutor to investigate and prosecute government and corporate abuse in Katrina disaster response contracting and expenditures, specifically including non-profit sector entities that raised or received monies in the name of Katrina victims.
- Amend all disaster laws to require local community and survivor participation in preparation, response and evaluation, with special emphasis on participation of women, people of color, renters and the most vulnerable.
- Establish binding post-disaster equitable rebuilding principles to guarantee local community participation, transparency, equity and accountability in rebuilding and prioritizing the needs of the most vulnerable in areas such as housing, health care, employment, education, public transportation and the right to vote.
- Reverse post-Katrina privatization of housing, health care, education and decision-making.
- Adopt the United Nations "Guiding Principles on Internal Displacement" and enforce right to return for everyone.
- Launch a national Wetlands Reclamation and Secure Levees Project.
- Establish a WPA-Style redevelopment project to employ 100,000 survivors of the disaster in rebuilding and reconstruction of their communities.

* * * * * * * * * * * * * * *

"If 9/11 was a failure of imagination, then Katrina was a failure of initiative. It was a failure of leadership."[1]

Hurricane Katrina and its aftermath was a historic U.S. disaster. The natural storm, and its all-too-human failures, made visible many deep social, political, economic and institutional problems. These range from the intentional reduction of the role of government; lack of investment in infrastructure; lack of decent affordable housing and accessible health care; destruction of the environment and the consequences of global warming; pervasive poverty; the high cost of the Iraq invasion and occupation; marginalization of entire communities; as well as continuing racism and sexism.

In Louisiana, 1,464 people died. Over 204,000 homes suffered severe or major damage. More than 200,000 people lost their jobs, and 81,000 businesses were damaged.[2] In Mississippi, over 230 people died and 200,000 were displaced from their homes, as the storm damaged 28,000 square miles, over 60 percent of the state.[3]

Further, as they say on the Gulf Coast, Katrina was a gift that keeps on giving. The consequences of Katrina now look to be generational, as the effects shape children and grandchildren and cities and counties and even states.

Katrina did offer opportunity. It offered a chance for the United States to look honestly at our failings and the opportunity to start over with a new mission of justice for all.

Our nation had the option of responding in a way that leveled the playing field and provided more opportunities for working families. Deep historic patterns of housing discrimination and exclusion based on race could have been challenged with the billions directed to housing. The consequences of the feminization of poverty, where women bear a much heavier burden from injustice, could have been addressed by demanding that all policies be gender-fair and by enforcing those laws. Families who rent could have been treated as fairly as families purchasing their homes. The public sector that has been subjected to dismantling for decades could have been reinvigorated to rise to the many challenges of infrastructure and institutional repair and redevelopment. Corporations that profit from public disaster funds could have been subjected to conditions of transparency and strict accountability. Those usually left behind when government and the powerful make decisions, those people left behind in New Orleans when Katrina hit, could have been made a part of the rebuilding, part of the review of what happened and part of the planning for what happens next.

But our nation declined those Katrina opportunities.

Instead, our nation chose to take up the other opportunities Katrina offered. Katrina and its aftermath offered a chance to those who profit politically and economically from the misfortunes of others and they took it. It offered an opportunity to accelerate those policies that rebalance the scales even more in favor of the powerful. The public sector was further diminished. Billions in public works that could have been done by the public sector were instead contracted to private corporations with little public oversight.[4] Over half the public schools in

New Orleans were turned into charter schools.[5] The government seized and sealed thousands of public housing apartments in order to demolish them and hand the land over to private developers.[6] Public health care and public transportation were dramatically cut back.[7] Local elected officials were pushed aside and replaced by unelected panels. Funds were prioritized to homeowners to leave out renters. Patterns of racism remained. Women, especially older and working-class heads of households were kept from returning home by the lack of public schools, housing, transportation, day care and health care.[8] All of this left billions available for the corporations and the connected to divide up as spoils.

These are the Katrina opportunities our national political leaders chose, and our nation and its people are the worse for it.

New national leadership offers one more, possibly last, chance to revive some of the hope that bloomed briefly after Katrina. The hope that people displaced through no fault of their own will be able to come home to a new and better and fairer and more just community. The hope that those whose actions contributed to the disaster and its horrifying aftermath will be held up to the light of public scrutiny and be held accountable. The hope that those who suffered so much will be an essential part of the rebuilding of their communities. This hope still lives.

Three years later, half the working poor, elderly and disabled people of New Orleans are not back. There has been a 50 percent reduction in people receiving Social Security; only half the number of Medicaid recipients are back; and the public school population is down 52 percent.[9]

People are heroically rebuilding their lives. But despite individual work and the kindness of volunteers and strangers, we still need our government to respond in order to have a chance to rebuild. Some have made independent decisions not to return, but most have had their choices limited by the lack of affordable housing, health care, decent schools and public transportation. Of course, there is a substantial racial overlay to this. Gender and class also dictate who has returned. As a result, the beauty of New Orleans that arose primarily from working-class family, African-American neighborhoods, the second-line parades, family cooking, music, work and culture is at real risk.

The people and communities of the Gulf Coast have a love-hate relationship with government. We curse its failures and its mistakes. Its delays force us to do more and more for ourselves with the help of the thousands of volunteers who have been by our side. But we know that it is only government, our common shared commitment embodied in our public institutions, which has the breadth and resources to help rebuild after such a disaster.

Does the current government leadership or the investor class really care about this? Current evidence appears to say no. The people of the Gulf Coast, however, are trying hard to preserve and revive. It is not wise to bet against the people in the long run, but it is also not wise to underestimate the power of exclusion in the short run.

The policy proposals outlined above are aimed at discovering what went wrong before that created the catastrophe called Katrina, analyzing the response to Katrina, working to include those left out in the planning, preparing for the future and helping rebuild the Gulf Coast in an equitable manner. The new Administration has the opportunity to radically reshape the national response to Katrina.

Katrina Commission

Democrats asked for a 9/11-like commission after Katrina, but Republicans did not allow it.[10] Without a full disclosure of the facts, the nation cannot have a realistic or fruitful discussion about what needs to happen differently next time. For example, there has been no investigation and hardly any discussion about the role the oil companies played in destroying the natural wetlands that should have provided protection for parts of the Gulf Coast. Different agencies and Congressional committees have looked into different parts of Katrina, but no one has been given the power to compel all the facts about all the phases of the preparation and immediate response. The Gulf Coast needs this. So does the nation.

Special Prosecutor

As a result of privatization of government work after Katrina, tens of billions of dollars went flying out of the national treasury to corporations without competitive bids.[11] Many of the same corporations working in Iraq—Bechtel, CHM2Hill, Shaw Group, Flour Corporation—received Katrina contracts, as have other politically connected firms.[12]

It appears that 98 percent of the money distributed in a disaster ends up enriching corporations. One example is the blue tarps that the government put on the roofs of houses after Katrina. The main contractor, Shaw Group, got $175 a square to put on the tarps. (A square is 100 square feet, a 10' x 10' section.) They subcontracted the work out to another corporation for $75 a square. The second corporation subcontracted the work out to a third corporation for $30 a square, and they in turn subcontracted it out again to guys who did the work for $2 a square. Two dollars a square for the actual worker is less than 2 percent of what the government paid out.[13]

Criminal prosecutions have begun against individuals who defrauded the government out of a $2,000 disaster check or other small crimes. Those prosecutions should continue. But a serious investigation into huge government contracts and their waste and criminality has not been launched. These investigations should extend to the non-governmental organizations that raised or spent money in the name of Katrina victims.

Mandate Real Community Participation

Once a disaster hits, it is too late to ask local communities what they need. Before disaster occurs, members the community need to be a real part of the planning and decision-making. Communities have wisdom. But working and poor communities have had no actual voice in disaster preparation and decision-making. As a result, others have spoken for them and others made plans for them. Disasters show that the plans made by people outside the community were grossly inadequate in the communities not represented. Therefore, there must be, in the legal requirements for all disaster planning, a conscious effort to include those usually left out, specifically women, communities of color, non-property owners, and the aged and disabled. Including these voices will not completely answer all the unanticipated problems of a disaster, but it will reduce them.

Guarantee Equitable Rebuilding

Katrina demonstrated that once disaster hits, those with the power and influence take charge. They start the rebuilding processes with their own interests in mind. For example, right after the hurricane hit Southern Mississippi, Vice President Dick Cheney's office called the Southern Pines Electric Power Association and ordered it to restore power to a substation that moves gasoline and diesel fuel from Texas to the Northeast. That call resulted in power workers being reassigned from restoring power to two hospitals and a number of water systems in rural Mississippi.[14]

Likewise, the Heritage Foundation issued a report days after Katrina containing its proposals for the reconstruction of the Gulf Coast: private entrepreneurial activity, not government, as the primary engine of rebuilding; public schools making way for increased charter schools; elimination of regulations on business to speed up private sector investment; repeal of environmental laws and regulations like the National Environmental Policy Act and the Clean Air Act; opening up the Arctic National Wildlife Refuge; and repeal of the estate tax.[15]

Before disasters hit, just principles must be incorporated into post-disaster rebuilding planning. Getting the oil and gas pipelines up and working is a part of the response to disaster, but it is not the only part, nor necessarily the most important part. The people need to know what is going on, hence transparency is important. The people need to know how to impact the decision-making process, hence participation and accountability are important. Prioritizing the needs of the most vulnerable did not happen after Katrina, so this must be incorporated into the legal requirements, particularly in the survival needs of housing, health care, employment, education, public transportation and the right to vote.

Reverse Post-Katrina Privatization

Katrina put privatization on steroids along the Gulf Coast. In New Orleans alone, the majority of public schools were flipped to charter schools; the main public health care facility closed and has been a political football ever since; the majority of public housing apartments were demolished and their land given to private developers; and the role of the City Council was diminished in favor of an appointed board. These decisions should be reversed and funds redirected into the public sector.

Enforce the Right to Return

Few in the United States know that the UN has developed principles for governmental action after a natural disaster. These are known as the "Guiding Principles on Internal Displacement."[16] These outline enforceable expectations to guide national governments.[17] Our country expects other nations to follow these principles, but says they do not apply at our country. They should. These principles give every victim of a natural disaster the right to return home if they want to, with full government support to do so, no exceptions. They require affordable housing and the other necessities of life for all who need it. The United States should adopt these principles and make them apply to Katrina and other victims.

Reclaim Wetlands and Secure Levees and Dams

Had Katrina hit a century before, much of its waves and winds would have been absorbed by scores of miles of wetlands. Those wetlands, swamps and marshes, which extended fifty miles out from New Orleans, are now mostly gone. The wetlands were victimized by oil and gas exploration and the navigation canals cut into them, mostly with federal and state approval.[18]

Reclamation is costly but the alternatives cost much more. Likewise, the levees and dams of our nation—they are expensive to survey, analyze and fix, but the alternatives are much more costly. Protecting our coasts and waterways will protect people.

Employ 100,000 Survivors to Reconstruct
Their Own Communities

President Franklin Delano Roosevelt initiated the Works Progress Administration during the Great Depression to help put the unemployed back to work so as to create much- needed infrastructure and civic improvements across our nation. In like manner, the Gulf Coast Civic Works Project is a national campaign to create 100,000 good-paying jobs for residents and evacuees from the area to rebuild the infrastructure and housing necessary to be able to return home. HR 4048 was introduced to do this, a concept that has been supported by numerous state and local communities, from the California Senate to the Louisiana Republican Party.[19]

What Katrina revealed is not unique to the Gulf Coast. Every one of our cities has its own Lower Ninth Ward and its own marginalized communities. The disempowering forces of race, class, gender and market-driven neoliberalism are working across the world and in communities across our country. What Katrina revealed about New Orleans is not unique to the Gulf Coast—it is just a more concentrated and vivid illustration of what is going on everywhere else. Social justice advocates can and should use the experiences of the people of Katrina to develop and promote a shift in our country's treatment of the most marginalized members of our society. If we do, what Katrina revealed will offer challenges and opportunities for us all.

Resources

ACORN Gulf Coast Recovery: http://www.acorn.org
Advancement Project: http://www.advancementproject.org
Facing South, The Institute for Southern Studies: http://southernstudies.org/facingsouth/
Greater New Orleans Community Data Center www.gnocdc.org
Gulf Coast Civic Works Project: www.solvingpoverty.com
Katrina Index at the Brookings Institution: http://www.brookings.edu
Mississippi Center for Justice: http://www.mscenterforjustice.org
Women of the Storm: http://www.womenofthestorm.net

References

"A Failure of Initiative: Final Report of the Select Bipartisan Committee to Investigate the Preparation for and Response to Hurricane Katrina." United States Congress, February 19, 2006. http://www.gpoaccess.gov/katrinareport/fullreport.pdf (accessed July 21, 2008).

William Quigley

Farber, Daniel A., and Jim Chen. *Disasters and the Law: Katrina and Beyond.* New York: Aspen Publishers, 2006.

Hartman, Chester, and Gregory D. Squires, eds. *There is No Such Thing as a Natural Disaster: Race, Class, and Hurricane Katrina.* New York: Routledge, 2006.

Troutt, David Dante, ed. *After the Storm: Black Intellectuals Explore the Meaning of Hurricane Katrina.* New York: W. W. Norton, 2006.

Wright, Beverly. "Katrina Reveals Environmental Racism's Deadly Force," New America Media, Commentary, September 21, 2005. http://news.ncmonline.com/news/view_article.html?article_id=74fb2e18f6e1c829ae731 81353442a61 (accessed July 21, 2008).

Wright, Beverly, and Robert D. Bullard. "Legacy of Unfairness: Why Some Americans Get Left Behind." Environmental Justice Resource Center, September 29, 2005. http://www.ejrc.cau.edu/Exec%20Summary%20Legacy.html (accessed July 21, 2008).

———. "The Real Looting: Katrina Exposes a Legacy of Discrimination and Opens the Door for 'Disaster Capitalism'." SeeingBlack.com, October 11, 2005. http://www.seeingblack.com/2005/x101105/411_oct05.shtml (accessed July 21, 2008).

van Heerden, Ivor, and Mike Bryan. *The Storm: What Went Wrong and Why During Hurricane Katrina.* New York: Viking, 2006.

Notes

1. "A Failure of Initiative: Final Report of the Select Bipartisan Committee to Investigate the Preparation for and Response to Hurricane Katrina," United States Congress, February 19, 2006, p. xi, http://www.gpoaccess.gov/katrinareport/fullreport.pdf (accessed July 21, 2008).

2. Hurricane Katrina Anniversary Data for Louisiana," *Louisiana Road Home*, August 20, 2006, http://lra.louisiana.gov/assets/LouisianaKatrinaAnniversaryData082206.pdf (accessed June 19, 2008).

3. A Failure of Initiative, supra, at 8.

4. "Big, Easy Money: Disaster Profiteering on the American Gulf Coast," Report. CORPWATCH, August 17, 2006, http://www.corpwatch.org/article.php?id=14023 (accessed June 19, 2008).

5. Jay Matthews, "Charter Schools' Big Experiment," *Washington Post*, June 9, 2008, A1, http://www.washingtonpost.com/wp-dyn/content/article/2008/06/08/AR20080 60802174_pf.html (accessed June 19, 2008).

6. See generally: William P. Quigley, "Obstacle to Opportunity: Housing That Working and Poor People Can Afford in New Orleans Since Katrina," *Wake Forest L. Rev.* 393 (2007).

7. William P. Quigley, *Thirteen Ways of Looking at Katrina: Human and Civil Rights*, 81 TUL. L. REV. 955, 977, 982 (2007).

8. Sarah Vaill, "The Calm in the Storm: Women Leaders in Gulf Coast Recovery" (2006), http://www.wfnet.org/documents/publications/katrina_report_082706.pdf; Erica

Williams et al., "The Women of New Orleans and the Gulf Coast: Multiple Disadvantages and Key Assets for Recovery, Part II," *Gender, Race, and Class in the Labor Market* (2006), http://www.iwpr.org/pdf/D465.pdf. (accessed June 19, 2008).

9. Bill Quigley, "Half New Orleans Poor Permanently Displaced: Failure or Success?" Common Dreams, March 4, 2008, http://www.commondreams.org/archive/2008/03/04/7462/ (accessed June 19, 2008).

10. "Senate Kills Bill for Katrina Commission," *USA Today*, September 14, 2005, http://www.usatoday.com/news/washington/2005-09-14-katrina-probe_x.htm (accessed June 19, 2008).

11. "Big, Easy Money: Disaster Profiteering on the American Gulf Coast," Report, CORPWATCH, August 17, 2006, http://www.corpwatch.org/article.php?id=14023 (accessed June 19, 2008).

12. William Quigley, "Trying to Make It Home," Counterpunch, August 22, 2006, http://www.counterpunch.org/quigley08222006.html (accessed June 19, 2008).

13. Gordon Russell and James Varney, "From Blue Tarps to Debris Removal, Layers of Contractors Drive Up the Cost of Recovery, Critics Say," *Times-Picayune*, December 29, 2005, http://www.pulitzer.org/year/2006/public-service/works/neworleansps19.html (accessed June 19, 2008).

14. Nikki Davis Maute, "Power Crews Diverted: Restoring Pipeline Came First," *Hattiesburg American*, Sept. 11, 2005.

15. Edwin Meese et al., "From Tragedy to Triumph: Principled Solutions for Rebuilding Lives and Communities," Report, Heritage Foundation, 2005, http://www. heritage.org/Research/GovernmentReform/sr05.cfm (accessed July 19, 2008).

16. "Guiding Principles on Internal Displacement," United Nations Office of the High Commissioner for Human Rights, February 11, 1998, http://www.unhchr.ch/html/menu2/7/b/principles.htm (accessed June 19, 2008).

17. William Quigley and Sharda Sekaran, "A Call for the Right to Return in the Gulf Coast," in *Bringing Human Rights Home: from Civil Rights to Human Rights,* Cynthia Soohoo et al. ed. (Westport: Greenwood Publishing, 2007), 291–94.

18. Oliver A. Houck, "Retaking the Exam: How Environmental Law Failed New Orleans and the Gulf Coast South and How It Might Yet Succeed," *Tulane Law Review,* Vol. 81 (2007), 1059.

19. Gulf Coast Civic Works Project, http://www.solvingpoverty.com/ (accessed July 21, 2008).

Chapter 28

From Newcomers to Americans:
An Integration Policy for a Nation
of Immigrants[1]

Tomás R. Jiménez

POLICY PROPOSALS

- Create a pathway to legal residency for unauthorized immigrants.
- Allow individuals brought at a young age to the United States without authorization to become legal permanent residents.
- Create an office within U.S. Citizenship and Immigration Services (US-CIS) devoted to immigrant integration.
- Set up a foundation within USCIS to make grants to non-profits and local governments for programs aimed at achieving immigrant integration.
- Create an information-sharing mechanism that allows local governments to share best practices for immigrant integration.
- Expand access to English-language classes for English-language learners, both adults and children.
- Create a mechanism for translating foreign credentials into Qualifications that employers understand.

* * * * * * * * * * * * * *

Immigrant integration has become a national issue as millions of America's newcomers adapt to communities that must in turn adjust to the social, economic and political changes resulting from the presence of these newcomers. Integration is an inevitable process wherein immigrants and the communities in which they settle mutually adapt to one another. But the inevitability of integration does not always guarantee positive outcomes. Integration may follow a path that

257

leads to divisiveness between newcomers and their receiving communities—a more likely outcome when integration is left to chance. A sound immigrant-integration policy can facilitate a more positive, unifying form of integration that benefits immigrants, their receiving communities and the nation as a whole.

Political pundits and policymakers have done a good deal of hand-wringing about integration, but government policies are virtually silent on this issue. The debate on immigration reform has largely revolved around the laws that govern who is admitted to the United States and under what circumstances, and very little attentions has been given to questions of integration. However, the United States needs much more than an overhaul of its immigration policy. This nation of immigrants also needs an immigrant policy that takes a more active role in the integration of newcomers, thereby maximizing the economic, social and cultural contributions that immigrants make to the United States.

The Need for an Integration Policy

Comparisons between contemporary and past waves of immigrants often lead to the conclusion that something is amiss with the way today's immigrants are integrating. Fears about their lack of integration are largely exaggerated, however. Though there is variation among groups, today's newcomers appear to be integrating into U.S. society in ways reminiscent of immigrants from previous eras, with the second-generation children and third-generation grandchildren of first-generation immigrants mastering English, improving their educational status and joining the U.S. workforce.[2]

Nearly all the children and grandchildren of immigrants speak English well, regardless of ethnic origin. For instance, according to the 2000 Census, 91.1 percent of the children and 97 percent of the grandchildren of Mexican immigrants spoke English well. Similarly, 93.8 percent of the children and 98.4 percent of the grandchildren of Salvadoran immigrants spoke English well in 2000.[3] Patterns in educational attainment also evince intergenerational improvement. Calculations from the 2004 Current Population Survey show, for example, that the share of Mexican immigrants without a high-school diploma was 58 percent, but only 16.9 percent of their children lacked a diploma. Conversely, only 5.7 percent of Mexican immigrants had a college degree, compared to 14.1 percent of their children.[4]

In addition, immigrants and their children are hardly idle when it comes to work. The 2004 Current Population Survey shows that adult immigrant men from Canada, Europe and Australia had the lowest employment rate (83.4 percent), while those from Mexico had the highest (87.3 percent). Immigrants actually tend to have somewhat higher rates of employment than their children. The employment rate of second-generation men from Canada, Europe and Australia was 82.6 percent, while that of second-generation Mexicans was 81.1 percent. Evidence of intergenerational improvement in employment rates is pronounced among women. For instance, only 45.3 percent of first-generation Mexican women were in the labor force, compared to 70.2 percent of their children.[5]

Mexicans, by far the largest immigrant group at 31 percent of all foreign-born individuals, are often cited as an exception to these larger integration trends. But they too appear to be integrating over time, even if at a slower pace compared to other groups. Sociologist Richard Alba finds that each new generation of Mexican-origin individuals born in the United States improves on their parents' educational attainment by an average of 2.5 years, though the third generation still lags behind non-Hispanic whites by 1–1.5 years (the gap is smaller among women).[6] Similarly, a 2006 study by RAND Corporation economist James P. Smith found that successive generations of Hispanics have experienced significant improvements in wages and education relative both to their fathers and grandfathers and to the native Anglos with whom they competed in the labor market.[7]

These positive trends belie reactionary "solutions" to the "immigrant problem." But the big picture also tends to gloss over challenges that both immigrants and their receiving communities confront on the ground. If left unaddressed, cultural and linguistic barriers, distrust between immigrants and receiving populations and institutions, and the economic, political and social marginalization of immigrants and their descendents may lead to a form of integration that results in mistrust and disunity. The United States simply cannot afford such an outcome. The imperative for adopting a policy that ensures positive integration becomes clearer when considering the following:

- *The future prosperity of the United States depends on the success of today's newcomers.* Immigrants who have arrived in the United States since 1960 make up almost one in ten individuals in the country, while the children of these immigrants comprise more than 10 percent of the total population. These children of immigrants, with an average age of seventeen, have not yet entered the full-time workforce, but soon will comprise a substantial proportion of American workers.[8] The nation's economic, political, and social futures thus rest on the successful integration of these "immigrant stock" individuals. Indeed, the nature of their integration will strongly influence the ability of the United States to compete in an increasingly global economy, the health of our democracy, the vitality of civic life, and even the well-being of native-born families who have lived in the country for generations. Perhaps the clearest link between integration and the prosperity of the nation is seen in the graying of the native-born population. As massive numbers of baby boomers age into retirement, today's second generation is the workforce on which aging baby boomers will depend for workers who provide both the direct services and the tax base that support programs for the elderly.[9]

The importance of immigrants and their children to the labor force is particularly acute in California, the most populous state in the union and a state in which 26.2 percent of the population was born abroad. Immigrants accounted for 66.9 percent of the growth in California's working-age population between 1980 and 2005. Over the next twenty-five years, however, the second-generation children of immigrants will account for the majority of this growth, at 59.5 percent, and immigrants will account for almost all of the remaining growth.[10]

- *Immigrant integration is a national issue.* Immigration is no longer a regional phenomenon concentrated in a few, mostly border states. While California, Florida, New York, New Jersey, Texas and Illinois remain the most popular immigrant destinations, since the early 1990s immigrants have fanned out to new Midwestern and Southern "gateways" that previously received few newcomers. The rate of growth of the immigrant population in these new gateways states has been enormous. All of the top-five immigrant-growth states from 1990 to 2005 are new gateways, and these states have experienced a rate of growth between 3.4 and 4.8 times that of the nation as a whole during this period.[11] The national nature of immigration means that communities throughout the country share a common set of challenges and opportunities related to immigrant integration. The benefits of a national integration policy, therefore, would reach into virtually every corner of the national map.
- *Any overhaul of immigration policy will have significant implications for integration.* An earned legalization program for undocumented immigrants now in the United States should be a centerpiece of any proposed immigration overhaul. Many of the unauthorized immigrants whose legal status would change under such a program already are experiencing some degree of integration. Unauthorized immigrants constitute nearly 5 percent of the U.S. labor force, and many have children who are U.S. citizens (64 percent of children living in an unauthorized family are U.S. citizens by birth).[12] A change in the legal status of undocumented immigrants would more deeply plant their roots in the United States, making their positive integration all the more necessary.

The inclusion of a guest-worker program in a larger immigration-reform package also has relevance for integration. Even if workers are in the country on a temporary basis, some degree of integration will take place. Guest workers will live in communities throughout the nation, and the way in which receiving communities and guest workers interact will determine the success of such a program.

Past Integration Policies

In looking ahead to an integration policy for immigrants to the United States, it is worth examining and learning from past efforts. The nation has historically taken two broad approaches to immigrant integration. The first sees a role for policies that actively encourage integration. This more pro-active approach first appeared on a large scale with the Americanization Movement of the 1910s and 1920s. Faced with large numbers of immigrants arriving primarily from Eastern and Southern Europe, communities throughout the country engaged in a massive effort to integrate and, in some instances, forcibly turn immigrants into "Americans." Programs coordinated by public- and private-sector organizations provided English-language training, civics classes and symbolic displays of patriotism—all aimed at expediting the removal of "old world ways" and the adoption of a singular American identity.[13]

The ideological underpinnings of the Americanization Movement resonate in many of today's policy initiatives. English-only campaigns at the state and national levels, efforts to limit immigrants' access to public resources, and bills that propose tightening citizenship requirements are all present-day policy cousins of the Americanization Movement that aim to preserve an un-changed ideal of American identity. The problem with this approach to integration is that it often achieves outcomes that contradict those which policymakers intend. Americanization-style initiatives become a significant basis for division. Instead of turning their allegiances towards an American mainstream, immigrants and their children may begin to turn their backs on a country that they believe has rejected them. Efforts to strip immigrants and their children of their ethnic allegiances altogether can also have deleterious academic and psychological outcomes that further inhibit positive integration.[14]

A more thoughtful, but equally active approach to integration is apparent in U.S. refugee policy. Refugees to the United States are greeted by an expansive web of government agencies and non-governmental organizations (NGOs) tasked with facilitating their integration into U.S. society. Established under the Refugee Act of 1980, the Office of Refugee Resettlement (ORR) in the Department of Health and Human Services heads refugee integration by providing funds for, "among other benefits and services, cash and medical assistance, employment preparation and job placement, skills training, English-language training, social adjustment and aid for victims of torture."[15] ORR's efforts appear to be successful, but the reach of their programs is limited to the 5 percent of the immigrant population annually admitted as refugees or asylees. The other 95 percent have no access to assistance aside from a small amount of funding for English-language acquisition and some workforce training provided by a patchwork of programs that together do not constitute a coherent integration policy.

A second and more predominant approach to immigrant integration involves virtually no policy intervention. This *laissez faire* method relies on a combination of immigrants' remarkable motivation and the ability of the labor market to provide jobs and income that, over time, facilitate the entrance of newcomers into the American economic, political and social mainstream. But the stakes are too high to rely on a *laissez faire* approach. The extent to which the prosperity of the United States depends on immigrants and their children, the national nature of immigration, and the sweeping changes that would result from enactment of comprehensive immigration legislation make an immigrant-integration policy essential.

Principles of an Immigrant-Integration Policy

The principles on which a national immigrant-integration policy might be based can be gleaned from successful local-level integration initiatives in places like Santa Clara County, California[16] and the State of Illinois,[17] as well as experimental efforts spearheaded by a coalition of government agencies and NGOs in Lowell, Massachusetts; Nashville, Tennessee; and Portland, Oregon.[18]

- *Integration is a two-way process.* Any integration policy must begin from the premise that immigrants influence the communities in which they settle as much as these communities influence the immigrants. Programs supported by a comprehensive integration policy, therefore, must place mutual responsibility for integration on both immigrant newcomers and their receiving communities. Accordingly, the aim of a successful integration policy is not just to help immigrants find their way in a new land, but also to help receiving communities adjust to the economic, political, and social shifts that immigration entails.
- *The federal government must take the lead.* Immigration has long been considered a federal policy issue, while integration is largely relegated to individuals, local governments and NGOs. But immigration and integration go hand-in-hand, and this division of labor thus makes little sense. Integration is a federal responsibility, and a federal integration policy should function alongside immigration policy. The federal government must serve as the "north star" for integration, setting guidelines and goals for integration programs implemented at the local level. Rather than dictate policy, the federal government should partner with state and local governments, NGOs and the private sector in carrying out the business of integration.
- *Integration takes place at the local level.* An integration policy must be spearheaded by the federal government, while allowing for flexibility in meeting challenges and opportunities that vary by locale. Although the effects of immigrant integration reverberate throughout U.S. society, it is at the local level where the proverbial rubber meets the road. Because some communities have a long history of immigration, they have existing institutional mechanisms that better equip them to carry out the business of integration. Other communities, however, have only a very recent history of immigration and lack these institutional mechanisms. The different immigrant groups that predominate in different locales also create an array of challenges and opportunities, requiring flexibility in the local implementation of integration programs. For example, Minneapolis, where the immigrant population is dominated by Southeast Asian refugees, likely

faces a different set of cultural, linguistic and social challenges and opportunities compared to Dalton County, Georgia, where nearly all immigrants are laborers from Latin America.

- *There are certain aspects of integration that are essential to the success of both immigrants and receiving communities.* If there is one aspect of integration that is preeminently important, it is English-language acquisition. There is little doubt that knowing English dramatically facilitates full participation in U.S. society, and an integration policy must have English-language acquisition as a centerpiece. Learning English does not require immigrants and their children to jettison their mother tongue, however. They are more successfully integrated, in fact, when they retain their native language while learning English,[19] and having a bilingual workforce makes the United States more competitive in the global economy. Civic integration of immigrants is essential, but should not be relegated to the memorization of basic facts about U.S. history and civics. It also must involve opportunities to participate in civil society that facilitate trustful relationships between immigrant newcomers and all facets of their receiving community, especially law enforcement, elected officials, and other civic leaders.
- *Integration is more than just U.S. citizenship.* U.S. citizenship is an essential goal of integration, but integration begins well before an immigrant takes the oath of citizenship. An integration policy should aim to develop important precursors to citizenship, like English-language acquisition, civic participation and socioeconomic mobility. These antecedents provide immigrants with a greater stake in their adopted communities and make them more likely to eventually become citizens.[20]
- *Integration requires the cooperation of many different actors.* Virtually every sector of U.S. society has a stake in successful integration, and all actors in receiving communities have an important role to play. As refugee resettlement programs suggest, integration is most successful when federal, state and local governments along with NGOs and the private sector work in collaboration with immigrant newcomers.
- *Integration policy works best as a complement to other institutions.* An integration policy is not a substitute for the key institutions that shape integration. Schools and legal institutions are particularly important engines of mobility. An integration policy will only work to the extent that immigrants and their children have access to high-quality and affordable primary, secondary, and post-secondary education. The success of an integration policy also requires U.S. legal institutions to protect immigrants from discrimination and human rights violations. Strong legal protections create mobility by tearing down the economic, political and social boundaries that impede integration.
- *Knowledge-sharing is essential.* No actor involved in the integration process should have to go it alone. An integration policy must create a

systematic way for NGOs and local governments from around the country to share best practices. Regional variation in the history of immigration means that some locales have more experience with integration than others. Local governments and NGOs in newer immigrant gateways no doubt have much to learn from the successes and failures in more established gateways, while the latter may bring fresh approaches to integration that would benefit the former.

Conclusion

Immigrant integration is inevitable and, for the most part, immigrants and their descendents are experiencing success in becoming American without the benefit of an integration policy. But the nature of integration will exert a powerful influence on the nation's prosperity in the years and decades to come, and there is simply too much at stake to rely on the current *laissez faire* approach. It is not in the best interests of the United States to make integration a more difficult, uncertain or lengthy process than it need be. Facilitating the successful and rapid integration of immigrants into U.S. society minimizes conflicts and tensions between newcomers and the native-born, and enables immigrants to more quickly secure better jobs, earn higher incomes, and thus contribute more fully to the U.S. economy.

The United States has long been a nation of immigrants, but its policies are out of step with this reality. Public policies with regard to the foreign-born must go beyond regulating who is admitted and under what circumstances. The nation needs an immigrant-integration policy that effectively addresses the challenges and harnesses the opportunities created by today's large immigrant population. An integration policy will help ensure a positive, unifying form of integration for newcomers and their receiving communities, thereby benefiting the nation as a whole.

Resources

Illinois Coalition for Immigrant and Refugee Rights–Immigrant Integration: www.icirr.org

Iowa Center for Immigrant Leadership and Integration: www.newiowans.org

National Center on Immigrant Integration: www.migrationinformation.org/integration

Santa Clara County Immigrant Relations and Integration Services : www.immigrant info.org

Notes

1. A version of this article was previously published by the Immigration Policy Center, April 2007 and it has reprinted with permission by the American Immigration Law Foundation. Copyright 2007.

2. Frank D. Bean and Gillian Stevens, *America's Newcomers and the Dynamics of Diversity* (New York: Russell Sage Foundation, 2003); Alejandro Portes and Rubén G. Rumbaut, *Immigrant America: A Portrait* (Berkeley & Los Angeles, CA: University of California Press, 2006), chaps. 7 and 8.

3. Richard Alba, *Language Assimilation Today: Bilingualism Persists More Than in the Past, But English Still Dominates* (Working paper 111) (La Jolla, CA: Center for Comparative Immigration Studies, University of California-San Diego, November 2004), Table 1 (Calculations based on 5-Percent Public Use Microdata Sample (PUMS) from the 2000 Census).

4. Roger Waldinger and Renee Reichl, "Today's Second Generation: Getting Ahead or Falling Behind?" in *Securing the Future: U.S. Immigrant Integration Policy, A Reader,* Michael Fix, ed. (Washington, DC: Migration Policy Institute, 2007), 29–30.

5. *ibid.*, p. 33.

6. Richard Alba, "Mexican Americans and the American Dream," *Perspectives on Politics* 4(2), June 2006: 289–296.

7. James P. Smith, "Immigrants and the Labor Market," *Journal of Labor Economics* 24(2), 2006: 203–233.

8. Alejandro Portes and Rubén G. Rumbaut, *Immigrant America: A Portrait*, 2006, 246–47.

9. Dowell Myers, *Immigrants and Boomers: Forging a New Social Contract for the Future of America* (New York: Russell Sage Foundation, 2007).

10. Dowell Myers, John Pitkin and Julie Park, *California Demographic Futures: Projections to 2030, by Immigrant Generations, Nativity, and Time of Arrival in U.S.* (Los Angeles, CA: Population Dynamics Research Group, School of Policy, Planning, and Development, University of Southern California, February 2005), 18.

11. Author's calculations based on U.S. Decennial Census and 2005 American Community Survey data compiled by the Migration Policy Institute.

12. Jeffrey S. Passel, *Size and Characteristics of the Unauthorized Migrant Population in the U.S.: Estimates Based on the March 2005 Current Population Survey* (Washington, D.C.: Pew Hispanic Center, 2006), 8–9.

13. John Higham, *Strangers in the Land: Patterns of American Nativism, 1860-1925* (New York: Atheneum, 1963 [1955]), chap. 9.

14. Alejandro Portes and Rubén G. Rumbaut, *Legacies: The Story of the Immigrant Second Generation* (Berkeley and Los Angeles, CA: University of California Press, 2001), chaps. 6–9.

15. Office of Refugee Resettlement, "Eligibility for Refugee Assistance and Services through the Office of Refugee Resettlement," http://www.acf.hhs.gov/programs/orr/geninfo/index.htm.

16. See ImmigrantInfo.org, sponsored by the Santa Clara County Office of Human Relations and IRIS (Immigrant Relations and Integration Services), http://www.immigrantinfo.org.

17. See immigrantIntegration.org, website of the New Americans Executive Order of the state of Illinois, http://www.immigrantintegration.org.

18. The Building the New American Community Initiative, which included the Office of Refugee Resettlement, the Migration Policy Institute, the National Conference of State Legislatures, the National Immigration Forum, the Southeast Asia Resource Action Center (SEARAC), and the Urban Institute. See www.migrationpolicy.org/news/2004_12 _9.php for more information.

19. Alejandro Portes and Rubén G. Rumbaut, *Legacies: The Story of the Immigrant Second Generation*, 2001, chap. 6.

20. Irene Bloemraad, *Becoming a Citizen: Incorporating Immigrants and Refugees in the United States and Canada* (Berkeley and Los Angeles, CA: University of California Press, 2006).

Chapter 29

Open the Government, A New Information Policy

Patrice McDermott

POLICY PROPOSALS

- **Make openness the default standard for government information.**
  - Issue a Presidential memorandum on day one of his administration making clear that government information belongs to the public and directing federal agencies to harness technology and the many skills of government employees to ensure that government information is open, authentic, accessible and usable.
  - Direct the executive branch to operate under the presumption that government information should be made available to the public except under limited and clearly articulated statutory or regulatory exceptions.
  - Direct the review of standards and guidelines created and implemented post-9/11 regarding information made publicly available online.
  - Direct the National Archives and Records Administration (NARA) to implement the framework for imposing order on the proliferation of "sensitive but unclassified"-type markings in a manner that minimizes the number, restrictions and duration of such markings and maximizes public access to information.
  - Issue a new Executive Order on national security classification to include the previous standard (in E.O. 12958-April 1995): "If there is significant doubt about the need to classify information, it shall not be classified."
  - Commit that executive branch officials and agencies will abstain from asserting executive privilege to shield the administration.

267

- Commit to not using signing statements as line-item vetoes or Constitutional challenges to legislation.
- Make the current structures for accountability and transparency work for the public.
  - Understand and clearly communicate to the President's staff and to all executive branch employees that all documents, including electronic communications, that are created, received or maintained as part of the work of government are federal records. Clearly communicate to all staff, all civil servants and all contractors that conducting government business on a non-government account or computer does not turn the documents into non-records.
  - Take immediate action to change course in the executive branch with respect to the Freedom of Information Act (FOIA). A presidential memorandum on government openness, including FOIA, should be issued, with an accompanying Attorney General's memo. The incoming President should direct all agencies to comply with both the letter and spirit of the law that establishes transparency as an essential feature of our democracy.
  - Remind agencies that the commitment to openness requires more than merely responding to requests from the public.
- Use technology to make government more open and accountable.
  - Direct an appropriate body, such as the Chief Information Officers Council or a taskforce, to identify models for the use of interactive technology as a vehicle to engage the public in open discussion.
  - Direct federal agencies to move rapidly to provide all new government information in open, structured, machine-readable formats that will permit the public—non-profits, companies, individuals—and other government entities to pull out the information, re-use it and combine it with other information.

*   *   *   *   *   *   *   *   *   *   *   *   *   *   *

What could access to government information look like in the incoming Administration? Will we have more of the same—secrecy, lack of accountability, expansive claims of executive privilege and state secrets, proliferation of "sensitive but unclassified" markings, destruction of electronic records (including e-mail), denials, stonewalling, and backlogs of FOIA requests—and, in general, a need-to-know culture? Or can we create the kind of government that James Madison envisioned when he said:

> A popular Government, without popular information, or the means of acquiring it, is but a prologue to a farce or a tragedy; or, perhaps, both. Knowledge will forever govern ignorance; and a people who mean to be their own governors

must arm themselves with the power which knowledge gives.
[Letter to W. T. Barry, August 4, 1822 (Madison, James. 1865. Letters and Other Writings of James Madison, Published by order of Congress. 4 volumes. Edited by Philip R. Fendall. Philadelphia: Lippincott., III, page 276]

The incoming Administration has great opportunities to restore the public trust in government and in our ability to participate meaningfully in governance. The March 2008 Sunshine Week poll found that three-quarters of American adults view the federal government as secretive, and nearly nine in ten say it's important to know Presidential and Congressional candidates' positions on open government when deciding for whom to vote. The survey showed a significant increase over the past three years in the percentage of Americans who believe the federal government is very or somewhat secretive, from 62 percent of those surveyed in 2006 to 74 percent in 2008. This is terrible news for our country and our system of government. The good news is that for nearly 90 percent it was a campaign issue (whether the media focused on the candidates' positions is a separate question) (http://www.sunshineweek.org/sunshineweek/secrecypoll08). Similarly, in exit polls during the 2006 Congressional elections, more than 40 percent of voters indicated that corruption and scandals in government were very important in their voting decisions. Sunshine on the workings of government is the first step toward winning back public trust.

Clearly, we cannot continue down the path on which we have been. Many of the pieces are in place for the incoming Administration to change the direction in which we have been heading. What is required is a demonstrated commitment to use them for the benefit of the public and, ultimately, of government itself.

Make Openness the Default Standard for Government Information

The incoming President has an immediate opportunity to define the relationship between his administration and the public by issuing a Presidential Memorandum on day one of his Administration that makes clear that government information belongs to the public and leads federal agencies to harness technology and personnel skills to ensure that government records that belong to the public are open and accessible. The public has come to expect instant and copious information on demand, and the federal government has to meet that challenge and make sure government information is not only instant, but accurate, authentic and usable.

This is not a drastic new step. The framework for openness is there—in statute and in regulation. Achieving more openness and transparency is a goal that transcends party lines and will allow the next President to demonstrate his commitment to the change the electorate has indicated it wants. The incoming

President has to immediately set the tone, make a commitment to transparency a keystone of his appointments, and task high-level officials in the Administration with responsibility for implementation of the openness mandate Executive-Branch-wide.

Our society and democratic form of government are based on an informed public. Our laws provide structures to guarantee the public's right to know what its government is doing. Over the last eight years, however, the Executive Branch has been transformed into a government that withholds information unless members of the public demonstrate a "legitimate" need to know. Keeping information secret has become the default position throughout much of the federal government. This trend has been apparent in responses to Freedom of Information Act requests and in the proliferation of markings, such as "Sensitive But Unclassified," to control access to unclassified information.

One of the first steps the incoming President should take is to direct agency heads to review information removed after the events of September 11 and the guidelines that agencies prepared to inform decisions about what has been allowed to be put online in the intervening seven years. The President should make clear that the benefit to the public of disclosure should be heavily weighted in considerations of disclosure and dissemination. If the security costs of disseminating the information do not heavily outweigh the societal benefits of dissemination, the information should be disclosed.

Similarly, the President should direct NARA to implement the framework for imposing order on the proliferation of "Sensitive But Unclassified"-type markings in a manner that minimizes the number, restrictions and duration of such markings and maximizes public access to information. We are all agreed that there is information that does need to be protected for some period of time. The tension, though, is not between openness and security; it is between information control for bureaucratic turf, power and, more than occasionally, political reasons and the reality that empowering the public makes us safer. Secrecy does not make for a more secure society; it makes for a more vulnerable society and less accountable governments.

Most Presidents issue an Executive Order on national security classification. The incoming President needs to do so early on in his Administration, allowing for public review and comment. At a minimum, the Order should restore the admonitions from the 1995 Order; "if there is significant doubt about the need to classify information, it shall not be classified." (Executive Order 12,958, Sections 1.2(b)), and that "significant doubt" about the appropriate level of classification should result in classification at the lower level (*Id.,* Section 1.3(c)). He should ensure continued automatic declassification, and fund and support the Public Interest Declassification Board.

The incoming President should also work to restore public faith in the workings of the Administration by reversing the practices of using signing statements as line item vetoes, assertions of his "inherent" powers, or as instructions to agencies to ignore or re-interpret Congressional mandates. Based on the best available numbers (as of July 1, 2008), President George W. Bush issued 157 signing statements, challenging 1,100 provisions of laws. In the 211 years of our Republic up to 2000, Presidents had issued, in total, fewer than 600 signing statements that took issue with the bills they signed. Among recent Presidents, President Reagan issued 71 statements challenging provisions of the laws before him; President George Herbert Walker Bush issued 146; and President Clinton issued 105.

The incoming President should further work to restore the public faith in the balance-of-powers on which our government is based, by invoking "Executive Privilege" only in rare circumstances and not to block accountability for actions that are unethical, illegal or against the public interest (such as suppression and rewriting of scientific findings). Executive Privilege refers to the assertion made by the President or, sometimes, other Executive Branch officials, when they refuse to give Congress, the courts or private parties information or records that have been requested or subpoenaed, or when they order government witnesses not to testify before Congress.

Make the Current Structures for Accountability and Transparency Work for the Public

It is time to restore trust in government, and the key step in achieving this trust is making available all the information the public needs to hold its government accountable. There are a number of steps the incoming Administration can take to further government transparency. Some of them can be implemented immediately while some others take a commitment of time and resources.

We already have some of the building blocks of transparency. Some of them are pretty mundane but are the cornerstones of accountable government. If records that belong to the public are to be open and accessible, they must be preserved appropriately and managed. Requiring agency heads to make management of government records, regardless of form, format or mode of creation is the fundamental step that the incoming President must take. The President must understand and must clearly communicate to his staff and to all Executive Branch employees that all documents, including electronic communications, that are created or handled as part of the work of government are federal records. He must clearly communicate to his staff, all civil servants and all contractors that conducting government business on a non-government account or computer does not miraculously turn the documents into non-records. The President and Vice-President and their advisors are obligated to preserve all their records under the Presidential Records Act. The President sets the example for the entire Executive Branch and must honor the law protecting the people's information. The example set by the Bush Administration, by contrast, is several hundred days of "missing" White House emails.

Records management is, of course, also essential to the effective working of FOIA. Preservation is the essential minimum. The existence of records, however, is no guarantee that the agency will disclose them pursuant to a FOIA request, even when disclosure is discretionary (not precluded by one of the nine exemptions to the Act or the many exemptions created by other statutes). The 1993 Attorney General Memorandum on FOIA said:

> The Department will no longer defend an agency's withholding of information merely because there is a "substantial legal basis" for doing so. Rather, in determining whether or not to defend a nondisclosure decision, we will apply a presumption of disclosure... In short, it shall be the policy of the Department of Justice to defend the assertion of a FOIA exemption only in those cases where the agency reasonably foresees that disclosure would be harmful to an interest protected by that exemption. Where an item of information might technically or arguably fall within an exemption, it ought not to be withheld from a FOIA requester unless it need be.

The George W. Bush Administration rescinded the 1993 Attorney General Memorandum on FOIA, but did not return to a "substantial legal basis" (as the basis on which it would defend agencies' withholding of records). Rather, the Memorandum issued by Attorney General Ashcroft told agencies:

> When you carefully consider FOIA requests and decide to withhold records, in whole or in part, you can be assured that the Department of Justice will defend your decisions unless they lack a sound legal basis or present an unwarranted risk of adverse impact on the ability of other agencies to protect other important records.

Against this background, the incoming President should take immediate action to change course in the Executive Branch with respect to the Freedom of Information Act. It is traditional for a new Administration to define its own FOIA policy. The incoming President should issue a Memorandum on government openness, including FOIA, with an accompanying Attorney General memo. The incoming President should direct all agencies to comply with both the letter and the spirit of the law that establishes transparency as an essential feature of our democracy.

The incoming President should also remind agencies that the commitment to openness requires more than merely responding to requests from the public. Agencies have obligations under the 1996 E-FOIA Amendments to post FOIA-related materials online. The incoming President must remind agency heads that each agency has a responsibility to distribute information on its own initiative, beyond this (and other statutory requirements), and to enhance public access through the use of electronic information systems.

Use Technology to Make Government More Open and Accountable

The digital technologies that are so ubiquitous in our lives offer great promise to make government both more open and more interactive. Not engaging citizens in the development of public policy feeds a growing cynicism and destroys trust. The need is for more than an opportunity to comment on rules (as important as that is); it is for meaningful discussion.

The federal government has begun to use wikis (collaborative websites where authorized users can contribute or modify content) for internal information-sharing and discussion, and government officials are using blogs to communicate *to* the public. A few, such as Dipnote (http://blogs.state.gov/), which offers the opportunity for participants to discuss important foreign policy issues with senior State Department officials, have made the move to interactivity. It invites comments from readers (subject, of course, to being moderated). Such moderating has not led to any First Amendment complaints, to date, and is a model that should be explored for replication. The President should direct an appropriate body, such as the Chief Information Officers Council or a taskforce, to identify models such as this and explore what might work for agencies across the government. The goal should be greater opportunities for the public to discuss issues, rules, etc. with government officials. Such discussions should be treated as records, of course.

Finally, the incoming President should direct federal agencies to move rapidly to providing all new government information (documents, data, etc.) in open, structured, machine-readable formats that will permit the public—nonprofits, companies, individuals—and other government entities to pull out ("grab," in the parlance of the profession) the information, re-use it and combine it with other information. There are numbers of sites based on such re-use and combinations ("mashups"), but to date they have all required cleaning up and reformatting government data. Whether the state of government information is deliberate (to make it hard to find and use) or a failure of imagination and/or resources, it is past time for the federal government to join the twenty-first century. This does not in any way absolve agencies of their responsibilities to ensure that government information is open, authentic, accessible and usable.

We need Democracy 1.0. It is up to us, as well as the incoming President, to meet Benjamin Franklin's challenge as he left the Constitutional Convention in Philadelphia: Asked, "Well, Doctor, what have we got—a Republic or a Monarchy?," he replied, "A Republic, madam, if you can keep it."

Resources

American Association of Law Libraries: www.aallnet.org/
American Booksellers Foundation for Free Expression: www.abffe.org/
American Library Association: www.ala.org/
American Society of Newspaper Editors: www.asne.org/
Association of American Publishers: www.publishers.org/
Association for Community Networking: www.afcn.org/
Association of Research Libraries: www.arl.org/
Bill of Rights Defense Committee: www.bordc.org/
Californians Aware: www.calaware.org/
Center for American Progress: www.americanprogress.org/
Center for Democracy and Technology: www.cdt.org/
Center for National Security Studies: www.cnss.org/
Center for Progressive Reform: www.progressiveregulation.org/
The Center for Public Integrity: www.publicintegrity.org
Center for Responsive Politics: www.opensecrets.org/
Citizens for Responsibility and Ethics in Washington:
    www.citizensforethics.org/
Common Cause: www.commoncause.org/
Defending Dissent Foundation: www.defendingdissent.org/
DownsizeDC.org, Inc.: www.downsizedc.org/
Electronic Frontier Foundation: www.eff.org/
Electronic Privacy Information Center: www.epic.org/
EnviroJustice: www.envirojustice.org/
Environmental Defense: www.edf.org/
Essential Information: www.essential.org/
Federation of American Scientists: www.fas.org/
Florida First Amendment Foundation: www.floridafaf.org/
Free Expression Policy Project: www.fepproject.org/
Friends Committee on National Legislation: www.fcnl.org/
Fund for Constitutional Government: www.epic.org/fcg/
Good Jobs First: www.goodjobsfirst.org/
Government Accountability Project: www.whistleblower.org/
Human Rights First: www.humanrightsfirst.org/
Humanist Society of New Mexico: nm.humanists.net/
Illinois Community Technology Coalition: www.ilctc.org/
Indiana Coalition for Open Government: www.indianacog.org/
Institute for Defense and Disarmament Studies: www.idds.org/
The James Madison Project: www.jamesmadisonproject.org/
League of Women Voters: www.lwv.org/
Liberty Coalition: www.libertycoalition.net
Mine Safety and Health News: www.minesafety.com/
Minnesota Coalition on Government Information: www.mncogi.org/

National Coalition Against Censorship: www.ncac.org/home.cfm
National Coalition for History: www.historycoalition.org/
National Freedom of Information Coalition: www.nfoic.org/
National Security Archive: www.gwu.edu/~nsarchiv/
National Security Whistleblowers Coalition: www.nswbc.org/
New Jersey Work Environment Council: www.njwec.org/
Northern California Association of Law Libraries: www.nocall.org
OMB Watch: www.ombwatch.org/
OpenTheGovernment.org: www.openthegovernment.org
PEN American Center: www.pen.org/
Pennsylvania Freedom of Information Coalition: www.openrecordspa.org/
People For the American Way: www.pfaw.org/
Political Research Associates: www.publiceye.org/
Progressive Librarians Guild: libr.org/plg/index.php
Project On Government Oversight: www.pogo.org/
Public Citizen: www.citizen.org/
Public Employees for Environmental Responsibility: www.peer.org/
ReadtheBill.org: www.readthebill.org/
ReclaimDemocracy.org: www.reclaimdemocracy.org/
Reporters Committee for Freedom of the Press: www.rcfp.org/
Secrecy News: http://www.fas.org/blog/secrecy/
Society of American Archivists: www.archivists.org/
Society of Professional Journalists: www.spj.org/
Special Libraries Association: www.sla.org/
Sunlight Foundation: www.sunlightfoundation.com/
Taxpayers for Common Sense: www.taxpayer.net
Transactional Records Access Clearinghouse: trac.syr.edu/
U.S. Public Interest Research Group: www.uspirg.org/
Voter Watch: www.voterwatch.org/
Washington Coalition for Open Government: www.washingtoncog.org/
Working Group on Community Right-to-Know: www.crtk.org/

References

McDermott, Patrice. *Who Needs to Know? The State of Public Access to Federal Government Information.* Lanham, MD: Bernan Press, 2007.

Chapter 30

Media and Communications Policy: Ensuring the Freedom of Expression Essential to a Democracy

Ben Scott

POLICY PROPOSALS

- Reduce the power concentrated in vertically integrated media industries while fostering greater ownership diversity in broadcasting and cable.
- Expand funding for public and community broadcasting: Provide resources for civic, cultural, educational and children's programming in non-commercial media.
- Make more FM licenses available for low-power radio; reduce postal rates for public affairs magazines; guarantee funds for public access TV; provide incentives for quality journalism.
- Ensure open and equitable access to content and services across all sectors of our network economy (from cable TV to broadband Internet to interconnection between local networks).
- Establish consumer protection rules that guarantee an open market for speech and commerce on the Internet and prohibit discriminatory interference by network owners.
- Open public airwaves allocated for broadcast TV but unoccupied by a station (so-called "white spaces") for wireless Internet.
- Transition the $7 billion annual Universal Service Fund programs from supporting telephone networks to supporting broadband infrastructure.
- Pair social programs that bring low-cost computers and technology training to underserved communities with incentives to deploy broadband infrastructure.

* * * * * * * * * * * * * * *

The country faces daunting challenges in the media and telecommunications sectors. Even though we understand the existing problems and know the desired outcomes, these challenges are daunting because success requires that we take on the entrenched interests of powerful industries. Cable, telephone, broadcasting and content companies have long sat astride our media system. A media policy appropriate to a democracy will require that our leaders address, and begin to dismantle, the concentrated power over news, information and cultural representation in the mainstream media.

In the twenty-first century, the corporations accustomed to dominating the traditional media seek to duplicate that control over the new digital media. Yet, the shift to an Internet-based media system provides an historic opportunity for the public to reclaim control of its media; we can translate an inherently decentralized technology form into a decentralized—and inherently democratic—media system. We must simply prevent history from repeating itself.

Policymakers interested in media democracy, thus, face two inter-related projects:
- Fix the problems in traditional media.
- Ensure that we don't duplicate such problems with new media.

Policies for Traditional Media

Television and Radio
The profit motive eclipses public-service objectives in the current broadcast and cable systems. Fewer owners, notwithstanding the seeming plethora of channel "choices," mean fewer voices in the mainstream media, obscuring the diversity of opinion and cultural representation in our increasingly pluralistic society. Marketplace concentration has also triggered a ratings-race-to-the-bottom in entertainment programming and dragged the quality of journalism into a public crisis of confidence in the press. Of course, not all programming has been corrupted; nor has every good reporter quit in disgust. But the trends are ominous, as is the alarming lack of public affairs knowledge carried by American voters into the voting booth.[1] Add to these the problems of hate speech, cultural stereotyping, and the simple omission of voices and faces from the media that feed American culture—and there is no shortage of reasons to use law to create better social and economic outcomes from the media.

To ensure a diversity of political voices, rich local culture, competitive media markets that catalyze innovation, and a variety of media channels that represent all sectors of society, we must place public-interest limits on ownership. It is neither partisan nor even particularly controversial outside the Beltway to argue that the outcomes of media consolidation (fewer voices in the media system) and the needs of a democracy (more voices in the media system for robust public debate) are in direct tension. This common-sense understanding in the U.S. polity explains why every recent effort by the Federal Communications Commission to relax media ownership limits has been met with overwhelming public opposition. This popular backlash has muted talk in Washington about permitting even more media concentration.

The challenge now is to shift the focus away from blocking industry efforts to lift ownership caps, and toward an array of public policies that cultivate independent, diverse and competitive media. Consider the shameful crisis in minority and female ownership in broadcasting and cable. Minority communities now make up nearly a third of the country—and yet own just 3 percent of TV stations and few of the national cable channels. Women make up more than half the population and yet own just 5 percent of TV stations and none of the major cable channels. In the current environment of vertical integration and cartelization among broadcasters and cable operators, opportunities to enter the national television market for independent or alternative programming are virtually nonexistent. The numbers for radio are not much better. Although throughout the economy, women and minorities are not represented in the ownership class in the same proportion as they are in the general population, the media industry lags woefully behind even that retrograde pattern. Such disparities will not be quickly corrected, but it is time to start.

The policy framework to accomplish these goals should combine structural ownership limits for existing media giants, fair competition to bring new entrants into the broadcasting and cable markets, and public support for noncommercial and community media outlets that serve the needs of a democratic society but go unmet in the current media marketplace. The first steps are straightforward:

- The Federal Communications Commission should concentrate on thoughtful ways to tighten limits on media ownership in local markets to promote competition in radio and television.
- Policymakers should look at ways to use pro-competitive policies to break the cartel of programmers that control the cable TV dial.

Given the explosion of outlets created by an increasingly digital cable system, a greater diversity of content could easily be available to American audiences. Programming could approximate the diversity of the country rather than simply default to formulaic, lowest-common-denominator television. The injection of competition from new, independent entrants into the cable programming market can meet this need. The emergence of telephone companies offering cable television services should also be a beneficial force. Such innovations can only be effective, however, in tandem with policies to guarantee access to cable programming at reasonable rates, terms and the conditions to be competitive.

Government can also expand the landscape for non-commercial, public service media forms by putting more dollars behind public broadcasting. Particularly in the areas of children's programming, news and current events, and cultural fare, the public media flagships—NPR, PBS and member stations—maintain a high standard. But corporate media's lobbyists and congressional surrogates have boxed in public broadcasting's reach by eroding its funding base and placing its future in doubt. We need creative thinkers from within the public broadcasting system to reinvent themselves in a multimedia environment. We need local partnerships, commitments to community service and an expanded mission to match the original intent of public broadcasting—to serve all segments of our society. Public broadcasters must speak more to different age groups, races and ethnicities, as well as cultural viewpoints. In some areas, this work has already begun. We must invest in its future on a scale that matches the public media sectors of other Western democracies (British government funding for the BBC, for example, is more than ten times the public broadcasting funding in the United States).

Policymakers must also support other forms of public media access, creating an interwoven fabric of public service outlets. Low-power FM radio is low-hanging fruit. Congress could quickly authorize thousands of new community radio licenses. These new stations would be exclusively local and non-commercial, vibrant new additions to the media-scape. Local cable television offers parallel opportunities. Public access TV, long a pillar of community service programming, is now jeopardized by recent policy decisions reducing the public service obligations of cable operators to support these channels. These stations should be nurtured and their funding guaranteed in the law as a condition of operating a cable TV system.

Print

Looming in the background of any discussion of public service media is the current crisis in journalism. Although newspaper *content* readership has never been higher, demonstrating a high demand for reporting, newspaper business models are under pressure as more readers go online rather than subscribe to print editions. Meanwhile, quality reporting and investment in the newsroom is contracting in order to offset near-term profit declines. This downturn may well be cyclical as developing models of revenue generation on the Internet help newspapers recover. In the interim, government policies could promote quality reporting essential to a functioning democracy, possibly through tax incentives. It could also invest in public affairs journalism education through scholarships and grants. Finally, the government should reverse 2007 postal rate increases that have hit small public affairs magazines the hardest.

New Media

Begin with the simple proposition that the broadband Internet is the central nervous system of our information society—the greatest engine of democratic speech, mass media and innovative commerce since the printing press. Then consider the reality that half of the nation's households are not connected and that the performance of our broadband marketplace is unimpressive, ranking the United States outside the top fifteen in the world and falling. Take into account that the Internet has become the means of distribution for much of the mass media, and we have not only an economic problem, we have a democracy problem.

Since ours is the nation that invented the Internet and led the world in technology markets, these realities constitute an astounding reversal. Yet recent U.S. broadband policy has not embraced a free-market approach that would encourage competition and innovation, tending instead to support the entrenched incumbency of a rigid duopoly of cable and telephone giants. In short, we're going down the same path we did with traditional media markets.

To address this crisis, Congress should explore a variety of broadband policy options and move toward a comprehensive national policy. Step one in this process must be an honest assessment of the problems.:

- Despite years of providers who promote "universal" availability, roughly 10 percent of American households still lack a terrestrial (as opposed to a prohibitively expensive satellite-based) broadband provider.
- We pay more for a lot less bandwidth than our global counterparts get.
- We lack a competitive market pushing speeds up and prices down at a rate sufficient to raise our stature relative to the rest of the world.

In sum, the U.S. broadband market has failed in the three metrics that matter most: availability, speed and value (cost per unit of speed).

Tackling these challenges will take bold leadership and action on a several policy fronts. There is no one answer to the broadband problem. Mindful of the history of traditional media, savvy policymakers must create a system that precludes market concentration and control over content distribution by a handful of corporate giants. This would be especially disastrous with a media form—the Internet—whose inherently decentralized properties make it fundamentally transformative.

Not since the popularization of radio in the 1930s have technological advances provided such a profound opportunity to transform the political economy of mass communications. The decisions made in Washington over the next few years will shape the future of the Internet. They will determine whether the power of unfettered access to online communications flows to everyone, or whether it is captured and limited by incumbent interests to the more narrow purposes of return on investment.

National broadband policy should instead be designed to achieve particular social and economic outcomes. We must concentrate on a straightforward set of aspirations and work backward to create the policy agenda to achieve them:

- **Access**: Every home, business and civic institution in America must have access to a high-speed, world-class communications infrastructure.
- **Choice**: Every consumer must enjoy real competition in lawful online content as well as among high-speed Internet providers to achieve lower prices and higher speed.
- **Openness**: Every Internet user should have the right to freedom of speech and commerce online without gatekeepers or discrimination.

- **Innovation:** The Internet should continue to create good jobs, foster entrepreneurship, spread new ideas and serve as a leading engine of economic growth.

Key Policies

Net Neutrality

When we log onto the Internet, we take much for granted. We assume that we'll be able to access whatever website we want, when we want to. We assume that we can use any feature we like, anytime we choose—watching online video, listening to podcasts, searching, emailing and instant messaging. We assume we can attach devices to make our online experience better—wireless routers, game controllers, or extra hard drives. What we assume is called "network neutrality," the principle, at the core of the Internet's DNA, that the Internet should be open and free, unrestricted by anyone. Unfortunately, we have no guarantee that such open conditions will endure.

Network owners—cable and telephone companies—would like to charge premiums for things we now take for granted: smooth access to websites, sufficient speed to run applications and permission to plug in a device. The network giants seek government sanction to charge website operators, application providers and device manufacturers for the rights to use their networks. Those who refuse to make deals or pay the network giants would experience discrimination. Unless these entities ante up—their sites will load more slowly or their applications and devices will perform less reliably those who do pay.

Without legal protection, consumers could find that a network operator has blocked the website of a competitor, or slowed it down so much that it is unusable. The fundamental nature of the Internet would change. Centralized powers would control access to content and services, and defeat the goal of maximizing free speech and innovation in an open marketplace.

As a first order of business, the government should guarantee network neutrality with clear consumer protection rules. This does not mean that networks will be forbidden to manage Internet traffic, block spam or comply with law enforcement. It does, however, mean that we will begin to prevent concentration of power in the new media.

Creating Adequate Infrastructure

How do we expand Internet access to everyone in America, increase the utility of the Internet by making it faster and more affordable, and encourage people to adopt it their homes and businesses? We can start by making access more widely available. One easy way is to open the public airwaves to deliver wireless connectivity to the public. The most valuable, unused chunks of the airwaves today are the TV channels that are not being used by a TV stations. These unused "white spaces" could be opened immediately for so-called "unlicensed" use. The result would resemble WiFi—but be faster and more ubiquitous. Anyone would be able to use these frequencies to connect to the Internet using an infinite number of devices and services. The sky is the limit in the unlicensed spectrum—a perfect free market with enormous public service benefits.

The Universal Service Fund programs, created by the Telecommunications Act of 1996, offer another ripe area for addressing infrastructure needs. Under current rules, USF programs channel up to $7 billion a year in fees taken from urban telephone customers directly to rural telephone providers to build and maintain traditional telephone networks. With a forward-looking strategy, the USF could foster broadband development in underserved areas. As we move from a dial-tone to a broadband world, these USF subsidies must also shift to broadband. Such a shift will also solve the telephone problem, as voice is simply one application among many available online. The lion's share of the USF money now heads toward subsidizing phone service that would never be profitable without public investment. But the USF also operates under a mandate to provide help in getting low-income families connected to the network and provided with basic services, as well as to fund network connectivity in schools, libraries and rural health clinics. If we use the transition to broadband to institute new measures of accountability and performance, the USF could be a central means of ensuring broadband access to meet twenty-first century social and economic needs.

The USF debate invites us to face the social challenge of increasing the demand for broadband- based communications. Assuming we meet the challenge of universal availability of Internet access, we remain far from accomplishing our goal of universal adoption of the technology. How do we get subscription rates for broadband up to the same levels as cable TV and cell phones? Policymakers must provide for systematic needs assessments for communities that do not adopt technology and respond with the resources—from computers to technology training to public education about the value of being connected—to facilitate adoption.

In addition to these social policies, federal policy must ensure that the Internet's delicate balance of cooperation between networks doesn't collapse in marketplace feuds or anti-competitive activity. The Internet is not one set of wires. It is an inter-connected set of networks owned by many public and private actors. It is critical that we establish clear, transparent, reasonable and non-discriminatory rules of interconnection to make sure that the myriad policies we set up at the edge of the network to facilitate network availability and adoption are not stymied.

Conclusion

The incoming Administration faces a unique opportunity to restore democratic values to media and communications policymaking. We are witnessing the decline of a media system whose *raison d'etre* became the pursuit of profit and into a new media system that rests on the inherently democratic foundation of the Internet. The policies we shape in the coming years must be designed to correct the imbalances of the current system, with at least as much emphasis on the public's interest as it has on private profit. We must both avoid the mistakes of the past as we manage new media forms and work to rejuvenate the traditional media marketplaces through competition, localism and diversity as they gradually transform, as well, into new media forms. Access to technology and control over content are common to both the old and the new media worlds— policymakers should move to address them successfully in both arenas, even as they converge into a new amalgam.

Resources

Consumers Union: http://www.hearusnow.org
Free Press: www.freepress.net
Media Access Project: http://www.mediaaccess.org
New America Foundation:
    http://www.newamerica.net/issues/telecom_and_technology
Prometheus Radio Project: http://www.prometheusradio.org
Public Knowledge: http://www.publicknowledge.org
Save the Internet: http://www.savetheinternet.com
Stop Big Media: http://www.stopbigmedia.com

References

Cooper, Mark N. "The Case Against Media Consolidation," January 2007: www.fordham.edu/images/undergraduate/communications/cooperbookinfo. pdf

Turner, S. Derek. "Broadband Reality Check II, Free Press Research," August 2006: www.freepress.net/files/bbrc2-final.pdf

———. "Out of the Picture, Free Press Research," October 2007: http://www. stopbigmedia.com/=research

———. "Off the Dial, Free Press Research," June 2007: http://www. stopbig-media.com/=research

Windhausen, Jr., John. "A Blueprint for Big Broadband," January 2008: net.educause.edu/ir/library/pdf/EPO0801.pdf

Notes

1. *"Public Knowledge of Current Affairs Little Changed by News and Information Revolution: What Americans Know, 1989-2007,"* Pew Research Center for People and the Press, April 15, 2007.

Chapter 31

Restoring Democratic Control over Corporations

Charlie Cray

POLICY PROPOSALS

- **Improve corporate accountability and oversight.**
  - Halt and reverse tort "reform" and other schemes to weaken corporate accountability.
  - Start tracking corporate crime.
  - Strengthen criminal liability for life-threatening harms.
  - Improve federal contractor accountability and oversight.
  - Rein in rabid financial speculation.
- **Free the public sphere from corporate control.**
  - Protect essential services and restrict corporations from government functions.
  - Cut corporate welfare.
- **Tame the giant corporations.**

* * * * * * * * * * * * * *

Business-friendly policies—including aggressive deregulation—have wrought all kinds of economic, consumer and ecological damage in recent years. In the past decade alone, we have witnessed Enron and the cornucopia of financial corruption that followed; unjustifiably stratospheric CEO pay packages and huge rake-offs by financial speculators; the doubling of oil prices between 2007 and 2008; an unending series of product safety scandals (including Vioxx, salmonella-tainted tomatoes and lead-painted toys imported from China); the epidemic of waste, fraud and human rights abuses by crony contractors and the new corporate mercenaries; the threat of global ecological calamity, and the mortgage market meltdown and the threat of a broader economic contagion—to name a few examples.

It is no coincidence that, at the same time, opinion polls consistently indicate the vast majority of Americans believe corporations have too much power, and are looking for ways to push the pendulum back in the other direction, toward a new era of reform and accountability.

We stand at the beginning of a very long process. There is much to do to rein in the giant multinational corporations that dominate our world and have brought us to the precipice of disaster.

Halt and Reverse Tort "Reform" and Other Schemes to Weaken Corporate Accountability

On December 1, 2006, *American Lawyer* magazine declared that after twenty years, the tort "reform" movement had won. "It's Over," the magazine crowed: Corporate America's massive investment in lobbying, public relations and various legal think tanks and front groups had resulted in deep and difficult-to-reverse changes in the civil justice system.

What they didn't say is that the real losers are not the trial lawyers, but the victims of corporate abuse, including defrauded investors and pensioners, medical malpractice victims and the many people injured by automobile design failures, toxic toys and other defective products.

The Chamber of Commerce and other big business lobbyists continue to press for more business-friendly judges, the construction of litigation trip-wires, and new liability shields.

In the Senate, a proposal was floated to constrict the Alien Tort Claims Act, one of the most effective tools in holding corporations accountable for their role in torture and genocide around the world. Fortunately, that proposal died a quiet death in committee. However, Congress passed the Foreign Intelligence Surveillance Act (FISA) bill, which included a provision granting telecommunication companies retroactive civil immunity for spying on Americans.

Other industries continue to press for immunity. The accounting industry has floated a proposal to cap auditor liabilities, claiming that another Arthur Andersen-style collapse would hurt the broader economy. Yet the proposed liability cap would create another moral hazard that could have its own devastating consequences, and should be resisted.

Another way corporations have managed to reduce accountability is by pressing the federal government to use its powers to persuade the courts to preempt state laws. In some cases, the push for preemption comes at the same time that industry has worked hand-in-glove with its allies on the inside to weaken federal health and safety standards—making state tort law protections all the more vital.[1]

Start Tracking Corporate Crime

What is measured is what matters. While there have been improvements in the federal government's tracking and reporting of federal spending, significant improvements are needed in the tracking and reporting of corporate crime and related abuses. Without such data, it is difficult for policymakers and the public at large to discern the magnitude and nature of this complex and multi-faceted issue, as well as the relative effectiveness of different sanctions as deterrents.

The last time the Department of Justice issued a comprehensive report on corporate crime was 1979.[2] By contrast, the Department of Justice issues a comprehensive report on street crimes each year, giving the law enforcement community a yardstick by which to measure the safety of our communities and the effectiveness of related law enforcement policies.

The same can and must be done with corporate crime. The Bureau of Justice Statistics at the Department of Justice should be directed to produce an annual report on corporate crime and related (civil and regulatory) violations, working with federal enforcement agencies (including the SEC, EPA, OSHA, CPSC, NHTSA and FTC) as well as state governments to develop consistent, Internet-accessible reporting standards.

In addition to better reporting, recent efforts to weaken the sanctions for corporate criminals should be resisted, including the use of deferred prosecution agreements, which has allowed over fifty companies suspected of bribery and other crimes to avoid the cost and stigma of defending themselves against criminal charges. Critics describe the use of these agreements as a kind of "get-out-of-jail-free" card since they undermine the general deterrent that results from corporate crime prosecutions and convictions.

Strengthen Criminal Liability for Life-Threatening Harms

To the extent that in can be quantified, corporate crime costs hundreds of billions of dollars in damages and tens of thousands of deaths and serious injuries each year.

The U.S. Consumer Product Safety Commission estimates that defective products alone cause 27,100 deaths and 33.1 million injuries each year,[3] while the Bureau of Labor Statistics reports that around 5,000 workers die each year on the job, with nearly sixteen workers dying each day from traumatic injuries.[4] Although corporations argue that there is no need to strengthen the law, the penalties for such harms are usually so insignificant that corporate managers see no need to report them to their own shareholders.

Loopholes in the law that allow specific industries to evade criminal prosecution for serious harms committed should be closed. This is particularly the case for auto safety violations (which have no criminal sanction under the law) and occupational manslaughter. According to the *New York Times*, between 1982 and 2002 OSHA identified 2,197 workplace deaths resulting from deliberate violations of workplace safety laws. And yet employers were sentenced to a total of just $106 million in fines and less than thirty years combined in jail sentences for those 2,197 deaths. In addition, at least seventy employers who avoided prosecution continued to violate safety laws, leading to scores of additional deaths.[5]

Criminal liability should be established for corporations and corporate managers who fail to warn potentially affected employees or the affected public about product and workplace dangers. Similar laws have recently been enacted in Canada and the UK. In addition to stiff sanctions (steep fines and jail time), a "Freedom from Harm" law could also empower individuals (including consumers, workers and other watchdogs) to initiate, participate in or intervene in any related court proceedings.

Improve Federal Contracting Rules and Regulations

An epidemic of waste, fraud and abuses resulted from the crony-riddled system of contracting and subcontracting in Iraq and elsewhere during the past eight years. The failure of federal officials to plan for and provide oversight, in combination with the outsourcing of government functions in the form of no-bid, cost-plus contracts for well-connected corporations, resulted in war profiteering on an epic scale. Similar abuses were witnessed in the post-Katrina contracts.

While Congress has begun to tackle the issue, a range of additional contracting reforms is still necessary. The number of auditors at the Pentagon and other major contracting departments should be increased to historical highs, while certain types of contracting that have effectively outsourced inherently-governmental functions over to the private sector should be eliminated. For example, the use of private security contractors (e.g., Blackwater) should be eliminated, as Rep. Jan Schakowsky (D-IL) proposed in the 2008 Stop Outsourcing Security Act (H.R. 4102).

In addition, the consequences for those who choose to rip off the taxpayer need to be so serious as to create an effective deterrent. Federal Acquisition Regulations—which require contracting officials to give taxpayer-funded contracts only to "responsible" companies—should be enforced to exclude recidivist violators.

A publicly available database of information related to the performance and integrity of federal contractors, including their record of convictions and violations, should be established, and contractors who have been convicted of two or more significant offenses (e.g., bribery, fraud and other crimes) within the previous five years should be automatically barred from eligibility.

Rein in Rabid Financial Speculation

As Robert Reich, Robert Kuttner and others have suggested, blind, ideologically driven deregulation has been a contributing cause of many of the worst corporate abuses of recent years, including the collapse of Enron and other companies and the spread of irresponsible and predatory lending practices and their dissemination throughout the broader economy through the securitization process. Many other disasters can be chalked up to deregulation and the failure to regulate as well: the deadly Sago mine collapse and other industrial accidents; the California energy crisis; the approval of Vioxx, Trasyol and other dangerous drugs; the contamination of tomatoes and other products in the wake of food inspection cutbacks; the failure to improve auto efficiency (CAFE) standards. Certain natural disasters, such as Hurricane Katrina, were also made worse by the failure to ensure a margin of safety.

The reforms passed in the wake of Enron and WorldCom have not only come under continuous attack, but they were designed at the outset to have a limited effect. As a result, the banking industry was able to put even more people at risk just years later, when it repackaged trillions of dollars in risky loans and dumped them on the wider market.

Just before she left her position as chair of the Commodity Futures Trading Commission (CFTC) in 1992, Wendy Gramm issued an order sought by Enron which exempted over-the-counter trades in exotic derivatives from CFTC supervision. (Just weeks later, Gramm joined Enron's board of directors.) This regulatory omission later came back to haunt consumers in the form of "rapacious speculation" by oil futures traders who, as Rep. John Dingell (D-MI) and other members of the House Energy and Commerce Committee have suggested, bear significant responsibility for the doubling of oil (and consequently, gas) prices between 2007 and 2008.

Aggressive new limits need to be established in the financial services industry as well as commodities trading markets in order to restrain speculation. Stronger disclosure and higher trading margin requirements would protect consumers and producers from being whipsawed by oil, grains and other commodities markets. Given the volume of trading, a barely noticeable transaction tax could be used to beef up market oversight and corporate crime enforcement budgets at the SEC and related agencies.

Protect Essential Services and Restrict Corporations from Government Functions

In November 2002, the Bush Administration announced plans to convert nearly half the federal civilian work force into positions held by private contractors. The stated goal was to save money. The unstated goal was an ideological assault on responsible government and unions, and the creation of new contracting op-portunities for corporate cronies.[6] By the end of Bush's second term, the mission was nearly accomplished: Huge sectors of the federal government had been pri-vatized. Private contractors now take home over 60 percent of the CIA's annual budget, manage the federal student loan program, process Freedom of Informa-tion Act requests, manage airport security and oversee the work of other con-tractors.

The incoming Administration should halt and reverse this process, recog-nizing that: a) turning over inherently governmental functions rarely results in a demonstrated benefit to taxpayers, as has often been claimed; and b) the corpo-ratization of certain inherently governmental functions has undermined govern-mental accountability and, in some cases, harmed the national interest.

Cut Corporate Welfare

While benefits for veterans, the poor and homeless, the disabled and unem-ployed continue to fall far short of social needs, corporate welfare programs continue to siphon funds from appropriate public investments.

The enormous variety and size of the largesse known as corporate wel-fare—bailouts, giveaways, tax loopholes, debt revocations, loan guarantees, insurance discounts and other benefits handed out to corporations—fuels anti-competitive and monopolistic behavior, undermines our national security and weakens our democracy.

Efforts to cut corporate welfare will require improved precision in federal spending reports; outright prohibitions and program cutbacks; the attachment of reciprocal obligations to existing benefits and their recipients; increased trans-parency in tax and other kinds of reporting; and across-the-board policy pre-scriptions, such as a ban on below-market sales and leases.[7]

Tame the Giant Corporations

The Constitution of the United States of America does not mention business corporations or define their relationship to the federal government. This omis-sion later allowed corporations to effectively reify themselves as "persons" able to claim Constitutional rights originally intended only for natural persons.

The omission also left the creation of corporations to state governments, a circumstance that originally led to greater levels of accountability, as charters were granted by state legislatures after considerable discussion—and usually only to businesses that demonstrated a public interest would be served: a canal built, a road constructed, etc. Over time, however, the process of incorporation devolved into a rote bureaucratic process, with states having little power to bargain for something in return for the rights and benefits (e.g., limited liability) automatically conferred through the corporate form itself.

The push for a federal chartering system to make up for these and other constitutional and regulatory gaps has been proposed before, at key moments in American history where corporate accountability has been deemed critical to the national interest.

At the peak of the Progressive Era (1904–1912), for example, federal chartering proposals were incorporated into the dominant political party platforms.[8] And in 1941, populist Senator Joseph O'Mahoney of Wyoming, chairman of the Temporary National Economic Committee—a massive examination of national industrial and economic policy—urged the creation of "a national charter system for all national corporations."[9] In the 1970s, in the wake of Watergate and related scandals, Ralph Nader and colleagues explored the potential strengths and weaknesses of a federal chartering system in their seminal book, *Taming the Giant Corporation.*

In today's era of corporate globalization, the federal chartering option could provide a new instrument of corporate accountability: Regardless of where a corporation chooses to incorporate (even if it relocates offshore), it would still be held to account if it were required to file for a federal charter or license to conduct business within the United States.

A federal chartering system could also be used in a variety of ways, providing a powerful tool for improved accountability across the entire corporate sector, within specific industries or even at specific companies. It can be used to limit the size of corporations, the activities they engage in (so that they do not engage in risky or manipulative behavior), and improve corporate governance and disclosure (e.g., of offshore operations), among other things.

Federal charters would re-establish the principle that corporations exist to serve some public purpose. This is a radical challenge to the current framework of corporate law, which treats corporations as a "nexus of contracts" between private parties, rather than creatures of law with public obligations.

Congress has issued charters periodically since 1791, most of them after the start of the twentieth century, particularly when the market fails to meet certain public needs. The National Railroad Passenger Corporation (Amtrak), for example, is a federally chartered corporation established to preserve inter-city passenger rail service. Fannie Mae is another federally chartered corporation that operates under an amended charter directing it towards a purpose that would not normally be served by for-profit corporations—providing assistance to secondary markets for residential mortgages, including activities related to mortgages on housing for low- and moderate-income families, as well as low-income loans and loans for energy conservation.

The federal government should be especially assertive in using its authority to alter any corporation's charter where there is a strong argument for serving the public interest. This could include financial bail-outs where the company relies on the taxpayer money to be restored to financial health. An important precedent was established in the case of WorldCom, which was allowed to re-emerge from bankruptcy only after addressing seventy-eight recommendations designed to address explicit abuses instrumental in the company's collapse, including a "maximum wage" for the new CEO.

Thus, rather than attempting a major overhaul of the entire corporate chartering system, policymakers can first take up this neglected tool as a way of addressing problems in specific industries or corporations where the case for public intervention is obvious. This might include industries that rely principally on public revenues or assets (e.g., the broadcast media and extractive industries reliant upon publicly owned natural resources); industries designed to serve the national interest (e.g., weapons manufacturers and others whose primary income is derived from federal contracts); industries whose restructuring is critical to national security objectives (e.g., energy and transportation); industries where an epidemic of corporate crime requires aggressive action and structural remedies; industries whose interests are in direct conflict with public health objectives (e.g., tobacco); and industries that provide an inherently public function (e.g., auditing firms).

There is no limit to the types of advances in corporate accountability that are possible in federal chartering. Entire industries could be restructured to make the profit motive subservient to a broader purpose.

In addition, the federal government could choose to charter new institutions—including cooperatives, community development corporations and trusts—which have the potential to displace corporations and serve the public interest more directly.[10]

The ultimate issue here is one of unchecked corporate power, which has managed to structure the laws and regulations in ways that relegate We the People to the margins, where we act as consumers and in other subordinate roles (e.g., as shareholders) rather than as citizens with sovereign authority.

Although compromises and regulatory capture could threaten the chartering process as much as any other regulatory framework, within a broader push for democratic reform the push for federal chartering as an instrument of corporate accountability could signal a shift toward restoring democratic control over important industrial and financial decisions.

As Theodore Roosevelt once put it: "The citizens of the United States must effectively control the mighty commercial forces which they have themselves called into being."

Resources

Association of Community Organizations for Reform Now (ACORN): http://www.acorn.org
Business Ethics Network: http://businessethicsnetwork.org/

Center for Justice and Democracy: http://www.centerjd.org/
Center for Progressive Reform: http://www.progressiveregulation.org
Collaborative Research on Corporations (Crocodyl): http://www.crocodyl.org
Commercial Alert (fights commercial excess): http://www.commercialalert.org
Community Environmental Legal Defense Fund: www.celdf.org
Consumer Federation of America: http://www.consumerfed.org
Consumer Project on Technology: http://www.cptech.org
Corporate Crime Reporter: http://www.corporatecrimereporter.com
Corporate Library: http://www.thecorporatelibrary.org
Corporate Research Project: http://www.corp-research.org/
Corporation 2020: http://www.corporation2020.org
CorpWatch: http://www.corpwatch.org
The Democracy Collaborative: www.community-wealth.org
Essential Information: http://www.essentialinformation.org
Fair Vote: http://www.fairvote.org
Food and Water Watch: http://www.foodandwaterwatch.org
Foundation for Taxpayer and Consumer Rights (CA): http://www.consumer
   watchdog.org
Good Jobs First: http://www.goodjobsfirst.org/gjf.htm
Government Accountability Project: http://www.whistleblower.org.
Institute for Local Self-Reliance New Rules Project: www.ilsr.org
Jobs With Justice: http://www.jwj.org
Just $6: http://www.just6dollars.org
Knowledge Ecology International: http://www.keionline.org/
Multinational Monitor Magazine: http://www.multinationalmonitor.org
National Community Reinvestment Coalition: http://www.ncrc.org
On The Commons: http://www.OnTheCommons.org
Pension Rights Center: http://www.pensionrights.org
Privatization Watch: http://privatizationwatch.org/
Program on Corporations, Law, and Democracy: www.poclad.org
Project on Government Oversight: http://www.pogo.org
Public Campaign: www.publiccampaign.org
Public Citizen: http://www.citizen.org
Public Employees Federation: http://www.stopprivatization.org/
Reclaim Democracy, Boulder, Colorado: www.reclaimdemocracy.org
Taming the Giant Corporation: http://www.tamethecorporation.org/
Too Much: A Commentary on Excess and Inequality:
   http://www.toomuchonline.org/
United for a Fair Economy: http://www.faireconomy.org
Wiser Earth: http://www.wiserearth.org/

References

Bakan, Joel. *The Corporation: The Pathological Pursuit of Profit and Power.* New York: Free Press, 2004.
Barnes, Peter. *Capitalism 3.0.* San Francisco: Berrett-Koehler, 2006.
Bollier, David. *Silent Theft: The Private Plunder of Our Common Wealth.* New York: Routledge, 2002.
Clinard, Marshall. *Corporate Crime.* 2nd ed. Piscataway: Transaction, 2006.
Drutman, Lee, and Charlie Cray. *The People's Business: Controlling Corporations and Restoring Democracy.* San Francisco: Berrett-Koehler, 2004.
Green, Mark. *Selling Out: How Corporate Money Buys Elections, Rams Through Legislation and Betrays Our Democracy.* New York: HarperCollins, 2002.
Hartmann, Thom. *Unequal Protection: The Rise of Corporate Dominance and the Theft of Human Rights.* New York: Rodale, 2002.
Mokhiber, Russell. *Corporate Crime and Violence.* San Francisco: Sierra Club Books, 1988.
Klein, Naomi. *The Shock Doctrine.* New York: Picador, 2008.
LeRoy, Greg. *The Great American Jobs Scam: Corporate Tax Dodging and the Myth of Job Creation.* San Francisco: Berrett-Koehler, 2006.
Nace, Ted. *Gangs of America.* San Francisco: Berrett-Koehler, 2003.
Nader, Ralph, et al. *Taming the Giant Corporation.* New York: Norton, 1976.
Nader, Ralph. *Cutting Corporate Welfare.* St. Paul: Seven Stories, 1999.
Phillips, Kevin. *Bad Money: Reckless Finance, Failed Politics and the Global Crisis of American Capitalism.* New York: Viking, 2008.
Rasmus, Jack. *The War at Home: The Corporate Offensive from Ronald Reagan to George W. Bush.* San Ramone: Kyklos Productions, 2006.
Ritz, Dean, ed. *Defying Corporations, Defining Democracy: A Book of History and Strategy.* New York: Apex, 2001.
Scahill, Jeremy. *Blackwater.* New York: Nation Books, 2008.

Notes

1. William Funk, et al., "The Truth about Torts: Using Agency Preemption to Undercut Consumer Health and Safety," September 2007. Center for Progressive Reform, http://www.progressiveregulation.org (accessed July 19, 2008). To learn more about the politics of tort "deform" see the Center for Justice and Democracy, www.centerjd.org.

2. See Marshall Clinard, et al., "Illegal Corporate Behavior," U.S. Department of Justice Law Enforcement Assistance Administration, National Institute of Law Enforcement and Criminal Justice, October 1979.

3. U.S. Consumer Product Safety Commission, 2008 Performance Budget Request, submitted to Congress February 2007. See page iv, http://www.cpsc.gov/cpscpub/pubs/reports/2008plan.pdf (accessed July 19, 2008).

4. Bureau of Labor Statistics, Census of Fatal Occupational Injuries, http://www.bls.gov/iif/oshwc/cfoi/cfch0005.pdf (accessed July 19, 2008).

5. David Barstow, "When Workers Die," *New York Times*, December 22, 2003, page A1. Available at http://www.nytimes.com/ref.national/work_index.html (accessed July 19, 2008).

6. Richard W. Stevenson, "Government May Make Private Nearly Half of Its Civilian Jobs," *New York Times*, November 15, 2002.

7. For additional information, see Ralph Nader, *Cutting Corporate Welfare* (New York: Seven Stories Press, 2000).

8. For a comprehensive analysis of the history, purpose and shortcomings of the federal chartering proposal, see Ralph Nader, Mark Green and Joel Seligman, *Taming the Giant Corporation*, 1976.

9. Senator Joseph C. O'Mahoney, "The Preservation of Economic Freedom." (final statement to the Temporary National Economic Committee, March 11, 1941), quoted in Nader et al., p. 70.

10. Gar Alperovitz, *America Beyond Capitalism: Reclaiming Our Wealth, Our Liberty, and Our Democracy* (2006). For more information, see http://www.community-wealth.org, and http://www.corporation2020.org (both accessed July 19, 2008).

Chapter 32

Making Our Democracy All It Can Be: An Agenda for Voting Rights and Election Reform

Miles Rapoport and Stuart Comstock-Gay

POLICY PROPOSALS

- Lower barriers and encourage participation.
  - Make registration easier.
    - Regularize and ease felony disenfranchisement laws.
    - Enact election day registration.
    - Improve implementation of the National Voter Registration Act.
    - Allow sixteen-year-olds to pre-register.
    - Register every American when he or she turns eighteen.
  - Maximize opportunities to vote.
    - Create a national early voting process.
    - Allow full use of mail-in balloting.
    - Grant DC residents full voting rights and representation.
  - Eliminate voter suppression and discouragement.
    - Enact laws prohibiting deceptive practices.
    - Prevent the passage of overly restrictive voter identification laws.
- Make votes and voices count.
  - Restore confidence in election administration.
    - Create a strong public open-source process for research, development and oversight of voting machines.
    - Fully fund state efforts to comply with national standards.
  - Support meaningful campaign finance reform, including public financing.

     □ **Restore the functioning of the Presidential Campaign Financing System.**
     □ **Support legislation for public financing of congressional campaigns.**
     □ **Support state legislation for public financing at the state level.**
■ **Create effective structures.**
   ■ **Create a strengthened Election Administration Commission with adequate funding and the authority to propose and enforce national standards.**
   ■ **Create a Justice Department committed to enforcing the right to vote.**
   ■ **Create a White House Office on Voting and Civic Engagement whose mission is to encourage policies that will produce a more vibrant and inclusive democracy.**

* * * * * * * * * * * * * *

As the incoming Administration begins to undo the damage of the last eight years, one question that will be asked is, "How did we let things get this bad?" One reason is that American democracy itself has had major deficits which made it far more difficult for the needs and voices of the full public to be heard.

From the start, let's be clear about one thing: The inequities in our economic policies and outcomes are completely intertwined with the deficits of our democracy. Inequalities in wealth and power will always find their way into the political process—through voting disparities, campaign contributions and unequal access to lobbying resources—to name a few. Conversely, the deficits in our democratic process make it harder for the political system to address the issues of those whose voices and votes are far more softly heard.

For a long time, concerns about how our election process functions have been dismissed as the sour grapes of a losing side or the province of a small band of "good government types." But the truth is there are important structural flaws in our democracy that can be fixed as a matter of public policy, and a critical responsibility and opportunity of the incoming Administration is to do just that.

It is a multifaceted agenda that the new administration and Congress must undertake, but the policies needed fall under two very broad categories. First, we need to ensure that each and every citizen has the maximum opportunity to participate in the process. And second, we must be sure that everyone's vote is counted and everyone's voice is fairly heard.

Lowering Barriers and Encouraging Participation

Expanding Voter Registration

Ideally, voter registration should be automatic and universal. Upon turning eighteen, every American should automatically be registered to vote. It should be a responsibility of the government to get us all signed up, as it is in the UK. Already, every American male who turns eighteen must register for Selective Service. Let's make voting similarly universal.

Short of universal registration, there are some policies that can make an extraordinary difference in the numbers of people registered, and the degree to which they mirror the population at large.

One such policy is Election Day Registration (EDR), often also called "Same Day Registration." Right now, eight states offer their voters the opportunity to register on Election Day. North Carolina allows citizens to register and vote on the same day during periods of early voting. A tenth, North Dakota, does not require voter registration. Maine, Minnesota and Wisconsin have allowed EDR for over thirty years, and New Hampshire, Idaho and Wyoming have been doing it for a dozen or more years. Montana, Iowa, and North Carolina have adopted EDR in the last three years. These states have administratively handled EDR with ease, without threatening the integrity of their elections.

The results are nothing short of extraordinary. In 2008, four of the top five states in voter turnout were EDR states. States with EDR typically have an average turnout rate that is 10–12 percentage points higher than the states without it. This year, in North Carolina, 22,293 brand new voters registered and voted at the early voting sites in the May 6 Presidential primary.

In the absence of real leadership from Washington, Election Day Registration has progressed in the states. But Congress could easily enact EDR for federal elections, which would have an enormous impact on the number of people who vote. It would also rectify the problem of registered voters arriving at the polls only to find that their names have been left off the voter list. They could simply re-register to vote and cast a ballot, eliminating the need for provisional voting.

A second way to facilitate voter registration is simple: We must vigorously enforce the National Voter Registration Act (NVRA), passed and signed into law by President Clinton in 1993. "Motor Voter" provides that people can register to vote at motor vehicle departments, but it also requires that all state public assistance agencies offer applicants and clients the opportunity to register to vote or update their voter registration records each time they apply for benefits, renew their benefits or report a change of address. Fifteen years after the law went into effect, compliance is abysmal in many states. Confronted with evidence of non-compliance, some states have recently improved their voter registration procedures in public assistance agencies, and have seen dramatic results. North Carolina, for example, recently saw a six-fold increase in the number of citizens registering in these agencies after implementing improved procedures.

Other states continue to ignore their responsibilities, leaving millions of low-income citizens unregistered. The Voting Rights Section of the Justice Department, which spent years ignoring evidence of non-compliance, has begun to investigate. A settlement agreement resulting from Justice Department enforcement in the early 2000s has made Tennessee a national leader in public assistance voter registration. A serious effort by the Justice Department to guarantee implementation could go a very long way.

These two policies—EDR and NVRA—help people who are unregistered but eligible to vote. However, an astonishing 5.3 million people are barred even from registering, because they are forbidden to vote. These are individuals who have been convicted of a felony and excluded by state law from participating in the electoral process. As is now well known, America incarcerates a higher percentage of its population than any other modern democracy. The prison population now stands at 2.3 million. In most states, a felony conviction carries collateral consequences for voting beyond the period of imprisonment. Thirty-five states bar voting for some period of time after a person is released from prison. This has been entirely a state function, and states have wildly different standards for restoration of the right to vote. In Maine and Vermont, you never lose the right to vote. In Kentucky and Virginia, you lose it for life. Most other states fall in between. Over 600,000 Florida residents were denied the right to vote in the 2000 Presidential election because of felony convictions, including more than 30 percent of African-American men who lived in the state.

What has been remarkably encouraging over the last ten years is how many states have improved their voting rights restoration statutes. In Connecticut, a 2001 law gave people on probation the right to vote. In Maryland, the lifetime ban on two-time offenders was repealed. Even in Florida, Governor Charlie Crist has streamlined the process and allowed tens of thousands—a significant number, though far from everyone—to regain the right to vote.

But once more, the patchwork quilt of laws hurts our democracy; many people who do have the right to vote don't exercise it because they assume they cannot. A federal law setting a single standard for federal elections, such as having one's voting rights restored when you leave prison in states that disfranchise felons, would re-enfranchise several million people.

Expanding the Ways to Vote

"Why Tuesday?" is the name of an organization which asks some simple yet profound questions about how American elections are conducted. Why Tuesday, indeed. Our national tradition of voting on a single day in November, which is not even a national holiday, began in our agrarian traditions. But in today's urban-suburban society, the practice is anachronistic and limits participation. It's past time for some modernization.

It used to be that banks closed at 3:00 pm on Fridays, and if you didn't make it in time to stand in an hour-long line, you didn't have any money for the weekend. Such an idea now seems ludicrous. Banks realized that if you want someone to do something, you make it as easy as possible for them to do it. Now every bank has ATMs, and if you want to make a withdrawal at 1:00 am rather than 1:00 pm, you can do it.

But in voting, the reigning assumptions are exactly the opposite. In most states, voters have to come to the polling place during or right after a workday to cast their votes. All states allow the opportunity to cast an absentee ballot, but in twenty-two states and the District of Columbia, you need an "excused absence" to vote by mail. Why is voting in person—on Tuesday between 8 am and 7 pm—superior to voting by mail, or voting on Sunday or at an early voting site? The overarching imperative is for people to have the greatest opportunity to vote.

In recent years, the trends have begun to come into modernity. Thirty-one states allow some form of no-excuse absentee ballots or in-person early voting. In 2008, one-third of all voters cast their votes early. Several of these states have established vote centers that are set up in convenient locations on or before Election Day. Early voting and vote centers dramatically increase the opportunities for voters to cast their ballot. Texas and Florida—among others—have seen a surge in early voting usage by residents there. In addition, more states have offered voters the opportunity to vote by mail, without requiring explanations. In Oregon, all elections are conducted through mail-in ballot. But no matter how it's done now, voters deserve an equal opportunity to cast a ballot in every state, making a national agenda of expanding voting opportunities clearly in order.

One additional means to expand people's opportunities to vote is to make sure that nothing and no one interferes with that right. The most outrageous stories from recent elections were the instances when people tried, with malice aforethought, to intimidate or trick people into not voting. Flyers were distributed in some neighborhoods alleging that if would-be voters had any outstanding parking tickets, they would be served with warrants while voting. In other places, letters were sent telling Democrats that to avoid long lines, Republicans were voting on Tuesday and Democrats on Wednesday. As ludicrous and amateurish as these efforts were in many cases, they undoubtedly discouraged people from voting, and the laws against such practices are ambiguous. As a Senator, Barack Obama introduced the Deceptive Practices and Voter Intimidation Act, to make such tactics clearly illegal. This legislation should be incorporated into the larger agenda of voting rights and election reform.

In the category of erecting barriers to voting, overly restrictive voter identification laws pose a serious danger, and don't even solve a real problem. The real instances of fraud by voters—the alleged target of voter ID laws—are almost non-existent. Professor Lorraine Minnite of Barnard College conducted an extensive study of the problem including a comprehensive analysis of thousands of news articles, prosecution records, interviews with state officials including secretaries of state and attorneys general, and the academic literature. She concludes that the allegations of fraud are almost always anecdotal and inaccurate, and the instances of real in-person fraud by a voter are infinitesimal in comparison to the numbers of votes cast. Yet, some states have enacted, and legislators in many states are pushing for, very strict voter verification requirements, including requirements for a government-issued photo ID, and even proof of citizenship. Studies have shown that significant numbers of people—disproportionately people of color, people with disabilities and the elderly—do not possess a drivers' license or other requisite ID, and the potential for discouragement of large numbers of voters is very real. These excessive requirements need to be resisted at all levels.

There is one place in our nation where discouragement of voting is a structural travesty, and that is in our nation's capital. The 580,000 residents of Washington, D.C., are denied the opportunity to cast a vote for meaningful representation in Congress. It is a totally unjustifiable restriction, and it is now a change that has clearly reached the tipping point. The last Congress came close to passing a bill granting the District of Columbia full voting representation in Congress. The incoming Administration's agenda must include granting full representational rights to voters in the District. The Administration should also fix the problem of the 4.4 million residents of various U.S. Territories (Puerto Rico, Guam, Virgin Islands and others) who not only have no voting representative in Congress, but don't even get any electoral votes.

Making Votes and Voices Count

Lowering the direct structural impediments to registering and voting will clearly be a major way to encourage voters. But there are many reasons people have not voted in the past. One reason, often cited by people who don't go to the polls, is that they don't believe their votes will be counted, and they have doubts that their voices will truly be heard in a political system tilted toward the wealthy. So, in addition to putting out the welcome mat to invite people in, we have to clean the house so that it is a truly welcoming process.

Election Administration We Can Believe In

It is essential that we improve the administration of our election process. Since the spectacle of administrative incompetence and confusion that have marked elections not just in Florida, but in many other jurisdictions, we have entered a real debate about how we run elections. President Jimmy Carter once remarked that he wouldn't send international election observers to the United States because we didn't meet minimum standards of uniformity and reliability.

To begin with, we need a strong set of national standards. Right now, elections are run separately in each of the fifty states, the District of Columbia and thousands of counties. Each of these entities can set different standards for machines operated by private companies in proprietary ways, for list maintenance, for poll workers and their training, for provisional ballots, and for voter identification requirements, in addition to having differing laws on registration and voter eligibility. The United States must have an election system where voters in different states are treated equally.

An important subtopic within the idea of national standards concerns voting machines. Eight years after the 2000 debacle, states are still floundering through the process of finding voting equipment that is modern, accessible and fully reliable. After an initial rush to direct recording electronic machines (DREs), followed by a counteracting movement against those machines and for paper ballots, there is no obvious answer as to the best system. This is certainly an area where national-level resources, research, standard-setting and decision-making, with clear public accountability, is in order.

Fixing Campaign Finance

Thirty-four years after Watergate spurred the first wave of campaign finance reform, the system is less reformed than ever. Campaigns continue to be more and more expensive. The Presidential public financing system has been breached and the water is pouring through. And the Supreme Court's excessive concern over the rights of the rich has made it extremely difficult to find ways to keep the sharpening divide of economic inequality from spilling over into our democratic system. But the basic critical principle is that in order to have voters truly control the system, and feel that their voices are truly heard, we cannot have a system in which the microphone volume available to the rich is so loud that it drowns out the voices of the rest of us.

One heartening development has been the massive increase in small donations, coming online, from over three million contributors in the campaign of Barack Obama. This is a truly democratic development, but it is a vast overreach to think that this has solved, or can solve, the deeper problems of our campaign finance system. For every high-profile candidate who can reach the kind of audience that Obama has, there are hundreds who slog every day through the old high-donor shakedown that has become a dreary ritual of American politics.

Creative and positive policy proposals are in the public debate. The Durbin-Larson bill would create public financing for Congressional elections. At the state level, Arizona, Maine and Connecticut have strong state public financing systems. New York has a strong matching system for candidates. Other states have partial systems covering judicial races or other steps forward.

The need for Presidential leadership is front and center. The incoming President must lead in refashioning a system that can work for the future, so that we don't have unlimited contributions and full-blown dominance of the process by large-scale donors. The Presidential system must be repaired.

Enacting public financing for Congressional races is another essential part of the process. The basic concept of requiring candidates to show a threshold of seriousness, and then to be able to concentrate on talking with voters instead of ministering to funders, is a concept that can work, and can make a serious difference in determining which candidates can enter the political arena. Passage of the Durbin-Larson bill would make a huge difference. And action at the federal level would undoubtedly encourage states—many of which are considering serious reform—to take those steps.

Marc Hanna, the moneyman behind the election of President William McKinley in 1896, is notorious for saying, "There are two things that are important in politics. The first is money and I can't remember the second." The incoming President must help change that calculus.

Creating Effective Structures

What has been laid out here is a welter of policy proposals that together form a coherent agenda for reform. Some are legislative, some administrative, some involve the use of the Presidential bully pulpit. But there are three organizational moves that seem essential to moving this agenda forward.

First, the Election Assistance Commission must be strengthened or replaced. It was set up under the Help America Vote Act (HAVA) intentionally as a weak agency with primarily advisory capacity. It is simply not enough.

After a very rocky start, the EAC found its footing and worked to give useful guidance to secretaries of state and other election officials. More recently, it has suffered from some of the partisan divide that has afflicted the Federal Election Commission. We need an agency that can set national standards for computerized list maintenance and purging, for voting machines that all can have confidence in, for a poll worker workforce able to administer a more and more complex set of tasks, and many others. And the agency needs significant funding in two ways: first, to have adequate research, administrative, and field capacity internally; and second, to have a significant and ongoing pool of funds to help states move forward. Election administration is not a one-shot fix, as HAVA imagined; rather, it is an ongoing, major aspect of our national life that needs care, attention and resources to change with the times.

Second, the Justice Department has to be turned into a genuine enforcement vehicle for voting rights. The politicization of the Justice Department during the Bush Administration has been painfully documented, but it was nowhere more damaging than in the voting rights arena. The Department has failed to heed voting rights concerns when pre-clearing new voting rights laws under the Voting Rights Act. It has failed to enforce, up until very recently, the National Voter Registration Act. It has dismissed prosecutors who would not drum up voter fraud claims against Democrats. Instead, it has mandated voter purges by states, and taken other steps that shrink the electorate and voting opportunities, rather than expand them. It was not the fault of the career staff, who have by all accounts struggled to do a fair job in an environment dominated by extreme partisans. They need leadership and an environment in which the real responsibilities of the Department can be exercised.

Lastly, we need a White House Office of Civic Engagement. The full achievement of a vibrant and inclusive democracy, with high levels of voting participation and also ongoing civic engagement, will require the active engagement of many parts of the government, and many partners at the state level and in the non-profit and civil society community at large. An office committed to making our democracy sing, with a leadership dedicated to making an agenda of legislative, policy and practice changes come into being, and Presidential support for the changes needed, would be an excellent focal point for much of what needs to be done.

There is no silver bullet of policy change that can cure our democracy's deficits and give the American people a democratic system of which we can be proud. But there are many steps that can be taken—by the incoming Administration, by Congress and by state legislators with the commitment to change—that will make an enormous difference in the ways we vote and participate. It's an agenda worth voting for.

Resources

Advancement Project: www.advancementproject.org
Brennan Center for Justice: www.brennancenter.org
Common Cause: www.commoncause.org
Demos: A Network for Ideas and Action: www.demos.org
Election Line: www.electionline.org
FairVote: www.fairvote.org
Lawyers Committee for Civil Rights Under Law: www.lawyerscomm.org
League of Women Voters: www.lwv.org
Moritz School of Law Equal Vote blog: http://moritzlaw.osu.edu/blogs/tokaji/
NAACP Legal Defense Fund: www.naacpldf.org
People for the American Way: www.pfaw.org
Project Vote: www.projectvote.org
Public Campaign: Clean Money, Clean Elections: www.publiccampaign.org
Voter Action: www.voteraction.org

References

Griffith, Benjamin E. *America Votes: A Guide to Modern Election Law and Voting Rights.* Chicago: American Bar Association, 2008.
Keyssar, Alex. *The Right to Vote: The Contested History of Democracy in the United States.* New York: Basic Books, 2001.
Overton, Spencer. *Stealing Democracy: The New Politics of Voter Suppression.* New York: W.W. Norton, 2006.
Waldman, Michael. *A Return to Common Sense: Seven Bold Ways to Revitalize Democracy.* Naperville: Sourcebooks, 2008.

Chapter 33

Restoring Balance to the Federal Courts

Nan Aron and Simon Heller

POLICY PROPOSALS

- The incoming Administration should promulgate guidelines and standards for the selection of federal judges that will shape a more diverse judiciary.
- Trial, appellate and Supreme Court-level federal judge nominations should reflect a diversity of prior legal experience.
- The Justice Department's Office of Legal Policy should consult with a broad range of civil rights, public interest and human rights organizations in its process for making judicial selection recommendations to the President.
- The Senate Judiciary Committee should prepare written committee reports on each nomination, at least for Courts of Appeals and Supreme Court appointments; should require advance consultation by the White House on judicial nominations; and should, whenever possible, broadcast confirmation hearings through the Committee website.
- Congress should repeal limitations on the ability of prisoners to file cases in federal courts; permit the recovery of attorney's fees in civil rights cases where the cases are the catalyst for a favorable settlement; and increase the hourly fees which lawyers can obtain under the Equal Access to Justice Act (EAJA), and expand the range of cases in which EAJA awards are permitted to include at least all cases vindicating federal Constitutional rights.
- Congress and the incoming President should respect the Supreme Court's decision on the scope of *habeas corpus* in *Boumediene v. Bush* by declining to enact special mechanisms for review of indefinite Presidential detention.

- Congress should enact the Fair Pay Restoration Act to undo the Court's decision in *Ledbetter v. Goodyear Tire & Rubber Co.*,[1] which severely limited the ability of workers to sue for pay discrimination.
- Congress should enact legislation to clarify the Federal Arbitration Act by establishing that mandatory binding arbitration is invalid in employment and consumer contracts and civil rights disputes.
- Congress should enact legislation to restore state damages actions for faulty medical devices to nullify the Supreme Court's decision in *Riegel v. Medtronic, Inc.*,[2] finding that such cases are pre-empted by federal law.

* * * * * * * * * * * * * * *

The past eight years have witnessed a dramatic conservative shift in the federal courts with the appointment of judges hostile to cherished rights and freedoms. As a result, Constitutional and statutory protections for millions of Americans have been curtailed. In addition, the Bush Administration has propounded an extreme view of sweeping Executive Branch power, power that has often been asserted to be (and in practice has been) unreviewable by either Congress or the courts.

The Need for a Balanced Judiciary

Because of the critical role life-tenured judges play in society and the damage done by the appointment of ultraconservatives during the Bush Administration, the incoming White House must make selection of judicial nominees a top priority. In tandem with this, the Senate must give top priority to its consideration of the President's judicial nominees and stand up to pressure from the Right to confirm only centrist and conservative judges. We must restore to the federal courts the lost voices of Justices William J. Brennan, Jr., and Thurgood Marshall.

The guidelines and standards promulgated by the incoming Administration should include the requirement that nominees have a proven record of commitment to equal justice under the law. The standards should, at a minimum, require a firm commitment to civil and women's rights; individual rights and liberties, including privacy; and environmental, worker and consumer protections.

Diversity in experience benefits courts, because federal judges handle an immensely diverse docket of cases. For this reason, selection of judicial nominees should increase the proportion of lawyers who have devoted a substantial portion of their careers to public interest law, including work as a public defender, civil rights lawyer, Legal Services attorney or labor lawyer. The increasing tendency to elevate sitting federal judges to higher courts risks isolating the federal judiciary from the American people.

Strengthening the Senate's "Advise and Consent" Role in the Confirmation Process and Enhancing Public Participation in and Knowledge of the Judicial Appointment Process

The Senate Judiciary Committee's written reports on each nomination should include transcripts of the confirmation hearing, copies of written materials submitted by the nominee and explanations of the Committee's action on the nomination—including the vote of each Senator and dissenting views if they exist. Too many judicial nominees have been reported to the Senate floor on voice votes. The confirmation process deserves the same level of documentation as does the Senate's legislative work.

The federal courts have a special and cherished role in our Constitutional system of government, providing a crucial check on the power of Congress and the President and giving ordinary citizens a forum in which the can seek to vindicate their federal rights before a neutral party. Over the past eight years, these roles of the federal courts have been attacked by a President who has relentlessly pursued unilateral powers and by a Congress that has failed to stand up to President Bush's schemes to pack the courts with ultraconservative judges and to whittle away at the jurisdiction of the courts.

Unilateral Selection of Judges by the President

Early in his Administration, President Bush signaled his unilateral intentions. The Bush Administration eliminated the vetting role the American Bar Association (ABA) had played in previous Administrations of both parties. It is no longer involved in the nominations process and has instead only evaluated nominees after their names have been sent to the Senate. The Bush Administration ended the time-honored practice of consulting with leaders of both parties in the Senate in an effort to settle on consensus nominees for higher courts. The Administration has also sought to steer the debate away from the legal views of judicial nominees, instead focusing on the credentials of nominees, and the Senate has failed to probe the judicial views of nominees in a meaningful manner.

The Senate's ability to withstand the Administration's court-packing plan was severely undermined when Republicans threatened to eliminate the possibility of filibustering judicial nominees. The resulting compromise of May 2005 by the bi-partisan "Gang of 14" Senators has virtually guaranteed that no controversial judicial nominee will be defeated, and indeed no nominee has been rejected since then, even after Democrats regained control of the Senate in January of 2007. In fact, nominees like Priscilla Owen (for the Fifth Circuit) and Janice Rogers Brown (for the D.C. Circuit), who had successfully been filibustered when the Democrats were in the minority, were confirmed after the Gang of 14 agreement.

An Increasingly Conservative Judiciary

The most prominent example of the rightward shift of the federal courts has been at the United States Supreme Court, to which President Bush has named two Justices, Chief Justice John Roberts, who replaced another conservative, Chief Justice William Rehnquist, in late 2005, and Justice Samuel Alito, who replaced Justice Sandra Day O'Connor in 2006. Justice O'Connor was often the "swing vote" between an ultraconservative bloc of Justices and a more moderate bloc, and she often sided with the more moderate Justices on issues ranging from the scope of the right to choose abortion[3] to the extent to which educational institutions can use race to achieve the goal of diversity in the student body.[4] With her replacement by Justice Alito, the new swing vote has become Justice Kennedy, who is, on many issues, more conservative than Justice O'Connor; Justice Alito is far more conservative than either Justice Kennedy or Justice O'Connor.

Even within just the Court's past two terms, it has already eroded several precedents that Justice O'Connor, together with the moderate bloc on the Court, established as the law of the land.[5] The newly conservative Court has not hesitated to construe statutes intended to protect employees in favor of employers instead,[6] and was just one vote away from blocking a challenge to the EPA's refusal to regulate greenhouse gases[7] and from granting the President the power to detain people indefinitely without any meaningful Court review.[8]

President Bush's appointments to the federal courts have also resulted in much more conservative federal Courts of Appeals, the courts of last resort for the overwhelming majority of federal litigants, and the federal District Courts. One study found that judges appointed by President Bush "turn out to be more conservative on civil rights, civil liberties, and worker and consumer protections when compared not only with Democratic appointees but also with judges named by previous Republican presidents."[9] By the end of his term of office, nearly one-third of all federal judges will have been appointed by Bush, and ten of the thirteen circuits will be dominated by judges appointed by Republicans. On the Tenth and Eighth Circuits, for example, President Bush himself has appointed half and nearly-two thirds of the active judges, respectively.

Though the seeds sown by these conservative appointments have yet to bear full fruit in terms of judicial decisions, we have already seen examples of these and other Courts of Appeals issuing extremely conservative decisions that undermine the basic rights of Americans. In one case, a conservative panel of the Eighth Circuit held that an employer could legally deny coverage for prescription contraceptives to women, while providing full coverage for all other prescription drugs, holding that contraception "is not 'related to' pregnancy."[10] Another telling example is provided by the Sixth Circuit, in which the conservative majority on the full Court often wields its power to set aside more moderate decisions made by three-judge panels.[11]

One of our key proposals to restore balance after the last eight years of judicial appointments is to select judicial nominees from a much wider range of professional backgrounds. Of the 237 district judges appointed by President George W. Bush who have not taken senior status, 107, or over 45 percent, have served as federal or state prosecutors or both, while only ten, or less than 5 percent, have worked as criminal defense lawyers. This sort of lopsided preference for appointing prosecutors creates a highly imbalanced bench.[12] The incoming President should rectify this imbalance by appointing judges from a wide range of professional backgrounds.

Expansion of Executive Power at the Expense of the Courts

In a number of arenas, the Bush Administration has asserted power that both threatens individual rights and undermines the authority of the federal courts to rein in Executive Branch excesses. The most dramatic example has been the President's assertion, in the wake of the September 11 attacks, of the power to imprison individuals indefinitely on the basis that they are connected to terrorism or otherwise pose national security threats, and the parallel assertion that the federal courts are without power to scrutinize the basis for the detention. These assertions have been struck down by a closely divided Supreme Court,[13] but continue to be pressed in the public debate.

Another assertion of judicially unreviewable Executive Branch power is the power asserted by the President to wiretap telephone and electronic communications without obtaining warrants from courts, including even the secretive Foreign Surveillance Intelligence Court, and the more general power to set aside any federal statute that the President believes conflicts with his understanding of his own powers under the Constitution. Similarly, the Bush Administration routinely invokes the "state secrets doctrine" to prevent courts from scrutinizing information that relates to "national security." Perhaps the most notorious assertion of Executive power has been that the President may have the power to authorize extreme interrogation techniques even if they violate federal criminal statutes prohibiting torture.

The expansion of Executive Branch power sought and often effectuated by the Bush Administration makes it essential that people appointed to the federal bench have an abiding commitment to our system of checks and balances, and a distrust of unilateral executive power.

Conclusion

The proposals summarized above would result in a judicial selection process that has the potential to restore much-needed balance to the federal courts and to make that process more transparent so that politicians can and will be held accountable for their roles in selecting judges. The only check on further polarization of the judiciary lies in the Senate and the public's insistence that the Senate assert its authority to reject nominees who are far to the right of the mainstream of American society.

Throughout much of our history, the federal courts have been called upon to decide difficult and controversial social issues. To fulfill this essential role effectively and fairly, the federal judiciary must merit the respect of all citizens, and must not stray from the basic values and rights we all cherish. Public confidence in our judiciary depends on the selection of judges who are fair, open-minded and committed to equal justice for all.

Resources

Alliance for Justice: www.afj.org
Federal Judicial Center: http://www.fjc.gov/history/home.nsf
Senate Judiciary Committee, Status of Article III Judicial Nominations: http://judiciary.senate.gov/nominations.cfm

References

Bass, Jack. *Taming the Storm: The Life and Times of Judge Frank M. Johnson, Jr., and the South's Fight over Civil Rights*. New York: Anchor Books, 2002.

Eisgruber, Christopher L. *The Next Justice: Repairing the Supreme Court Appointments Process*. Princeton: Princeton University Press, 2007.

Goldman, Sheldon. *Picking Federal Judges: Lower Court Selection From Roosevelt Through Reagan*. New Haven: Yale University Press, 1999.

Schwartz, Herman. *Right Wing Justice: The Conservative Campaign to Take Over the Courts*. New York: Nation Books, 2004.

Tribe, Lawrence H. *God Save This Honorable Court: How the Choice of Supreme Court Justices Shapes Our History*. New York: Random House, 1985.

Notes

1. 127 S. Ct. 2162 (2007).
2. 128 S. Ct. 999 (2008).
3. See, e.g., *Stenberg v. Carhart*, 530 U.S. 914, 947 (2000) (O'Connor, J., concurring).

4. See, e.g., *Grutter v. Bollinger*, 539 U.S. 306 (2003) (opinion of the Court by O'Connor, J.).

5. See, e.g., *Gonzales v. Carhart*, 127 S. Ct. 1610 (2007) (significantly eroding *Stenberg*); *Parents Involved in Community Schools v. Seattle School Dist. No. 1*, 127 S. Ct. 2738 (2007) (eroding *Grutter* and numerous other precedents).

6. *Ledbetter v. Goodyear Tire & Rubber*, 127 S. Ct. 2162 (2007).

7. *Massachusetts v. EPA*, 549 U.S. 497 (2007).

8. *Boumediene v. Bush*, 76 U.S.L.W. 4406 (June 12, 2008).

9. See Kenneth Jost, *Courts & The Law: The Bush Bench*, CONG. QUARTERLY, May 22, 2006; Press Release, Univ. of Houston, Bush-Appointed Judges Most Conservative on Record, New UH Study Finds (Feb. 6, 2006), http://www.uh.edu/media/nr/2006/02feb/020606jappointees_carp.html (last visited June 20, 2008).

10. *In re Union Pacific Railroad Employment Practices Litigation*, 479 F.3d 936 (8th Cir. 2007).

11. See, e.g., *Williams v. Taft*, 359 F.3d 811 (6th Cir. Jan. 15, 2004): Five circuit judges dissented from an order refusing to stay the execution of Mr. Williams, as to whose case rehearing *en banc* had been granted, in a case challenging execution procedures. The dissenters observed that two Senior Judges were improperly permitted to vote on the motion to stay execution though "the requested stay would have been granted in the absence of [their] votes. . . . Moreover, this unlawful denial of the motion to stay has eviscerated the results of the poll of active judges granting *en banc* review. Without a stay, the *en banc* review authorized by [statute] will never take place." Williams was executed.

12. One commentator has specifically examined the question of whether Supreme Court Justices appointed by Republican presidents "evolve" and has discovered "one single factor [that] has proven an especially reliable predictor of whether a Republican nominee will be a steadfast conservative or evolve into a moderate or liberal: experience in the executive branch of government. Those who lack such experience evolve; those who have had it do not." Michael C. Dorf, *Does Federal Executive Branch Experience Explain Why Some Republican Supreme Court Justices "Evolve" and Others Don't?*, 1 HARV. LAW & POLICY REV. 457 (2007).

13. *Boumediene v. Bush*, 76 U.S.L.W. 4406 (June 12, 2008).

Chapter 34

Unleash Democracy:
Policies for a New Federalism

Ben Manski and Karen Dolan

POLICY PROPOSALS

- **Remove federal obstacles to local and state innovation.**
  - Commission a thorough review of federal preemption law and its impact on the practice of local democracy in the United States.
  - Work with Congress to pass a "Local Democracy Act" affirming federal respect for local and state innovation by rooting out anti-democratic federal preemption laws. This omnibus legislation should centralize the "democracy question"—that is, what level government is most open to democratic participation and protecting democratic rights—in revoking federal regulations, rulings and acts that interfere with the sound practice of local democracy and participatory economics.
  - Convene a congress of municipalities and states to develop and advance a national agenda for the expansion of local democracy and democratic federalism.
- **Invest in cooperatives and participatory democracy.**
  - Work with Congress to establish the Bureau for Economic Democracy, a new federal corporation (like the Corporation for Public Broadcasting) intended to provide publicity, training, education and direct financing for development of cooperatives and for democratic reforms intended to make government agencies, private associations and business enterprises more participatory. Financed through public and private support, the Bureau would enable the creation and sustenance of innovative participatory democratic and economic initiatives at the local, state and regional level.

- Order federal agencies to revise contracting and granting guidelines with an eye toward fostering cooperative and participatory service models. This would entail inserting criteria to evaluate and reward applications for federal funding that demonstrate meaningful levels of participation and mechanisms for self-governance.
- Establish, support, and reward a new class of federally chartered co-operatives.
- Advocate for the creation of a new class of federally chartered cooperatives. Several states provide a state-level mechanism for coop incorporation; this initiative would bring that model to the national scene. Chartering requirements would include specific elements of community, social and ecological responsibility, as well as member control. To encourage and support the growth of this new cooperative class, this initiative would enact incentives similar to the tax breaks and zoning privileges now granted to for-profit private businesses operating within so-called "Free Enterprise Zones," as well as, in some economic sectors, start-up grants.

■ Restore the National Guard to its proper defense role.
  - Immediately order the return and release of the National Guard from service in Iraq and Afghanistan. The Militia Clause plainly limits National Guard service to domestic defense. Notwithstanding the limitations of the Militia Clause. Congress' 2002 Authorization for the Use of Military Force (2002 AUMF) established a limited Iraq mission whose objectives have been met: Saddam Hussein was removed from power; the threat of supposed Weapons of Mass Destruction is absent. The 2002 AUMF has expired, and there is no current lawful basis for the deployment of the Guard to Iraq. Furthermore, Congress's 2001 AUMF established an unconstitutionally limitless mission in the undeclared "War on Terror"; there is thus no lawful basis for Guard deployment to Afghanistan.
  - Work with Congress to pass a "Restore the Guard Act" affirming the plain meaning of the Militia Clause, ending dual enlistment, and restoring the republican character of the National Guard as primarily a creature of the States. What was done to the Guard in the twentieth century can be undone, and then improved upon, in the twenty-first century.
  - Commission a plan for the reform of the U.S. Armed Forces congruent to the original intent of the founders, placing homeland defense, not empire, at the center of American military policy. Key elements of this plan will certainly include shifting spending from the three Cold War military branches to the Guard, major cuts in overall military spend-

ing, and restoring the military supremacy of Congress at all times except in battlefield command under a lawful declaration of war.

* * * * * * * * * * * * * *

Dateline: May 4, 2018

(News)—Citizens of Anytown, USA, today marked that city's centennial year. A decade ago, when the area suffered from a weak economy, few services and a childhood asthma epidemic, this anniversary might have passed with little fanfare. But recent years have brought major changes to Anytown, and today the community has a great deal to celebrate.

Anytown's renaissance is visible throughout this all-American city, from the free municipal wireless communications service, to the new mass transit system, to the solar and wind energy provided by Anytown Public Power. Family incomes are improving as municipal minimum wage, rent control, drug enforcement and health insurance policies have lightened the poverty burden. The city's cooperative sector is booming, with coops and community-owned enterprises producing, processing and distributing nearly a third of all locally consumed foods.

All of these changes and more, city officials say, have been fueled by the national explosion of local democracy initiatives over the past decade. And, they add, the shift in federal priorities from military spending to helping local government has not hurt, either.

A decade from now, fictitious Anytown's story could become a reality in communities across the United States. Rich potential for the rebirth of America exists at the local and state level. Making good on that potential, however, will require a significant shift in the relationship between the federal, state and local governments, as well as a major national domestic investment in democracy.

The past century detoured the United States from its historic romance with decentralization, home rule and direct democracy. Beginning with the Spanish-American War and continuing on through two World Wars, the Cold War and the era of corporate globalization, power has aggregated generally in the federal government, particularly in the federal Executive. In the post-9/11 era, Presidential aggrandizement has become chronic, and the need is great for a new democratic federalism that returns power to the states, communities and the people themselves.

The incoming President, together with the new Congress, offers the possibility of democratic change. The incoming federal Administration can unleash local democracy from the constraints of federal preemption that bind it. The Administration can move America forward by investing in local, democratic and cooperative economic solutions. The new government can restore our nation's promise as a beacon of liberty, not a bastion of empire, by recognizing the war powers of the States and by ending federal abuse of the National Guard. In short, the incoming federal Administration can help, or hinder, the vital work of making American democracy possible, practical and prosperous.

Remove Federal Obstacles to Local and State Innovation

Progressive Era leaders knew the value of American federalism. Justice Louis D. Brandeis described the states as engines of social and economic experimentation. Senator Robert M. La Follette, Sr., hailed the states as "laboratories of democracy." More recent American leaders, however, seem to have forgotten the value of local and state innovation. Despite, or perhaps because of, the bubbling ferment of reform rising today from the grassroots, the federal government has of late acted to suppress local democracy through the application of preemption doctrine and the adoption of new global economic treaties.

The ferment of local democracy is potent, fed as it is by unprecedented dissatisfaction with the performance of the federal government, and supported by the decentralizing power of the Internet. In this new ferment, deliberation, education and activism have combined in the new connections made between local communities and global movements and ideas. Never before have localities and states had the capacity to drive social progress that they do now:

- As the federal minimum wage standard has fallen, over 130 localities have adopted higher living-wage and minimum wage ordinances of their own.
- In place of Harry Truman's unmet promise of universal health care for the entire nation, localities have begun to enact public universal health coverage and sick leave laws.
- As federal regulatory agencies have been captured by the telecom, energy and food corporations they were supposed to regulate, local people have established community wireless, community cable, public power and municipal food utilities.

Local communities and states are also connecting the dots for federal policymakers, as they take action on national and global issues:

- Over 825 cities have enacted their own versions of the Kyoto Protocol on climate change, which the federal government declines to sign.
- The citizens of nearly 200 communities have voted in plebiscites for U.S. withdrawal from Iraq; hundreds of municipal councils and state legislatures have joined them.
- Twenty states have divested from Sudan, following in the wake of the Burma and South Africa divestment campaigns of the 1990s and 1980s.
- The citizens of Humboldt County, California, adopted Measure T, a ballot measure that nullifies the doctrine of corporate constitutional rights.
- At least thirty cities, including the nation's capital, have declared themselves "Sanctuary Cities" for undocumented immigrants.

- Over 400 cities and some states are protecting civil liberties through ordinances that direct local officials to honor the Bill of Rights over the 2001 USA PATRIOT Act.

Yet as local and state governments innovate and advocate, the federal government has placed barriers in their way. Increasingly, Congressional legislation, Presidential mandates and Supreme Court rulings have undermined the 10th Amendment reservation of power to the states, and by extension, in home-rule states, to local governments. Scorning the Constitutional guarantee of a federal government of limited and enumerated powers, and belittling state constitutional provisions guaranteeing limited "home rule" authority to municipalities and counties, corporate lobbyists have developed a doctrine of "federal preemption" as a tool for obliterating local and state laws deemed threatening to business.

For example, Congress and the Federal Communications Commission (FCC) have repeatedly acted to preempt local telecommunications initiatives. The Telecommunications Act of 1996 severely limited the ability of local governments to regulate local cable markets, and recently introduced legislation would preempt municipal broadband networks. The FCC has issued rulings preempting even minor telecom regulations regarding satellite dish placement.

The Supreme Court has repeatedly sided with corporate interests in ruling that acts of Congress or federal regulations preempted state and local laws regarding divestment from Burma (*Crosby v. National Foreign Trade Council*), drug policy reform (*Gonzales v. Raich*), workplace health and safety (*Gade v. National Solid Wastes Management Association*), pre-Holocaust insurance claims (*American Insurance Association v. Garamendi*) and probate rules (*Egelhoff v. Egelhoff*), among other things.

Even federally negotiated global trade agreements pose preemption threats to local and state policies. The World Trade Organization and so-called Free Trade Agreements like NAFTA operate in anti-democratic ways that can work to eliminate laws and regulations at the local, state or federal levels considered impediments to trade. Under U.S. bilateral and regional free trade agreements, private foreign investors can also sue signatory governments for compensation for damages allegedly caused by state and local laws that significantly diminish the value of an investment.

Local and state governments innovate and advocate, the federal government preempts and ignores. The situation is more worthy of the word "antagonism" than it is of "federalism." This antagonistic relationship needn't persist; indeed, it should not persist. The incoming Administration can choose to recall that the task of the federal government is to look after the people's interests, not its own. The incoming Administration should take positive steps to encourage local innovation, avoid state-federal friction and become more responsive to the people's will as expressed through those governments closest to them.

Invest in Cooperatives and Participatory Democracy

The incoming Administration can do more to advance democracy than simply removing the obstacles to local innovation. The United States invests hundreds of billions of dollars annually in efforts allegedly intended to spread democracy to the rest of the world; imagine what might happen were those dollars spent instead on democracy-building here at home.

The United States is home to a thriving grassroots democratic culture, despite the failure of the federal government to support it. Vibrant expressions of grassroots democracy include producer, worker and consumer cooperatives; direct democracy as practiced in town hall meetings and ballot initiatives; neighborhood associations and assemblies; community-supported agriculture; and credit unions, local currency systems and community asset-building associations. These grassroots expressions of participatory democracy offer positive political alternatives to representative democracy and economic alternatives to the private business corporation.

The deeply rooted American cooperative movement is probably the most successful example of such an alternative. Today, more than 500,000 American workers are employed by cooperatives, over 120,000,000 people are member-owners of consumer cooperatives, nearly 40,000 businesses are organized as cooperatives, and another 11,000 that are not coops are employee-stock-owned companies known as ESOPs. Coops have been shown to be very effective producers and retainers of jobs and wealth. Yet the federal government does not reward cooperative development in the same way it supports private business corporations; the corporations have their U.S. Treasury Department, while coops have no such entity.

New innovations in participatory democracy are tackling pressing issues such as wealth inequality. Participatory budgeting (PB), for example, is one innovation that has taken hold in Latin America, Europe and some parts of Africa. Participatory budgeting uses neighborhood assemblies to bring tens of thousands of city residents directly to the municipal budget table, giving everyone a direct vote on how public funds are spent. The citizens most affected by budgeting decisions participate in determining the goals, implementation, funding and assessment of those decisions. Fledgling efforts at establishing PB in U.S. cities hold the promise of increased equality through participatory democracy.

Yet, despite all the energy, passion and success experienced by coops and other participatory economic initiatives, these forward-thinking efforts remain largely unsupported by federal funds and policies. Federal support in the form of tax incentives, seed grants, temporary subsidies, zoning accommodations and elimination of obstructive preemptive laws that favor private business at the expense of locally-owned and -operated cooperative businesses have huge potential in the movement to increase community participation, economic equality and sustainability.

Restore the National Guard to Its Proper Defense Role

The incoming Administration must take affirmative steps to restore to the states their historic war powers by de-federalizing the National Guard. In so doing, the United States can close the door on its imperial past and bring democratic federalism into the ambit of the most essential of questions—those involving war and peace.

Over 600,000 members of the U.S. National Guard and Reserves have made possible the occupations of Afghanistan and Iraq. Without the Guard, successive Secretaries of Defense have told us, the ongoing projection of U.S. military power to the ends of the Earth would be impossible. But unending wars of empire are not what the Guard was intended or designed for, and not what Guard members signed up for. As the U.S. Constitution's Militia Clause makes exceptionally clear, the Guard is intended exclusively to serve as America's primary line of defense against invasion, insurrection or domestic national emergency. It is largely that defensive mission that long has attracted so many young Americans to the Guard. Today, however, the Guard is imposing a failed military policy, not defending American soil, and the cost of their deployment is mounting.

Empire exacts a price, material and political. In material terms, estimates of the war dead run into the hundreds of thousands. The economic price is calculated in the trillions. Politically speaking, the staggering reality is that a majority of the citizens of every nation on Earth perceive the U.S. invasion of Iraq to have been baseless and illegal. The invasion and occupation have inflamed anti-American sentiment around the globe, including here in the United States. The ongoing inability of the majority of the American people to bring about an end to the Iraq War has further undermined what faith they retained in the federal government. Most dangerously, the unending "War on Terror" and the federal response to 9/11 have created a climate of fear and insecurity that is wearing away at the belief that America is, ever was, or could be, a democracy.

Among the many ironic tragedies of the War on Terror is that the National Guard—the very institution designed to prevent the United States from paying and doling out the price of empire—has been used to impose imperial policies. The Guard, of course, is the modern militia—that state-organized body of Americans called into national service to defend the nation in times of crisis. In the early years of the United States, defense meant something deeper than the protection of territorial borders; it meant the protection of America as a "land of liberty." By and large, the revolutionary generation was committed to creating a new society in which power was decentralized. A force made up of the people themselves, and controlled in times of peace by the states, not the federal government, was considered the greatest protection against the potential collapse of the American republic into imperial tyranny.

The Guard has been made into a tool for U.S. force projection, a far cry from the promise of a state-based system of homeland defense used only, in the

words of the Constitution, to "execute the laws of the union, suppress insurrec-
tions and repel invasions."

Towards a Democratic Federalism

These three major policy reforms—removing the preemption barrier, investing in democracy, restoring the Guard—can help move America along democracy's path. Together, they form the practical basis for a new democratic federalism, and also for something more: the opening of untold possibilities for prosperity, peace and progress.

Resources

Bring the Guard Home: www.bringtheguardhome.org
Cities For Peace: http://www.citiesforpeace.org
Community-Wealth.org: http://www.community-wealth.org
Deliberative Democracy Consortium: http://www.deliberative-democracy.net
Democracy Unlimited of Humboldt County: http://www.DUHC.org
Inequality.org: http://www.inequality.org
Liberty Tree Foundation for the Democratic Revolution:
     http://www.libertytreefdr.org
Local Democracy Convention: www.localdemocracy.org
National Cooperative Business Association: http://ncba.coop
National Priorities Project: http://www.nationalpriorities.org
ParticipatoryBudgeting.org: http://www.participatorybudgeting.org
Program on Corporations, Law and Democracy: http://www.POCLAD.org
U.S. Solidarity Economy Network: http://www.populareconomics.org/ussen

References

Albert, Michael, and Robin Hahnel. *Looking Forward: Participatory Economics
     for the Twenty-First Century*. Boston: South End Press, 1991.
Alperovitz, Gar. *America Beyond Capitalism*. Hoboken: John Wiley & Sons,
     2004.
Gastil, John, and Peter Levine, eds. *The Deliberative Democracy Handbook*.
     San Francisco: Jossey-Bass, 2005. http://www.deliberative-democracy.net/
     hand book.
Hahnel, Robin. *Economic Justice and Democracy: From Competition to Coop-
     eration*. New York: Routledge Press, 2005.

Kittrie, Nicholas, and Eldon Wedlock, eds. *The Tree of Liberty: A Documentary History of Rebellion and Political Crime in America,* Vol. 1–2. Baltimore: The Johns Hopkins University Press, 1998.

Lappé, Frances Moore. *Rediscovering America's Values.* New York: Ballantine Books, 1989.

———. *Democracy's Edge: Choosing to Save Our Country by Bringing Democracy to Life.* San Francisco: Jossey-Bass, 2005.

Lummis, C. Douglas. *Radical Democracy.* Ithaca: Cornell University Press, 1996.

Manski, Ben, ed. *Liberty Tree: Journal of the Democratic Revolution.* Vol. 1–2. Madison: Liberty Tree Foundation, 2005-2008.

Morris, Jane Anne. *Gaveling Down the Rabble.* New York: Apex Press, 2008.

Nace, Ted. *Gangs of America: The Rise of Corporate Power and the Disabling of Democracy.* San Francisco: Barrett-Koehler Publishers, 2005.

Raphael, Ray. *The First American Revolution: Before Lexington and Concord.* New York: W. W. Norton, 2002.

Raskin, Jamin. *Overruling Democracy: The Supreme Court Versus the American People.* New York: Routledge Press, 2003.

Ritz, Dean, ed. *Defying Corporations, Defining Democracy: A Book of History and Strategy.* New York: Apex Press, 2001.

Rogers, Joel. "Cities: The Vital Core." *The Nation,* June 2, 2005. http://www.thenation.com/doc/20050620/rogers (accessed July 16, 2008).

———. *Devolve This! The Nation,* August 12, 2004. http://www.thenation.com/doc/20040830/rogers (accessed July 16, 2008).

Shuman, Michael H. *Going Local: Creating Self-Reliant Communities in a Global Age.* New York: Free Press, 1998.

International
Issues

Chapter 35

Ending the Iraq War and Occupation

Erik Leaver and Phyllis Bennis

POLICY PROPOSALS

- End the U.S. occupation of Iraq by bringing home all the troops and contractors and closing the bases as the first step in moving closer to peace and reconstruction.
- Engage Iraq's neighbors and the international community helping post-occupation Iraq rebuild.
- Support the troops when they get home with proper medical and mental health care.
- Accept more refugees and pledge greater financial support to UNHCR and encourage international donors to do the same.
- Commit new funds for reconstruction; with the end of U.S. occupation, the international community will be more likely to make good on their previous pledges.
- End dependence on private corporations to fight U.S. wars.
- Drop all efforts to impose an oil law on Iraqis.

* * * * * * * * * * * * * * *

Two years ago, the public demanded a change in Iraq policy. Encouraged by popular support behind Ned Lamont's 2006 Senate campaign in Connecticut highlighting his anti-war credentials against Sen. Joe Lieberman, Democratic candidates across the nation ran against the war, resulting in huge victories. Shortly after the elections, the bipartisan Iraq Study Group's report was released calling for a change in course. Nearly 70 percent of the public disapproved of Bush's Iraq policy and 65 percent supported bringing some or all of the troops home.

Yet instead of heeding calls for withdrawal, President Bush surprised the nation by announcing in January 2007 that he would be sending a "surge" of an additional 30,000 more troops to Iraq. Nearly two years later, the benefits and limitations of the "surge" are clear. The combination of added U.S. forces, putting 90,000 Sunni militiamen ("Sons of Iraq") on the U.S. payroll, Shia cleric Muqtada al-Sadr's ceasefire, and a year of ethnic cleansing in the capital has lowered the U.S. casualty rates dramatically, and somewhat lowered Iraqi casualties. But this development has the serious side-effect of promoting warlordism and fueling sectarianism, destroying any hopes for the political reconciliation needed for the long-term stability of Iraq. In short, temporary gains in stability from the "surge" have greatly damaged hopes for long-term reconciliation.

To promote the long-term reconciliation needed for a stable and free Iraq, the answer is clear but counter-intuitive: Negotiate terms for complete withdrawal with Iraqis and the international community. Instead of being an act of cowardice, as some suggest, withdrawal is actually the best option for Iraq in the long term.

A thoughtful plan for withdrawal would have three main elements: a clear, fast timetable with measurable benchmarks for complete withdrawal of troops, contractors and bases; engaging with Iraq's neighbors, the UN and the international community to promote political reconciliation and address potential Iraqi security needs; and finally, making firm commitments to provide financial and technical assistance for reconstruction.

How withdrawal is done must not continue our existing legacy from this ill-fated war and occupation. Instead, our legacy should be based upon returning to Iraqis true control over their country and its political, economic and security conditions—meaning that withdrawal of troops and ending the occupation of Iraq isn't the last step—it is only the first step in a long commitment the U.S. will have to this country.

Effects of the War

So far, over 1.5 million U.S. service members have deployed to Iraq and Afghanistan. More than 4,000 young women and men serving in the U.S. military have died. Over 30,000 have been seriously physically injured. But it's the "hidden" injuries that will have the greatest toll. Already roughly 300,000 individuals suffer from post-traumatic stress disorder (PTSD) or major depression and an additional 320,000 individuals suffered traumatic brain injury (TBI) during deployment. Despite the "successes" that are reported, these numbers climb every day.

Those at home have suffered, too. Civil rights, particularly those of Muslims, Arab immigrants and Arab-Americans, have been shredded. The $657 billion in U.S. tax dollars already spent directly on the war (and counting) have wrought havoc on our economy and continues to escalate the deficit. Recent studies estimate the long-term costs of the war will easily top $3 trillion.

Iraqis have suffered far more. While seldom seen on the front pages of U.S. newspapers, estimates of Iraqi deaths range up to 1.2 million. The people of the United States don't know because, as General Tommy Franks said, "We don't do body counts." Further hollowing Iraq, out of a nation of 25 million people, over 2 million have fled to neighboring countries, and there are over 3 million internally displaced Iraqi refugees.

Beyond the lack of physical security in Iraq is a lack of social, economic and political security. Electricity, clean water, sanitation services and access to medical care all remain in short supply, far below pre-war levels. For example, before the war Iraq had 34,000 doctors, now there are roughly 12,000. Iraq's unemployment rate is estimated to be between 25–40 percent, higher than U.S. unemployment rates during the Great Depression. Politically, Iraq's government has not reached any of the benchmarks set by its own U.S. sponsors. Political parties are determined more by ethnicity than political ideology, and the government and parliament both are weak and ineffective.

The costs to the rest of the world from this conflict are often overlooked. Coalition partners took on significant casualties and absorbed financial costs as well. But the most significant cost was to the United Nations. The global body was cast aside in order for the United States to pull together a coerced "coalition of the willing," and the impact was severe. Rejecting the UN undermines UN democracy and international law, makes double-standard enforcement more likely, and makes it more difficult to activate the Security Council for non-military internationalist responses to other global crises.

Bush's Iraq War strategy of unilateral militarism has proven to be too costly in human and financial terms, both to the Iraqi people and U.S. troops. And ironically, it has failed to achieve even Bush's own stated goals. Five years after the invasion, Iraqis still lack meaningful security, and political stability remains a distant mirage.

The "Surge" and Its Aftermath

With violence at an all-time high towards the end of 2006 and a clear lack of political progress from Iraqi politicians, there was intense political pressure on the Bush Administration to begin withdrawing troops.

However, instead of retreating from a disastrous position Bush decided escalating U.S. military involvement was the answer. Key to his plan was minimizing the role of U.S.-backed Iraqi leaders, such as Maliki, and bringing in additional U.S. forces and engaging directly with Iraq's Sunni militias. The first six months after the "surge" began in January 2007 were a disaster, bringing some of the highest levels of violence and internal displacement since the war began. But by the middle of the year, around the time al-Sadr's ceasefire took hold and Sunni tribal leaders accepted U.S. bribes to stop attacking U.S. troops, the level of violence reportedly began to drop, with December being the second least violent for U.S. troops since 2003. But even those preliminary gains were short-term; by June 2008 U.S. troop casualties were rising again, and no matter what improvements have been made, life is still deadly for Iraqis. In 2008, documented civilian deaths are on track to exceed 12,000 and the figure is sure to be much higher when undocumented deaths are added.

The single-minded focus on casualties, however, masks the internal problems in Iraq that have arisen due to the policies of the "surge" itself.

Over the past five years, the United States has spent over $20 billion training the largely Shi'a Iraqi army and police, while also arming and training the Kurdish Peshmerga troops in Northern Iraq. But since the "surge" began, the United States has also been arming, training and financing the largely Sunni "Sons of Iraq" militias, numbering 90,000. The consequence of this dual policy is that all actors on the ground have greater fire power and training and now have less interest in a negotiated solution.

Not only is the security situation worse because of the U.S. occupation, but even Washington's own political "benchmarks" imposed on Iraq were never achieved. Provincial elections and the referendum on the status of Kirkuk were postponed. The Iraqi parliament was often stalemated, and when it was able to function, it served primarily to oppose virtually everything the United States and its supporters in the Iraqi cabinet wanted. And the period for amending the constitution in a fast-track manner, which was the carrot for the Sunnis to help pass the constitution, was extended for the fourth time.

In 2008, the United States began to exert more pressure for local elections to take place, which would allow it greater influence at the local level. Simultaneously the United States waded back into Iraq's national political scene, backing the sectarian Iraqi government in their attacks on the forces loyal to Muqtada al-Sadr, thus fueling the Shi'a-Shi'a conflict in Iraq's south and in Baghdad itself. By supporting Maliki against Sadr's al-Mahdi army, the United States is now more deeply involved than ever in the politics of Iraq's sectarian war. By getting rid of Sadr and the other anti-occupation nationalists left in Iraq, the United States seeks to solidify a government that will be friendly to the United States and allow continued occupation of Iraq for decades to come.

The United States has set the pieces in place, hoping for this scenario of permanent occupation: There are 140,000 troops in Iraq; our embassy (the largest in the world) is now completed; four or five of the major U.S. military bases are the size of mini-cities unto themselves; and dozens more are scattered around Iraq.

But these policy goals ignore the Iraqi people and the reality they face in the U.S. occupation of Iraq. It is precisely the occupation that fuels the Iraqis' resistance. Developing an even closer alliance with the U.S.-created and occupation-backed Iraqi government and/or imposing a long-term military presence will only further alienate this Iraqi government from its people. And by having armed all actors in the conflict, if or when the current Iraqi government falls, the resulting struggle for control may be a far bloodier affair than would otherwise have been the case.

A False Solution

Since the war began, there have been many competing plans for re-aligning Iraq policy and bringing troops home. Several plans use the rhetoric of ending the war, but the details only call for pulling "combat troops" out of Iraq, keeping significant U.S. forces in Iraq for counter-terrorism, military training, diplomatic protection and other tasks. These plans would easily leave 30,000–80,000 troops inside Iraq for decades, not to mention permanent U.S. bases and an untold number of military contractors. That means permanent occupation.

In addition, there are specific policy problems with these plans.

- U.S. counter-terrorism programs are dependent on free movement of U.S. troops within Iraq. Their actions on the ground would still constitute military occupation, albeit a slightly smaller one. U.S. troops and mercenaries would maintain the power to detain Iraqi prisoners, attack Iraqi targets, and remain immune from Iraqi law. With fewer troops, more air power would be used, resulting in even higher civilian casualties. The U.S. occupation forces would remain a target for attack and would remain a powerful recruiting tool for extremists and terrorists as well as legitimate resistance forces.

- The idea that U.S. occupation forces will be "required" to remain in Iraq to train Baghdad's military assumes the independent legitimacy of those Iraqi forces. For many Iraqis, and many outside observers, the Iraqi Army functions essentially as simply one more militia among the plethora of armed groups contributing to the instability in Iraq. For many, the Iraqi Army, despite being armed, trained and funded by the United States, is simply a larger version of assorted other party-linked militias, this one controlled (more or less) by Prime Minister al-Maliki and his Dawa Party. The Army's problem is not a lack of training, but a lack of accountability to the nation as a whole.

- The construction of the largest embassy compound in the world sets in motion an inevitable "necessity" of thousands more U.S. troops being required to protect that compound. But an embassy that is to truly function as a normal embassy instead of the imperial center of an occupying power does not require the 5,000 diplomats currently planned for in the U.S. embassy. The huge new embassy and its small-town-sized population will continue to demonstrate to the world the non-sovereignty of any Iraqi government and the clear U.S. intention of maintaining permanent control of the country.

How to End the War

Almost from the moment of the U.S. invasion of Iraq in 2003, politicians and political figures were talking about "ending" the war. Definitions changed, depending on who was doing the talking. For George Bush and others in his Administration, "ending the war" meant "winning" the war, with whatever transitory definition of victory was current at the moment. For others, it meant bringing the troops home.

In fact, the United States does not have the capacity to end the entire complex of wars currently being waged in Iraq. The U.S. invasion and occupation are not only directly responsible for massive death and destruction across Iraq, but they set in motion a convoluted set of sectarian and civil battles, conflicts over money and power, and clashes over control of Iraq's future.

What the United States does have the capability of doing—and what it must do if Iraq is to have any hope of reclaiming its sovereignty, its unity and its future—is to end the *occupation* of Iraq, and allow Iraq and Iraqis the opportunity to work through their own crises and end, on their own terms, their own wars.

Ending the U.S. occupation of Iraq is the first step in moving closer to peace and reconstruction. U.S. and coalition troops are both the cause of and the magnet for the violence in Iraq, not a solution to that violence. A goal that would support both the Iraqi people and the U.S. troops deployed in Iraq would be to bring all the foreign troops and contractors home by December 2009.

Setting a firm date to end the occupation will transform the dynamics in Iraq. Iraqis will begin to reclaim control of their own country, and this will give them hope that they will yet again be an independent nation with the power to rebuild their nation on their own terms.

It is unlikely that all the violence will completely disappear with the end of the occupation or that the Iraqi military can rebuild itself instantly after U.S. troops are withdrawn. As a result, the United States should support temporary peacekeeping or security assistance if Iraq requests it. Temporary on-the-ground security assistance cannot be provided by U.S. (or the U.S.-led coalition) forces. Nor can an international, even United Nations, peacekeeping force function safely if it assisted by the United States (or U.S.-led coalition). The bombing of the UN compound on August 19, 2003, resulting in the death of UN Special Representative Sergio Vieira de Mello and 21 other UN staffers is a poignant reminder of the dangers of being allied with the occupation.

Only a truly multilateral force, not controlled by the United States, can be credible to the Iraqi people. For example, a combination of United Nations blue-helmet peacekeepers and temporary forces accountable to the Arab League and/or the Organization of the Islamic Conference in coordination with the UN could provide international legitimacy as well as regional accountability. The effect would be to reduce regional tensions and encourage neighboring countries to provide support throughout Iraq's reconstruction process.

Essential to helping post-occupation Iraq rebuild is engagement by Iraq's neighbors and the international community. A new international, not U.S.-controlled, "diplomatic offensive" is needed. Diplomatic goals should include a U.S.-supported regional non-aggression pact (one that includes Iran), commitments to help enhance border security for neighboring nations, and encouraging other nations to establish embassies in Iraq.

The United States should also commit new funds for reconstruction; with the end of U.S. occupation, the international community will be more likely to make good on their previous pledges. Economic assistance should be purposely aimed to unify instead of divide the country. Reconstruction is not an impossible task. Iraq has gone through two major reconstruction campaigns during the last two decades: one after the Iraq-Iran war and the other after the 1991 Gulf War. Both times, Iraqis managed to mobilize their human resources and fix the country on their own. With the financial help of the United States and the international community, they can do it again.

Given the rise of militias under the "surge" strategy and the massive amount of U.S. aid and training provided to the Iraqi Army, the timetable for withdrawal must include benchmarks for zeroing out funding to all these groups. Iraq's future cannot be built upon a set of warlords and an Army largely loyal to Shia Prime Minister Maliki. In its place, the United States should provide funding for jobs training and demobilization programs to be carried out by the international community. Any training for Iraq's military undertaken by the international community should adhere to the principles of the Leahy Law, which prohibits any funding to military units implicated in human rights abuses.

One of the worst side-effects of the war has been the refugee and internally displaced people crisis. Jordan and Syria have received a large majority of refugees, but nations across the region, including Egypt, Iran, Lebanon and Turkey, have all been touched by the crisis. Western countries, in particularly the United States, have done a completely inadequate job of resettling Iraqis—by the end of September 2008 the United States had accepted only 12,000 Iraqi refugees, while Sweden has taken in 40,000. In addition to accepting more refugees, the United States should pledge greater financial support to UNHCR and encourage international donors to do the same.

Reinforcing Iraqi concerns about our long-term intentions in their country has been the relentless pursuit by U.S. officials to secure the passage of an oil law that would favor private companies and particularly privilege U.S. companies, wresting control out of the hands of Iraqis. The United States should drop all efforts to impose an oil law on Iraqis. Ending occupation has to include explicit renunciation of efforts to control Iraq's oil industry. Key to this would be dismantling the Development Fund for Iraq, which requires oil revenues be kept in U.S. banks. Instead, Iraq should be able to manage and keep its own oil funds. Finally, the role of contractors in this conflict has shown why depending on private corporations to fight U.S. wars must be ended. Congress should clamp down on the rampant war profiteering that has caused widespread waste, fraud and abuse, and create a standing oversight committee. Any existing contracts with U.S. corporations must be cancelled altogether, so that reconstruction funds can be made available directly to Iraqi companies and other institutions to take control of the reconstruction of their own country.

Conclusion

The illegal U.S. invasion and occupation of Iraq have brought enormous death and destruction to that country. The United States has no perfect options, perhaps not even any good options, in Iraq. All possible scenarios in today's war-ravaged Iraq pose potential risks. Maintaining the U.S. occupation, with U.S. troops continuing to kill and die in Iraq, is the worst possible choice.

Those who fear a larger war when the United States withdraws should heed the lesson learned in the southern city of Basra that had been occupied by British troops since 2003. When British forces withdrew, attacks dropped by 90 percent. Analyzing the impact of his 5,000 troops moving out of the heart of Basra, British General Graham Binns said there had been "a remarkable and dramatic drop in attacks. The motivation for attacking us was gone, because we're no longer patrolling the streets."

Certainly the violence in Basra has not completely ended; there was a temporary week-long spike in fighting in Spring 2008 in response to a U.S.-backed Iraqi government military attack on the dominant Shi'a militia in Basra. But there is no question that the withdrawal of occupation troops led to a massive reduction in overall violence.

The U.S. invasion launched war in Iraq, but the United States on its own can no longer end the entire Iraq War. What the United States can—indeed must—do first, is to end its occupation so as to allow Iraq to begin the difficult task of rebuilding its shattered country. Then, and only then, can the United States move on to step two: providing compensation and real assistance to a once-again sovereign nation of Iraq.

References

Allawi, Ali A. *The Occupation of Iraq: Winning the War, Losing the Peace.* New Haven: Yale University Press, 2007.

Baker III, James A., and Lee H. Hamilton, *The Iraq Study Group Report.* New York: Vintage Books, 2006.

Bennis, Phyllis. *Ending the Iraq War: A Primer.* New York: Interlink Books, 2008.

Burner, Darcy, et al. "A Responsible Plan to End the War in Iraq." http://www.responsibleplan.com/ (accessed July 18, 2008).

Burnham, Gilbert, et al. "Mortality After the 2003 Invasion of Iraq: A Cross-Sectional Cluster Sample Survey." *The Lancet*, October 2006, 1421–1428.

Chandrasekaran, Rajiv. *Imperial Life in the Emerald City*. New York: Vintage, 2007.

Cockburn, Patrick. *The Occupation: War and Resistance in Iraq*. London: Verso, 2006.

Mokbel, Madona. "Refugees in Limbo: The Plight of Iraqis in Bordering States." *Middle East Report* (Fall 2007).

O'Hanlon, Michael E., and Jason H. Campbell. "Iraq Index: Tracking Variables of Reconstruction & Security in Post-Saddam Iraq." Brookings Institute (June 26, 2008). http://www.brookings.edu/saban/~/media/Files/Centers/Saban/Iraq%20Index/index.pdf (accessed July 16, 2008).

Scahill, Jeremy. *Blackwater: The Rise of the World's Most Powerful Mercenary Army*. New York: Nation Books, 2007.

Simon, Steven. "The Price of the Surge." *Foreign Affairs* 87 (2008). http://www.foreignaffairs.org/20080501faessay87305/steven-simon/the-price-of-the-surge.html (accessed July 16, 2008).

Stiglitz, Joseph, and Linda Bilmes, *The Three Trillion Dollar War*. New York: W.W. Norton, 2008.

Tanielian, Terri, and Lisa H. Jaycox, eds. *Invisible Wounds of War: Psychological and Cognitive Injuries, Their Consequences, and Services to Assist Recovery*. Santa Monica: Rand, 2008.

Chapter 36

U.S. Policy toward Afghanistan: Rethinking the "Good War"

Erik Leaver

POLICY PROPOSALS

■ Set forth a timetable for withdrawal of U.S. and NATO forces while considering support for future post-occupation peacekeeping involving the United Nations and regional forces such as the Organization of the Islamic Conference.

■ Promote reconstruction and development inside Afghanistan and Pakistan.

■ Support international policing of terrorist activities.

■ Encourage the Afghan and Pakistani governments to negotiate with the Taliban.

■ Relinquish the relationship with the Pakistani army and instead turn to supporting civilian institutions.

■ Shift from drug eradication and supply reduction programs to nation-building and development initiatives.

* * * * * * * * * * * * * *

In the early dawn on October 7, 2001, the United States and Great Britain launched an aerial assault against the Taliban and al-Qaeda in retaliation for the 9/11 attacks against the United States. A fateful decision was made as those missiles were launched to seek vengeance instead of justice. Instead of engaging in serious negotiations with the Taliban regime and others in the region to bring Osama bin Laden to justice, the United States and the UK went to war.

What was an area of the globe that had ceased to be a priority for the United States after the Soviet withdrawal in 1989 was now supposed to be the center-piece of the "Global War on Terrorism." In speeches after 9/11, President Bush signaled that the destruction of bin Laden and the al-Qaeda network would be his highest priority

But what started out seven years ago as "The Good War" is largely today the forgotten war. Just as our nation abandoned Afghanistan after the Soviets withdrew in 1989, so do did our attention wane as Bush engulfed the United States in a second war, the Iraq War. The death and destruction caused in the Iraq War eclipsed the fighting in Afghanistan. The public eye faded, despite the fact that Osama bin Laden remained on the loose as the Bush Administration made the claim that Iraq, not Afghanistan, was the new centerpiece in the "War on Terror."

The inattention to Afghanistan has produced similar results to what was seen in the aftermath of 1989. When the Soviets retreated from Afghanistan that year, it was expected that Western powers would come to its aid and assist with reconstruction, reconstituting democratic structures, and implementing a rule of law. Mostly, they didn't. Today, these vital steps for helping Afghanistan escape the violence it is trapped in are once again missing.

Instead, as violence is on the rise, the Taliban has become much stronger, and as al-Qaeda is freely moving between Afghanistan and Pakistan, the focus of the United States and much of the international community is on a military solution. For most of 2007 and 2008, the United States has urged NATO members to send more troops. And there are widespread calls within the U.S. political establishment to draw down troops from Iraq and send them to Afghanistan.

But after seven years of fighting in Afghanistan and five years in Iraq, there are clear lessons to be learned about "surging" troops and continuing occupation. Our counter-insurgency tactics are ineffective, resulting in greater fighting rather than less. The United States has failed to provide the needed funds for meaningful reconstruction. And heavy-handedness by the United States and international partners in both the formation and the daily operations of the Afghan government has undermined their legitimacy.

Afghanistan Today

After the 9/11 attacks, well over 90 percent of the American people supported the invasion of Afghanistan. Today, less than half believe the mission is going well.[1] Skepticism has increased due to the failure to have captured Osama bin Laden, a lack of credibility from the Bush Administration, the failure of the Iraq War, and more recently, the rising death toll inside Afghanistan.

In the last two years, particularly as U.S.- and NATO-caused civilian casualties have escalated, the Taliban gained increased support. In fact, they have regrouped and taken over large and strategic areas in the south. Perhaps their most notable action occurred in June 2008, when the Taliban attacked a jail in Kandahar, freeing 600 prisoners, including hundreds of suspected supporters. Al-Qaeda has apparently set up residence in the Federally Administered Tribal Areas (FATA) in Pakistan and is now able to move freely back and forth between Afghanistan and Pakistan. And the illicit drug trade has flourished. Afghanistan now produces 93 percent of the world's opium, and the drug trade accounts for one-third of the country's gross domestic product.[2]

Despite these alarming events, Afghanistan didn't creep back into the mainstream news until late 2007/early 2008 when attacks on civilians and coalition forces increased, causing a rise in the death toll. U.S. attention was particularly driven by the rise in U.S. military casualties. The use of roadside bombs jumped from 1,931 in 2006 to 2,615 in 2007.[3] Suicide bombings, a tactic not seen in Afghanistan before the invasion, increased from 21 in 2005 to over 140 in 2007.[4] As a result, by June 2008, casualty rates for American and NATO force troops were higher than any other month since the war began.[5] Likewise, 2007 was the deadliest since the invasion for Afghan civilians, with the UN estimating more than 6,200 Afghan casualties due to insurgent-related violence.[6]

The increase in casualties corresponds directly with the increase in U.S. and NATO troop strength. According to the Department of Defense, as of April 1, 2008, the United States had 33,000 military personnel deployed in Afghanistan. In April 2007, the United States maintained 24,310 troops on the ground. Of the current troops, 25,200 are active duty and 7,800 are National Guard and Reserves.[7] In addition to the U.S. forces, there are 38,000 troops from dozens of other countries who are operating under NATO command.

While the United States has sought to bolster the military, social conditions on the ground continue to be ignored, and for ordinary Afghans they are seriously deteriorating. Heading into battle, the Bush Administration promised to rebuild Afghanistan, transform its economy and liberate its women from the oppression of the Taliban. These promises turned out to be hollow. In a country of 32 million, Afghanistan's social indices rank it 174th out of 178 nations in the UNDP Human Development Index. Infant mortality rate is one of the highest in the world—one child out of every four does not survive his/her fifth birthday. Two million primary school-aged children (60 percent) are out of school, an estimated 1.3 million of whom are girls. Only 23 percent of the entire population has access to safe drinking water and a mere 12 percent have access to sanitation facilities.[8]

Though severe challenges exist on the military and social fronts, the biggest challenge for Afghanistan is political. The U.S.-backed government of President Hamid Karzai has little credibility within the country. A survey released by Integrity Watch Afghanistan noted that 60 percent of the respondents believed the Karzai government was more corrupt than the Taliban or the prior Soviet-backed government.[9]

The United States is responsible for a good portion of the lack of legitimacy for the Afghan government. The U.S.-managed Presidential elections in 2004 were organized without meaningful input from the Afghan people. U.S. officials actively pressured a number of prominent Presidential candidates to drop out of the race to help ensure Karzai's election.[10] And while often unspoken, the occupation itself is the largest contributor to undermining the legitimacy of the Afghan government. It certainly didn't help that once in power Karzai gave senior police posts to former warlords and human rights abusers.

The conditions on the ground indicate a serious problem. After seven years of war, Afghanistan is not safer, better off economically or more free.

The pressure is on from the U.S. public and the growing international community for a quick fix, such as seen in Iraq—a "surge" in military troops and aligning closer with warlords. However, these approaches further undermine the democratic principles that are needed for Afghanistan to stand up over time. Increasing troop numbers and escalating a military occupation is not going to help Afghanistan rebuild its shattered country.

The Problem with NATO and the Military Mission

The war in Afghanistan was NATO's first deployment outside of Europe. Engaged partially as an attempt to keep NATO relevant, instead it now is a prime example of how military multilateralism à la carte has failed.

When the United States and UK first started the Afghanistan war, the UN had not provided a mandate for war—indeed the U.S.-drafted UN Security Council Resolution responding to the 9/11 attacks did not even mention a military attack on Afghanistan. Instead, the United States and UK rationalized the strikes as legal under the act of collective self-defense provided for under Article 51 of the UN Charter. When the UN did authorize a force to protect the Afghan Interim Authority, its scope was limited to protecting the capital. It was nearly two years later when NATO took over the UN-authorized International Security Assistance Force (ISAF). The entire process of going to war fell outside of the proper legal framework. It set the stage not only for a poorly managed mission but one that violated international law and the UN Charter. A contributing factor to the current disarray in the mission can be blamed on this rush to war.

On the ground today, there are two separate military missions the United States is involved in. The first, Operation Enduring Freedom (OEF), undertakes training of local security forces and counter-insurgency operations. The second is participation in the NATO-commanded International Security Assistance Force.

ISAF has forty contributing nations with five regional commands and twenty-six national-led Provincial Reconstruction Teams. Most of the nations involved have restrictions where the ISAF commander can send troops and what actions they can undertake. Few are permitted to go to the areas of heavy fighting.

The sheer number of participants and the numerous restrictions contribute to the disorganization of the overall planning. There is also reluctance by United States and other major nations to be directed or even coordinated by another nation or UN commander. Furthermore, each country involved often appears to assess the overall situation in Afghanistan largely through the lens of where its troops are based.[11] The result is the fragmentation of the international community and an ineffectual response on the ground.

Demands by the United States for greater troop levels from the other participants are creating a greater tension in the coalition over burden-sharing. These tensions are now threatening the foundations of multilateralism, including NATO's future.[12] The United States must realize that its military and political unilateral actions and its demands for greater commitment from others weaken the motivation of others in the coalition. The lesson to be learned is that the UN must be central to the mission, and that true multilateral cooperation is a needed component if any future action—either military, political or economic—is to have a greater chance of success.

Pakistan

Since the Afghanistan war began, Pakistan has been praised as a staunch ally. But instead of being the stable partner Bush has often claimed, the world watched in fear when crisis gripped Pakistan as 2007 ended after President Musharraf dismissed judges questioning the constitutionality of his moves to consolidate power. The situation became worse with the assassination of Benazir Bhutto. As riots fell over Pakistan, concern grew about the ability of the military to guard the nuclear weapons in its possession. A rash of suicide bombings compounded fears in the West—the resurgence of al-Qaeda and the Taliban.

Despite Pakistani negotiations with tribal leaders to quell the Taliban and al-Qaeda, the situation has only become worse. Across the border from Pakistan, attacks have increased by 40 percent.[13] The effects are also being felt inside Pakistan—the bombing of the Indian embassy in July 2008 that killed forty-one people is one cogent example of the new wave of violence.

Increasing violence is not only due to the influx of fighters from Afghanistan, in part it is a reaction to Musharraf's power grab over the last decade. The Bush Administration has reinforced this trend by consistently rewarding Musharraf, claiming his government is a strong ally in opposing the "War on Terror." Watching the aftermath of the U.S. invasions of Afghanistan and Iraq, and the deepening U.S. involvement in Pakistan many Pakistanis are wary about U.S. intentions. A May 2008 poll by the Pakistan Institute for Public Opinion found that 44 percent of Pakistanis believe the United States is the greatest threat to their personal safety.[14]

The United States has few options available. Joint U.S.-Pakistani military missions fuel anger inside of Pakistan and have been ineffective. Similar tensions arise due to air strikes taken by the United States without informing Pakistan's military or leadership, undermining its sovereignty. The territory in which al-Qaeda and the Taliban operates in is largely outside the control of Pakistan's government. Throwing money at the problem hasn't helped either. Since 2002, the United States has given Pakistan nearly $11 billion in military and economic aid (70 percent of which was for military aid), with few to no results.[15] A scathing report by the Government Accountability Office found that there was no plan for meeting U.S. security goals in the Federally Administered Tribal Areas.[16]

As in Iraq with the "surge," the inclination will be to ramp up the use of force, engaging in wider and more deadly missions across the border. The results will further alienate the Pakistani population by causing greater civilian casualties and reminding the Pakistanis that their sovereignty is not respected by the United States.

Similar to Afghanistan, the United States has paid far too much attention to military solutions and not enough to the other conditions inside the country that are enabling the insurgency. In Pakistan today these issues are: the economy, the electricity load-sharing, the water shortage and the political instability.[17] Addressing these core issues is the best way to reduce the influence of the Taliban and al-Qaeda in FATA and the North-West Frontier Province.

Drugs and Development

Briefly interrupted during the Taliban's rule, Afghanistan's opium production quickly rebounded once the U.S.-NATO mission began, setting record levels in 2006 and 2007. Today, Afghanistan produces 93 percent of the world's opium and receives roughly $4 billion in revenue from the drug trade—about half of its Gross Domestic Product.[18]

With the revival of the drug trade, the overwhelming response has been military. The United States favors aerial fumigation eradication programs, while NATO and the UN prefer to focus on disrupting the drug trade by targeting kingpins, production labs and drug transport. Evidenced by the increase in cultivation, neither of these approaches has proven to be effective.

Clearly, the drug trade is harmful for Afghanistan. It fuels corruption in the Afghan government, contributes to the violence in the country and presents a global health crisis. Yet Afghanistan is overwhelmingly dependent on the drug trade for its economy. The dependency on military solutions from the United States, NATO and the UN fails to offer a credible alternative to the drug economy. Moreover, the militarization of drug control has failed to win "hearts and minds," driving poor peasant farmers into the hands of the Taliban and the insurgency. Shifting away from dependency on the drug trade requires not only an economic transition plan for farmers but also a political plan for the elites who have gained power through the profitable trade.

Aid is not a panacea, but it has been sorely lacking—Afghanistan is dependent on the international community for 90 percent of all public expenditure in the country.[19] In June 2008, donors gave pledges of less than half of the five year, $50 billion plan unveiled at the June 2008 Paris conference by Karzai. The United States pledged only $10.2 billion over the next two years—less than what is spent each month in Iraq.

Much of the aid that is distributed has not been effective. Aid programs, such as provincial reconstruction teams, have militarized the distribution of aid, jeopardizing both recipients and providers. And many aid programs have been designed and carried out with little or no input from the local populations. The priorities for aid programs aimed at shifting farmers away from poppy production would include providing lines of credit, improving access to markets and improving local infrastructure, including roads and irrigation.

The drug trade developed in Afghanistan in response to the destruction of the economy, infrastructure and the abandonment by the international community. Increased aid is just part of the solution. For alternative development to be successful, it must be accompanied with a long-term commitment by the international community to assist in building a stronger economy, reconstructing the war-torn infrastructure and strengthening the state.

A New Way Forward

Just as there was an alternative path in the aftermath of the 9/11 attacks, there is another way to bring peace, democracy and justice to Afghanistan. Noted Afghan scholar Barnett Rubin correctly argues that the solution requires an integrated response to promote reconstruction and development over drug eradication; encourages the Afghan and Pakistani governments to negotiate with the Taliban; relinquishes the relationship with the Pakistani army and instead turns to civilian institutions; and promotes international policing of terrorist activities.[20]

Rubin recognizes the dilemma U.S. and NATO forces present, noting that the Afghan forces should be structured to operate independently. But he does not take the logical next step of calling for a timetable to withdraw all troops and contractors. Without such a commitment, the Taliban and insurgent elements will continue to thrive. Afghanistan will likely continue to need peacekeeping support in the aftermath of the U.S.-NATO withdrawal. A withdrawal allows for the international community to revise the current ill-conceived mission and devise a truly international solution involving the United Nations and regional forces such as the Organization of the Islamic Conference.

These steps recognize the true threats in the region—a lack of governance and little access to economic development. Al-Qaida and the Taliban, while dangerous actors, must be recognized for what they really are—a band of 2,000–3,000 fighters and the remnants of a failed government that was not very popular until it claimed the mantle of opposing occupation.[21] And while no action can truly protect our nation from terrorist attacks, getting the policy right is a key step in making the United States and the world a safer place.

References

"Afghanistan: Development and Humanitarian Priorities." Oxfam. January 2008. Available at: http://www.oxfam.org.uk/resources/policy/conflict_ disasters/downloads/afghanistan_priorities.pdf

"Afghanistan: The Need for International Resolve." International Crisis Group. February 6, 2008.

Bidwai, Praful, "Changing Pakistan." *Frontline*, June 26, 2008, http://www.hin duonnet.com/fline/fl2513/stories/20080704251309300.htm (accessed July 16, 2008).

Coll, Steve, *Ghost Wars: The Secret History of the CIA, Afghanistan, and Bin Laden, from the Soviet Invasion to September 10, 2001.* New York: Penguin, 2004.

Jelsma, Martin, Tom Kramer, and Cristian Rivier, "Losing Ground: Drug Control and War in Afghanistan." Transnational Institute. December 2006.

Rashid, Ahmed, *Descent into Chaos.* New York: Viking, 2008.

Rubin, Barnet, and Jake Sherman, "Counter-Narcotics to Stabilize Afghanistan: The False Promise of Crop Eradication." Center on International Cooperation. New York University. February 2008.

Notes

1. Pew Research Center survey conducted by Princeton Survey Research Associates International, Feb. 20–24, 2008; CNN/USA Today/Gallup Poll, July 19–21, 2004, available at: http://www.pollingreport.com/afghan.htm.

2. David Rohde, "Second Record Level for Afghan Opium Crop," *New York Times,* August 28, 2007.

3. Mark Mazzetti, "Military Death Toll Rises in Afghanistan," *New York Times*, July 2, 2008.

4. Ann Scott Tyson, "NATO's Not Winning in Afghanistan, Report Says," *Washington Post*, January 31, 2008.

5. Mark Mazzetti, "Military Death Toll Rises in Afghanistan," *New York Times*, July 2, 2008.

6. "Afghan, International Forces Retake Town Held by Taliban since February," *The Associated Press*, December 10, 2007.

7. JoAnne O'Bryant and Michael Waterhouse, "U.S. Forces in Afghanistan," Congressional Research Service, May 9, 2008, http://www.fas.org/sgp/crs/natsec/RS22633.pdf (accessed July 17, 2008).

8. UNICEF Humanitarian Action Report 2008, United Nations Children's Fund (UNICEF), 2008.

9. "Current Afghan Government More Corrupt than Taliban, Survey Finds," *The Associated Press*, March 19, 2007.

10. Stephen Zunes, "Afghanistan: Five Years Later," Foreign Policy in Focus, October 13, 2006, http://www.fpif.org/fpiftxt/3597 (accessed July 17, 2008).

11. Mark L. Schneider, "Strategic Chaos and Taliban Resurgence in Afghanistan," Testimony to the House Committee on Foreign Affairs Subcommittee on the Middle East and South Asia, April 2, 2008.

12. International Crisis Group. "Afghanistan: The Need for International Resolve," Asia Report 145, February 6, 2008, http://www.crisisgroup.org/home/index.cfm?id= 5285 (accessed July 17, 2008).

13. Gerry J. Gilmore, "General Cites Security, Development, Governance Gains in Afghanistan," American Forces Press Service, June 24, 2008.

14. Terror Free Tomorrow. "Pakistan National Survey," New America Foundation (May–June 2008), http://www.terrorfreetomorrow.org/upimagestft/PakistanPollReport-June08.pdf (accessed July 17, 2008).

15. Alan Kronstadt, "Direct Overt U.S. Aid and Military Reimbursements to Pakistan, FY2002–FY2009," Congressional Research Service, July 10, 2008, http://www.fas. org/sgp/crs/row/pakaid.pdf (accessed July 17, 2008).

16. "Combating Terrorism: The United States Lacks Comprehensive Plan to Destroy the Terrorist Threat and Close the Safe Haven in Pakistan's Federally Administered Tribal Areas," Government Accountability Office, April 2008, http://www.hcfa.house. gov/110/GAO041708.pdf (accessed July 16 2008).

17. Fouad Pervez, "The Real Pakistan Crises," Foreign Policy in Focus, July 11, 2008.

18. "Opium Amounts to Half of Afghanistan's GDP in 2007, Reports UNODC," UN Office on Drugs and Crime Press Release, November 16, 2007, http://www.unodc.org/ unodc/en/press/releases/opium-amounts-to-half-of-afghanistans-gdp-in-2007,-reports-unodc.html (accessed July 17, 2008).

19. Matt Waldman, "Falling Short: Aid Effectiveness in Afghanistan," Agency Co-ordinating Body for Afghan Relief, March 2008.

20. Barnett Rubin, "Afghan Dilemmas: Defining Commitments," *The American Interest*, May/June 2008.

21. David Rohde, "Foreign Fighters of Harsher Bent Bolster Taliban," *New York Times,* October 30, 2007.

Chapter 37

A New U.S. Policy on Terrorism

John Feffer and Daniel Scheer

POLICY PROPOSALS

■ Retire the Global War on Terror framework.
■ Withdraw U.S. troops from Iraq.
■ Shift from a military response to terrorism to a criminal justice response.
■ Pursue diplomatic resolutions to outstanding conflicts in the Middle East and Southwest Asia.
■ Close Guantanamo detention facilities and end policies of rendition and torture.
■ Subject domestic surveillance programs to strict rule of law.

* * * * * * * * * * * * * * *

On February 28, 2008, five former U.S. Secretaries of State recommended that the next President should close the military prison of Guantanamo Bay. The infamous holding area, where 759 suspected terrorists have been detained at one time or another since January 2002, had become such a symbol of the universally unpopular counter-terrorism policy of the Bush Administration that shuttering the facility had attracted bipartisan support. Colin Powell, Henry Kissinger, James Baker, Warren Christopher and Madeleine Albright all agreed that shutting down Guantanamo Bay detention centers would improve the U.S. reputation in the world.

Baker, who served under Bush senior, expressed criticism of the Bush Administration's use of Guantanamo Bay facilities to serve counter-terrorism efforts. "I have a great deal of difficulty understanding how we can hold someone, pick someone up, particularly someone who might be an American citizen, even if they were caught somewhere abroad, acting against American interests, and hold them without giving them an opportunity to appear before a magistrate," Baker said. [1]

Closing down Guantanamo, while important and symbolic, would roll back only one of the dramatic changes that the Bush Administration made in U.S. foreign and domestic policy under the rubric of the Global War on Terrorism (GWOT). The incoming Administration could certainly gain crucial political capital by changing U.S. policy on unlawful detention, rendition, torture and domestic surveillance. It could more effectively reduce extremist violence by withdrawing U.S. troops from Iraq, negotiating political settlements in Afghanistan and Pakistan, and more vigorously pursuing peace in the Arab-Israeli conflict. And it could score more successes in apprehending those who continue to plan for follow-up actions to September 11 by following the European example of treating terrorism as a crime rather than as a military threat.

In short, the incoming Administration can try to rewind the tape back to September 12. It can thereby try to reverse the damaging policies of the last eight years and attempt to put in their place the measures the U.S. government should have pursued to take advantage of global sympathy in the aftermath of the attacks.

It is not, however, possible to return to September 12 any more than it is possible to go back two days before that and pretend that September 11 never happened. The Bush Administration's policy on terrorism has left a deep stain on the U.S. reputation. Closing down Guantanamo is not enough. In fact, any rollback in counter-terrorism policies can have only partial success if the incoming Administration does not directly challenge the GWOT framework that justified so many departures from international law, the U.S. Constitution and common sense over the last eight years. Without this overall conceptual change, the United States will continue to find itself in a Guantanamo of its own, built from fear and over-reaching arrogance.

Retire the Global War on Terrorism

During the 1990s, the Clinton Administration began to restructure U.S. foreign policy around a new concept: the "rogue state." These were countries, according to the U.S. government, that posed a cross-border threat to regional or international stability. "Rogue" did not refer to their internal policies, only to their intentions, stated or otherwise, to invade other countries, pursue weapons of mass destruction and otherwise cause or threaten mayhem in the world beyond their borders. In a foreshadowing of the Bush Administration's "axis of evil," the Clinton Administration identified a set of "irrational" countries, including Iraq, Iran and North Korea, that were bent on subverting international law and challenging U.S. regional interests.

The "rogue state" framework suffered from many of the same conceptual flaws that would later emerge in the Bush Administration's response to the September 11 attacks. The concept, like the Bush Administration's doctrine of "preventive war," had no standing in international law. The notion that the leaders of "rogue states" were irrational suggested that they could only be dealt with militarily and were impervious to the pragmatic bargaining that takes place through the normal channels of diplomacy. And any suggestion to negotiate with countries deemed beyond the pale of accepted international norms was open to charges of appeasement. [2]

The appropriate response to the "rogue state" concept was not to argue about this or that country's inclusion in the framework. Exceptions only proved the rule. For instance, the Clinton Administration decided to negotiate with North Korea in 1994 and again in 1999, only to come up against hard-line objections that the leadership of such a rogue state could not be trusted. The Administration's adherence to the overall "rogue-state" framework with respect to Syria, Afghanistan, Iraq, Iran and others proved to be self-defeating when it came time to shift gears, abandon the concept and negotiate with North Korea.

The GWOT framework has had a similarly pernicious effect on U.S. foreign policy. The very terms of the framework are problematic. Terrorism is a tactic, not a country or an ideology: One does not, for instance, wage a war on espionage or blitzkrieg. Wars, meanwhile, are conducted between countries—to declare a war on an organization like al-Qaeda elevates its participants from their status as criminals to the level of warriors, which is how they prefer to see themselves. And the conflict is not global. The United States has largely confined its military operations to Iraq, Afghanistan and a portion of Pakistan.

The GWOT framework also suggests that terrorism is the single greatest threat to U.S. interests. It is not. Half the victims of terrorism in 2007 were Muslim, and most were from Iraq. Only seventeen U.S. citizens died in terrorist attacks in 2007.[3] Indeed, as political scientist John Mueller has argued in *Foreign Affairs*, the terrorist threat to the United States has been greatly exaggerated. No terrorist attacks have taken place on American soil since 2001, and investigators have not turned up any real al-Qaeda cells in the United States. "The massive and expensive homeland security apparatus erected since 9/11," Mueller writes, "may be persecuting some, spying on many, inconveniencing most, and taxing all to defend the United States against an enemy that scarcely exists." [4]

Casting the fight against terrorism as a war allowed the Bush Administration free rein to engage in extraordinary measures across borders—to invade and occupy countries, to pour money into the Pentagon in pursuit of these objectives, and to seize suspects and "render" them to countries that permit torture in their interrogations. Each of the elements of the campaign, which might have been successfully opposed on the grounds of their illegality, were justified as part of the larger goals articulated by the Administration.

The incoming Administration will necessarily have to challenge the individual components of the Bush Administration's approach to terrorism. But if the overall framework is left untouched, the way still will be open for politicians to hold the new Administration to the yardsticks established by the Bush team: the stated necessity to wage an unlimited war, to break whatever domestic and international laws are necessary to expedite such a war, and to lump all putative terrorists into a single category of actors who lie outside the "civilized" discourse of diplomacy. Just as the "rogue state" formulation misstated the problem, so does GWOT miss the point. In place of a "war on terror," the incoming Administration must articulate an appeal based not in a culture of fear but on the rule of law.

Iraq Troop Withdrawal

The Iraq War and the U.S. occupation that followed have done more than anything else to increase the ranks of al-Qaeda and like-minded organizations. The United States launched a crusade against Saddam Hussein that naturally generated a crusade (or jihad) in return. Specific U.S. policies—torture and mistreatment at the Abu Ghraib prison in Iraq, the failure to turn over political authority to Iraqis, the emphasis on military solutions—have only compounded the errors made by invading in the first place.

The initial reason for al-Qaeda's campaign against the United States was the location of U.S. Army bases in Saudi Arabia. The U.S. occupation of Iraq has served as a similar rationale for a succession of terrorist attacks against countries like England and Spain that served in the "coalition of the willing." The U.S. occupation has not simply inspired bombings in Europe or Asia. Iraq itself has become a center of terrorist activities. The greatest number of terrorist attacks, according to U.S. government statistics, takes place in Iraq itself.[5]

The Iraq War has also revealed the underlying goals of U.S. counterterrorism policy. Since Saddam Hussein had nothing to do with the attacks of September 11, the invasion and occupation had nothing to do with preventing future attacks. Instead, the war was about securing access to oil and creating U.S. client states in the region. Resentment toward U.S. resource policies and ham-fisted attempts at "bringing democracy" to the region have translated into greater support for terrorism.

Withdrawal of U.S. troops from Iraq will deprive al-Qaeda of its chief recruiting tactic. It will send a clear signal that the United States is finally leaving Iraq in the hands of Iraqis. A portion of the money now spent on war should be devoted instead to large-scale reconstruction—both in Iraq and in Afghanistan. When the United States becomes associated with constructive rather than destructive acts, it will no longer serve as the inspiration for acts of violence.

Shift to Criminal Justice Approach

The greatest successes in fighting al-Qaeda have not taken place in Iraq. They have not taken place on the field of battle. Rather, they have happened in England. And the successful actors were not soldiers, but police. In 2004, Scotland Yard arrested eight Britons planning to use 1,300 pounds of ammonium nitrate fertilizer. Later the same year, the British police disrupted a plot to set off a dirty bomb in London. In 2006, it foiled a plot to blow up planes at Heathrow.

In contrast, the U.S. government has argued that only war "over there" can prevent terrorism from happening "over here." But war has only increased the frequency of terrorist attacks. Indeed, the sheer number of civilian deaths in Iraq as a result of the war—anywhere from thirty times the number of fatalities on September 11 to 300 times the number—suggests that at the moment the United States is the greatest state sponsor of terrorism in the world, and the U.S. Army is the instrument of this policy.

The criminal justice approach to terrorism is a better conceptual fit because terrorism is a crime rather than an act of war. Of equal importance, as the British cases suggest, the criminal justice approach works. But the British have not pursued just any criminal justice approach. "In each instance," writes David Cole of the British successes, "the plots were disrupted not by using rendition, torture, disappearances or indefinite detention without trial, but through the kind of old-fashioned police work that is commonly dismissed in the United States these days as 'backward-looking.'"[6]

While the British foiled actual plots, U.S. authorities proceeded to bend and break laws in order to uncover plots that never existed, including the infamous "dirty bomb" of José Padilla and the imaginary plot to attack the Sears Tower in Chicago. British methods are far from ideal, given the greater controls on speech and weaker protections of privacy in British law. But they demonstrate that a criminal justice approach can be both legal and effective.

Pursue Diplomatic Solutions

Terrorists are, by and large, attacking the policies of the U.S. government, not a Western way of life. If these policies change, particularly in the Middle East, terrorist organizations would lose a major organizing tool. A change in U.S. policy in the Middle East—withdrawing from Iraq, providing more reconstruction assistance to Afghanistan, pressuring Arab allies to democratize, brokering a two-state peace deal between Israel and Palestine—would demonstrate that Washington is siding with the majority of citizens in the region rather than simply backing elites and their repressive activities. Despite its myriad divisions, the Islamic world has united in opposition to current U.S. military policy. If U.S. policy changes, then diversity will return to the foreground, and al-Qaeda's notion of a global Islamic caliphate will become even more improbable a goal than it currently is.

By turning a cold shoulder on organizations such as Hamas in Palestine, Hezbollah in Lebanon and the Muslim Brotherhood in Egypt (and elsewhere), the United States has failed to facilitate the transformation of these groups into viable political entities. More importantly, by refusing to negotiate with these groups—as well as others deemed beyond the diplomatic pale—the United States has missed opportunities to bring a measure of political stability to the very conflicts in the Middle East that serve as the training grounds for anti-American extremists. As Madeleine Albright has said, "We have to understand what diplomacy is really about. It's talking to your enemy."[7]

Instead of trying to impose democracy through the barrel of a gun, which has failed so far in Iraq, the United States should support the efforts of those in the region to create viable democratic states, in Palestine, Lebanon and elsewhere. Only by talking with the current government in Iran, and joining with the European Union in finding a package deal that substitutes civilian nuclear cooperation for the country's potential nuclear weapons program, can the United States undercut the Iranian hardliners' strategy of using the threat of war to bolster their own position.[8]

Close Guantanamo

After the urging of key allies, the UN and every major human rights organization, a bipartisan consensus has emerged in the United States on closing the Guantanamo detention facilities. In practice, that would mean ending the policy of indefinite detention and either trying the detainees in U.S. courts or releasing them to countries where they will not be tortured. Such a change in policy would, at a minimum, bring the United States into compliance with the Geneva Conventions regarding the treatment of enemy combatants and with the principle of *habeas corpus* that the Supreme Court ruled in June 2008 applies even to the detainees at Guantanamo.[9]

Guantanamo is not, however, the only problematic detention facility. The treatment of detainees at the Bagram facility in Afghanistan was much worse, particularly from 2001 to 2003.[10] The detention facilities, which were built by the Soviets, currently hold over 600 detainees. The Pentagon plans a $60 million facelift, and human rights organizations fear a second Guantanamo facility. Closing the camp in Cuba is therefore only dealing with part of the network of shadowy detention facilities that the United States runs. Part of any plan to pull the United States out of the shadow of Guantanamo must involve not only closure of facilities but a thorough investigation into the abuses that took place in them and the punishment of those responsible.

The Bush Administration's permissive position on torture lost the United States considerable credibility as an upholder of human rights. Even the Justice Department raised concerns about the techniques used by military interrogators, concerns shared by top FBI personnel who kept a "war crimes" file about what they observed.[11] The incoming Administration has to move quickly and firmly to a "just say no" policy on torture.

Return to Rule of Law

The Global War on Terrorism has not simply been conducted overseas. GWOT has been waged at home as well. The assault on civil liberties over the last eight years has eroded the very Constitutional foundations of U.S. law. The Bush Administration imprisoned over 5,000 foreign nationals, subjected 80,000 Arab and Muslim immigrants to fingerprinting, and allowed another 8,000 to be interrogated by the FBI.[12] It sent 30,000 "national security letters" every year to U.S. businesses demanding information about their customers. It engaged in large-scale, warrantless wiretapping of citizens.

Federal courts declared unconstitutional some of the provisions of the Administration's domestic policy as articulated in the USA PATRIOT Act. There have been efforts in Congress to subject the Administration's programs to the rule of law. Individuals have filed suit to overturn certain pieces of the policy.

But it is up to the incoming Administration to send a clear signal to the American people that the days of "emergency powers" are over. The new President must return to the legally accepted procedures for initiating wiretaps and revert back to the use of national security letters only for individuals involved in criminal investigations.

From GWOT to GDOL

The elements of a fair, just and effective counter-terrorism policy are clear, from an end to the Iraq War to the closure of Guantanamo. But how do these policies all hang together?

In place of a Global War on Terrorism (GWOT), the incoming Administration must adopt a Global Defense of Law (GDOL). This new counter-terrorism approach is built on two key principles: the priority of international and domestic law, and the defense of the homeland, rather than the use of military force beyond our borders.

To treat terrorism effectively as a crime, the United States must take the law very seriously: the international laws governing institutions such as the International Criminal Court as well as the domestic laws that safeguard the civil liberties of those living in the United States. Bending or breaking laws in order to apprehend terrorists ultimately destroys the foundations of the American way of life more surely than any actual or imagined terrorist attack. Meanwhile, the United States is justified in spending resources to protect the country: securing ports, upgrading the Coast Guard, improving coordination among law enforcement agencies. In this case, the best defense really is the best defense. Offensive measures have only increased the threats against the United States.

The Bush Administration did not put a time limit on its Global War on Terrorism. This framework must be retired before it can do more damage. The only feasible alternative is a new framework that is global, law-abiding and attentive to the real security needs of Americans.

Resources

3D Security: http://www.3dsecurity.org/
Foreign Policy in Focus: www.fpif.org
Oxford Research Group: http://www.oxfordresearchgroup.org.uk/

References

Clarke, Richard. *Against All Enemies*. New York: Free Press, 2004.
Cole, David. "Are We Safer?" *New York Review of Books*, March 9, 2006, http://www.nybooks.com/articles/18752 (accessed July 19, 2008).
———. "The Brits Do It Better," *New York Review of Books*, June 12, 2008, http://www.nybooks.com/articles/article-preview?article_id=21513 (accessed July 19, 2008).
Gordon, Philip. *Winning the Right War*. Washington, D.C.: Brookings Institution Press, 2007.
Litwak, Robert. *Rogue States and U.S. Foreign Policy*. Washington, D.C.: Woodrow Wilson Center Press, 2000.
Lustick, Ian. *Trapped in the War on Terror*. Philadelphia: University of Pennsylvania Press, 2006.
McClatchy series on detainees in U.S. facilities abroad: http://www.mcclatchydc.com/detainees/story/38773.html
Mueller, John. "Is There Still a Terrorist Threat?" *Foreign Affairs* 85 (September/ October 2006).
———. *Overblown*. New York: Free Press, 2006.
Rashid, Ahmed. "Jihad Suicide Bombers: The New Wave." New York Review of Books, June 12, 2008, http://www.nybooks.com/articles/21473 (accessed July 20, 2008).
United States Department of State. *Country Reports on Terrorism 2007*. Prepared by the Office for the Coordinator of Counterterrorism. Washington, D.C., April 2008.

Notes

1. "Former Secretaries of State: Close Guantanamo," *Atlantic Journal-Constitution*, March 28, 2008, http://www.ajc.com/news/content/news/stories/2008/03/27/secstate_0328.html (accessed July 20, 2008).

2. See Robert Litwak. *Rogue States and U.S. Foreign Policy* (Washington, D.C.: Woodrow Wilson Center Press, 2000); and Michael Klare, *Rogue States and Nuclear Outlaws* (New York: Hill and Wang, 1996).

3. United States Department of State, *Country Reports on Terrorism 2007*, prepared by the Office for the Coordinator of Counterterrorism, Washington, D.C., April 2008.

4. John Mueller, "Is There Still a Terrorist Threat?," *Foreign Affairs* 85 (September/October 2006).

5. Country Reports on Terrorism 2007, op cit.

6. David Cole, "The Brits Do It Better," *New York Review of Books*, June 12, 2008, p. 69.

7. "Former Secretaries of State: Close Guantanamo," op. cit.

8. Vali Nasr and Ray Takeyh, "How Iran's President is Being Undercut," *Christian Science Monitor*, December 14, 2007, http://www.csmonitor.com/2007/1214/p09s02-coop.html?page=1 (accessed July 20, 2008).

9. BBC News, "Major Guantanamo Setback for Bush," June 12, 2008, http://news.bbc.co.uk/2/hi/americas/7451139.stm (accessed July 20, 2008).

10. See five-part series done by the McClatchy news service in June 2008, http://www.mcclatchydc.com/detainees/story/38773.html (accessed July 20, 2008).

11. Robert Scheer, "Even the FBI Is Outraged over U.S. Torture," AlterNet, May 29, 2008, http://www.alternet.org/story/86651/ (accessed July 20, 2008).

12. David Cole, "Are We Safer?" *New York Review of Books*, March 9, 2006.

Chapter 38

Eliminating Nuclear Weapons

Marcus Raskin and Robert Alvarez*

POLICY PROPOSALS

- Cut the large U.S. and Russian nuclear stockpiles of intact warheads by 90 percent over the next five years.
- Establish security assurances with Russia, halting the expansion of NATO; re-instating the Anti-Ballistic Missile Defense Treaty, contingent on restoration of the Conventional Forces Agreement; and résumé negotiations for nuclear arms reductions under a START II agreement.
- Establish an office in the White House National Security Council to coordinate the development and implementation of an Administration plan for nuclear abolition and general disarmament.
- Expand the Cooperative Threat Reduction Program in the Department of Defense to accommodate a START II Agreement.
- Ratify the Comprehensive Test Ban Treaty.
- Establish a multilateral Fissile Material Cut-Off Agreement.
- Place fissile materials resulting from arms cuts under International Atomic Energy Agency (IAEA) inspections.
- Establish a modern infrastructure in the Department of Energy to dismantle nuclear weapons and to ensure safe, secure storage and disposition of fissile materials.

* * * * * * * * * * * * * *

The United States has the opportunity to take several steps in the next few years that demonstrate its leadership in ridding the world of nuclear arms. The incoming Administration should make clear that it will move forward with a revitalized general disarmament program. Obviously, the purpose of nuclear abolition should not be to make the world safe for non-nuclear war.

*Special thanks to Kathleen Tucker for her able editing.

The incoming Administration and U.S. Congress will enter an important historic moment in the nuclear age. Both Republican and Democratic Congresses have consistently rejected proposals to design and build new nuclear weapons. The expiration of the START I Treaty in 2009 will become an important benchmark for the future of nuclear arms reductions. The Nuclear Non-Proliferation Treaty Review Conference in 2010 provides an important opportunity for the United States to take bold steps in reducing nuclear arms. Restructuring the U.S. government's programs will be required to meet NPT policy goals.

Today, the power stemming from the threat of ultimate destruction by nuclear weapons continues to exact a bitter price on those who have the most. Some 28,000 intact nuclear warheads (93 percent of all nuclear arms in the world) remain in the United States and the Russian Federation. The momentum that began in the twilight of the Cold War to get rid of nuclear weapons has long stalled, and they remain ever more attractive to nations, terrorists and free-wheeling entrepreneurs on the international free market.

We now have the opportunity to change course and eliminate nuclear weapons. Even the prime architects of U.S. nuclear Cold War strategy—George P. Shultz, William J. Perry, Henry A. Kissinger and Sam Nunn—who in large measure helped foster these monstrous arsenals, are alarmed by these prospects and call for "setting the goal of a world free of nuclear weapons." In the April 4, 2007, *Wall Street Journal,* they declared:

> Unless urgent new actions are taken, the United States soon will be compelled to enter a new nuclear era that will be more precarious and psychologically disorienting, and economically even more costly than was Cold War deterrence.

It's been nearly twenty years since the last new weapons were made by the former Cold War enemies. Missiles have been de-targeted, and the vast industrial complexes that churned out nuclear arms are decaying and crumbling. Once-secret nuclear facilities in the United States are now turning to tourism for survival.

This necrosis is nowhere more felt than in the loss of institutional memory formed over sixty years by the artisans, engineers and scientists who made the current generation of weapons and will likely die off in the next couple decades. Ironically, because of all this, the intractable problems of having nuclear weapons not only endure but thrive.

A major reason is that neither the United States nor the Soviet nuclear weapons bureaucracies ever envisioned stopping, and they had no contingencies to come to terms with an abrupt end to the nuclear arms race. As a result, tens of tons of excess nuclear explosive materials, such as plutonium and highly enriched uranium in the United States and the former Soviet Union, had to be stored in aged and deteriorated structures, including wooden buildings. They were even stored outside exposed to the elements. The collapse of the former

Soviet nuclear program was more severe and still poses a significant danger of theft and diversion of these materials.

Heralding the collapse of the U.S. and Russian nuclear arms infrastructures was one of the largest environmental disasters ever, the 1986 Chernobyl nuclear power reactor accident. More than 100,000 people were permanently evacuated and about one million emergency responders and clean-up workers were sent into this radiological charnel. Two decades later, 6,000 square miles, an area greater than the State of Connecticut, are severely contaminated and remain uninhabitable.

The shock of Chernobyl jarred the thinking of the Soviet leadership from the isolated abstractions of military Cold War strategy. Looking back twenty years later, Mikhail S. Gorbachev, the last President of the USSR, said:

> Chernobyl opened my eyes like nothing else: It showed the horrible conse-
> quences of nuclear power....One could now imagine much more clearly what
> might happen if a nuclear bomb exploded. According to scientific experts, one
> SS-18 rocket could contain 100 Chernobyls.

Chernobyl also brought to light the dangerous and decrepit state of the nuclear weapons production infrastructures that served as the industrial engines of the nuclear arms race. Between the late 1980s and early 1990s, efforts by the U.S. Congress and Energy Secretary Hazel R. O'Leary, and Alexie Yablokov, former Science and Environmental Advisor to Boris Yeltsin, released previously secret information revealing that millions of workers, military personnel and residents living near weapons sites were put at greater risk of radiation disease and death. Water supplies in large regions in the United States and the former Soviet Union are contaminated and remain threatened by the enormous amounts of wastes containing long-lived carcinogens in leaking tanks or dumped into the ground.

By 1988, Senator John Glenn (D-OH), a staunch advocate of nuclear arms, was now challenging their legitimacy, asking, "What good does it do to protect ourselves with nuclear weapons, if we poison our people in the process? "

The aftermaths of Chernobyl and the end of the Cold War gave way to a dam burst of nuclear arms reductions:

- The Intermediate-Range Nuclear Forces Treaty, which, for the first time in the Cold War, eliminated deployment of nuclear weapons from Europe, went into force.
- The Strategic Arms Reduction Treaty (START I) was signed and ratified to downsize strategic nuclear arsenals. (The START II treaty, which banned the use of multiple warheads on long-range ballistic missiles, was being finalized for adoption.)
- Nuclear testing had ceased in the United States and Russia, and the Comprehensive Test Ban Treaty was signed.

- The United States purchased 500 metric tons of highly-enriched uranium from Russian nuclear weapons to be blended down for use in power reactors,
- The United States withdrew 800 tactical nuclear weapons from South Korea and closed down major portions of its nuclear weapons production complex.
- The Cooperative Threat Reduction Program was established in the U.S. Defense Department to secure safe and secure storage of nuclear weapons materials in the former Soviet Union, championed by Senators Sam Nunn (D-GA) and Richard Lugar (R-IN).

Unfortunately, the political momentum for nuclear arms reduction halted in the United States in the mid-1990s. The Clinton Administration found itself up against a Republican-dominated Congress determined to thwart further arms control, and to restore the status of nuclear weapons.

A sobering reality for the United States and Russia also set in: Elimination of nuclear weapons required large unanticipated expenses to assure verification, perform wholesale warhead dismantlement, and complete the difficult challenge of storing and disposing of large amounts of excess weapons plutonium. The Clinton Administration froze into place a policy to maintain a large strategic arsenal and a substantial reserve of intact warheads, until the START II Agreement was ratified. With the U.S. Senate in 1999 voting down the Comprehensive Teat Ban Treaty, this ended further nuclear arms reduction prospects with Russia by the Clinton Administration.

Adopting the demands of the Republican hardliners in the Congress, the George W. Bush Administration has sought to undo the work of his father's Administration in order to restore the legitimacy of nuclear weapons. In a drastic shift in U.S. nuclear weapons policy, President Bush issued a directive on September 14, 2002 (NSPD-17), which named Syria, Libya, Iran and North Korea as potential nuclear targets. Preemptive nuclear attacks against nations that may pose *imminent* threats of possessing weapons of mass destruction were subsequently authorized in 2005. In 2006, this doctrine was reaffirmed in the President's "National Security Strategy."

In 2002, Bush also withdrew from the Anti-Ballistic Missile Treaty and has been aggressively pushing for the expansion of NATO and the deployment of missile defense systems close to Russia's borders. The promise made by then-Secretary of State James Baker to President Gorbachev that the United States would refrain from expanding NATO, if the USSR agreed to the unification of Germany, was broken during the Clinton Administration.

This has prompted Russia to withdraw from START II (which had yet to enter into force) and, more ominously, the Conventional Forces Agreement. In its place, the United States and Russia agreed to reduce operationally-deployed warheads by 1,200 to 2,200 by the year 2012. Unlike the previous treaties, there are no verification provisions, and reductions are not required to be permanent—

allowing for large "war reserves" to be redeployed within three months. If reduction targets are not reached by 2012, the Treaty simply expires.

With the departure of the second Bush Administration, the opportunity presents itself for the United States and Russia to resume where they left off in the early 1990s. An important first step would be the elimination of 90 percent U.S. and Russian arsenals within the next five years. The grip that nuclear weapons have on the United States and Russia can be broken, setting the stage for their elimination.

Origins and Illegitimacy

The U.S. nuclear weapons program began with the launch of the Manhattan Project, which cost $23 billion in 2007 dollars and employed over 130,000 people at more than thirty sites. The United States was the first to use nuclear weapons as a terror weapon, against Hiroshima and Nagasaki. Their use communicated very specific messages to the world. First, the United States had the will to use nuclear weapons, as well as play the nuclear card against the war-devastated Soviet Union. Second, the United States had a technological edge over the Soviet Union and didn't need its help in achieving victory over Japan.

By the mid-1990s, according to a Brookings Institution report, the cost for nuclear weapons exceeded $6 trillion. By this time, however, the rationale for their stockpiling and use had shifted considerably from the World War II and Cold War contexts. The Soviet Union no longer existed, and the potential had emerged of nuclear material falling into the hands of an adversary or terrorist. Nevertheless, certain types of realists within the U.S. government continued to argue for the "rational" use of nuclear weapons: to deter the use by other nuclear powers, as strategic counterforce in the event of war, as tactical weapons in battlefield conditions, and so on.

George W. Bush and his Pentagon have tried to extend this realist tradition by continuing to look for a rational use of nuclear weapons. To this end, they sought to build the so-called "bunker buster" bombs. These small, low-yield weapons ostensibly could be used against adversaries hiding out in mountain caves. In this way, nuclear weapons have become just another "niche" weapon that can be used on the orders of the President or any battlefield commander.

And yet, at the same time, the Pentagon itself had run dozens of war games that showed the inherent danger to American forces that these weapons posed. Depending on sudden shifts in wind conditions, bunker busters could cause devastating radiological damage to American forces, not to mention civilians and the environment.

Although the utility of nuclear weapons has declined for major powers such as the United States, other countries have come to see these weapons as shortcuts to shoring up their own national security. Leaders in Iran or Israel, for instance, have come to believe that nuclear weapons reduce their dependency on others and the risk of attack. Their belief in the benefits of nuclear weapons flies in the face of the experience of the Soviet Union, which couldn't maintain its hold over Eastern Europe even with a massive nuclear arsenal, or of the United States, which couldn't win victories in Vietnam or Korea even with the threatened use of nuclear strikes. Even deterrence, the fundamental pillar of nuclear policy, has begun to fray. The very stonemasons of these foundational policies—Shultz, Perry, Kissinger, Nunn and others—have concluded, in the *Wall Street Journal* article cited above, that "reliance on nuclear weapons for this purpose is becoming increasingly hazardous and decreasingly effective."

The Non-Proliferation Approach

Advocates of the nuclear abolition view the use and manufacture of nuclear weapons as a cataclysm waiting to happen. This conclusion found its institutional expression in the Nuclear Non-Proliferation Treaty (NPT), which entered into force in 1970 and has been signed by 189 countries. According to the underlying assumption of the NPT, the nuclear weapons states would undertake serious negotiations to reach nuclear abolition through general and complete disarmament.

Over a generation ago, non-nuclear states accepted the path of nuclear abolition—and were willing to give up their research and development of nuclear weapons—if the nuclear powers would travel a well-defined road toward nuclear disarmament. But this road has not been traveled. And the fears of nuclear proliferation grow even among the most powerful states. The result is the toxic double standard in which the weak must follow the law and the powerful are free to do as they wish.

The U.S. approach to the NPT is hypocritical in two ways. First, the United States has accepted certain states into the nuclear club (India, Israel) for geopolitical reasons while threatening to go to war with other countries (North Korea, Iran) that it wants outside the clubhouse. Second, the United States has not moved toward nuclear abolition and general disarmament.

There have been some countervailing trends in the United States. Important segments of U.S. society have campaigned for the United States to take its NPT obligations seriously. The U.S. Catholic Bishops, for instance, argued in 1977 that neither deterrence nor mere arms control were moral ends and that nuclear abolition was a moral necessity for humanity. Even the U.S. government itself has, at one time or another, acknowledged the importance of disarmament. For instance, the United States has signed at least six arms control treaties meant to be steps on the way toward general and complete disarmament. The Kennedy Administration took disarmament seriously enough to create the Arms Control and Disarmament Agency to balance the advice of the Pentagon and prepare comprehensive peace alternatives. After Kennedy's death, however, interest dried up in comprehensive disarmament and economic conversion with the escalation of U.S. military involvement in Indochina. Under George W. Bush, the United States moved even further from its NPT obligations. It served notice that it would not abide by treaties that placed limits on American sovereignty or, indeed, the actions of the Bush Administration itself.

Beyond Nuclear Weapons

Nuclear weapons and their missile launchers are more than hardware. They are a social and economic system that requires structural transformation. Eighteen years after the end of the Cold War, the United States and Russia maintain nuclear "entitlement" cultures that dominate the economies of large geographical areas.

Consequently, any alternative to the present state of affairs must begin with two objectives: a shift in consciousness about nuclear weapons and the application of international law to the nuclear question. We are seeing the first in terms of the abandonment of the realist position by former realists such as Shultz and Kissinger. They see that nuclear weapons no long have utility, in terms of furthering U.S. national security objectives as they understand them. Equally important, and dependent on this shift in consciousness, is the recognition that nuclear disarmament is a legal matter—subject to treaty obligations.

With these important conceptual shifts as a backdrop, the United States has the opportunity to take the several steps in the next few years outlined in our Policy Proposals.

The nuclear Non-Proliferation Treaty Review conference will commence in 2010, as noted above, and major opportunities and pressures will arise for the nuclear weapons states to significantly reduce their nuclear arsenals. The goal of the NPT group is to secure a halt to the expansion of nuclear weapons states, with the major states laying out a time schedule for ten-year dismantlement. Stages of the process would not be interrupted.

In the longer term:

- The federal government will have to be restructured in order to establish a meaningful programmatic mission dedicated to nuclear weapons elimination and non-proliferation.
- Methods will need to be formulated to provide for regional defense and security plans through the United Nations Military Committees, with the understanding that planning and defense of regional and national states are to conform to the UN Charter, of which the United States was the original signatory and expositor.
- National defenses should become transparent, but clearly aimed at the defense of a nation's own territory rather than the spread of nuclear weapons bases around the world or the proliferation of weapons. The nuclear

umbrella would be discarded as would weapons of mass destruction and nuclear weapons development for threat or aggressive use.

Resources

Bulletin of the Atomic Scientists: http://www.thebulletin.org
Peace Action: http://www.peace-action.org

References

Alvarez, Robert. "U.S.-Russian Nuclear Agreement Raises Serious Concerns." *Bulletin of Atomic Scientists,* June 16, 2008.
Cirincione, Joseph. *Bomb Scare: The History and Future of Nuclear Weapons.* New York: Columbia University Press, 2007.
Raskin, Marcus. *Abolishing the War System: The Disarmament and International Law Project of the Institute for Policy Studies and the Lawyers Committee on Nuclear Policy.* Amherst, MA: Aletheia Press, 1981.
———. *Essays of a Citizen: From National Security State to Democracy.* New York: M. E. Sharpe, Inc., 1991.

Chapter 39

U.S. Policy on the Global Economy: A New Development Agenda

Sarah Anderson and John Cavanagh

POLICY PROPOSALS

- **Trade and Investment:** Renegotiate existing trade agreements, starting with the North American Free Trade Agreement (NAFTA), as part of a broad development agenda aimed at promoting good jobs and healthy communities here and abroad.
- **Finance:** Shut down the global financial casino by increasing regulation and cooperating with other nations to create a currency transaction tax.
- **Debt:** Support cancellation of external debts for impoverished countries, without onerous conditions.
- **World Bank and IMF Overhaul:** Condition U.S. support for these institutions on a transformation of their lending policies, including an end to harmful economic policy conditions and a phase-out of fossil fuel lending. Support new regional alternatives, such as the Bank of the South and the Chiang Mai Initiative.
- **Aid:** Increase effectiveness in fighting poverty, including ending the practice of tying aid to purchases from U.S. firms and supporting the creation of a UN Commissioner to strengthen international aid accountability.
- **Corporate Accountability:** Support the right to bring corporate violators of international human rights to justice in U.S. courts and cooperate with other nations to establish an international court for the most egregious corporate crimes.
- **Worker and Consumer Protections:** Support labor law reforms and increased training and unemployment benefits for U.S. workers and

dramatically increase monitoring of imported food, toys and other consumer products.

* * * * * * * * * * * * * *

A U.S. mortgage meltdown gone global. Food riots. Untraceable tainted products. The continued hemorrhaging of U.S. manufacturing jobs.

All around us are signs of a global economy in big trouble. And as a consequence, the institutions and policies that have long set the rules of the road for international trade, investment and finance are in a crisis of legitimacy.

Nowhere is this more apparent than at the International Monetary Fund (IMF). For more than two decades, this institution has demanded that borrowing countries slash public spending and lift barriers to trade and financial flows—despite the failure of such "reforms" to generate growth or reduce inequalities. In the past five years, new sources of credit have liberated one country after another from the IMF's misguided loan conditions, causing the Fund's portfolio to shrink by more than 80 percent. IMF economists' credibility sank even further when they failed to predict the global financial crisis that erupted in 2007 and is now expected to cost nearly $1 trillion.

Likewise in the trade arena, the World Trade Organization (WTO) is mired in dysfunction, with negotiations for a new round of market openings stalled for years. Bush Administration officials also failed to forge a hemispheric trade pact, having to settle for only a handful of bilateral deals. Meanwhile, opinion polls in the United States and in many other countries are showing growing opposition to the current approach to free trade.

The incoming U.S. Administration should view this legitimacy crisis as an opportunity for long-needed change. The current outmoded approach to the global economy started with the Reagan Administration in the 1980s. Driven by textbook free market theory, U.S. officials pressed other governments to shrink their traditional functions of regulating and stimulating the economy, leaving their nations' fates up to the whims of the market. Philosopher-philanthropist George Soros has aptly called this approach "market fundamentalism."

Why did other countries accept this? In the 1960s and 1970s, irresponsible lenders funneled large sums of money to non-democratic governments, where it often wound up in rulers' pockets or boondoggle projects with dubious benefits for the poor. By the early 1980s, impoverished nations were having trouble servicing their external debts, and the richer nations came up with an unequal solution.

The Reagan Administration and conservative European governments instructed the global financial institutions, particularly the World Bank and IMF, to impose "austerity" measures on poor nations in exchange for renegotiating the debts. Countries were told to cut government workers, sell off government enterprises such as water systems to for-profit corporations, and plunder their natural resources to boost export earnings.

Governments accelerated this market-opening mania in the 1990s through the WTO, NAFTA and other deals that further knocked down trade and investment barriers and gave corporations new rights. In the process, five major problems emerged:

- *Climate Chaos:* Pressure to boost exports contributed to rampant over-use of the world's water, forests, fisheries and natural resources, pushing the planet to the verge of ecological collapse and climate catastrophe.
- *Volatility:* Starting with Reagan, the U.S. government and then the global institutions pushed for financial deregulation, removing checks on hot money that zips around the world seeking the highest short-term return, no matter how risky the investment.
- *Obscene Inequality:* As corporations and billionaires have reaped enormous benefits from global trade and investment, the rest of us have gotten the crumbs. According to the IMF, inequality has risen in five of seven world regions in the past two decades, after a general decline during much of the first eighty years of the twentieth century. The world's 1,125 billionaires today have combined wealth that is bigger than the combined wealth of the poorest two-thirds of humanity.
- *Excess Corporate Power:* Trade and investment agreements have granted corporations unprecedented powers, including the right to sue governments in international tribunals when regulations threaten their profits.
- *Race to the Bottom:* Since corporations can now move nearly anywhere in the world, they use this as leverage to bargain down wages, working conditions and environmental standards everywhere.

To fix these problems, the U.S. government must rethink the logic of its interactions with the global economy, based on a broad re-examination of:

- what works not just for the largest corporations, but for the broadest set of U.S. interests (workers, environment, communities, farmers, small businesses);
- what respects the interests and needs of other peoples around the world;
- what respects the urgent ecological limits of the planet.

In the past two years, there have been some hopeful signs of change in this direction. In May 2007, Democratic House leaders struck a trade deal with the White House that reflected a major shift in the globalization debate. The most significant step was an agreement to revise pending trade agreements to require compliance with core international labor standards and multilateral environmental treaties. Thea Lee, the AFL-CIO's veteran trade analyst, is quoted in the Fall 2007 issue of New Labor Forum as remarking, "We've always said that adding labor and environmental standards was not the only thing that needed to be fixed about our trade agreements, but it was the first thing that needed to be fixed. Yet even that idea wasn't taken seriously when we were negotiating NAFTA. Now it's at the center of the debate."

However, the 2007 "deal" on trade was far too limited. Here are a few of the most glaring problems:

- The deal does not eliminate investment provisions in trade agreements and bilateral investment treaties that are fundamentally anti-democratic. Under these rules, private foreign investors can bypass domestic courts and sue governments in unaccountable international tribunals. They can sue over alleged violations of a long list of "investor protections," the most controversial being the protection against government actions, including public interest regulations, that significantly diminish the value of an investment. For example, a Canadian company is currently using NAFTA to sue the United States over California laws to reduce the damage of a gold-mining project.
- The investment rules also ban governments from imposing controls on capital flows, even though such measures have helped insulate some nations from the financial crises that have hit countries from Korea to Mexico, throwing millions of workers out of their jobs.
- The deal completely ignores agriculture, even though existing trade pacts subject small farmers to massive displacement by pitting them in direct competition with global agribusiness. For example, more than a million Mexican farmers have lost their livelihoods due to an influx of heavily subsidized U.S. corn. This contributes to migration pressures and the crushing unemployment that makes it harder to organize unions and push up wages.
- The deal would allow procurement rules in trade pacts that undermine the ability of governments to use tax dollars to invest in job creation and other legitimate social objectives.

Dialogue Around a New Development Agenda

The incoming U.S. Administration should declare a moratorium on all new trade agreements and carefully examine the impact of past policies. It should open a dialogue with international governments and civil society organizations that are promoting alternatives. And rather than focusing on minor reforms to the existing trade model, the incoming Administration should build consensus around a broad development agenda that puts people and the environment first.

In recent years, there has been a flourishing of innovative proposals originating in the developing world. For example, in Asia, through the Chiang Mai Initiative, and in South America, through the Bank of the South, governments are cooperating to develop mechanisms for sharing regional financial resources. Several South American governments are also developing new approaches to trade and investment that emphasize respect for national sovereignty and cooperation rather than cut-throat competition. The incoming Administration should welcome input from these innovative policymakers as it works towards a cohesive U.S. development agenda.

A first step should be to renegotiate existing trade agreements, beginning with NAFTA. Bush Administration officials ignored widespread concerns over this 1994 trade pact, the basic blueprint for subsequent agreements. In fact, they actually expanded NAFTA's failed policies through a so-called "Security and Prosperity Partnership" with Mexico and Canada. Based on exclusive consultations with large corporations, the three governments chipped away at remaining restrictions on trade and investment through regulatory changes carried out without Congressional approval. For example, they weakened NAFTA's "rules of origin" to give products with a lower level of national content preferential tariff treatment, making products from third countries like China even more profitable and undercutting local producers.

New international economic rules should set a floor for basic labor and environmental standards, while also allowing governments sufficient policy space to pursue their own national economic strategies. This means allowing countries to use trade and investment restrictions to protect sensitive products, like staple foods, or to advance other social and environmental goals.

This broad new agenda should also include more effective international lending, debt and aid policies. Creating a more level playing field by lifting up our poorer economic partners would benefit us all.

The incoming President should call on the World Bank, IMF and other international financial institutions to discontinue their practice of imposing harmful economic policy conditions, such as demands to privatize water or other essential services, apply user fees on health care, and adopt labor market reforms that undermine workers. In the past two years, the UK and Norwegian governments have developed policies limiting these types of conditions.

The International Trade Union Confederation has documented how these institutions continue to undermine workers. In one of the most outrageous cases, the World Bank threatened to cut off budget support to King Gyanendra of Nepal in 2006 unless he decreed labor market deregulation. Gyanendra did as the World Bank ordered, only to see unions join the pro-democracy movement and overthrow his absolute rule. One of the democratic government's first acts was to annul the labor decree. In Iraq, the IMF in 2008 supported cuts in public rations and pension benefits. The World Bank is also continuing to fund fossil fuels, despite its purported commitment to combating climate change.

On debt, the Bush Administration took some positive steps by supporting debt relief for some of the poorest countries, mostly in Africa. However, the international financial institutions imposed onerous conditions on these countries and left out dozens of nations that desperately need to be freed from unrepayable debts. These impoverished countries should no longer need to pay debt service to wealthy nations and institutions at the expense of providing basic services to their citizens. The incoming Administration should support the call of Jubilee Campaigners to expand debt cancellation to more countries, without harmful conditions.

On aid, ActionAid reports that some 86 percent of U.S. foreign assistance is so ineffective in fighting poverty that they call it "phantom aid." This international development group charges that much of U.S. aid supports geo-strategic interests (e.g., Pakistan and Colombia), rather than poverty reduction. The U.S. government also continues to tie some aid to purchases of U.S. goods and services, which benefits U.S. corporations but lengthens delivery time and raises costs. The incoming Administration should end this scandalous "tying" of aid, de-politicize all assistance, focus on helping the poorest of the poor, and ensure full transparency and genuine consultation with affected citizens. It should also channel increasing amounts of aid through UN agencies, such as the International Fund for Agricultural Development and the World Food Programme.

Shutting Down the Global Financial Casino

The global financial turmoil sparked by the U.S. mortgage crisis reinforces the need for effective international regulation. And yet the body created to promote financial stability, the IMF, has an abysmal track record. In the late 1990s, the IMF contributed to the Asian financial crisis by promoting full and rapid capital account liberalization, and then deepened the crisis by conditioning emergency loans on harsh austerity measures.

Ten years later, IMF officials not only failed to foresee the current crisis (they even revised economic growth forecasts upwards two weeks before the crisis broke out), they also initially expressed confidence that markets alone would resolve it. Six months later, they reversed their position, supporting a coordinated fiscal stimulus led by rich countries. However, if the IMF limits its endorsement of anti-recession policies to only a select number of developed countries, this policy shift will be of limited impact.

Even more disturbing is the IMF's failure to develop a new international regulatory framework to prevent future crises. National regulators need to do their job too, but they can only go so far in controlling speculators whose borderless activities inflated the housing bubble that led to the current global economic slowdown.

The incoming Administration must urge the IMF to abandon its failed deregulatory policies and return to its original mission of stabilizing the international financial system. It should lead a process to establish an international currency transaction tax, targeting very short-term transactions, to discourage destabilizing speculation. It should support countries seeking to control "hot money" flows and those that require emergency assistance to overcome balance-of-payments problems. If the IMF proves incapable of change, the incoming U.S. Administration should work with other nations to develop alternatives.

Reining in Excessive Corporate Power

While institutions like the IMF and WTO and agreements like NAFTA have laid down the rules of the road for globalization, corporations have been the real drivers. And while global firms have received tremendous new rights and benefits under current policies, they face no new responsibilities. Even the Congressional Democrats' proposed labor rights enforcement mechanisms for new trade deals would apply only to governments, leaving corporate violators off the hook.

In recent years, pioneering lawyers have opened a legal avenue to end the impunity of U.S.-based corporations that commit human rights abuses abroad, using the once-obscure 1789 Alien Tort Claims Act (ATCA). Thus far, more than forty such cases have been brought in U.S. courts, but the corporate lobby and the Bush Administration have launched a major assault to undermine this legal tool.

The incoming Administration should allow human rights lawyers to continue to make use of this important strategy. At the same time, the Administration should work with other nations to begin developing an international mechanism to punish corporate criminals, following the precedent of the International Criminal Court. Initially, this court might focus on the most egregious corporate crimes, such as slave labor and the worst forms of child labor.

U.S. Worker and Consumer Protections

Labor rights abuses are not just a developing country problem. The current U.S. labor law system allows employers to use harsh intimidation tactics to thwart union organizing drives. The incoming Administration must champion labor law reforms to protect these basic rights. To ensure a healthy economy for the future, they must also invest in training and other benefits for jobless Americans and develop a robust program to create green jobs.

American consumers also need increased protections. Tainted products, from deadly dog food to toxic toys, have revealed the inadequacy of import controls. Today, less than 1 percent of non-meat food imports are inspected. It's hardly a surprise that China is the source of many of these tainted products, as trade rules have only encouraged that country to pursue a low-road development strategy. The Clinton Administration made no demands for human rights improvements in exchange for China's entry to the WTO. As a result, global corporations found a virtual paradise that offered low export barriers combined with a lack of basic labor rights and lax environmental and safety enforcement. U.S. workers and consumers are paying the price.

In today's world, the welfare of American workers is more than ever before linked to the welfare of those in impoverished countries. The worse things get for workers in China, Ghana or Nicaragua, the worse off we'll be here. We need someone in the White House who is a bold new internationalist, committed to rewriting the rules of the global economy to put the rights of all workers, communities, and the environment first.

Resources

AFL-CIO: http://www.aflcio.org/
Alliance for Responsible Trade: http://art-us.org/
Institute for Agriculture and Trade Policy: http://www.iatp.org/
International Forum on Globalization: http://www.ifg.org/
International Labor Rights Forum: http://www.laborrights.org/
International Trade Union Confederation: http://www.ituc-csi.org/
Jubilee USA: http://www.jubileeusa.org/
Public Citizen's Global Trade Watch: http://www.citizen.org/trade/

References

ActionAid. "Making Aid Accountable and Effective." 2008. http://www.
    actionaid.org/docs/making%20aid%20accountable%20and%20effective.pdf
    (accessed July 17, 2008).
Alliance for Responsible Trade, et al. "NAFTA Must Be Renegotiated: A
    Proposal from North American Civil Society Networks." March 2008.
    http://art-us.org/node/334 (accessed July 17, 2008).
Anderson, Sarah. "What the Next President Should Do About Globalization."
    New Labor Forum. Fall 2007.
Anderson, Sarah, et al. "Strategic Corporate Initiative." Corporate Ethics
    International, September 1, 2007. http://www.ips-dc.org/getfile.php?id=151
    (accessed July 17, 2008).

Broad, Robin, and John Cavanagh. *Development Redefined: How the Market Met Its Match*. Boulder: Paradigm Publishers, 2008.

Cavanagh, John, and Jerry Mander. *Alternatives to Economic Globalization: A Better World Is Possible*. San Francisco: Berrett-Koehler, 2004.

International Trade Union Confederation. "Renewed Financial Turbulence and Global Economic Slowdown Demand Major Policy Shifts by the IFIs." Statement by Global Unions to the 2008 Spring Meetings of the World Bank and International Monetary Fund (April 2008).

Chapter 40

Elements of a Just
International Climate Policy

Daphne Wysham and Janet Redman

POLICY PROPOSALS

■ Fully and constructively engage in negotiations for a post-2012 climate regime under the auspices of the United Nations Framework Convention on Climate Change.

■ Globalize a carbon- and nuclear-free, sustainable future beginning with the United States.

■ Establish an International Renewable Energy Agency.

■ Help advance a Clean Technology Bank accountable to the UN and independent of the World Bank.

■ Support a Climate Crisis and Adaptation Fund under UNFCCC auspices and overseen by developing countries.

■ Enact the UN Declaration on the Rights of Indigenous Peoples.

■ Target women's energy needs in developing countries.

■ Develop innovative financing mechanisms to generate revenue for taking just climate action.

* * * * * * * * * * * * *

The United States finds itself with an unparalleled opportunity to regain a leadership role in global climate negotiations under the incoming Administration. The integrity of an international climate deal in many ways is dependent on what binding commitment the United States is willing to make to reduce its carbon footprint, and whether that commitment is able to engender global trust that can be leveraged to bring developing countries to the table to negotiate actions that "measurably, reportably, and verifiably" reduce greenhouse gases.

The facts are clear: We have already passed the point at which dangerous, runaway climate change is a possibility. We now need to bring our global atmospheric concentrations of CO_2 from their current levels of 383 parts per million to 350 ppm, and quickly.

To be successful at meeting the reduction benchmarks called for by the scientific community, and in order to build global good will, any U.S. international climate policy must be, at its core, just. Climate justice is predicated on the notion that the disparate impacts of a shifting global climate, and the solutions proposed to address it, are centrally addressed in the architecture of domestic and international policies, programs and treaties. In order to move beyond rhetoric, U.S. climate policy must support, and be grounded in, the principles of participation, democratic resource allocation, historical responsibility, local innovation, and the right to self-determination.

Constructively Engage in the United Nations Framework Convention on Climate Change Process (UNFCCC)

The United States was until recently the world's leading greenhouse gas emitter. While our annual greenhouse gas emissions have recently been overtaken by China, we remain one of the countries with the highest per-capita emissions in the world—owing in large part to our energy use, transportation infrastructure and resource-intensive consumption patterns.

Cutting emissions domestically, and committing to binding targets internationally, is a key aspect of international climate policy actions. Given our historical and current contribution to rising greenhouse gas emissions, the United States should take a leadership role in pushing global emissions cuts of 20–30 percent below 1990 levels by 2020; and 80 percent below 1990 levels globally by 2050. This translates to between 90–95 percent cuts in the United States by 2050. It is incumbent upon the United States to commit to binding targets, regardless of reduction levels assumed by developing countries.

Globalize a Carbon- and Nuclear-Free, Sustainable Future

On July 17, 2008, former Vice President Al Gore gave a speech in which he urged the United States to source 100 percent of its electricity from renewable energy within ten years. Although his vision is perhaps the most ambitious of any high-level figure in the climate debate thus far, he is not alone in calling for a shift to a renewable future. U.S.-based scientist Dr. Arjun Makhijani released the book *Carbon Free and Nuclear-Free: A Roadmap for U.S. Energy Policy* in

June 2007, which sets forth a plan to reach national emissions levels of 95 percent below the 1990 benchmark by 2050. The roadmap outlines the elimination of fossil fuels and nuclear power from the entire U.S. energy sector—going beyond electricity to include industrial fuels, feedstocks, aircraft, non-electric home and commercial building heating, and fuel for combined heat and power.

Portions of this agenda could be globalized.[1] Makhijani also favors using microalgae to make liquid fuel alternatives to petroleum-based fuels. Microalgae can be created in bioreactors at existing coal-fired or other biomass-fired power plants. Similarly, the water hyacinth, a prolific aquatic plant, could serve a dual purpose of wastewater treatment and energy production.

Makhijani also lays out an ambitious agenda for solar electricity, wind and other clean energy supply technologies, as well as energy efficiency approaches available now to help the United States exceed the targets necessary to stabilize the climate. In the United States, parking lot and commercial rooftop areas are large enough to supply most of its electricity requirements from solar power. What is unique about these ideas is that they allow the United States to reach parity with large developing economies in terms of per capita greenhouse gas emissions, a key demand of heavily populated developing countries. These ideas could be further developed for international deployment.

Establish an International Renewable Energy Agency

Congressman Ed Markey (D-MA), chair of the House Select Committee on Energy Independence and Global Warming, has introduced legislation calling for the establishment of an International Renewable Energy Agency (IRENA). Germany and other countries are also eagerly pushing for an IRENA (see www.irena.org).

Currently, the International Atomic Energy Agency (IAEA) in Vienna is the only special energy agency of the United Nations, but this agency is ill-suited to manage a transition to a clean energy future. Similarly ill-suited to the task is the International Energy Agency, created in the aftermath of the first Organization of the Petroleum Exporting Countries (OPEC) oil crisis; the IEA is accountable only to Organization for Economic Cooperation and Development (OECD) countries, and largely focused on managing fossil fuel energy resources.

The basic electricity needs of 1 billion people could be covered with a generating capacity of 56 gigawatts.[2] A program to create 56 gigawatts of capacity with low- or no-carbon technologies (including capacity building) would cost an estimated $100 billion.[3] In comparison, the world-wide subsidies for conventional sources of energy (particularly fossil fuels) are estimated to amount to at least $150–250 billion per year.[4] The IRENA could work to ensure that member states' subsidies to dirty, unsustainable energy were identified and phased out, with the exception of those subsidies targeted at low-income persons, and redirected toward sustainable forms of energy.[5]

The IRENA could also assist in implementing an "oil, gas and coal deple-tion protocol." Such a protocol, similar to that proposed by petroleum geologist Dr. Colin Campbell,[6] Dr. Richard Heinberg and others, would encourage all countries to more accurately assess their fossil fuel reserves as well as their im-ports and exports, and more transparently manage their steady reduction in con-sumption, imports and exports by at least the world depletion rate, in order to avoid the economic shocks due to the "peaking" and collapse of these markets.

Help Advance a Clean Technology Bank Accountable to the UN and Independent of the World Bank

A Clean Technology Bank, charged with the task of coordinating project and policy financing by enhancing capital sourcing from all possible investors and lenders for sustainable energy and transportation, is urgently needed. Currently, lenders such as the World Bank Group and export credit agencies, private sector banks, foundations, donors and governments are trying without success to re-spond to the climate and energy crisis in developing countries—often funding "slightly less dirty" technologies in the name of incremental emissions reduc-tions.

Parties to the UN Framework Convention on Climate Change, of which the United States is one, have an obligation to provide "measurable, reportable and verifiable" support to developing countries to lower their emissions. As develop-ing countries have stipulated, any clean technology funding falling outside the authority of the Convention will not meet this obligation. Thus, such a bank must be created under the authority of, and accountable to, the UNFCCC.

A Clean Technology Bank is not a new idea. Created in 1992 at the Rio Earth Summit, the Global Environmental Facility comes closest to this concept. Charged with managing the financial mechanism for the international conven-tions on biodiversity, climate change, persistent organic pollutants and desertifi-cation, the GEF is a repository for clean energy funds. However, the GEF is not singular in its focus, and perhaps better tasked with the charge of financing the other environmental conventions.

A Clean Technology Bank should provide financing for transformational energy projects—not necessarily on a large scale, but technologies that move developing, as well as developed, countries away from dependence on fossil fuel energy. Funding should be in the form of grants or concessional micro-loans that prioritize bringing down the price of clean technologies to equal or lower than that of dirty technologies, so as to encourage developing countries to embrace a clean development path without putting themselves at an economic disadvan-tage.

Where appropriate, micro-loans and grants could be coupled with technological capacity-building to ensure that recipients of clean energy and transportation technologies become self-reliant in maintaining and repairing infrastructure.[7] Emphasis should be given to building in-country expertise in developing and deploying locally or regionally appropriate clean energy and energy-efficient technologies.

Patents should not be a barrier to clean technology transfer. Among other items, clean technology financing should help pay for technology transfer to technology developers. Additionally, the agreement reached at the Doha Round of the World Trade Organization that poor countries should have the right to waive or override patents to produce and import generic medicines should be applied to the production and import of affordable, clean, renewable technologies to mitigate greenhouse gas emissions and climate change—a multifaceted threat to global public health.

Support a Climate Crisis and Adaptation Fund under UNFCCC Auspices and Overseen by Developing Countries

Communities in the developing world are already feeling the impacts of climate change—a problem they did little to create, but for which they will shoulder a disproportionate burden. Estimates of the cost to developing countries for adapting to climate change impacts range from $50–100 billion per year. A just international climate policy should acknowledge the disproportionate role of the United States in causing the climate crisis by supporting a Climate Crisis and Adaptation Fund to manage financial flows for response to crises—such as Cyclone Nargis—and adaptation to the known impacts of climate change and long-term resilience for facing unforeseeable consequences.

Like clean energy and transportation funding, financing for adaptation should fall under the auspices of the UNFCCC, with representation on governing bodies that reflects the composition of the Parties to the Convention. Funds should be disbursed as grants. Loans would exacerbate indebtedness, rendering developing countries less able to deal with climate-related disasters. Climate Crisis and Adaptation Funds should support local solutions to climate change impacts, taking into account the importance of land rights, sovereign food and energy systems, conservation and localization, and emphasizing decentralized funding. Adaptation funding must be additional to current levels of foreign assistance. To show leadership in addressing the impacts of climate change internationally, the United States should provide at least a proportion of funding equal to its greenhouse gas emissions, or at least $25 billion a year.[8]

Enact the UN Declaration on the Rights of Indigenous Peoples

Up to a fifth of global greenhouse gas emissions come from deforestation in tropical regions,[9] most of which is cleared for agriculture, timber and, ironically, large-scale biofuel plantations. Much of the world's remaining forests are inhabited by indigenous peoples who have developed knowledge over generations specifically attuned to forests in which they live.

U.S. enactment of the UN Declaration on the Rights of Indigenous Peoples (UNDRIP) would put pressure on governments to take their commitment to uphold the rights of indigenous peoples seriously. Perhaps most pertinent in terms of avoiding deforestation, the UNDRIP calls for the recognition and protection of customary and collective land rights. Granting indigenous land rights in tropical countries would give indigenous peoples, long stewards of sustainable co-existence with forests, greater resources and legal protection when fighting illegal clearing and incursions into standing forest.

U.S. implementation of the UNDRIP would also help hold any institution proposing development activities that would affect indigenous communities to the principle of "free, prior and informed consent." This is critical to ensuring that indigenous peoples can block dirty energy projects, large-scale forest clearing and other climate-threatening activities. The UNDRIP also opens political space for the recognition of indigenous knowledge and the role it can serve in developing low-carbon, small-scale adaptation techniques.

Target Women's Energy Needs in Developing Countries

So-called "survival" emissions are often the result of fuel burned in developing countries for cooking and heating. In virtually every developing country the task of gathering these energy resources largely falls on women. As cooking fuel becomes more limited, women are investing more time and caloric energy gathering increasingly scarce fuel. This has consequences for both their health and the health of their children who end up accompanying them on long hunts for fuel or breathing smoke from indoor fires.

Empowering women, on the other hand, with sustainable energy resources would accomplish multiple goals. It would provide them with more time and energy for their families, which has multiple potential dividends, including income-generating opportunities. It would improve their health and that of their children, by making their indoor air less polluted. And it would allow the forest cover to regenerate itself.

Develop Innovative Financing Mechanisms that Generate Revenue for Taking Just Climate Action

The revenue required to make a dent in the more than $8 trillion needed by 2030 for developing countries' energy infrastructure development is massive. Where clean energy, transport, or other climate-related technology loans are required, the Clean Technology Bank could provide the financing. In addition, current energy lending originating with international financial institutions, export credit agencies and other public institutions targeted at fossil fuels should be halted. Where grants are required, the Clean Technology Bank could oversee this as well. However, where revenue for these grants would come from remains an open question.

A variety of sources of revenue could be marshaled for these tasks. Among the possibilities:

- A share of the revenue generated under any sort of cap and auction scheme and/or carbon tax that is developed in the United States (and elsewhere).
- A border carbon fee.
- A tax on international currency transactions, arms trades, or oil trades;
- Debt relief;
- An increase in overall Overseas Development Assistance (ODA).

Conclusion

The United States could spearhead a global transition to clean energy which would in turn help build new economic drivers both in the United States and in the developing world to offset the drain on the global economy that volatile oil prices now impose. Impoverished countries, less vulnerable to the rising debt from rising non-renewable energy prices, could become strengthened trading partners. Clean energy policies could help jump-start the renewable energy industry into a new and major engine of growth for the global economy. These changes could lead to a new era of global peace, cooperation and progress. But bold leadership, taken swiftly, is absolutely critical in achieving these goals.

Resources

Carbon Trade Watch: http://www.carbontradewatch.org/
"Carbon Trading, Climate Justice and the Production of Ignorance: Ten Examples" by Larry Lohmann, The Corner House: http://www.the corner-house.org.uk/summary.shtml?x=561681

ENERGIA, International Network on Gender and Sustainable Energy: http://www.energia.org/

Institute for Energy and Environmental Research: http://www.ieer.org/carbon free/index.html

"Preparatory Conference for the Foundation of the International Renewable Energy Agency (IRENA)": www.irena.org

Sustainable Energy and Economy Network: www.ips-dc.org/seen

United Nations Declaration on the Rights of Indigenous Peoples: http://www.un. org/esa/socdev/unpfii/en/declaration.html

United Nations Framework Convention on Climate Change: http://unfccc.int/ 2860.php

References

Hansen, James. "Target Atmospheric CO2: Where Should Humanity Aim?" *Open Atmospheric Science Journal.* 2008.

Notes

1. Arjun Makhijani, "Carbon-Free and Nuclear-Free: A Roadmap for U.S. Energy Policy," Nuclear Policy Research Institute and the Institute for Energy and Environmental Research, July 2007, http://www.ieer.org/carbonfree/summary.pdf (accessed July 20, 2008).

2. See William Fulkerson, et al., "Sustainable, Efficient Electricity Service for One Billion People," *Energy for Sustainable Development*, June 2005, pp. 26–34 and 31.

3. Ibid.

4. See REN 21, Renewables 2005, p. 16

5. See the statute put forth: The International Sustainable Energy Agency, http:// www.abolition2000.org/atf/cf/%7B23F7F2AE-CC10-4D6F-9BF8- 09CF86F1AB46%7D/ISEA.PDF (accessed July 20, 2008).

6. See http://www.oildepletionprotocol.org/theprotocol (accessed July 20, 2008), also known as the "The Rimini Protocol" and "The Uppsala Protocol."

7. The Renewable Energy Task Force of the G-8 produced a report in 2001 which found that renewable energy could be provided to 1 billion people by grants and loans by 2010. This overview could help inform the financial mechanisms for the Clean Energy Bank.

8. Friends of the Earth US, "International Adaptation to Climate Change."

9. Smita Nakhooda, "Correcting the World's Greatest Market Failure: Climate Change and the Multilateral Development Banks," World Resources Institute, http://pdf.wri.org/correcting_the_worlds_greatest_market_failure.pdf (accessed July 20, 2008).

Chapter 41

Immigration and Migration Policies for a Sustainable Future

Oscar Chacón and Amy Shannon

POLICY PROPOSALS

■ Substantially elevate the social and economic standards of living in migrant-sending countries.

■ Modify the trade and development policies the United States has pursued in Latin America.

■ Immediately halt all immigration-related workplace and residential raids.

■ Grant people residing in the United States without proper authorization the right to become legal permanent residents and open the pathway to pursue future U.S. citizenship.

■ Fast-track to permanent residency every relative of a U.S. citizen or a legal permanent resident who has been waiting more than a year for their visas.

■ Create a national immigrant integration program.

■ Create a foreign worker program to match available workers outside the United States with U.S. labor market needs.

■ Strengthen humanitarian protection programs for refugees and asylum seekers.

■ Establish minimum standards of treatment for migrants in sending, receiving and transit countries.

* * * * * * * * * * * * * *

Immigrant populations represent an invaluable asset for the United States of America, bringing an unparalleled cultural richness and economic agility. Unfortunately, political forces motivated by racist and xenophobic hate have man-

aged to dominate the political and legislative debate on immigrants and immigration policy. Since the early 1990s, these forces have succeeded in creating a
perception of today's immigrants as a political, economic, social and cultural
threat to the nation. Consequently, public attitudes about immigrants, as well as
policy changes that have occurred since at least 1996, have centered around a
punitive approach towards immigrants, as well as a restrictive approach towards
immigration. Neither of these strategies is leading our nation to desirable outcomes. Nor are they equipping the country with the best policy solutions to rec-
oncile our social, economic and political interests at the nexus between migration and the nation's future.

A quick review of our history can help us understand how we got to this
point. It turns out that fears about newcomers to America are as old as the nation
itself. At many points in our history, politicians and opinion leaders have raised
concerns about new arrivals, in particular those who didn't speak English, had
"foreign" cultural practices, hailed from an "inferior" country or practiced a
"strange" religion. This pattern of xenophobia, or fear and prejudice against foreigners, has been directed at Germans, Italians, Irish, Asians and, more recently,
at Latin Americans, as the country experienced successive waves of immigration.

In addition to xenophobia, we also have a troublesome history when it
comes to issues of race. This history dates from prior to the formation of our
nation, when European immigrants managed to decimate the indigenous populations that inhabited North America. That sad trend continued when slave traders
first began bringing people of African origin to the New World as slaves. The
legacy of slavery, and its accompanying ideology of white supremacy over other
races, has cast a long shadow over the way in which we have dealt with immigrants throughout our history.

However, the undercurrents of today's highly charged and polarized national policy debate over immigration cannot be reduced neatly to racism and
xenophobia. Another key factor that has come into play in recent years is the
pattern of increasing socio-economic inequities in American society.

Put simply, many working people find it increasingly difficult to keep up
the middle-class lifestyle that their parents took for granted. The trend is a sobering one: 50 million people in the United States lack health insurance; hundreds
of thousands have seen retirement benefits withdrawn or curtailed; tens of thousands of well-paying manufacturing or technology jobs have vanished in just the
past few years. A growing segment of U.S. society has failed to participate in
the long-term overall growth that our economy has enjoyed over the past three
decades. The deep sense of insecurity, fear and confusion caused by these
changes leaves many people looking for someone to blame. Unfortunately, foreigners have proven easy targets.

Objectively, the foreign-born population residing in the United States bears
little responsibility for the economic policies that are causing millions of middle-class American families so much anxiety. In fact, many immigrants found

themselves obliged to leave their homes due to the same policies that contribute to an ever more unfair distribution of wealth in their countries of origin, as well as in the United States. But the facts have not stopped those who find it convenient to blame immigrants for the ills of globalization. Politicians from both parties have found immigrants to be a convenient scapegoat for policy failures they would prefer their constituencies not to examine too carefully.

In spite of the reality that migration does not begin when people arrive to our borders, we have failed so far to incorporate a new course of action when it comes to the international economic, social, cultural and political factors that play critical roles in determining the dynamics of migration in today's global reality. If we are truly to transcend our failed policy solutions of the past, we must dare to go beyond questions of what immigration status we grant foreigners once they are already here, and begin to address the factors that have kept pushing so many people out of their own countries in search for a better quality of life.

In the global economic landscape in which most of the peoples around the world live today, migration will continue to be part of our reality, as it is embedded in the very nature of the increasingly interdependent global economic system. The real question is not how to put an end to migration, but how to manage it in a humane manner that justly serves everyone's interests.

To craft a brand new policy framework to handle immigration is no easy task. For all practical purposes, we continue to approach immigration reform by mending a policy architecture first put in place in 1965. A lot of things have changed since then. The fact that at least 10 million foreign-born human beings in the United States of America find themselves living, working, paying taxes, and contributing to the progress and well-being of the nation, but lacking permanent residency status or the condition of naturalized citizens, represents a major failure in our ability to modernize our immigration law and to bring it into sync with our times.

One of the major factors that stymies our efforts to reform the ancient policy architecture around immigration has been our decision to ignore the forces driving so many people to emigrate from their respective countries. In 1986, the last time we tried to solve the issue of the "out of status" foreign-born population, neither Congress nor activists were willing to tackle the thorny question of root causes of migration. In recent political debates about immigration, we continue to avoid this question, often with facile assurances about the benefits of free trade. The sad truth remains: As long as we keep pretending that we will reduce migration by militarizing our borders and threatening even more Gestapo-like interior enforcement, we will continue to move farther away from sensible and equitable policies.

The best way to bring equilibrium between economic demands for foreign-born workers and legitimate demands for a better quality of life for people in the United States as well as in our neighboring countries, will be to tackle migration in a two-pronged manner: First, we must develop a more realistic immigration policy that recognizes the primarily positive nature of migrants and migration and, consequently, embraces immigrants as an asset for the progress and well-being of the United States of America. Second, we should develop and promote an international economic policy model that emphasizes social investments and human development, particularly in the nations known to be the largest sources of U.S.-bound migrants, and makes a major investment in the development and consolidation of micro, small and medium-sized rural and urban enterprises.

What we need now is a real exercise in democratic accountability. Missing from the national debate are the wise and practical, solution-oriented voices of local elected officials, businesspersons, religious leaders, immigrant community leaders, law enforcement officers and others who truly care about these matters and who are often misrepresented by those who claim to speak for them. A real solution to our nation's challenges when it comes to immigrants and immigration policy requires us to go beyond the surface.

Substantially Elevate the Social and Economic Standards of Living in Migrant-Sending Countries

In order to address the root causes of migration, we must engage in a thorough revamping of our economic and development policies, with the urgent goal of substantially elevating social and economic standards of living in migrant-sending countries. Economic policies in place since at least the mid-1980s have proven to be a dismal failure in achieving these goals. Unless we significantly reduce the current asymmetries between the United States and its neighbors in the South, not even the most generous immigration policy will provide lasting solutions.

Modify the Trade and Development Policies the United States Has Pursued in Latin America

Current policies have largely failed to lift the majority of people out of poverty and have deepened economic inequality in the region. Instead of moving forward with more ill-conceived trade agreements, American development assistance policies should support strengthening local economies and laying the groundwork for long-term, sustainable development. The collapse of rural economies is one factor driving people to migrate. Given the importance of local agricultural production in the livelihood of many Latin Americans, we should give priority to building strong local and regional markets and to environmental sustainability by revising American subsidies to agricultural production.

Immediately Halt All Immigration-Related Workplace and Residential Raids

As a transitional measure on the way to truly humane and visionary immigration policy reform, the incoming U.S. President should immediately halt all immigration-related workplace and residential raids, as well as the deportation of all immigrants whose only crime is to have been residing and/or working in the United States without immigration status.

Create Pathways to Legal Permanent Residency and Citizenship

The incoming President should then work with Congress to grant the opportunity to people who are residing in the United States without the proper authorization to become legal permanent residents, and open up the pathway for them to pursue U.S. citizenship in the future. Anyone who, having been given this opportunity, decides to remain outside the margin of the law, should be identified, investigated and if proven to be a threat, deported from the United States.

Fast-Track to Permanent Residency Every Relative of a U.S. Citizen or a Legal Permanent Resident Who Has Been Waiting More than a Year

In the future, a maximum six-month limit should be mandatory for all immigration benefits applications. Family unity should remain a central consideration in our overall immigration policy. We must correct, once and for all, the long, painful waiting periods that break up immigrant families.

Create a National Immigrant Integration Program

A national immigrant integration program should be created with the purpose of supporting immigrants and local communities to fully integrate newcomers harmoniously into the social, economic, cultural and political fabric of our nation. Such a program should go far beyond the current assimilationist rhetoric that emphasizes, almost exclusively, English-language learning. To be truly successful, an integration program should include efforts to stimulate local dialogue and cultural exchange, civic participation programs, youth programs—including efforts to increase educational success—and workforce development programs that would benefit both immigrants and U.S.-born workers.

Create a Foreign Worker Program to Match Available Workers outside the United States with U.S. Labor Market Needs

A temporary guest worker program should not be the keystone of immigration reform. However, if after enacting the above reforms, the economy continues to need workers, a foreign worker program should be created, intended to match available workers outside the United States with the needs of the U.S. labor market. Such a program should enable foreign workers to come in with equal labor rights to those of U.S. citizens and residents. If within a reasonable period of time, a worker has maintained good standing under this program and wishes to remain in the United States, there should be a pathway for pursuing legal permanent residency and citizenship. Given the horrible abuses by private recruiters for temporary workers in recent years, the practice of outsourcing temporary worker recruitment should be ceased. Any temporary worker program should be administered directly by the sending and receiving governments.

Strengthen Humanitarian Protection Programs for Refugees and Asylum Seekers

Humanitarian protection programs for refugees and asylum seekers should be strengthened in line with the highest international standards. The United States must reclaim its role as a beacon of hope for those requiring humanitarian protection.

Establish Minimum Standards of Treatment for Migrants in Sending, Receiving and Transit Countries

Because all the countries of our hemisphere are now experiencing migration in ever more complicated dynamics, we should work across borders to establish minimum standards of treatment for migrants in sending, receiving and transit countries. These standards should be based on the principles of respect for human rights and human dignity. Migration should be decriminalized in all countries as a first step toward reducing the extreme vulnerability of migrants to exploitation and abuse.

Current immigration policies, patched together in a piecemeal basis over the past two decades, are increasingly proving inadequate for advancing the best interests of the nation. In both the short and long terms, it would be more effective and humane to embrace a new comprehensive set of migration and development policies that respond to current challenges and will equip our nation with the human resources to be successful into the next century. Migration is not a phenomenon exclusively affecting the United States of America. It is a challenge for many nations around the world. As a nation that prides itself on being a nation of immigrants, we have an opportunity to design a coherent set of best practices that can serve as a model for other nations.

Policy proposals like these are the best means to ensure the national security of the United States in a way that is humane, efficient and effective. However, in order for this to happen, the American people need to take back this debate from those who want us to embrace fear and hate as the way of the future. This proud nation of immigrants needs its citizens to reclaim the best traditions of our nation and to build a better America for all.

Will the incoming President have the will to provide leadership on this issue? Both parties have trended toward a downward spiral on immigration issues. The national political and legislative debate has degenerated to the point where all manner of nastiness toward immigrants is fair game. In the face of the economic downturn brewing over the past decade or so, which has become very obvious over the past year with the financial crisis, there is an imminent danger to sink even lower in the trap of blaming foreigners for the hardships affecting us all. Recent events in South Africa have warned the entire world about the dangers of letting blind xenophobic prejudice go unchecked, especially in a time of growing economic insecurity for most people. Given how complex our national debate on immigrants and immigration has become, it will be imperative for the incoming President to provide economically and morally sound leadership on how best to resolve this public policy challenge.

Resources

Americas Program: http://americas.irc-online.org/
First Latin American Migrant Community Summit: www.cumbrede.migrantes. org
International Network on Migration and Development: www.migracionydesar-rollo.org
National Alliance of Latin American and Caribbean Communities: http://www. nalacc.org.

References

Anderson, Sarah, Oscar Chacón, and Amy Shannon. "Inviting Immigrants Out of the Shadow." *Yes Magazine* (Summer 2006). http://www.yesmagazine. org/article.asp?ID=1455 (access-ed July 16 2008).

Castles, Steven, and Raul Delgado Wise. *Migracion y Desarrollo: Perspectivas desde el Sur.* Mexico City: Miguel Angel Porrua, 2007.

Hing, Bill Ong. *Defining America Through Immigration Policy.* Philadelphia: Temple University Press, 2004.

Ngai, Mae M. *Impossible Subjects: Illegal Aliens and the Making of Modern America.* Princeton: Princeton University Press, 2004.

Chapter 42

U.S. Policy toward Africa: Advancing a Twenty-first Century Vision

Emira Woods, Nicole Lee and Gerald LeMelle

POLICY PROPOSALS

- Redefine U.S. Africa policy, giving primacy to human rights, poverty reduction and civilian oversight.
- Work proactively to scale back to cessation U.S. military operations on the continent of Africa not specifically mandated by the UN and support multilateralism, regionalism and cooperative action as the solution to the problems of human security in Africa.
- Resist the expansion of the U.S. War on Terror and hyper-militarism to Africa; instead, adopt a global human security framework as a basis for assessing the national security of the United States.
- Advance economic justice and a green economy for Africa.

* * * * * * * * * * * * * * *

The incoming President of the United States will have an opportunity to turn the page on decades of flawed policies and usher in a new era of U.S. engagement with Africa, based on mutual respect and mutual benefit. Bold actions are needed to demilitarize U.S. Africa policy, advance human rights and propel Africa into a global green economy.

The United States has a long, checkered history in Africa. It is a past defined largely by support for colonial governments and reprehensible regimes like the Apartheid tyrants in Southern Africa. While these regimes have fallen, failed twentieth century policies remain the cornerstone of U.S.-Africa engagement well into the twenty-first century. The United States government continues to prop up "friendly" dictators; promote disastrous and impoverishing IMF/World

Bank policies; and prioritize corporate access to the continent's vast resources, particularly oil, over the needs of the African people. The United States remains the largest supplier of arms to Africa, and defense/security dominates the U.S. foreign policy toolkit in Africa, as elsewhere. The democratic development and consolidation African countries experienced during the 1990s and early 2000s has been slowed, even reversed in some cases, by this misguided U.S. foreign policy framework. So far, six African leaders who have strongly cooperated with U.S. counter-terrorism programs have maneuvered to stay in power against the democratic will of their people, by either changing or ignoring their national constitutions and routinely using violence. In each instance, the U.S. government not only failed to directly criticize the leader's actions, but also quickly endorsed their new and illegitimate term.

The Bush Administration has resisted making human rights a centerpiece of U.S. foreign policy. The result has been a blind eye or active support for multiple "friendly" African government initiatives that have resulted in massive numbers of deaths, internal displacements and governance failures. Human rights considerations in U.S. foreign policy would have mandated a comprehensive plan for human security, building the infrastructure for healthy communities—food, shelter, education, jobs health care and peace. Instead, U.S. policy has focused primarily on arming and training national militaries without regard to human rights safeguards. These armies in turn operate with impunity. The Leahy provision, included in every annual Foreign Operations Appropriations bill since 1997, is designed to prohibit U.S. military assistance to foreign military units that violate human rights, yet today it is rarely mentioned, let alone followed. In 2007, close to half of the people displaced world-wide by conflict were in Africa, spread across twenty countries. The numbers are staggering. UNHCR estimates that there are an estimated 12 million people internally displaced and over 2 million refugees strewn across the continent. Despite these historic humanitarian challenges, the Bush Administration continues its callous prioritization of access to resources and counter-terrorism programs, instead of addressing human needs on the continent.

The incoming Administration must make human rights an unconditional priority of U.S.-Africa policy, not just because of the moral imperative to do so, but because human rights are an essential part of a smart, just global and national security framework. It is often the case that international human rights standards are the only thing standing between militias with guns, including ones the United States has trained, and innocent men, women and children. The Bush Administration has invested billions of dollars in arming, training and, most blatantly in the case of Ethiopia, encouraging Africans to fight what are often proxy battles. History shows this is a failed approach. In the past, support for the perceived geo-strategic allies *du jour* without a human rights standard has created devastating enemies for the United States, such as Osama Bin Laden, the Taliban and Saddam Hussein. Was the world really made safer by the crimes and legacies of U.S. clients like the Apartheid regime in South Africa, Liberia's Samuel Doe and/or Zaire's Mobutu Sese Seko?

The incoming Administration must be resolute in its support for the rights of African people to choose their leaders and hold them accountable. Today, President Bush rarely mentions democracy in Africa, and in fact suggests that African interests are best protected by "strong leadership," a veiled return to the racist historical view that African societies are incompatible with any form of democracy and can only be ruled by force. The incoming President must support organic African democracy by promoting the right of African people to decide their own definition of what strong leadership is and whether that standard is being met.

The incoming Administration must change the perception that American people and their government ignore the negative impact of U.S. policies on Africans. The incoming President can advance a concerted and sincere effort to bolster and empower African civil society groups by consistently consulting them and acknowledging their analysis and recommendations prior to embarking on U.S. or U.S.-led multilateral initiatives. The 1990s saw an explosion of civil society groups across the continent, raising an honest and empowering voice for the real concerns of African people. These voices are not heard in the echo chambers of Washington defense- and intelligence-driven policy circles. Yet the fact remains that African civil society is best positioned to speak to the impacts of U.S. actions on ordinary Africans. The U.S. government must support ways to get African civil society perspectives in foreign policy discourse and decision-making.

The incoming Administration must engage the African Union regarding its policies, strategies and long-term vision for the continent. At a political level, the interests of African people are well served by strengthening the capacity of collective bodies like the African Union (AU), the Southern African Development Community, the Economic Community of West African States, the East African Community and the Northern African Community of Sahel-Saharan States. Africa's challenges are rarely constrained by the colonial constructions that are political boundaries—this same logic applies to solutions. Regional organizations must be engaged and equipped by the United States and the broader international community to mature as effective, transparent agents of peacebuilding, conflict resolution and economic empowerment for the African people—as mechanisms of defense for human rights. The current trajectory of prioritizing bilateral relations that facilitate military cooperation or unfettered trading access to African resources over multilateral regional engagement does not accomplish these goals, and in certain instances continues to bolster antidemocratic forces.

Essential to the Bush Administration's strategy to ensure U.S. security and economic interests is the further shift of U.S government interests to the dominance of the Department of Defense. Through this lens, economic and neoliberal ideological interests are dressed up in a national security package that often ignores human needs. In fact, the U.S. "war on terror" has exacerbated conflicts and deepened humanitarian and human rights crises in the Sudan, Somalia, the Democratic Republic of the Congo and elsewhere on the continent.

The situation is complicated by a historic pattern of U.S. military aggression and a long record of problematic and unjustified military interventions in Africa, despite our unwillingness to act to save African lives when it is not in U.S. "strategic" interests. This dichotomy has led many to mistrust U.S. military intentions in Africa.

In spite of this mistrust, the Bush Administration plans to stand up a new Unified Command, the Africa Command, or AFRICOM. Touted as an "administrative solution to an administrative problem," neo-cons as early as 2000 saw a unified command as a way to extend U.S. government and corporate interests on the continent in order to surpass the holdings of European and Asian countries. AFRICOM will be operational as a stand-alone command less than four months before the incoming U.S. Administration takes office.

The incoming Administration must heed the call of democratic African leaders and civil society that security in their respective countries can only be achieved by sustainable economic development and indigenous democracy. There will be many opportunities for the Administration to provide support and cooperation in these endeavors. Support of the AU in peace-keeping operations is vital to the long-term interests of regional cooperation within the continent. Presently, the AU has taken on peace-keeping missions in Darfur and Somalia. Consistent U.S. support, not just rhetoric, is necessary to ensure the continued growth of the AU's capacity to take on the human security concerns in Africa. Trade rules that are fair and just, development assistance and respect for sovereignty are important benchmarks for a good relationship. These measures would encourage positive governance and democratic economic development. Expanding the U.S. military onto the continent will not.

Despite the claims, as reported on the U.S. Africa Command Transition Team website, that AFRICOM's "foremost mission is to help Africans achieve their own security, not to extend the scope of the war on terrorism or secure African resources," U.S. interests have always been, in relation to the African continent, about security of resources. Early in 2007, Nigeria surpassed Saudi Arabia as the largest supplier of oil to the United States. The United States currently imports more oil from the African continent than from the entire Persian Gulf. The African continent has also risen in importance as a key theatre to fight the U.S. government's Global War on Terror. These changes in U.S. energy and foreign policies position the African continent in a place of greater public and strategic importance, and largely set the stage for the creation of the new combat command for Africa, AFRICOM.

Theresa Whelan, the Assistant Secretary for Defense, writing in an August, 2007 Institute for Security Studies report, argued that Africa "possesses 8 percent of the world's petroleum; and it is a major source of critical minerals, precious metals and food commodities." This sentiment is coupled with the reality that the United States is nervous about Chinese economic penetration into the African continent; currently, there are an estimated 750 Chinese companies operating in fifty countries on the continent. Many of these investments are in the form of debt relief, grants, soft loans and buyer credits to African countries, without economic structural adjustment demands or human rights overtures. Thus, the competition for Africa's resources wage on, now with additional opponents. The impending resource conflicts will, without a doubt, cloud any efforts at real African-centered soft diplomacy engagement.

Through this lens, once again, U.S. policy attempts to carve up Africa into fiefdoms based on resources and strategic positioning. History has shown us this is a losing battle for the stability of African nations, as it destabilizes democracies and takes the decision-making power out of the hands of civil society. The incoming Administration must learn from the past and be prepared to work in partnership with the African Union and African governments and communities, supporting indigenous rights to resources and fair trade relationships.

Since the beginning of the Iraq War, President Bush has funneled over $1 trillion through the Department of Defense. Little known, however, is that, increasingly, Defense Department funding also includes monies for economic development, also known as foreign assistance programs. The Administration is progressively placing more funding for humanitarian and diplomatic efforts, typically State Department functions, into the hands of the Pentagon. In Africa, AFRICOM has provided the newest vehicle for this inter-agency collusion.

Like in the Middle East, U.S. military presence in Africa has meant reliance on military contractors. The result has been disjointed coordination, fragile chains of command for armed personnel and impunity from crimes committed in the country. Many military contractors are anticipating new significant contracts in Africa due to the new Africa Command.

The impact of a hyper-militaristic foreign policy is that basic human security has decreased. An honest assessment of the global human security status is vital to assessing U.S. national security. The United States must not continue to play a duplicitous role in Africa, but instead acknowledge that human need breeds human and national insecurity.

From Sudan to Chad to the DRC, Africa is home to conflicts where sovereign states have failed to protect or are actively violating the human rights of their populations, and the international community must honor its responsibility to protect civilians. Yet history shows us unequivocally that unilateral intervention—real or purported humanitarian intent notwithstanding—is ineffective and illegitimate. The incoming President of the United States can bolster UN and AU peace-keeping efforts to protect innocent civilians, internally displaced people and refugees. The United States owes an estimated $668 million in arrears for UN peace-keeping. To date, the United States has refused to provide the necessary support for the Mission de l' Organisation des Nations Unies en République Démocratique du Congo (MONUC); has allowed "war on terror" ties to compromise pressure on the government of Sudan to stop obstructing the deployment of the 26,000-person strong United Nations/African Union hybrid peace-keeping operation for Darfur; and woefully underfunded the African Union Mission to Somalia (AMISOM), which is largely in Somalia to help clean up the damage the United States had a huge hand in producing.

A demilitarized U.S. Africa policy must be combined with a comprehensive, bold package on debt, trade and development finance that can propel Africa into the twenty-first century global green economy.

According to the UN Economic Commission for Africa, only 55 percent of people living in Sub-Saharan Africa have access to clean drinking water. Illiteracy and infant mortality rates are highest in the world. UNICEF's report, "The State of Africa's Children 2008," reminds us that Africa is the only continent that has seen rising numbers of deaths among children under five years old since the 1970s. Although Africa accounts for only 22 percent of births globally, half of the 10 million child deaths annually occur on the continent.

Despite these grim statistics, Africa has entered the twenty-first century in a position of heightened importance. Africa's strategic resources are the lynchpin of a global economy racing towards nanotechnology and other advances in information technology. Without the coltane that comes from the heart of Africa, cellphones and state-of-the-art computers could not be produced. Africa's oil is steadily surpassing the Middle East in the world market. A full 24 percent of U.S. oil comes from Africa, up from 12 percent in the last five years alone. Uranium, diamonds, gold—the list of Africa's resources vital to the world economy is long. However, commodity pricing, local dealmakers and irresponsible global firms have meant that Africa's strategic resources have not benefited its people or created sustainable economies on the continent.

The incoming U.S. President can reverse decades of exploitative trade by creative new measures that redirect the resources of the continent for development finance. According to a new report by the Political Economy Research Institute, "Since the mid-1970s, Africa has lost some $420 billion in capital flight." The UN reminds us that current trade rules are rigged in favor of powerful countries and their corporations, costing developing countries $700 billion a year. Creative instruments are needed to ensure that the resources of Africa benefit her people, foster healthy communities and build twenty-first century economies throughout the region.

One bold effort that could bring U.S. leadership is the Global Fund for Africa's Green Economy. This new fund, created under African Union auspices, could institute an across-the-board global green tax on oil, gas and mining concession agreements in Africa. With these three sectors accounting for 90 percent of U.S. trade with Africa, a small tax of 1 percent could yield millions of dollars that can be directed to greening Africa's economy. U.S. leadership under a new President can bring political leverage for technology transfer, as well as private-public partnerships with solar, wind and tidal industries. Creating innovative green jobs can sustain the environment while allowing Africa to leapfrog its development in creative new ways.

U.S. and other foreign direct investors need to uphold core labor and environmental standards. The incoming U.S. President can use the power and visibility of the White House to advance standards of accountability that reverse the "race to the bottom" and other negative impacts of globalization and unfair trade. With the increasing pressure on global food markets, a visionary U.S. President can also encourage the U.S. Treasury and the international financial institutions to remove conditions on African governments that limit their ability to protect their small and medium-sized farmers and other at-risk sectors. Agricultural reform can be the centerpiece of new U.S. engagement with the continent. This would mean the elimination of subsidies to large U.S. agribusiness. coupled with support for farmers and other marginalized sectors in Africa.

Fairer trade, aimed at improving the lives of all, rather than an elite few, can dramatically revitalize African economies and unleash the potential of the continent. Debt elimination and removal of external constraints can further advance this goal. From 1970-2002, Africa received some $540 billion in loans and paid back $550 billion in principal and interest. Yet Africa remains today with a debt stock of $244 billion. Sub-Saharan Africa pays an estimated $13 billion to wealthy creditors each year. A new President committed to a fully functioning global economy could advance a plan for 100 percent bilateral and multilateral debt cancellation for all African countries. Cancellation should not be dependent on harmful economic restructuring and must be implemented outside the constraints of the flawed IMF/World Bank Highly Indebted Poor Country Initiative. Debt elimination could responsibly be financed through the sale of IMF gold, with leadership from a new U.S. President toward that end.

The Bush Administration squandered the hope of the millennium as it established a unilateral aid program, the Millennium Challenge Account (MCA). The MCA is a politicized aid apparatus that rewards "friends" who fulfill a unilateral set of Bush Administration criteria. This program is not targeted on poverty reduction, adds costly overhead, and may undermine African countries' democratic structures and accountability measures. The incoming President must examine critically the impact and implications of the MCA and work towards a comprehensive development finance plan that advances global poverty-elimination goals.

The Bush Administration also established a unilateral program in the critical area of the HIV/AIDS pandemic. The President's Emergency Plan for AIDS Relief (PEPFAR) is bridled by conservative ideological constraints that limit the effectiveness of the program and limit women's right to health around the world. PEPFAR also relies on costly procurements that advance the interests of big U.S. pharmaceutical companies at the expense of the poor. A new U.S. President can move to finance AIDS care, treatment and prevention by supporting multilateral efforts like the Global Fund for HIV/AIDS, Malaria and TB. The Global Fund is less prone to ideological manipulation, has proven its effectiveness, and should serve as the principal vehicle to support anti-AIDS efforts. The incoming President can also show U.S. leadership on agreements on intellectual property rights to ensure that such agreements protect public health and promote access to medicines for all. The new President can commit the United States to global goals that strengthen the health infrastructure of Africa by supporting the World Health Organization's campaign to support and sustain health care workers in developing countries.

The incoming U.S. President can amplify the emerging role of African women in the continent's political landscape. Women are generating hope for the future of the continent and raising the bar for democracy world-wide. Few Americans would guess that the country that leads the world in political gender balance is Rwanda, where women make up half of the members of parliament, a development that started in the mid-1990s. South Africa and Mozambique, also high on the list, are both countries with women composing more than 30 percent of their parliaments. This stands in stark contrast to the United States, where women make up only 18 percent of Congress. African countries also have higher percentages of women in cabinet-level positions. In South Africa, thirteen out of twenty-eight are women, and in Rwanda there are nine women to twenty-two men. In the United States, there are only three women in President George W. Bush's twenty-person cabinet. The incoming U.S. President should go on a listening tour of Africa in his first year. This tour should focus on engaging women and civil society, while also re-inforcing the importance of continental governing structures like the African Union.

The incoming U.S. Administration must take immediate steps to:

1) Establish a Presidential Council on African Affairs, with a mandate to engage Africa and the Diaspora in the design of a road map for comprehensive engagement with the continent. A key element of the road map must be people-focused development that propels Africa into a global green economy.

2) Appoint a Treasury Secretary who will fight global poverty by working to provide full debt elimination to African countries, without harmful economic conditions.

It is time for the incoming U.S. President and his Administration to engage with Africa in strategic twenty-first century ways that meet the needs of the continent and her people, while also bringing the region into a global green economy and a less militarized world.

Resources

Africa Action: http://africaaction.org
Africa Faith and Justice Network: http://www.afjn.org
Africa Focus: http://www.africafocus.org
Africa Forum and Network on Debt and Development: http://www.afrodad.org
Foreign Policy In Focus: http://www.fpif.org
Jubilee USA Network: http://www.jubileeusa.org
Pambazuka News: http://www.pambazuka.org

Resist Africom: http://www.resistafricom.org
Third World Network-Africa: http://www.twnafrica.org
TransAfrica Forum: http://www.transafricaforum.org

References

Abugre, Charles. "A Leaking Ship: The Role of Debt, Aid and Trade." *Pambazuka News*, February 2, 2006. http://www.pambazuka.org/index.php? issue=240 (accessed July 21, 2008).

Brown, Michael Barrett. *Africa's Choices*. Boulder: Westview Press, 1997.

Ghazvinian, John. *The Scramble for Africa's Oil*. San Diego: Harcourt Books, 2007.

Hertz, Noreen. *The Debt Threat*. New York: Harpers-Collins, 2005.

Juhasz, Antonia. "Will the next war for oil be in Africa?" Foreign Policy in Focus, June 18, 2008. http://www.fpif.org/fpiftxt/5301 (accessed July 27, 2008).

Rodney, Walter. *How Europe Underdeveloped Africa*. Dar-Es-Salaam: Bogle-L'Ouverture Publications, 1973.

Rynn, Jonathan. "How to Enter the Global Green Economy." Foreign Policy in Focus, June 16, 2008. http://www.fpif.org/fpiftxt/5299 (accessed July 18, 2008).

Whelan, Theresa. "Why AFRICOM? An American Perspective." Situation Report, Institute for Security Studies, August 17, 2007, p. 1.

Chapter 43

U.S. Policy toward the Middle East: Elevating Peace by Resolving Crises

Phyllis Bennis and Farrah Hassen

POLICY PROPOSALS

- **No war on Iran.**
  - Remove the military option from the table and end the bellicose rhetoric towards Tehran.
  - Pursue immediate negotiations with Iran without preconditions in order to address existing grievances, including the nuclear issue and Iraq.
  - Recognize that new sanctions against Iran are not an acceptable compromise. Nor will they change Iran's behavior or enhance U.S. interests in the region.
- Support a just, comprehensive and lasting peace between Israel and Palestine.
  - Ensure that a just peace is based on ending occupation, international law and United Nations resolutions, human rights and equality for all.
  - End military aid to Israel.
  - Demand an end to Israeli settlement building on Palestinian land and the construction of the separation Wall in the West Bank, which both violate international law and challenge the creation of an independent, contiguous Palestinian state.
- Redefine relations with Syria and Lebanon.
  - End the Bush Administration's failed policy of isolating Syria by restoring full diplomatic relations, including the return of the U.S. Ambassador to Damascus.
  - Engage Syria on stabilizing Iraq, resolving the Israeli-Palestinian conflict and supporting political reconciliation in Lebanon.

- Play a leading role in brokering a just and lasting peace between Israel and Syria, in the wake of resumed indirect talks occurring between the two countries.
- Stop undermining Lebanon's fragile democracy by interfering in Beirut's internal affairs. Recognize the legitimacy of the new unity government in accordance with the May 2008 Doha Agreement.

* * * * * * * * * * * * * * *

During the 2006 summer war between Israel and Hezbollah in Lebanon, Secretary of State Condoleezza Rice declared, "It is time for a new Middle East."[1] She was only half right. The Bush Administration's policies have not brought about the desired outcome for a new Middle East. Instead, the war in Iraq, unresolved Israeli-Palestinian conflict, U.S. threats of a new war on Iran and interference in Lebanese affairs ensure that the old Middle East remains in bloody difficulty, if not worse. A "new" Middle East, where peace and political, social and economic development can reign supreme, also necessitates a new U.S. policy geared towards resolving ongoing crises in the region, instead of creating new ones and inflaming existing ones.

The dynamics of the region have changed dramatically, especially driven by the 2003 invasion and ongoing occupation of Iraq. As a result of the war, 2.7 million Iraqis are internally displaced and over 2.4 million refugees have sought safety in Jordan, Syria and elsewhere in the region, creating new stresses and new instabilities. The overthrow of Saddam Hussein's regime has also altered the balance of power between Iraq and Iran, with Iran asserting more influence in neighboring Iraq and far more powerful elsewhere in the region.

Anti-Americanism is also on the rise, which should concern the incoming U.S. President and provide further impetus for reversing the current path of U.S. policy in the Middle East. Already, according to the 2008 Arab Public Opinion poll conducted in Saudi Arabia, Egypt, Morocco, Jordan, Lebanon and the United Arab Emirates, eight out of ten Arabs hold an "unfavorable" view of the United States. Aside from concerns about the instability of Iraq, over 80 percent of respondents identified the Arab-Israeli conflict as a key issue.[2]

After eight years in office, President Bush has provided the incoming U.S. President with clear guidelines for what *not* to do in the Middle East: threatening Iran with war; championing sanctions and the policy of isolation with Syria; and acting as a less-than-honest broker in the Israeli-Palestinian peace process. Instead of adhering to this failed policy script, the incoming President should apply diplomacy with Iran and Syria. and act impartially in brokering a meaningful, just and comprehensive peace between Israel and Palestine.

No War on Iran

The Bush Administration has claimed, almost since coming into office, that Iran is a "threat" to the United States. On December 3, 2007, the National Intelligence Estimate on Iran, reflecting the consensus view of all sixteen U.S. intelligence agencies, made clear that Iran did not have a nuclear weapon, did not have a program to build a nuclear weapon, and was less determined to develop nuclear weapons than U.S. intelligence agencies had earlier claimed. Despite this conclusion, the NIE's release has not quelled Washington's bellicose rhetoric.

Speaking before the Israeli Knesset on May 15, 2008, in language reminiscent of the run-up to the invasion of Iraq, President Bush reassured Israeli leaders that "America stands with you in firmly opposing Iran's nuclear weapons ambitions. Permitting the world's leading sponsor of terror to possess the world's deadliest weapons would be an unforgivable betrayal for future generations."[3] Bush avoided—as he has repeatedly done—any reference to the facts, such as those from his own NIE. In early June, reports surfaced that Israel conducted a military exercise targeting Iran's nuclear facilities, raising the threat of war with Iran even further.[4]

A closer examination of the facts suggests that the incoming U.S. President should elevate diplomacy with the government of President Mahmoud Ahmadinejad, instead of pushing for another unprovoked war in the region. Indeed, Iran does have an active nuclear power program, including a program to enrich uranium to fuel the program. Iran was one of the original signers of the 1968 Nuclear Non-Proliferation Treaty, and like all other "non-nuclear weapon states" that sign the treaty, Iran has a legal right to produce and use nuclear power for peaceful purposes. Despite Iran's legal right to nuclear power, the Bush Administration still didn't like it and pressured other countries to impose UN Security Council sanctions against Iran for exercising that internationally guaranteed right.

Aside from the nuclear issue, the Bush Administration has blamed Iran for the ongoing violence and instability in Iraq. In his testimony to Congress in early April 2008, then General David Petraeus (now head of Central Command) claimed, "Iran has fueled the violence in a particularly damaging way through its lethal support to the special groups." Those special groups (meaning the militias) pose the biggest threat to the United States, he added. Petraeus also accused Iran of launching rocket attacks on the Green Zone and warned, "We should all watch Iranian actions closely in the weeks and months ahead." But neither Petraeus nor Bush mentioned the role Iran played in mediating a ceasefire between the Iraqi government and Shiite militias in Basra in March 2008, which offers a snapshot of the more constructive role Iran could play in Iraq if relations between Iran and the United States improved.

A war with Iran would bring deadly and counter-productive consequences to Iran's neighbors and U.S. interests in the region. The incoming President should remove the military option from the table and end the bellicose rhetoric towards Tehran. This includes vetoing the launching of a "surgical" or "precision" strike on Iranian installations, which Tehran would legitimately interpret as an act of war. In response, Iran could send troops across its border to attack U.S. occupation troops in Iraq. Iran could attack U.S. troop concentrations in Kuwait, Oman, Qatar or elsewhere in the region, or go after U.S. ships in Bahrain, home of the Navy's 5th Fleet. It could attack Israel. It could close the Strait of Hormuz, through which 45 percent of the world's oil passes. The incoming President should recognize that supporting new sanctions against Iran is not an acceptable policy compromise. Nor will they change Iran's behavior or enhance U.S. interests in the region.

Instead of the saber-rattling, crippling sanctions and military strikes, the incoming President should take seriously the Iraq Study Group's recommendation: "engage directly" with Iran to "obtain their commitment to constructive policies toward Iraq and other regional issues."[5] This entails pursuing immediate negotiations with Iran without pre-conditions in order to address existing grievances. Ultimately, Iran wants a security guarantee (guaranteeing no invasion, no attack on nuclear facilities and no efforts at "regime change"), a recognition of its role as a regional power and a reaffirmation of its rights under the Non-Proliferation Treaty. On the nuclear issue, the incoming President should recognize that the UN, through the International Atomic Energy Agency (not through the enforced transfer of the issue to the UN Security Council), should be the main actor in orchestrating international negotiations with Iran. The next President should also acknowledge that the United States needs to implement its own obligations under the Non-Proliferation Treaty for full and complete nuclear disarmament, in order to convince other countries, like Iran, to take their obligations seriously.

Recent history confirms that diplomacy with Iran is possible. Like almost all governments, Iran's leaders condemned the September 11 terror attacks in the United States. Despite the ongoing U.S. sanctions in place against Iran, the government of President Mohammed Khatami assisted the United States in stabilizing Afghanistan. According to James Dobbins, President Bush's first post-September 11 envoy to Afghanistan, "perhaps the most constructive period of U.S.-Iranian diplomacy since the fall of the Shah of Iran took place in the months after the 2001 terrorist attacks."[6]

In addition, in 2003, only a few weeks after the U.S. invasion of Iraq, Iran had offered to negotiate a comprehensive solution with the United States. Iran acknowledged the need to address Washington's concerns regarding Iran's nuclear program and raised specific concessions it would be willing to make, including the possibility of ending support for Hamas and Islamic Jihad in Israeli-occupied Gaza, and ending the arming of Hezbollah in Lebanon. In return, Iran wanted a security guarantee that the United States would not attack or invade. The Bush administration, however, rejected such an agreement. The incoming President should revive this diplomatic initiative and discard the more destructive military option.

Support a Just, Comprehensive and Lasting Peace between Israel and Palestine

Elsewhere in the region, the realities of Israeli occupation—characterized by land grabs and expanding settlements across East Jerusalem and the West Bank; the complete isolation of the 1.7 million people of the Gaza Strip; continued construction of the separation Wall; and over 700 checkpoints and other barriers to Palestinian movement within the West Bank—continue to prevent any realistic hope of a just and comprehensive agreement or a viable two-state option, as the Bush Administration has called for. Since the collapse of the Camp David talks in 2000, Israel has built 143,000 new housing units in West Bank settlements (all of which are illegal under the Geneva Conventions, "authorized" by the Israeli government or not).

The withdrawal of settlers from Gaza and the 2006 legislative elections that brought Hamas to power there did not mean an end to occupation but simply a change in the nature of Israeli control. Gaza remains surrounded, and trapped—subjected to a virtually complete U.S.-orchestrated international boycott of goods and services. Israel maintains control over entry and exit of people and goods, control over the borders, the air space, even the waters off the Gaza coast. Some Palestinian resistance has sent rockets targeting Israeli civilians over the Gaza border; those attacks are illegal under international law (which does allow resistance against military targets), but any serious effort to stop that rocket-fire must take into account the desperation rising within the besieged community.

The Bush Administration's November 2007 summit in Annapolis was understood by many at the time, and today, as unquestionably a charade. It had far less to do with a new Israel-Palestine initiative than it did with consolidating regional support for Bush's anti-Iran mobilization. And, true to form, settlement-building escalated even further after Annapolis. Six months after the summit, Israeli Prime Minister Ehud Olmert approved the construction of nearly 1,000 housing units in settlements throughout the West Bank.[7] Under the Bush Administration's 2003 Road Map initiative, Israeli-Palestinian talks may have proceeded in form, but not in substance. The Palestinian political divide between Fatah and Hamas—exacerbated by the U.S. arming of the Fatah militia in Gaza—has made current Israeli-Palestinian Authority talks a sham, and it remains to be seen how long the June 2008 truce between Israel and Hamas will last.

Since 1967, Palestinians have continued to live under Israeli occupation. The Israeli-Palestinian conflict remains the longest running unresolved crisis in the Middle East. As one major consequence, the Bush Administration's invasion and occupation of Iraq has diverted much-needed U.S. attention and commitment towards resolving the conflict between Israel and Palestine. The incoming President must not make this same mistake. Instead, he should support a just, lasting and comprehensive peace based on ending occupation, international law and UN resolutions (including Nos. 194, 242 and 338), human rights and equality for all. That requires the incoming President to speak to all parties of the Israeli-Palestinian conflict, even those with whom we disagree, like Hamas. In addition, as Oslo, Camp David II, the Road Map and Annapolis have demonstrated, any peace process that avoids addressing the final status issues (Palestinian refugees' right to return, water, borders and the status of Jerusalem) is doomed to fail.

Real support for peace requires that the incoming President demand an end to Israeli settlement building on Palestinian land and construction of the wall (known to Palestinians as the "Apartheid Wall") in the West Bank, which both violate international law and challenge the creation of an independent, contiguous Palestinian state. Certainly, the U.S.-Israel relationship is real, but Israel should not be able to keep receiving 25 percent of total foreign aid while continuing to create further obstacles to peace. That's why the incoming President should also end military aid to Israel. Presently, all U.S. aid to Israel is military, to be employed at Israel's discretion. That means the United States is responsible for violations of international humanitarian law, including the 4th Geneva Convention on Civilian Persons in Time of War, because the violations visited upon Palestinian civilians and their homes have occurred with U.S.-provided weapons. This only enhances anti-American sentiment in the Middle East, which makes Americans more vulnerable at home and abroad.

Redefine Relations with Syria and Lebanon

The invasion of Iraq led to declining relations between Washington and Damascus, not in the least part due to Syria's opposition to the war. During and following the invasion, President Bush accused Syria of supporting terrorism, facilitating the entry of foreign fighters into Iraq and providing Iraqi fighters with military equipment. In December 2003, President Bush signed the Syria Accountability and Lebanese Sovereignty Restoration Act (SALSA), legislation which banned U.S. exports to Syria and Syrian aircraft from flying into and leaving the United States (never mind that Syrian planes don't fly to the United States in the first place).

Since 2004, Bush has continued to renew sanctions under SALSA, without questioning what impact they've had on changing Syria's behavior or enhancing U.S. interests. On February 13, 2008, he signed additional sanctions into law, targeting Syrian officials with assets in the United States. Following the assassination of former Lebanese Prime Minister Rafik Hariri on February 14, 2005, the Bush Administration blamed the government of Bashar al-Asad and withdrew the U.S. Ambassador to Syria in protest. Thereafter, the United States continued to isolate Syria, demanding that it accede to U.S. demands on Iraq, Lebanon and the Arab-Israeli arena as conditions for improved relations. On October

26, 2008, American Special Operations forces allegedly pursuing a "top opera-tive" of Al-Qaeda in Iraq carried out a helicopter attack on Sukkariyah, a small Syrian village six miles from the Iraqi border, killing eight civilians.

Contrary to the Administration's accusations, however, Syria has cooper-ated with the United States in the "War on Terror" and Iraq. Damascus provided intelligence on Al-Qaeda to U.S. officials after 9/11 and helped thwart an attack on the U.S. fleet in Bahrain. In a more gruesome example of counter-terrorism cooperation, Syria participated in the Bush Administration's "extraordinary ren-dition" program. And following the invasion of Iraq, Syria, sharing a porous 400-mile border with its neighbor, welcomed 1.5 million Iraqi refugees and has engaged with Iraq's various political players.

The July 2006, thirty-four-day war waged between Israel and Hezbollah in Lebanon highlighted the root of the problem exacerbating U.S.-Syrian relations. U.S. demands, plus the rhetoric of "fighting terrorism" and "spreading democ-racy," fall short of coherent "policy." The absence of a U.S. policy on Syria in-validates solutions to resolving continued tensions in Lebanon, Iraq and the lar-ger Middle East peace process. Instead, during the Lebanon war, U.S. officials repeated enigmatically that as one of Hezbollah's supporters, "Syria knows what it needs to do," as though those words would have somehow helped resolve the devastation in Lebanon. In the midst of the war, the Bush Administration re-fused to recognize the fundamental issue: Israel's continued occupation of Pales-tinian land and Syria's Golan Heights since 1967.

The incoming President must acknowledge that sanctions and isolation have not worked in changing Syria's regional posture—including its influence in Lebanon and relations with Hamas, Hezbollah and Iran. Damascus plays an in-fluential role in the region, as the Baker-Hamilton Iraq Study Group acknowl-edged. But instead of readily bowing down to U.S. dictates, Syria also seeks to have its interests recognized. They include the resumption of the Middle East peace process and the return of its occupied Golan Heights.

Rather than maintaining President Bush's failed approach, for the sake of stabilizing Iraq and the larger region, the incoming President should prioritize the redefining of relations with Syria, elevating peace and justice over bullying, contradictory policy and politics as usual. This requires restoring full diplomatic relations, including the return of the U.S. Ambassador to Damascus. U.S. inter-ests would also benefit from the incoming President engaging with Syria on stabilizing Iraq, resolving the Israeli-Palestinian conflict, and supporting politi-cal reconciliation in Lebanon. Indeed, Syria's involvement—and not the United States'—in the Doha Summit helped end the eighteen-month political stalemate in Lebanon in May 2008.

Under Turkey's leadership, indirect peace talks between Israel and Syria—which broke down in March 2000—have resumed. The incoming President should not only support continuation of these talks, but play a leading role in brokering a just and lasting peace between Israel and Syria. The incoming Presi-dent should take seriously former U.S. President Jimmy Carter's insights on brokering peace in the region. Before meeting with Hamas political bureau chief Khaled Meshaal and President Asad in Damascus in mid April 2008, Carter stated: "I think it's absolutely crucial that in a final dreamed-about and prayed-for peace agreement for this region that Hamas be involved and that Syria be involved." The International Crisis Group further concluded that Syria's "regional posture and relationships with Hamas, Hezbollah and Iran inevitably would change following a peace deal."[8]

Finally, instead of parroting President Bush's empty promises of "supporting Lebanon's democracy," which in translation has meant challenging Hezbollah's political and social influence, the incoming President should stop undermining Lebanon's fragile democratic processes. This means an end to interfering in Beirut's internal affairs. Since the withdrawal of Syrian troops from Lebanon at the end of April 2005, President Bush has demanded that Syria open an embassy in Beirut, which it announced it would do in October 2008, and end its influence there. But the United States has no right to control bilateral relations between Syria and Lebanon. Instead, the incoming President should recognize the legitimacy of the new Lebanese unity government in accordance with the May 2008 Doha Agreement.

Resources

American Friends Service Committee: www.afsc.org

Campaign Against Sanctions and Military Intervention in Iran: www.campaign iran.org/casmii/

Center for Arms Control and Non-Proliferation: www.armscontrolcenter.org

Just Foreign Policy: http://www.justforeignpolicy.org/iran

Peace Action: http://www.peace-action.org

United for Peace and Justice: http://www.unitedforpeace.org

U.S. Campaign to End the Israeli Occupation: http://www.endtheoccupation.org

References

Bennis, Phyllis. *Iran in the Crosshairs: How to Prevent Washington's Next War.* Institute for Policy Studies (2008): 5–36.

———. *Understanding the Palestinian-Israeli Conflict: A Primer.* Northampton: Olive Branch Press, 2007.

Ebadi, Shirin, and Hadi Ghaemi. "The Human Rights Case Against Attacking Iran." *New York Times*, February 8, 2005.

Hersh, Seymour M. "The Syrian Bet." *The New Yorker* (July 28, 2003). http://www.newyorker.com/archive/2003/07/28/030728fa_fact (accessed July 18, 2008).

————. "Shifting Targets: The Administration's Plan for Iran." *The New Yorker*, October 8, 2007. http://www.newyorker.com/reporting/2007/10/08/071008fa_fact_hersh (accessed July 18, 2008).

International Crisis Group. "Restarting Israeli-Syrian Negotiations." *Middle East Report* 63 (April 10, 2007).

Lesch, David W. "Missed Opportunities: Cooperation and Confrontation in the U.S.-Syrian Relationship." The Century Foundation (2007): 3–30.

Nasr, Vali. *The Shia Revival: How Conflicts Within Islam Will Shape the Future*. New York: W.W. Norton, 2006.

Ottaway, Marina, Nathan J. Brown, et al. "The New Middle East." Carnegie Endowment for International Peace (2008): 1–38.

The Iraq Study Group Report (December 6, 2006). http://www.usip.org/isg/iraq_study_group_report/report/1206/index.html

Yacoubian, Mona, and Scott Lasensky. "Dealing with Damascus: Seeking a Greater Return on U.S.-Syria Relations." Council on Foreign Relations Special Report Number 33 (June 2008): 1–43.

Notes

1. "Rice Regrets Mid-East 'Suffering'," BBC, July 25, 2006.

2. Shibley Telhami of the University of Maryland and Zogby International conducted the 2008 Arab Public Opinion Poll. For results, see http://sadat.umd.edu/surveys/2008%20Arab%20Public%20Opinion%20Survey.ppt.

3. See transcript of President Bush's address to the Knesset: http://www.whitehouse.gov/news/releases/2008/05/20080515-1.html.

4. Michael R. Gordon and Eric Schmitt, "U.S. Says Israeli Exercise Seemed Directed at Iran," *New York Times*, June 20, 2008, http://www.nytimes.com/2008/06/20/washington/20iran.html?_r=1&hp=&pagewanted=print&oref=slogin.

5. Iraq Study Group Report, December 6, 2006, p. 37. See http://www.usip.org/isg/iraq_study_group_report/report/1206/index.html.

6. James Dobbins, "How to Talk to Iran," *Washington Post*, July 22, 2007. http://www.washingtonpost.com/wp-dyn/content/article/2007/07/20/AR20070 72002056.html.

7. Adri Nieuwhof, "Israel Accelerates Settlement Expansion after Annapolis," *The Electronic Intifada*, June 11, 2008, http://electronicintifada. net/v2/article9606.shtml.

8. International Crisis Group, "Restarting Israeli-Syrian Negotiations," Middle East Report Number 63, April 10, 2007.

Chapter 44

U.S. Policy toward Asia:
For a Policy of Equitable Engagement

John Feffer

POLICY PROPOSALS

- Freeze U.S. military spending, stop new military base construction and cap levels of military exports to Asia—as a first step toward reversing the militarization of the region.
- Support a regional security mechanism in Northeast Asia to eefuse an emerging divide between maritime and continental powers.
- Engage China in a new partnership on issues vital to both the United States and China.
- Build on the Bush Administration's engagement policy with North Korea by focusing not only on denuclearization but also strengthening Pyongyang's relationship with the international community.
- Work with China, India and Southeast Asian nations to help guide Burma toward democracy and economic rehabilitation.
- Cancel the nuclear deal with India and replace it with a sustainable energy program that addresses India's needs and international concerns about global warming.
- Support Democratic alternatives in Pakistan and offer a Marshall Plan for South Asia that addresses the roots of extremist violence in the region.

* * * * * * * * * * * * * * *

For such a vast, wealthy and conflict-ridden region, Asia merited relatively little attention from the Bush Administration. Distracted by ground wars in Afghanistan and Iraq and the windmill-tilting of the "global war on terror," the United

States watched North Korea join the nuclear club, missed important opportunities to engage China, ignored Southeast Asia and made a hash out of its South Asian policy.

This policy of neglect raised the ire of Republicans and Democrats alike. "It's not that we're ignoring Asia a little bit," complained Richard Armitage, former Deputy Secretary of State in the George W. Bush Administration. "We're ignoring it totally. We're playing foreign policy at the moment like five-year-olds play soccer, everyone is going after the ball at once rather than covering the whole field."[1] The United States is "behind the curve," argued James Laney, former Clinton Administration envoy to South Korea, in a *Foreign Affairs* article on "Washington's Eastern Sunset."[2] Critics were particularly anxious that China would quickly fill the vacuum created by U.S. indifference.[3]

Examples of specific neglect certainly abound, from Secretary of State Condoleezza Rice's unprecedented decision to skip two ASEAN Regional Forum meetings to President Bush's postponing of a major summit with ten Southeast Asian leaders in Singapore in September 2007.

But if the Administration punted on a number of specific Asia policies, it nevertheless paid attention to the bigger picture. Over the last eight years, the United States has pursued a traditional geopolitical strategy in the region. With China mending fences with Russia and India in order to consolidate its influence over a vast Eurasian "heartland," the United States has been busy strengthening alliances on the periphery, from Japan in the Northeast, through Indonesia, the Philippines and Thailand in Southeast Asia, down to Australia in Oceania, and over to India in Southeast Asia. This alliance-strengthening can be seen in new arms deals with Jakarta, more military exercises with Manila, a vastly expanded security partnership with Tokyo and a proposed nuclear deal with New Delhi.

These discrete policies suggest that Washington is not like a five-year-old playing soccer. Rather it is a coach pursuing a distinct strategy against a specific opponent. Connect the dots from Japan to Indonesia to Australia to India and you get a string of alliances that form a choker around China.

Al-Qaeda, the Iranian leadership and Iraqi insurgents feature prominently in the rhetoric of Washington policymakers. But the Pentagon acknowledges that China is the only power on the horizon that can challenge U.S. global might and therefore the only threat that can justify the billions of dollars of traditional military spending in the Pentagon budget.[4] This Chinese "threat" has served to focus the minds of policymakers in Washington. "In the future, we are likely to see a world in which the challenges to peace and stability come from the Pacific Rim," asserts Sen. Daniel Inouye of Hawaii. "Today most people are focused on missiles from North Korea. But they ignore that the Chinese have this and much, much, much more."[5] The Pentagon's most recent annual assessment of China's military underscored this view of China as an imminent danger by re-asserting its 2006 conclusion that China "has the greatest potential to compete militarily with the United States and field disruptive military technologies that could over time offset traditional U.S. military advantages."[6]

It is not a simple Cold War shaping up between continental powers led by China and maritime powers led by the United States. After all, China holds too many Treasury bonds and is too important a trade partner for the United States to confront directly. And many countries in the region are reluctant to choose sides. India is striking deals with both Beijing and Washington. Even Australia, under new Mandarin-speaking Prime Minister Kevin Rudd, is looking to bridge the divide. But the with-us-or-against-us philosophy of the Bush administration has nevertheless helped to further polarize a region that is already deeply divided economically, politically and culturally.

Unlike some other regions of the world where the legacy of Bush Administration policies will be more difficult to undo, the U.S. Administration can readily resolve the paradox of U.S. policy toward Asia. With a modicum of political and financial capital, the incoming President can reverse both the perceived neglect of Asia and the slide toward a new geopolitical divide between continental and maritime powers in the region.

Stop Pouring Oil on the Fire

The Asian region today is in the middle of a sharply escalating arms race. Spurred in part by large increases in U.S. military spending—a 74 percent rise during the Bush Administration[7]—Asia-Pacific countries are the leading drivers of the global military-industrial complex. Of the world's top dozen military spenders, seven are Asia-Pacific powers (United States, China, Russia, Japan, India, South Korea and Australia).[8]

Washington, responsible for half of all global military spending, is at the front of this flying-geese formation. A sizable portion of the $607 billion Pentagon budget request for 2009 will go to maintaining and expanding the U.S. military presence in the Pacific. The big-ticket items in next year's budget—the CVN-78 Advanced Aircraft Carrier, the DDG-1000 Zumwalt-Class Destroyer—are of little use in fighting terrorism. These assets are part of the Pentagon's long-range plan to build a 313-ship navy meant to counter the only potential great power that the United States sees on the horizon: China.

The United States is also flooding the region with arms. Following the Clinton administration strategy, when Japan was our second largest purchaser of weapons,[9] the Bush Administration's push for Japan to field a "normal" military rather than simply a defensively-arrayed army has translated into increased sales of military hardware (though Congress wisely rejected the Administration's effort to sell Tokyo F-22 Stealth jet fighters).[10] Japan was the fifth largest purchaser of U.S. weapons from 2003 to 2006, spending $3.4 billion. Other Asian countries in the top ten include Australia at $3.9 billion, South Korea at $1.9 billion and Taiwan at $1.1 billion.[11]

To arrest this trend, the incoming Administration should revive the approach of the Bush Sr. administration, which undertook a substantial reduction of U.S. troops in the Asia-Pacific region through the East Asia Strategic Initiative (EASI). A new EASI would acknowledge the dangers of the new arms race in the region. It would explore ways of cooperating with our allies and negotiating with our competitors to first freeze and then reduce military expenditures. The United States would lead the way by putting a cap on military exports to the region—negotiated in conjunction with other leading suppliers—and cancel new base constructions, particularly in Okinawa and Guam. Troops scheduled to relocate to the new bases would be demobilized. The savings could go to a new regional climate change adjustment fund.

Start with Regional Security

Reducing the U.S. military presence in Asia must be done in tandem with creating a new security architecture that can maintain the peace. This is particularly important in Northeast Asia, where no regional security mechanism exists. Here the arms race is particularly acute. Of the countries negotiating in the Six Party Talks over North Korea's nuclear program, five have increased their military spending by 50 percent or more in the last half decade.[12] The six countries are responsible for over 65 percent of global military spending.

The Six Party Talks can serve as the building block for such a regional peace and stability structure. Indeed, this rather loose negotiating structure already sponsors a working group on this topic. But without strong support from the United States, this idea will not go anywhere. Traditionally, the United States is anchored in the region through bilateral alliances—with Japan, South Korea and to a certain extent Taiwan. This bilateralism allows the United States, much the larger partner in all these cases, to control the security equation more easily. These bilateral alliances are also perfectly suited to the United States' new approach of strategic flexibility: that is, rapid response with new technologies to crises throughout the region. Strategic flexibility requires lightning-fast decisions concluded at the highest level with one or two governments, not the deliberative consultations of multilateral bodies.

Nevertheless, there is support across the political spectrum in the United States for some kind of regional security structure. Influential U.S. figures such as political scientist Francis Fukuyama have backed a permanent forum for addressing security issues in the region.[13] In his book *Failed Diplomacy*, former Bush Administration point person on North Korea Charles Pritchard devotes an entire chapter to enumerating what such a forum would look like.[14] In a 2007 issue of *Foreign Affairs*, former Bush Administration official Victor Cha and former U.S. Ambassador to South Korea James Laney disagree about virtually everything related to U.S. policy toward East Asia—except that they both support a peace forum for the region.[15]

In its last year in office, the Bush Administration floated the idea of a kind of Pacific coalition of the willing with Japan, South Korea and Australia.[16]

Should this coalition come to pass, perhaps under the deceptively benign label of "strengthened coordination," it will deepen the nascent divide in the region and undercut promising developments in trade and diplomacy. China has become the major trading partner for many Asian countries, and the traditional disputes such as the spats over the South China Sea islands. are now open to diplomatic solutions. It is time for the United States to work with China to create an inclusive rather than an exclusive multilateral security structure in Northeast Asia to address common problems.

Engage China and North Korea

The Bush Administration began on a low note with China over the downing of the U.S. spy plane in 2001. Since then, relations have been more-or-less cordial. The Bush Administration enlisted China as a willing ally in its global war on terrorism, relied on Beijing to help on negotiations with North Korea, and restrained the Taiwanese government from disrupting the status quo in cross-Straits relations. U.S. economic dependency on China also grew since 2001, as the trade deficit tripled[17] and Chinese investments in U.S. Treasury bonds grew to nearly $1 trillion.[18] As such, China and the United States are economically linked in a way no other adversaries have been in recent history.

Some analysts have forecast head-to-head competition between the United States and China in soft power—that is, economic aid and trade, political deals, and the like.[19] The incoming Administration, however, should be wary of such zero-sum analyses. As the Congressional Research Service has argued, China's projection of soft power beyond its borders is overrated (much as the hard-power potential of its military has been exaggerated).[20]

Instead, the incoming Administration should look for overlapping interests with Beijing. The United States has tried to improve U.S. access to Chinese markets by pushing Beijing to reduce tariff barriers and float its exchange rate. Instead of setting off a trade war similar to the U.S.-Japan conflict of the 1980s, Washington should look for ways to engage China on win-win economic projects. Japan, for instance, has reached various agreements with China on energy and environmental cooperation, which could serve as a model for the United States. The countries of Northeast Asia have been negotiating ways to bring the energy resources of Far-East Russia to the energy-hungry economies of China, South Korea, and Japan. By working with China on, for instance, a regional climate adjustment fund—which could provide targeted funding for sustainable sources of energy, help countries meet new efficiency standards at the workplace and in households, and train workers to transition to a new Green economy—the United States can address problems in way that integrates rather than divides the region. Analyst Michael Klare proposes an annual Energy Summit where the two countries "eliminate areas of possible friction, such as disputes over contested foreign oil and gas deposits" and "review and finalize proposals on the joint development of alternative, climate-friendly sources of energy."[21] Finally, the victory of Ma Ying-jeou of the Koumintang (KMT) in Taiwan's March 2008 presidential elections reflects the Taiwanese majority's preference for maintaining the status quo with China and moving closer in economic relations. The United States can help foster better relations by encouraging rapprochement and overseeing a gradual demilitarization of the cross-Straits relationship.

In the last two years, prompted in part by the failures of its Iraq policy and by North Korea's explosion of a nuclear device in October 2006, the Bush Administration made an about-turn in its policy toward North Korea. The State Department began to negotiate seriously with Pyongyang, address North Korean negotiators in bilateral meetings, and offer incentives throughout the denuclearization process rather than just at the end. Despite some inevitable complications, a deal trading North Korea's denuclearization for a package of diplomatic recognition, security guarantees and economic offers has moved through the first two stages of the three-stage process, culminating in the Summer 2008 with North Korea's declaration of its nuclear programs and destruction of a cooling tower at its Yongbyon facility and Washington's announcement of the lifting of key sanctions against Pyongyang.

The incoming Administration must continue this engagement process. The problem inherent in these negotiations, however, is a profound asymmetry—not only in the respective power of Washington and Pyongyang but in their perspectives. North Korea is interested in a long-term relationship with the United States. In contrast, the United States is fixated on a single goal: the denuclearization of North Korea. It is not likely that the negotiations will complete the third stage unless the United States begins to understand that the normalization of relations with North Korea and its integration into a regional security structure are essential components of a new U.S. policy toward Asia.

Broker a Deal on Burma

The military regime in Burma, which has renamed the country Myanmar, has resisted pressures to change from the outside (sanctions) and the inside (popular protests). It has promised reform—for instance, holding democratic elections in 1988—only to violently reverse itself. The cyclone that struck the country in May 2008 left tens of thousands dead, and the junta scrambling to control both the physical and the political damage. This humanitarian disaster, compounded by the regime's reluctance to allow in international aid workers to minister to the survivors, interrupted the junta's top-down reform initiative, which included a new constitution, a referendum on the new document and multi-party elections in 2010.

The United States and China have taken very different positions on Burma. By and large, Washington has favored sanctions. Beijing, on the other hand, has supplied the junta with arms, made significant investments in the country, and long coveted Burma's numerous resources, including energy. India is somewhere in the middle, having initially supported the democracy movement and more recently edged toward *realpolitik*.

Neither sanctions nor protesting monks nor high winds have yet dislodged the junta in Rangoon. So it is time for the United States to work with China and India—as well as ASEAN and the European Union—to hammer out a consensus position. Washington must abandon the regime change option in favor of using economic carrots to encourage the military junta to work with the democratic opposition. This deal would make way for a parliament with real decision-making power, a federal arrangement with real power-sharing among the different regions, and a role for the military that would ultimately be separate from the political realm. Only when Burma finds its way back to the international community will the region of Southeast Asia finally realize its accelerated efforts at economic integration.

Marshall Plan for South Asia

The Bush Administration pursued a particularly misguided *realpolitik* toward India and Pakistan. Washington negotiated a nuclear deal to cement a military alliance with India and lock in India's position as a nuclear power. With Pakistan, Washington supplied strong-arm leader Pervez Musharraf with a bonanza of arms, including F-16 fighter jets, even as new democratic movements were gaining ground in the country.

On the face of it, the deal with India seems like a reasonable quid pro quo. India gets access to civilian nuclear technology and nuclear fuel. In exchange, the country maintains a moratorium on nuclear tests and opens its nuclear facilities to inspections. In fact, however, this deal threatens the non-proliferation regime. For one thing, eight of India's military-controlled nuclear plants would be off-limits to inspections. For another, India would be able to import technologies that would enable it to reprocess more material for bombs. Finally, India wouldn't have to limit the production of nuclear material or nuclear weapons.[22]

This U.S. offer to India also tilts the balance of power on the subcontinent. The incoming Administration should cancel the nuclear deal, which has attracted considerable opposition in India, and instead support the country's thriving sustainable energy field, much as Japan has taken a leading role in this regard in China.[23]

With Pakistan, the United States must abandon its attempt to influence through military means the country and the border areas with Afghanistan. More weapons will not stabilize this volatile region. Instead, the United States should work with the international community and the South Asian Association for Regional Cooperation to come up with substantial funds to build schools, hospitals, roads and other infrastructure—in short, a Marshall Plan for this volatile region of the world. Such a plan, which would be a far more effective counter-terrorism strategy, should encompass Bangladesh as well, given the emergence there of groups such as Harkat-ul-Jihad-e-Islami, which has attempted to establish Islamic law in the country through violent means.

To reduce tensions in South Asia more generally, the United States must devise a more comprehensive non-proliferation agreement for both India and Pakistan that both caps and secures their nuclear programs. This can only be accomplished, however, if Washington commits, in negotiations with Russia, to steep reductions in its own nuclear arsenal. Moreover, the United States must seek to restrict the flow of arms into both India and Pakistan and promote instead a cooperative security arrangement in the region.

Out of the Rubble

After World War II, few observers believed that either Japan or Korea would quickly recover from the devastation. Burma and the Philippines, with their plentiful natural resources, were considered more likely to succeed. As the Cold War developed, however, a series of autocrats bilked Burma and the Philippines while both Japan and South Korea built economic miracles.

After the Cold War, both Burma and North Korea are the two basket cases of Northeast and Southeast Asia, along with Bangladesh in South Asia. The economic impoverishment and relative isolation of these countries pose substantial barriers to integration in the respective regions.

The United States can help change this situation. By working to engage North Korea more fully, sitting down with China and India to work out a feasible solution to the Burmese standoff, and pulling together, with other international actors, a substantial development package for South Asia, the United States can play a constructive rather than destructive role. Such a policy depends on a shift away from using arms as a primary instrument of policy and backing true regional security arrangements. Alternatively, ignoring Asia and promoting a new geopolitical divide between continental and maritime powers will do nothing to rescue U.S. international reputation or advance peace and prosperity in the region.

Resources

Asia-Pacific Freeze: http://pacificfreeze.ips-dc.org/
Foreign Policy in Focus: http://www.fpif.org
Japan Focus: http://www.japanfocus.org
Korea Report: http://koreareport2.blogspot.com/

Renewing India: http://www.renewingindia.org/

References

Bleicher, Samuel. "China: Superpower or Basket Case?" Foreign Policy In Focus, May 8, 2008. http://fpif.org/fpiftxt/5210 (accessed July 19, 2008).

"China's Foreign Policy and 'Soft Power' in South America, Asia, and Africa." Congressional Research Service, April 2008. http://www.fas.org/irp/ congress/ 2008_rpt/crs-china.pdf (accessed July 19, 2008).

Cumings, Bruce. *Another Country*. New York: New Press, 2003.

Feffer, John. "Asia's Hidden Arms Race." TomDispatch, February 12, 2008. http://www.tomdispatch.com/post/174893 (accessed July 19, 2008).

———. *North Korea, South Korea: U.S. Policy at a Time of Crisis*. New York: Seven Stories, 2003.

———. "Pacific and Not-So-Pacific Oceans." Inter Press Service (March 7, 2008).

Klare, Michael. *Rising Powers, Shrinking Planet*. New York: Henry Holt and Company, 2008.

Lankov, Andrei. *North of the DMZ*. Jefferson: McFarland and Co., 2007.

McCormack, Gavin. *Client State: Japan in the U.S. Embrace*. Brooklyn: Verso, 2007.

Oo, May. "Change in Burma?" Foreign Policy in Focus, March 13, 2008. http://fpif.org/fpiftxt/5063 (accessed July 19, 2008).

Pan, Esther, and Jayshree Bajoria. "The U.S.-India Nuclear Deal." Council on Foreign Relations, February 8, 2008. http://www.cfr.org/publication/9663/ (accessed July 19, 2008).

Pastreich, Emanuel. "The Frankenstein Alliance." Foreign Policy in Focus, May 9, 2007. http://fpif.org/fpiftxt/4066 (accessed July 19, 2008).

Pervez, Fouad. "The Real Crisis in Pakistan." Foreign Policy in Focus, July 11, 2008. http://fpif.org/fpiftxt/5360 (accessed July 19, 2008).

Rashid, Ahmed. *Descent Into Chaos*. New York: Viking, 2008.

Samuels, Richard. *Securing Japan*. Ithaca: Cornell University Press, 2007.

Selig Harrison. *Korean Endgame*. Princeton: Princeton University Press, 2003.

Shaplen, Jason, and James Laney. "Washington's Eastern Sunset." *Foreign Affairs* (November/December 2007)

Shirk, Susan. *China: Fragile Superpower*. New York: Oxford University Press, 2007.

Notes

1. Greg Sheridan, "China Wins As U.S. 'Neglects Region," *The Australian*, September 3, 2007.

2. Jason Shaplen and James Laney, "Washington's Eastern Sunset," *Foreign Affairs* (November/December 2007), http://www.foreignaffairs.org/20071101faessay86606-p30/jason-t-shaplen-james-laney/washington-s-eastern-sunset.html (accessed July 19, 2008).

3. Leon Hadar, "U.S. on Sidelines in Asia," *Orange County Register*, August 7, 2007, http://www.ocregister.com/opinion/east-middle-asia-1792866-arf (accessed July 19, 2008).

4. Michael Klare, "The China Syndrome," Foreign Policy in Focus, March 5, 2008, http://www.fpif.org/fpiftxt/5041 (accessed July 19, 2008).

5. As quoted in: John Feffer, "Pacific and Not-So-Pacific Oceans," Inter Press Service, March 7, 2008, http://ipsnews.net/news.asp?idnews=41493 (accessed July 19, 2008).

6. Department of Defense, "Military Power of the People's Republic of China," (Washington, DC: Office of the Secretary of Defense, 2008), p. 1, http://www. defenselink.mil/pubs/pdfs/China_Military_Report_08.pdf (accessed July 19, 2008).

7. Office of Management and Budget, "FY2009 Defense Department Budget," http://www.whitehouse.gov/omb/budget/fy2009/defense.html (accessed July 19, 2008).

8. Christopher Hellman and Travis Sharp, "FY 2009 Pentagon Spending Request — Global Military Spending," The Center for Arms Control and Non-Proliferation, February 22, 2008, http://www.armscontrolcenter.org/policy/securityspending/articles/fy09_dod_request_global/ (accessed July 19, 2008).

9. "A Good Defense is a Good Offense," *Mother Jones,* http://www.motherjones.com/news/special_reports/arms/japan.html (accessed July 19, 2008).

10. Tomoko Hosaka, "U.S. Ambassador: Japan Should Expand Military Budget," Associated Press, May 20, 2008, http://ap.google.com/article/ALeqM5gQALHsK-FVcNGUluJTlRHaSLkCVQD90P9IOO2 (accessed July 19, 2008).

11. These arms trade figures are for contracts between 2003 and 2006 and come from: Richard Grimmett, "U.S. Arms Sales: Agreements with and Deliveries to Major Clients, 1999-2006," Congressional Research Service, December 20, 2007, p. 2 and 4, http://www.fas.org/sgp/crs/weapons/RL34291.pdf (accessed July 19, 2008). The delivery figures differ, but Japan, South Korea, Australia, and Taiwan remain in the top ten globally.

12. John Feffer, "Asia's Hidden Arms Race," TomDispatch, February 12, 2008, http://www.tomdispatch.com/post/174893 (accessed July 19, 2008).

13. Francis Fukuyama, "Re-Envisioning Asia," *Foreign Affairs*, January/February 2005, http://www.foreignaffairs.org/20050101faessay84107/francis-fukuyama/re-envisioning-asia.html.

14. Charles Pritchard, *Failed Diplomac* (Washington: Brookings Institution, 2007).

15. Victor Cha, "Winning Asia," *Foreign Affairs* (November/December 2007), http://www.foreignaffairs.org/20071101faessay86607/victor-d-cha/winning-asia.html; Shaplen and Laney, op. cit.

16. Kim Yon-se, "US, Korea, Japan Studying Joint Regional Security Entity," *Korea Times*, April 11, 2008.

17. Foreign Trade Statistics, U.S. Census Bureau, http://www.census.gov/foreign-trade/balance/c5700.html (accessed July 19, 2008).

18. Ambrose Evans-Pritchard, "China Threatens 'Nuclear Option' of Dollar Sales," *Daily Telegraph*, August 10, 2007, http://www.telegraph.co.uk/money/main.jhtml?xml=/money/2007/08/07/bcnchina107a.xml (accessed July 19, 2008).

19. Joshua Kurlantzick, *Charm Offensive* (New Haven, CT: Yale University Press, 2007).

20. Congressional Research Service, "China's Foreign Policy and 'Soft Power' in South America, Asia, and Africa," April 2008, http://www.fas.org/irp/congress/2008 _rpt/crs-china.pdf (accessed July 19, 2008).

21. Michael Klare, *Rising Powers, Shrinking Planet* (New York: Metropolitan Books, 2008), pp. 247–48.

22. Esther Pan and Jayshree Bajoria, "The U.S.-India Nuclear Deal," Council on Foreign Relations, February 8, 2008, http://www.cfr.org/publication/9663/ (accessed July 19, 2008).

23. See, for example, http://www.renewingindia.org/.

Chapter 45

U.S. Policy toward Latin America: Supporting Democratic Diversity

Sarah Anderson, John Cavanagh, Saul Landau and Manuel Pérez-Rocha

POLICY PROPOSALS

- **Turn the page on failed free trade, drug war and Cuba policies.**
  - **Engage Latin American governments and civil society organizations in a dialogue over fresh approaches to economic and political cooperation.**
  - **Revise existing trade and investment agreements to ensure mutual, broadly shared benefits.**
  - **Lift the embargo and travel ban on Cuba, close the Guantánamo Bay detention facility, and develop a plan with Cubans for converting the facility into a jointly administered hospital.**
- **Become a better neighbor.**
  - **Work with Congress to achieve genuine and realistic immigration reform, as part of a long-term vision for stability and prosperity that would allow free labor mobility with our neighbors.**
  - **Call for a summit with Mexican and Canadian government and civil society leaders to launch a transparent process for North American cooperation that puts people and the environment first, demonstrating a clear break with the secretive and corporate-driven Security and Prosperity Partnership.**
- **Wipe away Cold War relics.**
  - **Acknowledge past U.S. support for dictatorships and further declassify information to help Latin American countries pursue justice for crimes committed under military regimes.**

■ **Support the investigation and cancellation of odious debts accumulated under non-democratic regimes.**
■ **End politically biased aid.**

* * * * * * * * * * * * * *

Imagine these three bold actions in the first year of the incoming Administration:

- The U.S. President stands on the U.S.-Mexico border and offers a twenty-year plan of cooperation that could tear down the shameful wall between our countries.
- The President invites prominent survivors of oppression under Latin American dictators to a conference in Washington to discuss ways to address the past as we strengthen democratic ties in the future.
- The President flies to Guantánamo to mark the closing of the notorious detention facility and plans for its conversion into a cutting-edge Cuban-U.S. children's hospital, and an inter-hemisphere research and development center.

These are just a few examples of the tremendous opportunities the incoming U.S. President will have to sweep away the policy relics of times past and launch a new era of U.S.-Latin American relations based on mutual respect and mutual interests. As the Council on Foreign Relations Latin America Task Force and others have noted, the notion of U.S. hegemony in the region has become obsolete. The Monroe Doctrine, if not completely dead, has exhausted itself.

This historic moment is the result of citizen pressure on governments, particularly in South America, to assert greater independence in their economic and foreign policies. In Brazil, trade unionists, small farmers and church leaders pushed their President to fulfill a campaign promise to oppose the U.S. model for a hemispheric free trade pact. In Venezuela and Bolivia, governments are renegotiating contracts with U.S. and other foreign investors to ensure that a fair share of natural resource profits stay in the country. In Ecuador, the President has responded to calls from indigenous and other activists to shut down a U.S. military base. And even in traditional close U.S. allies Chile and Mexico, leaders carried out the will of the vast majority of their people when they instructed their UN Security Council representatives to oppose the invasion of Iraq.

It's no coincidence that these and other signs of increased independence occurred during the regime of George W. Bush. The image of a superpower run amok, launching pre-emptive war, institutionalizing torture and burying habeas corpus, made convenient fodder for those seeking change. But it would be a mistake to dismiss the political shifts in South America as merely knee-jerk "anti-Americanism." Rather, Latin Americans have responded to the failure of the major long-standing U.S.-backed policies: 1) fighting a "drug war," 2) expanding "Washington Consensus"-style economic reforms, 3) sanctions against Cuba, and 4) U.S. intervention and support for dictatorships.

The U.S. government's costly "War on Drugs" has neither reduced coca cultivation in Latin America nor cocaine use in the United States. The region has gone through more than two decades of World Bank- and International Monetary Fund-imposed reforms, including trade and investment liberalization and privatization that have driven a dramatic rise in inequality and poverty. According to the World Bank, the number of Latin Americans living on less than $2 per day jumped 16 percent to 121 million between 1981 and 2004. The region has the highest level of income inequality, thanks in part to privatizations that made the rich even richer, while causing layoffs and reduced services for ordinary citizens. The IMF's bungling of the 2001 financial crisis in Argentina (previously an IMF star pupil) delivered a severe blow to the legitimacy of these U.S.-backed institutions and policies.

And so it is an entirely healthy development that social movements have organized in so many countries, particularly in South America but also in Central America and the Caribbean, to advance a new, more independent path. These movements represent a push for *greater* democracy, not a threat to democracy. So too is it healthy that most Latin American economies have diversified trade and investment partners, and are less tied to the U.S. market (although the diversification is more advanced in South America).

The incoming U.S. President should go on a listening tour to learn more about the innovative proposals for regional economic cooperation in South America. In May 2008, twelve countries signed a treaty to launch the Union of South American Nations (UNASUR), a supranational body modeled to some extent on the European Union. Some of these countries are already cooperating to develop the Bank of the South, a regional alternative to the Washington-based international financial institutions. The long-term vision for UNASUR includes plans for common external tariffs and the eventual formation of a common currency, central bank and parliament. The U.S. government should bring the same spirit of constructive engagement to UNASUR as it brought to the European Union during its early days of formation. European integration has made that region not a threat but a stronger, more stable partner.

The incoming Administration should also work with Latin American government and civil society leaders to find solutions to the many concerns related to existing trade agreements and bilateral investment treaties, which go far beyond the issues of labor and environmental standards that have dominated the U.S. debate. Throughout the region, there are growing demands to revise these policies in order to allow governments to play a more responsible role in ensuring that trade and investment meet social and environmental goals, such as the creation of good jobs, technology transfer, and supports for small and medium businesses and farmers. A major new report by the Global Development and Environment Institute, for example, finds that trade and investment agreements are currently restricting Latin Americans' ability to use policy instruments that have contributed to development in Asia and elsewhere.

U.S. officials should engage constructively with alternative proposals that have originated in Latin America. For example, the Bolivian government, at the Bush Administration's request, proposed guidelines for an alternative approach to fair trade and cooperation that would allow governments to protect indigenous communities and small farmers from trade liberalization rules; place conditions on foreign investment to support national development goals; and include pro-active measures to reduce inequality. The Ecuadorian government has made an innovative proposal whereby that country would forego oil extraction in a biodiversity-rich area of Amazon rainforest that holds 20 percent of the country's oil reserves. In exchange, they are asking for foreign donations worth only about half what could be generated from drilling in the oilfield. Support for this proposal would be one important step towards a U.S.-Latin America energy partnership, focusing on reducing fossil fuel dependence and increasing renewable energy sources.

With regard to Cuba, the incoming Administration should acknowledge the failure of a half-century of sanctions. In their attempts to "punish Castro," U.S. officials have only inflicted suffering on the Cuban people. A 2008 report by a Council on Foreign Relations Task Force on Latin America supporting a lifting of the embargo is a sign of the widespread support for this policy change. The incoming Administration should reflect on the inconsistencies between the hardline approach to Cuba versus U.S. policies towards other countries that lack free elections (e.g., China, Saudi Arabia) and develop a flexible, yet coherent response. Beyond lifting the travel ban, the State Department should discuss with the Cuban government the possibility of cultural and people-to-people exchanges. A deeper understanding of Cuba's government, institutions and civil society will lead to opportunities for collaboration around common concerns.

Finally, the incoming U.S. Administration should shut down the Guantánamo Bay detention facility, now a notorious symbol of the Bush Administration's disregard for international human rights, and work with Cuban officials to convert the facility into a symbol of positive cooperation, perhaps a jointly administered hospital for Latin American and Caribbean children or an inter-hemispheric research and development center. They should also set up a working group to address other issues that could be obstacles on the path to normal relations with Cuba, including compensation for expropriated U.S. companies, Cuban claims for the costs of damage caused by the embargo and U.S.-backed terrorist attacks.

Become a Better Neighbor

Within the first 100 days, the incoming U.S. President should travel to the walled U.S.-Mexico border, the most dramatic symbol of the current divisions between the United States and Latin America. There he should commit to working with Congress to address the urgent need for genuine immigration reform that offers undocumented workers the opportunity to become legal permanent residents, facilitates family reunification, and opens up a path to U.S. citizenship.

Just as important, the President should lay out a long-term vision for reducing the economic and security gaps so that it could one day be possible to relax border controls, without significant disruption. The European Union offers some lessons from its experience with integrating the former "poor four" countries of Spain, Portugal, Ireland and Greece in the 1980s. The richer countries of the EU invested in infrastructure and training in these poorer neighbors (as well as poorer areas in the richer nations) and insisted on stronger social safety nets, including unemployment insurance. These measures helped level the playing field so that when borders were lifted after a transition period, there was no exodus. The EU is currently preparing to lift borders in 2011 with ten new countries, many of them much poorer nations in Eastern Europe.

It's important not to romanticize the EU. A recent directive aimed at swiftly expelling undocumented immigrants and banning their reentry into any EU member state is a chilling reminder that the Europeans have their own xenophobia problems. Europe has also pursued the same failed "Washington Consensus-style" policies towards developing countries outside the Union. Nevertheless, we can learn from the EU's general principle of focusing on narrowing the gaps as a necessary part of a transition to free labor mobility.

Step one should be to renegotiate existing trade agreements with Mexico and Central America. NAFTA became a "push factor" in migration by pitting small farmers in Mexico against heavily subsidized U.S. agribusiness. More than a million persons have been squeezed off their land. Likewise, small and medium-sized Mexican businesses have had difficulty competing in an unregulated export-oriented economy increasingly dominated by large global firms. While the pact attracted some new factory jobs to the border, many of these swiftly departed to China. For those that remained, NAFTA's labor side-agreement failed to protect basic labor rights. Rampant employer abuse has created additional migration pressures.

The incoming President should begin to address these issues by calling for a Summit with Mexican and Canadian government and civil society leaders. Under the Bush Administration, the official tri-national dialogue centered around the so-called Security and Prosperity Partnership (SPP), a series of regulatory reforms hammered out behind closed doors without public or even Congressional participation. Only the North American Competitiveness Council, made up of thirty large corporations, was allowed to give input. And while little information has been made public, it's clear that the SPP has resulted in increased pressure to intensify exploitation and privatization of natural resources like oil and water and further deregulation of trade policies to serve large corporations' intra-firm trade, at small businesses' expense; and increased militarization of the borders and the region as a whole. The SPP must be terminated and replaced with a "bottom up," transparent approach focusing on NAFTA renegotiation and other pressing social and economic issues.

Make a Clear Break with Misguided Cold War Policies

Anti-American rhetoric resonates among many Latin Americans because of the painful history of U.S. interventions, as well as U.S. support for brutal dictators and death squads. In the name of "protecting American freedom from the scourge of Communism," U.S. governments, at times in cahoots with large corporations, financed and propped up murderous regimes that killed and tortured hundreds of thousands of innocent people and set back democracy and human rights for decades.

The incoming President should strive to heal these wounds by convening a group of Latin Americans representing the many thousands who have fought doggedly to bring human rights violators to justice. He should invite heroes like Argentina's Mothers of the Plaza de Mayo who have held weekly marches for more than three decades to demand justice for family members "disappeared" by the military junta of the 1970s and 1980s. These activists' efforts helped push the Argentine Supreme Court in 2005 to withdraw amnesties that had shielded hundreds of former officers from prosecution.

From Chile he should invite Judge Juan Guzmán, who was the first to indict the notorious dictator Augusto Pinochet, and President Michelle Bachelet, who, as a former torture survivor herself, stands as one of the most inspiring symbols of just how far Latin America has come in the promotion of human rights. The President should also invite prominent victims now living in the United States, such as Dr. Juan Romagoza Arce, a trained surgeon who successfully sued the Salvadoran generals responsible for mutilating his fingers, or Sister Diana Ortiz, who has bravely demanded accountability for a brutal attack by Guatemalan government agents.

The incoming President should thank these human rights champions for their courageous efforts, acknowledge U.S. government involvement, and promise to never again allow U.S. agents to support dictators or death squads. This would go significantly beyond the small steps made under the past two Administrations. Former Secretary of State Colin Powell once remarked that the Nixon Administration's support for Chilean dictator Augusto Pinochet was "not a part of American history that we're proud of." President Clinton ordered the declassification of documents related to the U.S. role in Chile and once acknowledged that U.S. support for the Guatemalan death squads was "wrong."

At this conference, the President should do more than make symbolic gestures by announcing concrete actions to move beyond the Cold War, such as:

- Resolving the issue of debt burdens accumulated by U.S.-supported dictators. The victims of these un-elected regimes should not be held accountable for their debts. The incoming President should recognize the culpability of irresponsible lenders and support efforts to conduct independent audits to determine the extent of these "odious" debts, as a step towards cancellation. This action should apply to relevant Caribbean nations, most notably Haiti, which is saddled with some $1.2 billion in external debts, 40 percent of which were amassed under the Duvalier dictatorship.
- De-politicizing and de-militarizing aid. Too often in the past, ideology, rather than economic needs, has driven aid decisions. Increased transparency and clear criteria aimed at achieving the Millennium Development Goals would go far to address concerns that the U.S. government uses aid as a tool for political manipulation. The incoming Administration should consider ending all military aid to the region, since in the past such funds have been used for repression rather than security. It should also ensure that the 4th Fleet, re-established in 2008 as the naval component of the U.S. Southern Command, is not used for mindless and anachronistic "shows of force."
- Declassifying additional documents that could support the pursuit of justice in Latin America and forming an independent Commission to investigate the culpability of U.S. officials who aided these murderous regimes. As Latin American governments grapple with the wrenching process of exposing and holding accountable those responsible for crimes against humanity, the U.S. government should be willing to examine its own role in this history.

The incoming President could conclude this conference by laying a wreath at the memorial that marks the site of the assassination of Orlando Letelier and Ronni Karpen Moffitt, just two miles from the White House, on Massachusetts Avenue. On September 21, 1976, agents of Chilean dictator Augusto Pinochet detonated a car bomb that killed Letelier, a former Chilean ambassador to the United States, and Moffitt, his twenty-five-year-old American colleague at the Institute for Policy Studies. This act of terrorism symbolizes the long reach and tragic cost of the U.S.-supported Latin American dictatorships. At the same time, this memorial has become a symbol of hope for the future, as Chile has made such remarkable progress in putting its dark past behind.

It's time for the United States to do the same.

Resources

Alliance for Responsible Trade: http://art-us.org/
Facultad Latinoamericana de Ciencias Sociales (FLACSO):
    http://www.flacso.org/

Hemispheric Social Alliance: http://www.asc-hsa.org/
Integración Sur: http://www.integracionsur.com/
Latin America Working Group: www.lawg.org
Unión de Naciones Suramericanas:
   http://www.uniondenacionessuramericanas.com/
Washington Office on Latin America: www.wola.org

References

Anderson, Sarah, and John Cavanagh. "After the FTAA: Lessons from Europe for the Americas." Institute for Policy Studies (2005): 1–15.

Anderson, Sarah, and Manuel Pérez Rocha. "Three Amigos Summit." Institute for Policy Studies (2008). http://www.ips-dc.org/articles/324 (accessed July 17, 2008).

Barshefsky, Charlene, and James T. Hill. "U.S.-Latin America Relations: A New Direction for a New Reality." Council on Foreign Relations. (2008): 1–110.

Boedt, Piet, and Esperanza Martinez. "Keep Oil Underground: The Only Way to Fight Climate Change." Oilwatch (2007): 1–74.

Bolivian Government. "Guidelines for a Fair Trade and Cooperation Treaty with the US." Alliance for Responsible Trade (2006). http://www.art-us.org/bolivia_guidelines (accessed July 16, 2008).

Hemispheric Social Alliance. "Alternatives for the Americas." Alliance for Responsible Trade (2002): 1–115. http://www.art-us.org/Alternatives_ for _the_Americas_html (accessed July 16, 2008).

Washington Office on Latin America. "Forging New Ties: A Fresh Approach to U.S. Policy in Latin America." Washington Office on Latin America Report (2007): 1–20.

Working Group on Development and Environment in the Americas. "Foreign Investment and Sustainable Development: Lessons from the Americas." Working Group on Development and Environment in Latin America Report (2008): 1–48. http://ase.tufts.edu/gdae/WorkingGroup_FDI.htm (accessed July 17 2008).

Chapter 46

Restoring Government Leadership on Human Rights at Home

Catherine Albisa, Martha F. Davis and Cynthia Soohoo*

POLICY PROPOSALS

- The incoming President should seek full implementation and, where necessary, ratification, of all human rights treaties.
- The incoming Administration should develop an economic and social rights agenda, with National Plans of Action to protect housing, health and education.
- The incoming President should issue an Executive Order requiring preparation of Human Rights Analyses of proposed budgetary, statutory and regulatory provisions.
- The incoming Administration should exercise leadership in promoting comprehensive Human Rights Education.
- In nominating members of the federal judiciary, the incoming President should take into account nominees' support for international human rights law.
- The incoming Administration should support subnational governments' efforts to promote human rights in the United States and abroad.

* * * * * * * * * * * * * *

* The authors wish to thank Amanda Shanor for her assistance in preparing this chapter.

Human rights are deeply embedded in the United States' identity as a nation, as reflected in its founding documents and history. However, U.S. protection of human rights has been uneven over time, and particularly degraded in recent years. In light of this, the incoming Administration should launch a Human Rights Restoration Initiative to restore the United States' world leadership with regard to human rights. Such an initiative should seek to establish the United States as an exemplar on the world stage in the protection of human rights at the national level.

The incoming President should seek full implementation and, where necessary, ratification, of all human rights treaties

The incoming Administration should lift unnecessary reservations, understandings and reservations from human rights treaties. Although the United States has ratified several major human rights treaties, including the International Covenant on Civil and Political Rights (ICCPR), the Convention on the Elimination of All Forms of Racial Discrimination (CERD) and the Convention Against Torture (CAT), these treaties have been subject to debilitating reservations, understanding and declarations ("RUDs") that undermine implementation. There are substantive reservations, such as the reservation to the ICCPR's prohibition on treating juveniles as adults in the criminal justice system, which are not constitutionally mandated and should be removed. There are also understandings and declarations that severely impede implementation of the treaties more generally. For example, the federalism understanding asserted by the United States each time it ratifies an international human rights treaty states that, despite the reference to treaties in the Constitution's Supremacy Clause, treaty ratification would not alter the balance of authority between the federal and state government. In effect, this makes it impossible for the federal government to enforce the treaty if faced with a recalcitrant state government. There are also declarations with regard to the ICCPR, CAT and CERD stating that the treaties are not self-executing, precluding almost any enforcement of treaty obligations by U.S. courts. Finally, there are understandings stating that the treaty obligations are co-extensive with U.S. law without any serious assessment of whether this in fact is the case, and without consideration of the fact that U.S. law changes over time. The incoming President should rescind unnecessary and harmful RUDs attached to human rights treaties, retaining only those that are mandated by differences between U.S. Constitutional law and treaty law, such as those preserving First Amendment protections.

The incoming Administration should also seek ratification—without reservations, and without the understandings or declarations discussed above which have hampered treaty implementation in the past—of all remaining major human rights treaties. There are several major human rights treaties the United States should ratify, including the International Covenant on Economic, Social and Cultural Rights; the Convention on the Elimination of Discrimination Against Women; the Children's Rights Convention; the Convention on Rights of

Persons with Disabilities; and the International Convention on the Protection of the Rights of All Migrant Workers and Members of their Families.

The incoming Administration should develop an economic and social rights agenda, with National Plans of Action to protect housing, health and education

Following in the footsteps of great American Presidents such as Franklin D. Roosevelt, who have made history with their visionary commitment to economic and social rights, the incoming Administration should announce an economic and social rights plan for the twenty-first century. This plan should recognize that fundamental human needs are basic human rights, and are essential to the functioning of a healthy democracy.

To be effective, policies impacting basic rights should be constructed within a unified, integrated and complementary framework. By looking at policies affecting core rights in their totality and in relationship to each other, the incoming Administration can create a cohesive, systemic approach to resolve the biggest social issues of our time, and address the inadequate patchwork system currently in place. Our current ragged patchwork of protection for economic and social rights allows and enables financial, geographic and cultural barriers to health care access, obscenely low levels of funding for HUD, demolitions of public housing, predatory lending, abusive zero tolerance approaches in schools, and chronic funding inequities leading to uneven teacher quality and other disparities. These plans should seek comprehensive solutions that, in their totality, fulfill the national government's responsibility for ensuring basic human rights. These plans should also ensure that the states have adequate resources to protect human rights; that geographic disparities are minimized to the greatest degree possible; and that effective accountability mechanisms, such as monitoring agencies, are put in place to guarantee a sufficient minimum of protection for every person within the United States. To evaluate the success of these plans, the incoming Administration can utilize the "progressive implementation" standard found in human rights covenants that requires governments to take steps that are targeted and concrete in order to realize economic and social rights over time. This standard requires continuous improvement efforts.

The economic and social rights agenda should be developed in a transparent and participatory manner. The incoming Administration will build public support for its plans if it ensures that policy solutions emerge from a participatory process that involves civil society—in particular, affected communities. A constructive dialogue framed by human rights standards, undertaken with full transparency and accountability to the public, will also ensure success of these plans.

The incoming Administration should issue an Executive Order requiring preparation of Human Rights Analyses of proposed budgetary, statutory and regulatory provisions

The federal budget and major federal legislation have often been vetted for their impacts on the environment and on families, and this should be extended to human rights. Significant budgetary, legislative and regulatory proposals may also have major impacts on U.S. compliance with its international human rights obligations. The incoming Administration can provide leadership in identifying these human rights impacts by issuing an Executive Order requiring Executive Branch departments and agencies to identify proposed budgetary, statutory and regulatory provisions that may have potential negative impact on U.S. human rights obligations, and to provide adequate rationale why such proposals should be submitted. These Analyses should be paired with independent review of the quality of these statements.

The incoming Administration can draw upon many effective models. While the Executive Branch will take the lead in developing the methodology for its Human Rights Analyses, the federal government already has much experience with environmental impact statements through the National Environmental Policies Act and with family impact statements through compliance with Executive Order 12606. Further, domestic localities such as San Francisco have undertaken human rights audits of their city agencies. Many countries, such as Britain and New Zealand, have a range of processes that assess pending legislation for its impact on human rights. Such analyses are important to ensuring that federal legislation respects human rights concerns. Without such an assessment, lawmakers may well underestimate or ignore entirely the human rights impacts of proposed legislation. Importantly, such Human Rights Analyses may be particularly beneficial in assessing the impact of a particular policy approach on the conduct of foreign relations.

The incoming Administration should exercise leadership in promoting comprehensive Human Rights Education

The federal government must play a leadership role to ensure that Human Rights Education is as comprehensive and universal as possible. The national government need not re-invent the wheel. For example, educators in Minnesota have already partnered with the Minnesota Department of Human Rights to pioneer implementation of human rights curricula in the state's public elementary and secondary schools. Other state human rights commissions have made similar efforts. But a few states' visionary efforts are not enough to discharge the national government's obligations to educate citizens about their human rights. While states have traditionally exercised responsibility for public school curricula, the federal government has often used its spending clause authority to expand state resources consistent with national educational priorities. The incoming Administration should propose legislation to support local school systems' teacher training and curricular development for Human Rights Education. To oversee this funding and to work with states and localities to develop best practices, the incoming President should immediately establish the position of Assistant Secretary for Human Rights Education within Department of Education.

Human Rights Education is also critical to state lawmakers in all branches of government. Because so much human rights implementation is left to states under our federal system, Human Rights Education of state and local leaders is essential. As a first step, to ensure that subnational lawmakers are aware of their human rights obligations, the incoming President should propose that federal matching funds be offered to states to support Human Rights Education for state and local lawmakers, including judges and law enforcement personnel.

Finally, Human Rights Education should extend to federal lawmakers in all branches of government. It should also be a key component of the training for any federal employment that relates to substantive policy development and lawmaking—including the Executive Branch, and Members of Congress and their staffs. Funds should likewise be provided to the Federal Judicial Center to promote Human Rights Education for the federal judiciary.

In nominating members of the federal judiciary, the incoming President should take into account nominees' support for international human rights law

Support for international law and for its domestic relevance is part of the bedrock of our national legal system. The Supremacy Clause in Article VI of the Constitution provides that Treaties constitute the "Supreme Law of the Land." Similarly, the Declaration of Independence calls on the newly constituted United States to give proper regard to the existing law of nations. Recognizing this, the U.S. Supreme Court has, since its inception, looked to international and comparative law for interpretive guidance.

In reviewing possible nominations to the federal judiciary, the incoming President should explore the potential nominees' views on international law and comparative law. The tradition of breadth and depth in federal judicial analysis should continue. While no single issue should be a "litmus test" for a nominee, a potential federal jurist who rejects the relevance of international law to domestic adjudication is asserting out an out-of-the-mainstream, ahistorical position that should be disfavored in the nomination process.

The incoming Administration should support subnational governments' efforts to promote human rights in the United States and abroad

In the past century, subnational governments have been increasingly active on the international stage: Among other things, local and state governments provided leadership in combating South Africa's apartheid policies through divestment legislation. More recent state and local efforts have focused on Burma, Sudan and Iran. Some federal courts have questioned whether these state efforts are preempted by the federal government's responsibility for foreign policy. In response to these challenges, and recognizing the positive impact that such local action can have in curbing human rights abuses, in 2007 Congress enacted the Sudan Accountability and Divestment Act, which specifically permits state and municipal governments to engage in certain divestment activity relating to Sudan. However, when signing the legislation, President Bush attached a statement that re-asserts supreme Executive authority in the area and effectively undermines the Congressional intent to give states and municipalities a safe haven for Sudan divestment activities.

The incoming Administration should abandon the Bush Administration's approach undermining state efforts to promote human rights. Subnational governments have much to contribute to the implementation of human rights norms within the United States and abroad. Reflecting the democratic process in its most vibrant form, subnational human rights initiatives are responsive to grassroots constituencies while also capitalizing on the increased global visibility of states and localities. Certainly when these subnational governments act to further implementation of human rights here and abroad, these acts should not be easily rescinded by either the judiciary or the Executive. To take full advantage of the power and dynamism of the U.S. federal system, the incoming President should revoke the signing statement attached to the Sudan Accountability and Divestment Act. Further, the incoming Administration should work closely with leaders in states and localities to develop more nuanced foreign policy approaches that recognize a role for subnational governments in promoting and implementing human rights at home and abroad.

Conclusion

In promoting a federal Human Rights Restoration Initiative, the incoming Administration can build on the nation's past successes, such as those watershed moments where the United States recognized the equality of all people irrespective of race or gender, or provided trail-blazing leadership resulting in the comprehensive human rights vision of the Universal Declaration on Human Rights protecting civil, political, economic, social and cultural rights. But in the wake of a Presidential Administration that has been hostile to human rights both within the United States and abroad, new Presidential vision and leadership is necessary to restore and expand the basic human rights of U.S. citizens.

Resources

Columbia Law School Human Rights Institute: http://www.law.columbia.edu/
    center_program/human_rights
National Economic and Social Rights Initiative, http://www.nesri.org

Opportunity Agenda: http:www.opportunityagenda.org
Program on Human Rights and the Global Economy, Northeastern School of
    Law: www.slaw.neu.edu/clinics//rights.html
U.S. Human Rights Network: http://www.ushrnetwork.org
U.S. Human Rights Online, http://www.ushumanrightsonline.net

References

Anderson, Carol. *Eyes off the Prize: The United Nations and the African-American Struggle for Human Rights, 1944-1955*. Cambridge, UK: Cambridge University Press, 2003.

Black, Charles. *A New Birth of Freedom: Human Rights, Named and Unnamed.* New Haven: Yale University Press, 1999.

Dudziak, Mary. *Cold War Civil Rights*. Princeton: Princeton University Press, 2000.

Smedly, Brian, and Alan Jenkins. *All Things Being Equal: Instigating Opportunity in an Inequitable Time*. New York: New Press, 2007.

Soohoo, Cynthia, Catherine Albisa, and Marthia F. Davis, eds. *Bringing Human Rights Home*. Westport: Greenwood Publishing, 2008.

Sunstein, Cass. *The Second Bill of Rights: FDR's Unfinished Revolution and Why We Need It More Than Ever*. New York: Basic Books, 2004.

Chapter 47

The Role of Organizing and
Movement-Building: The Sine Qua Non

Frances Fox Piven, Rinku Sen and Eric Mann

As noted in the Editor's Introduction, bottom-up, boots-on-the-ground organizing is the key to converting the dozens and dozens of good policy proposals offered in the foregoing chapters into political reality—building a movement that can hold progressive elected and appointed politicians accountable. And so we asked three leading figures in the community organizing world, movement-builders, to offer their views on the relationship of organizing to policy, via a set of questions we posed to them. The respondents are Rinku Sen, President/CEO of the Applied Research Center, based in Chicago, Oakland and New York, and Publisher of their magazine, *ColorLines* [RS]; Eric Mann, Director of the Labor/Community Strategy Center in Los Angeles [EM]; and Frances Fox Piven of the City University of New York Graduate Center and one of the leading writers/theorists of social movements [FP].

How should organizers approach the incoming Administration?

RS: Organizers should look upon the next Administration with honorable flexibility. Whether we've got Obama or McCain, we need to understand that neither will be an all-or-nothing President. Obama won't support all our solutions, and McCain won't reject them all out of hand. Organizers should be thinking through all of the factors that will be in play—popular sentiment, the shape of Congress, pressure from governors and mayors, and the state of the news media. If it's an Obama White House, we will need to prepare ourselves simultaneously to challenge him and protect him, knowing that he will both continue moving to the center and be the target of insane racist stereotyping. In addition, if he wins, both liberals and conservatives will characterize the victory as proof that we have finally arrived at the post-race state, and both will insist that class is the real and only problem.

EM: With optimism, assuming it is President Barack Obama, and also great independence, pressure and at times trepidation. The progressive agenda must begin by confronting the role of our government in imposing a heavy carbon, economic and military footprint on the world. A progressive agenda must begin by supporting the right to sovereignty and self-determination of Third World nations—Iran, Venezuela, Cuba, Iraq, Afghanistan, Pakistan, Palestine, North Korea. We can't let an Obama Administration demonize certain governments as pretense for blockade or invasion. When Obama says, "I am solid as a rock on women's choice" and he appoints a strong Office of Contract Compliance to monitor sex and racial discrimination, that is a major step. When he says he will talk to other governments, that is very encouraging. When he then characterizes so many governments as "our enemies" and "two-bit dictators"—meaning those governments who challenge U.S. policy, as opposed to carrying it out—we must be vigilant and independent. When Obama says that we are fighting two wars, one we shouldn't have gotten into (Iraq) and still proposes a big U.S. presence there, and one where we are not fighting hard enough (Afghanistan) and proposes more troops and assaults, we should be gravely concerned. The approach to the incoming Administration—that of Obama, hopefully, or McCain, regrettably—must be to reject the entire premise of "the war against terrorism." How can we fight for a progressive "domestic" agenda if government is invading, subverting, torturing, and has all of us under surveillance? In that Obama's main foreign policy advisor is cold warrior Zbigniew Brzezinski, not Cindy Sheehan, organizers must approach the incoming Administration with a strong independent political program and a tactical plan to carry it out.

FP: I think a Democratic Administration will spark a good deal of organizing. This is not, however, because the Administration will automatically be an ally. Instead, I think organizers—or activists or agitators—should approach the new regime as the political operation it is. Barack Obama will try to position himself in ways that build support among powerful interest groups without antagonizing too many voters. In this he is no different than any other President. What might make him different is the possibility, even the likelihood, that his voter constituency, because it includes large numbers of African Americans and young people, will be responsive to the issues raised by social movements on the left. Put another way, organizers do better when they attack governments that have reason to be at least somewhat friendly.

What do you see as openings in the incoming Administration on key issues such as poverty, inequality, education and health care?

RS: The green economy will be a major element of federal policies for the next several years, as will immigration and, to a lesser extent, health care. While these aren't the only issues Americans care about and need addressed, they will get traction because people from all ideological fronts are heavily invested in them, including corporations and environmentalists. Mainstream interest, however, won't guarantee that we get the most progressive possible versions of green jobs or immigration bills. In the green economy, for example, we need not just job training, but actual jobs, and they need to be directed toward poor people and people of color, even in an anti-affirmative action context. In immigration, the business community wants legal workers, but they'd be perfectly happy with guest workers whose right to be present is bound to an employer and who have no path to citizenship. We need to be prepared to take advantage of real openings on these issues—it would be bad to get a call from the White House and not be prepared to move.

EM: I hope the Obama Administration appoints courageous and principled government officials and judges. In Los Angeles, the Strategy Center and our Bus Riders Union are opposing exorbitantly priced rail projects and environmentally destructive highway projects. We propose clean fuel, 24/7, low-fare urban bus systems as the centerpiece of an expanded public transit system. The LCSC and BRU, along with attorneys and allies, will be approaching federal officials at the EPA, DOT, Department of Justice's Civil Rights Division to intervene in LA against rail and auto lobbies. We will be bringing further civil rights and environmental lawsuits. I hope the Democrats control the Judiciary Committee, but also that Obama has the courage to appoint judges and department heads who will respond to grassroots pressure.

These appointees and judges also preside over key issues of public participation and due process that are essential to grassroots organizing—public hearings on fare increases, community right to know, right to speak and right to intervene on chemical emissions. We need emission reductions that are based on strict enforcement, not the buying and selling of air pollution credits. In this context, we can't expect the Obama Administration to lead—what we hope is that there are people there who will listen and respond to more militant and structural proposals from below.

FP: I agree these are the important domestic issues, and so far the Obama campaign has said little that should give us reason to expect that by themselves they will take bold new initiatives to reduce poverty or inequality. Rather, the openings will have to be created by the trouble and turmoil made by the social movements whose hopes have been excited by the campaign and the extraordinary fact of an African-American President.

What lessons did you learn from the failure of Bill Clinton's health care initiative in the first two years of his Administration?

RS: Bill Clinton failed to lead, not just on health care, but also on gays in the military (Don't Ask, Don't Tell), on affirmative action (Mend it, Don't end it) and on welfare (Personal Responsibility). Most liberals and some of the leftists who helped elect him were so relieved that he wasn't Reagan or Bush that they explicitly decided not to criticize him and not to press too hard. Not only did he realize that he was free, but we also let our activist muscle atrophy—the base got used to not responding as he did horrible things, and it became more and more difficult to arouse outrage as time went on.

EM: The lesson wasn't that he lost. The negative lesson was that by 1994 Clinton had capitulated to Newt Gingrich, raised triangulation to a principle and attacked the most vulnerable—women on welfare, those on death row—to get re-elected.

Thus, the main lesson is that Obama is not coming to office to be our friend. He is subject to so many conflicting obligations and constraints—e.g., his strong ties to the ethanol lobby, a corn-based fuel that is an environmental disaster and is making the price of corn for tortillas in Mexico unaffordable.

The next lesson is not from Bill Clinton's treachery but the shame of those who conciliated with him under the rationale of "not playing into the hands of the Right." A movement has to make an objective assessment of the Obama program, support him and push him to the left on his better instincts and be a strong independent force to his left and take him on with passion and intelligence when we disagree.

In our dealings with Mayor's Tom Bradley, Richard Riordan and Antonio Villaraigosa, at times the struggle is quite sharp but always principled. Because we have some power and know how to operate as effective allies when possible and adversaries when necessary, the lines of communication are always open. At the Bus Riders Union we have 200 active members, 3,000 dues-paying members, 100,000 on-the-bus supporters and hundreds of thousands of others in LA and throughout the United States who look to us for leadership. The job is to put the interests of our members, our allies, and our program at the center of our relationship with the new Administration.

FP: The lessons are, I think, very clear. A health care initiative that tries to appease the big health care provider interests, especially the powerful HMO's and pharmaceutical companies, by giving them stakes in the policy, will be extremely costly and complicated. The Clinton plan was a Rube Goldberg contraption. As a result, it was doomed to be susceptible to pressure from the provider interests for ever more concessions, and once these interests decided they could do better without compromise, it was virtually impossible to rally popular support for an incomprehensible policy.

Why is organizing a necessary complement to policy work?

RS: We have to have a constituency supporting not just a particular policy solution, but, more importantly, the values and principles that elevate one solution over another. That constituency also has to be built to scale. The power of a dedicated constituency should be clear by now, as we've watched nativist anti-immigration organizations like Numbers USA harass every politician who ever considered legalizing undocumented immigrants into backing away from it. Yet, organizing as it has been done traditionally is not going to get the job done. In today's world, media, technology and politics have merged. It will be increasingly difficult to get political attention, particularly at the federal level, if we are not using new technology to put out our ideas. The digital divide is shrinking by the day—black Broadband users now outnumber white, and nearly everyone has a cell phone. We can do amazing things with emerging technology, not to send messages out to a passive audience, but to actually encourage people to participate, on- and off-line.

EM: Organizing goes beyond being a complement, it is the core of effective policy work. The key to advocating policies to the government is to represent a real grassroots base with grassroots participation. Informed working people and communities of color are the most powerful, sophisticated lobbyists. If you are known as a force in Los Angeles, Houston, Detroit, New Orleans, New York, Atlanta, Chicago, when you come to your Representative or Senator's "home" office or visit them in D.C., they will open their doors and suggest other elected officials for you to visit—even when they disagree with you. In 1964, when the Mississippi Freedom Democratic Party came to the Atlantic City Convention, they were carrying out the most profound policy work—demanding the seating of their delegation and the un-seating of the racist "regular" Mississippi Democrats. They were met by Hubert Humphrey, Walter Reuther and Bayard Rustin who told them to accept an unacceptable compromise. Fannie Lou Hamer, the leader of the MFDP and a Black Mississippi sharecropper, told us: "You can always compromise, but never make a compromise that is not in the best interests of the people you represent and that you can't defend back home." She was a great organizer and a great policy advocate. The lesson: It is essential we do not break the connection between organizing and policy, and make sure it is those doing the organizing who represent us in front of the new administration. If there are differences, which there will be, at least it will be among forces that represent significant constituencies.

FP: Organizing is not a necessary complement to policy work. It is only a necessary complement to policy work that tries to counter the advantages that market and state-based interest groups ordinarily enjoy. Most policy work goes forward in a political environment dominated by government insiders and lobbyists, which is why the historical moments of genuine progressive reform are so rare. However the policy initiatives that are so desperately needed in the United States today are only imaginable in the aftermath of extraordinary grassroots pressure. This is not likely to take the familiar forms of consultation and litigation, and popular mobilizations may not target specific policy initiatives. Really massive pressure from the bottom is not so neatly organized and channeled. Nevertheless, the broad policy thrust of such movements is clear. Martin Luther King rightly dismissed the critics who said that the poor people assembled at Resurrection City in 1968 has failed to present a policy agenda. The authorities, he said, knew what to do. The problem was to force them to do it.

Describe a concrete example of how a policy proposal can be implemented or made more effective when undergirded with an organizing strategy effort.

RS: It's really critical that we don't just fight for the idea, but also for the details of how the idea will be applied in real time. In New York, we have a great example in the campaign to change the schools' funding formula and get more money for the state's neediest schools, most of which serve kids of color in the inner cities. The work started years ago with the Campaign for Fiscal Equity's lawsuit against the state for failing to meet its own constitutional standard of providing an adequate education for all. The lawsuit generated both positive and negative rulings over the course of fifteen years, resulting in a stalemate. It was the organizing of the Alliance for Quality Education (AQE), a coalition of community organizations, including Citizen Action of New York, the Northwest Bronx Community and Clergy Coalition and Mothers on the Move, that led to former Governor Eliot Spitzer's campaign promise to devote $1.8 billion new dollars to the education budget, and it was their organizing that kept the pressure on when he scaled back the amount during the predictable budget crisis of his first term. Parents, students and teachers immediately confronted the state legislature to win restoration of the education budget. AQE released a report on how the cuts disproportionately affected students of color and English language learners. When Spitzer's extracurricular activities forced him to resign, it was the Alliance again that worked with Governor David Paterson to make sure the restored budget went through. The minute it did, New York City Mayor Michael Bloomberg decided to cut the city's contribution to the education budget, and the NYC members of the Alliance had to shift their strategy to target him. AQE has put out its own plan for new money coming into education budgets. Their work will be key to ensuring that the money actually helps kids learn and graduate, robbing conservatives of their next tactic, arguing that more money makes no difference when it comes to "those kids."

EM: In 2008, 2009 and 2010 and beyond, the federal government will be voting on a Federal Transit Bill involving more than $200 billion. Much of this will be pork and terrible give-aways to the highway lobby. The Strategy Center is initiating a national network to intervene in the T4 process (the fourth version of the transit bill). Our policy demands focus on: 1) Ending the 80 percent highway, 20 percent public transit funding. We propose all funds go for public transportation. 2) More funding for bus systems and operations of existing bus and rail systems. 3) A Title VI civil rights provision preventing any transportation funds being allocated in a racially discriminatory manner.

The Strategy Center and Bus Riders Union and our National Center for Transportation Strategies will be working with more than 100 low-income groups located in communities of color, and mainstream environmental groups as well, to reach unity on this program. Then, we will do organizing in key districts, have LA legislative meetings, send out monthly legislative updates and organize grassroots lobbying days in D.C. The same people who draw up the policy will be leading the movement, and many groups doing work on immigration, women's reproductive rights, AIDS education, civil rights, criminal justice—whose members are poor and transit dependent—will be brought into a new coalition in which the needs of the inner city are primary. We will then take this to the incoming Administration and will fight to win.

FP: I would reverse the question. Are there any important progressive initiatives in the absence of a mobilized constituency? I can't think of any. Progressive policies have never been initiated without tremendous upheavals from the bottom of American society that depend on "organizing," broadly conceived. From the early achievements of Revolutionary-era mobs in forcing the creation of the elements of electoral-representative arrangements, to the emancipation of the slaves, to the labor, regulatory and social welfare reforms of the New Deal, to the great civil rights and anti-poverty initiatives of the 1960s, there are no exceptions. And there are also no guarantees that policy reforms once won will not be eroded without the periodic revival of popular movements.

What are the most noteworthy instructive examples of organizing that led to effective policy implementation?

RS: The Restaurant Opportunities Center of New York (ROC-NY) and its national offshoot, ROC-United, have proven that a small group can force policy change in corporations and government by surrounding an industry with organizing, research, coalition-building and policy design.

EM: In 1964, I worked with the Congress of Racial Equality and helped lead the boycott of the Trailways buses. That resulted in the hiring of hundreds of Black and Puerto Rican ticket agents, information clerks, and bus drivers and integrated the entire company and the New York City Port Authority terminal.

In 1967, the Newark Community Union Project organized to impact the local "area board: of the War on Poverty. Our entire slate was elected and we helped the poverty program to support rent strikes and school protests. The federal government (and Democratic Party mayors) shut us down because we were too successful.

In 1994, the BRU sued the Metropolitan Transportation Authority. In 1998, I negotiated with MTA CEO Julian Burke an "accelerated bus replacement plan" that created a new bus fleet. We had a slogan, "Billions for Buses." So far we have won 2,500 new compressed natural gas buses, new bus lines, lower fares, for a total of more than $2.7 billion in new funds for urban transportation.

In 1982, I organized the UAW Campaign to Keep GM Van Nuys Open. I built a large coalition of elected officials (Congresspeople Howard Berman and Maxine Waters), religious organizations (Baptist Ministers Conference, La Placita church) and Black and Latino student organizations, led by our UAW Local where I worked on the auto assembly line for ten years. Our tactic was to meet GM's threat of a plant shut down, which was imminent in 1982, with the threat of a boycott of GM products in Los Angeles, the largest new car market in the United States. In a protracted negotiation with F. James McDonald, the GM President, he agreed to a three-year extension of the plant. Maxine Waters, who was on our negotiating committee, turned to me and said: "Well, check this out. I introduce legislation asking the corporations to give three months advance notice before they close a plant and I am told my bill is too radical and anti-business. You organize a coalition that threatens a boycott of GM in the largest new car market in the U.S. and GM gives us a three-year commitment. What do we learn from that story?"

In 2007, Barack Obama, a Black U.S. Senator decided to run for President. He was seen as a long-shot. His chief rival, Sen. Hillary Clinton, was the prohibitive favorite with a bold tactical plan, a former President as one of her chief tacticians, a formidable war chest and lead in the polls. In one of their first disagreements, Obama argued that it was Martin Luther King and the Civil Rights Movement who changed history and LBJ who implemented it. Hillary disagreed, arguing that grassroots pressure is good and all, but it is the power-brokers at the top who make the change. Obama put together an amazing movement on the ground, and his top organizers taught young activists to become organizers—as our National School for Strategic Organizing has done since 1990. Obama makes fundraising into a grassroots campaign and outraises and outspends Sen. Clinton. He tells folks he was a community organizer in Chicago and shows he can walk the walk, bringing those lessons to a campaign process that had been reduced to big money, big ads and passive Internet advocacy. His on-the-ground organizing work is the decisive factor. What do we learn from that story?

One thing that makes an Obama Presidency the most attractive to me is that he will respect and understand power, pressure, confrontation if necessary, if it is based on grassroots organizing and a genuine base of low-income Black, Latino, Asian/Pacific Islander working people. No matter what deals he may choose to cut, his organizing background is now in his blood. I may be wrong, but I want to believe he will respond to righteous pressure because he knows we are doing our job and because he will care, in the tradition of George McGovern, Bobby Kennedy and Ted Kennedy, in a way that he can be reached with a moral argument rooted in the lives of Blacks, Latinos, working people and women. The challenge is not primarily to him, but to us.

FP: I am struck by the word "implementation" because mass organizing is more successful at forcing new policy initiatives than in ensuring their effective implementation over the longer run. Movements fade, partly because they require people to break with the routines of their everyday lives, and partly because they depend on an unstable constellation of political conditions that generate hope and possibility. Once the Abolitionists drifted back into the Republican Party, the great promises of the 13th, 14th and 15th Amendments were eviscerated by resurgent Southern planter elites. Similarly, after the great strike upsurge of the 1930s, the promises of the Wagner Act were whittled away both in subsequent legislation and in implementation by an increasingly pro-employer National Labor Relations Board. To be sure, legislative design matters because it can make the corruption of policy in implementation more difficult. But there are no silver bullets to guarantee effective implementation in the absence of the reality or threat of popular movements.

Index

Contributors

Catherine Albisa (info@nesri.org) is Executive Director of the National Economic and Social Rights Initiative in New York City.

Robert Alvarez (kitbob@erols.com) is a Senior Scholar at the Institute for Policy Studies, where he is currently focused on nuclear disarmament, environmental and energy policies. His articles have appeared in many publications, including *Science Magazine*, the *Bulletin of Atomic Scientists*, *Technology Review* and the *Washington Post*.

Sarah Anderson (saraha@igc.org) is the Director of the Global Economy Project at the Institute for Policy Studies. She is co-author (with John Cavanagh and Thea Lee) of *Field Guide to the Global Economy* (New Press, 2004) and numerous studies and articles on the global economy.

Nan Aron (naron@afj.org) is the President of Alliance for Justice in Washington, D.C., a national association of environmental, civil rights, mental health, women's, children's and consumer advocacy organizations. She is the author of *Liberty and Justice for All: Public Interest Law in the 1980s and Beyond* (Westview Press, 1989).

Dean Baker (dean.baker1@verizon.net) is an economist and Co-Director of the Center for Economic and Policy Research in Washington, DC. Among his numerous articles and books is *The Conservative Nanny State: How the Wealthy Use the Government to Stay Rich and Get Richer* (Lulu.com, 2006 - free download at www.conservativenannystate.org)

Phyllis Bennis (phyllis@ips-dc.org) is a Fellow at the Institute for Policy Studies, where she directs the New Internationalism Project. Her recent books include *Understanding the US-Iran Crisis: A Primer* (Olive Branch Press, 2008) and *Ending the Iraq War: A Primer* (Olive Branch Press, 2008).

Angela Glover Blackwell (ablackwell@policylink.org) is the founder and chief executive officer of PolicyLink, a national research and action institute advancing economic and social equity. She co-chaired the Center on American Progress Task Force on Poverty.

Earl Blumenauer has represented Oregon's Third Congressional District, which includes Portland, since 1996. A former member of the Transportation & Infrastructure Committee, Rep. Blumenauer now serves on the Ways and Means Committee, the Budget Committee, and the Select Committee on Energy Independence and Climate Change.

Robert L. Borosage (borosage@ourfuture.org) is the President of the Institute for America's Future and Co-Director of its sister organization, the Campaign for America's Future, both in Washington, D.C. He is a Contributing Editor at *The Nation* magazine.

Kate Bronfenbrenner (klb23@cornell.edu) is Director of Labor Education Research at Cornell ILR. A former organizer and union representative with the United Woodcutters in Mississippi and SEIU in Massachusetts, her most recent publication is the edited volume, *Global Unions: Challenging Transnational Capital through Cross-Border Campaigns* (ILR Press, 2007).

John Cavanagh (jcavanagh@igc.org) has been the Director of the Institute for Policy Studies since 1998. He is the co-author of twelve books and numerous articles on the global economy, most recently (with Robin Broad) *Development Redefined: How the Market Met its Match* (Paradigm Publishers, 2008).

Oscar Chacón (info@nalacc.org) is Executive Director of the National Alliance of Latin American & Caribbean Communities (NALACC), a Chicago-based group that seeks to improve the quality of life for Latinos and Latino immigrants in their communities, both in the United States and in countries of origin. Until December 2006, he served as Director of Enlaces América, a project of the Chicago-based Heartland Alliance for Human Needs and Human Rights.

Chuck Collins (chuckcollins7@mac.com) is Senior Scholar at the Institute for Policy Studies, where he directs the Program on Inequality and the Common Good and the Working Group on Extreme Inequality (www.extremeinequality. org). He is a contributor to *Ten Excellent Reasons Not to Hate Taxes* (New Press, 2008).

Stuart Comstock-Gay (scomstock-gay@demos.org) is the Director of the Democracy Program at Démos: A Network for Ideas and Action. Démos is a New York-based public policy and advocacy center for democratic values.

Charlie Cray (ccray@corporatepolicy.org) is Director of the Center for Corporate Policy in Washington, D.C. He is co-author of *The People's Business: Controlling Corporations and Restoring Democracy* (Berrett-Koehler, 2004).

Sheila Crowley (sheila@nlihc.org) has been the President and CEO of the National Low Income Housing Coalition since 1998. NLIHC is a research and policy advocacy organization solely dedicated to ending the affordable hosing crisis in the United States and led the eight-year campaign that resulted in the enactment of legislation to establish the National Housing Trust Fund in 2008.

Martha F. Davis (m.davis@neu.edu) is Professor of Law and Co-Director of the Program on Human Rights and the Global Economy at Northeastern University. She is co-editor of *Bringing Human Rights Home* (Praeger, 2008), a three-volume series chronicling the U.S. human rights movement.

Karen Dolan (reachable via http://www.CitiesforPeace.org) is a Fellow at the Institute for Policy Studies and Director of its Cities for Peace program, working with citizens, national peace and human needs organizations, locally elected officials and federal lawmakers.

Peter Edelman (edelman@law.georgetown.edu) is a Professor of Law at the Georgetown University Law Center and directs the Georgetown Center on Poverty, Inequality and Public Policy. He co-chaired the Center on American Progress Task Force on Poverty.

Carroll L. Estes (carroll.estes@ucsf.edu) is Professor of Sociology, founding Director of the Institute for Health and Aging, and past Chair of the Dept. of Social & Behavioral Sciences at the Univ. of California, San Francisco. She is past President of The Gerontological Society of America and The American Society on Aging. Among her twenty-four books are *Social Policy and Aging* (Sage, 2001) and the forthcoming *Social Insurance, Social Justice, and Social Change* (Springer).

John Feffer (johnfeffer@gmail.com) is Co-Director of Foreign Policy in Focus at the Institute for Policy Studies. He is the editor of *Power Trip: U.S. Foreign Policy After September 11* (Seven Stories Press, 2003) and the author of *North Korea/South Korea: U.S. Policy & the Korean Peninsula* (Seven Stories Press, 2003).

Bill Fletcher, Jr. (papaq54@hotmail.com) is Executive Editor of Black Commentator and Co-Founder of the Center for Labor Renewal. He serves as Director of Field Services & Education for the American Federation of Government Employees in Washington, D.C. His new book is *Solidarity Divided: The Crisis in Organized Labor and a New Path Toward Social Justice* (Univ. of California Press, 2008).

Maria Foscarinis (mfoscarinis@nlchp.org) is founder and Executive Director of the National Law Center on Homelessness & Poverty in Washington, D.C., the legal arm of the national movement to end and prevent homelessness. She is a primary architect of the landmark McKinney-Vento Homeless Assistance Act; has litigated to enforce critical legal rights of homeless people; and written widely on homelessness and poverty.

Kim Gandy (president@now.org) is serving her second term as President of the National Organization for Women in Washington, D.C., elected by the group's grassroots members in 2001 and 2005. An attorney, she oversees NOW's multi-issue agenda, which includes: ending sex discrimination, advancing reproductive freedom, promoting diversity and ending racism, stopping violence against women, winning LGBT rights and ensuring economic justice.

Jaime Grant (jgrant@thetaskforce.org) is Director of the Policy Institute at the National Gay and Lesbian Task Force in Washington, D.C. For six years, she directed the Union Institute's Center for Women, the nation's only academic women's center dedicated to collaborations between scholars and activists.

Mark Greenberg (mgreenberg@americanprogress.org) is a Senior Fellow at the Center for American Progress (CAP) and previously directed CAP's Task Force on Poverty. He is Executive Director of the Georgetown Center on Poverty, Inequality and Public Policy.

Jim Harkness (jharkness@iatp.org) is President of the Institute for Agriculture and Trade Policy in Minneapolis. Before joining IATP he lived for sixteen years in China, working on rural development and sustainability issues.

Chester Hartman (chartman2@aol.com) is Director of Research at the Poverty & Race Research Council in Washington, D.C. and an Associate Fellow at the Institute for Policy Studies. His recent books include *There Is No Such Thing As a Natural Disaster: Race, Class and Hurricane Katrina* (Routledge, 2006), *A Right to Housing: Foundation for a New Social Agenda* (Temple Univ. Press, 2006) and *City for Sale: The Transformation of San Francisco* (Univ. of Calif. Press, 2002).

Farrah Hassen (farrah@ips-dc.org) is the 2008 Carol Jean and Edward F. Newman Fellow at the Institute for Policy Studies. She has been writing about and researching U.S.-Syrian relations and the Middle East for the past five years.

Simon Heller (simon@afj.org) is Legal Director for the Alliance for Justice in Washington, DC, a national association of environmental, civil rights, mental health, women's, children's and consumer advocacy organizations. He is responsible for their Judicial Selection and Justice Watch Projects, as well as their broader Access to Justice Program. Before coming to the Alliance, he was a reproductive rights litigator at the American Civil Liberties Union and the Center for Reproductive Rights.

Katrina vanden Heuvel is editor and publisher of *The Nation* magazine. Her latest books are *Taking Back America: And Taking Down the Radical Right* (Nation Books, 2004), co-authored with Robert L. Borosage, and *Dictionary of Republicanisms: The Indispensable Guide to What They Really Mean When They Say What They Think You Want to Hear* (Nation Books, 2004).

Alan W. Houseman (ahouse@clasp.org) has been Director of the Center for Law and Social Policy since 1982. CLASP is a public policy organization that focuses on improving the lives of low-income persons, reducing poverty and advancing racial equity.

Tomás R. Jiménez (tjimenez@stanford.edu) is an Irvine Fellow at the New America Foundation and Assistant Professor of Sociology at Stanford University.

Barbara B. Kennelly (kennellyb@ncpssm.org) is President and CEO of the National Committee to Preserve Social Security and Medicare, following her seventeen years as Member of the U.S. Congress from Connecticut, where she served as ranking member of the House Ways & Means Subcomm. on Social Security. In 2006, Speaker of the House Nancy Pelosi appointed her to the Social Security Advisory Board.

Gloria Ladson-Billings (gjladson@wisc.edu) is the Kellner Family Chair in Urban Education at the Univ. of Wisconsin-Madison. She is the author of *The Dreamkeepers: Successful Teachers for African American Children* (Jossey-Bass, 1994).

Saul Landau (saul@ips-dc.org) has been with the Institute for Policy Studies since 1972 and is currently Vice Chair of its Board. His newest book is *A Bush and Botox World* (AK Press, 2007). His most recent award-winning film is *We Don't Play Golf Here.*

Erik Leaver (erik@ips-dc.org) is Research Fellow at the Institute for Policy Studies. He has been writing about and organizing around the Iraq War for the past six years.

Nicole Lee (nlee@transafricaforum.org) is Executive Director of Transafrica Forum in Washington, D.C. Prior to that, she was the Managing Director of Global Justice, a Washington advocacy group focused on HIV/AIDS and child survival policy.

Gerald LeMelle (gerald@africaaction.org) is Executive Director of Africa Action in Washington, D.C. He formerly was Deputy Executive Director for Advocacy at Amnesty International (USA) and Director of African Affairs with the Phelps-Stokes Fund.

Ben Lilliston (BLilliston@iatp.org) is Communications Director at the Institute for Agriculture and Trade Policy in Minneapolis and editor of IATP's *Think Forward* blog.

Bart Lubow (blubow@aecf.org) is the Director of Programs for High-Risk Youth and a Senior Associate at the Annie E. Casey Foundation in Baltimore.

Eric Mann (ericmann@ericmannauthor.com) is Director of the Labor/Community Strategy Center in Los Angeles and a veteran of CORE, SDS and the United Auto Workers. His forthcoming book is *The Twenty-Five Qualities of the Successful Organizer*.

Ben Manski (reachable via http://www.LibertyTreeFDR.org) is a Wisconsin attorney and Executive Director of the national pro-democracy group, the Liberty Tree Foundation for the Democratic Revolution in Madison, WI.

Marc Mauer (mauer@sentencingproject.org) is Executive Director of The Sentencing Project, a Washington, D.C.-based national non-profit engaged in research and advocacy on criminal justice policy. His book *Race to Incarcerate* (New Press, 1999) was a semi-finalist for the Robert F. Kennedy Book Award, and he is co-editor of *Invisible Punishment* (New Press, 2002), a collection of essays examining the social costs of incarceration.

Patrice McDermott (pmcdermott@openthegovernment.org) is Director of OpenTheGoverment.org, a coalition of journalists, consumer and good government groups, environmentalists, library groups and others united to make the federal government a more open place in order to make us safer, strengthen public trust in government and support democratic principles. She is the author of *Who Needs to Know? The State of Public Access to Federal Government Information* (Bernan Press, 2007).

Dedrick Muhammad (dedrick@ips-dc.org) is the Senior Organizer and Research Associate for the Program on Inequality and the Common Good at the Institute for Policy Studies. He formerly was National Field Director for Rev. Al Sharpton's National Action Network and Coordinator for the Racial Wealth Divide Project of United For A Fair Economy. He is author of the report "40 Years Later: The Unrealized American Dream" (available at http://www.ips-dc.org/reports/#249).

Douglas W. Nelson (dnelson@aecf.org) is President and CEO of the Annie E. Casey Foundation in Baltimore.

Miriam Pemberton (miriam@ips-dc.org) is a Research Fellow at the Institute for Policy Studies, writing and speaking on demilitarization issues for its Foreign Policy In Focus project. She leads a group that produces the annual "Unified Security Budget for the United States." With William Hartung of the New America Foundation, she is co-editor of *Lessons from Iraq: Avoiding the Next War* (Paradigm Publishers, 2008).

Manuel Pérez-Rocha (manuel@ips-dc.org) is Associate Fellow at the Institute for Policy Studies, where he directs an advocacy and research project, "The Security and Prosperity Partnership and the NAFTA Plus Agenda." He works in coordination with the Alliance for Responsible Trade in the United States and is a member of the Mexican Action Network on Free Trade.

Frances Fox Piven (FFox-Piven@gc.cuny.edu) is on the faculty of the Graduate Center of the City University of New York. Among her many books are *Regulating the Poor* (Vintage, 1993); *Poor People's Movements* (Vintage, 1978); *Why Americans Still Don't Vote* (Beacon Press, 2000); and *Challenging Authority: How Ordinary People Change America* (Rowman and Littlefield, 2006).

Sam Pizzigati (editor@toomuchonline.org), an Associate Fellow at the Institute for Policy Studies, edits "Too Much," an online weekly on excess and inequality. His most recent book, *Greed and Good: Understanding and Overcoming the Inequality That Limits Our Lives* (Apex Press, 2004), won an "outstanding title" of the year rating from the American Library Association.

Ron Pollack (rpollack@familiesusa.org) is Founding Executive Director of Families USA in Washington, D.C., the national organization for health care consumers. He also was Founding Executive Director of the Food Research and Action Center (FRAC) and Dean of the Antioch University School of Law.

William Quigley (quigley77@gmail.com) is a human rights lawyer and Professor at Loyola Univ. New Orleans College of Law. His new book is *Storms Still Raging: Katrina, New Orleans and Social Justice* (Book Surge Publishing, 2008). He has advocated with organizations and individuals in New Orleans for thirty years.

Miles Rapoport (mrapoport@demos.org) is the President of Démos: A Network for Ideas and Action. He served for fourteen years in Connecticut state government, as State Representative from 1985 to 1994, and as Secretary of the State from 1995 to 1999.

Marcus Raskin (mraskin@igc.org) is Co-Founder and Distinguished Fellow at the Institute for Policy Studies and currently directs its Paths for the 21st Century project. He was a member of the special staff of the National Security Council in President Kennedy's Administration, as is the author of over a dozen books.

Janet Redman (janet@ips-dc.org) is a Research Associate for the Sustainable Energy and Economy Network at the Institute for Policy Studies. She is the author of the recent reports "World Bank: Climate Profiteer," and "Dirty is the New Clean" (both available at wwwips-dc.org/seen).

Michael A. Replogle (mreplogle@edf.org) is Transportation Director for the Environmental Defense Fund in Washington, D.C., and President/founder of the Institute for Transportation and Development Policy. A civil engineer, sociologist and planner, he has been a consultant to The World Bank, Environmental Protection Agency and many state, local and foreign governments

Jon Rynn (jonathanrynn@gmail.com) is a regular contributor to the blog for *Grist Magazine*. He holds a Ph.D in political science from the City Univ. of New York.

Rebecca Sawyer (Rebecca.sawyer@gmail.com) served as a Vaid Fellow at the National Gay and Lesbian Task Force's Policy Institute during the Summer of 2006. She is currently a graduate student in the joint MBA/MPP program at the University of Maryland.

Daniel Scheer (daniels@ips-dc.org) is a junior at Hampshire College in Amherst, Massachusetts.

Ben Scott (bscott@freepress.net) is Policy Director at Free Press in Washington, D.C., where he oversees all governmental and legislative affairs for the country's largest public interest organization working exclusively on communications policy. Before joining Free Press, he was a Legislative Aide to then-U.S. Congressman (now U.S. Senator) Bernie Sanders of Vermont.

Rinku Sen (rsen@arc.org) is the President and Executive Director of the Applied Research Center (ARC) and Publisher of *ColorLines* magazine. She has written extensively about immigration, community organizing and women's lives for a wide variety of publications including *Third Force*, AlterNet, tompaine.com, *Race, Poverty & the Environment*, *Amerasia Journal* and *ColorLines*.

Amy Shannon (amyshannon@earthlink.net) is a consultant for non-profit organizations, and former Associate Director of Enlaces America.

Cynthia Soohoo (csooho@reprorights.org) is Director of the Domestic Legal Program at the Center for Reproductive Rights in New York City.

Nancy Starnes (starnes@nod.org) is Senior Vice President for the National Organization on Disability (NOD) in Washington, D.C.

Betsy Taylor (betsytaylor@gmail.com) is President of 1Sky (www.1sky.org), a Takoma Park, MD-based national campaign of over 100 diverse organizations working to ensure that the next President and Congress enact bold policies at the scale of the climate change problem.

Sanho Tree (stree@igc.org) is a Fellow and Director of the Drug Policy Project at the Institute for Policy Studies. The project works to end the domestic and international "War on Drugs" and replace it with policies that promote public health and safety as well as economic alternatives to the prohibition drug economy.

Dorian Warren (dw2288@columbia.edu) is Assistant Professor in the Dept. of Political Science and the School of International and Public Affairs and a Faculty Affiliate at the Inst. for Research in African-American Studies at Columbia Univ. His most recent work is the co-edited collection *Race and American Political Development* (Routledge, 2008).

Emira Woods (emira@ips-dc.org) is Co-Director of Foreign Policy in Focus at the Institute for Policy Studies and serves on the Board of Directors of Africa Action, Just Associates, Global Justice, and the Financial Policy Forum. She is also on the Network Council of Jubilee USA.

Daphne Wysham (daphne@ips-dc.org) is a Fellow and Board member at the Institute for Policy Studies. She is founder and director of its Sustainable Energy and Economy Network. She serves on the board of Nuclear Information and Resource Service, is on the advisory board of the Carbon Free Nuclear-Free Alliance, and co-hosts the one-hour weekly broadcast of Earthbeat Radio, which airs on 50 radio stations in the U.S. and Canada.